MW01515085

HEALING NATURE
PATHWAYS FOR LIVING

HEALING NATURE
P R E S S

Healing Nature Press is committed to publishing works that have a positive impact on the health and wellness of our readership. Our authors are all on their individual journeys toward health and are committed to sharing their lifestyles, understanding that the hardest journey you can make is the one you make alone. We invite you to participate in our collective journey led by experts in their fields of nutrition and health care. The subject matter you'll find covered by our products range from healthy living, raw food diets, living food diets, benefits of juicing, benefits of fasting, lifestyle change, baby steps to healthy lifestyle, living disease free, to health and wellness coaching. We invite you and the countless others in your quest for healthy living to further both your knowledge and application of it, through our ground-breaking *Healing Nature Institute*.

www.healingnaturepress.com

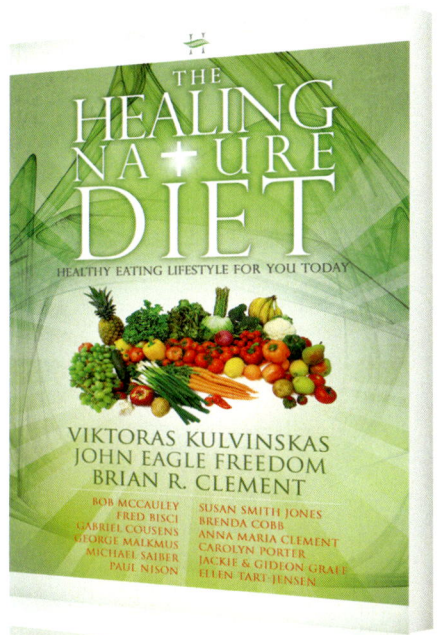

A well-written life is almost as rare as a well-spent one.

- Thomas Carlyle

HEALING NATURE

I N S T I T U T E

Healing Nature Institute is committed to providing ongoing education in the arena of health and wellness. In the coming year, an online learning center will be taking shape with the expert help of our growing network of authors and practitioners, developing and offering courses on their material to aid you in not only deepening your understanding of healthy living, but becoming an advocate for that life change as well.

THE HEALING NATURE OF JESUS

DYNAMIC HEALING PATHWAYS FOR YOU TODAY

JOHN EAGLE FREEDOM
SUSAN SMITH JONES

FOREWORD BY BRIAN R. CLEMENT, PHD, NMB, LNC

REV. VIKTORAS KULVINSKAS, GRANDFATHER OF LIVING FOOD

T. COLIN CAMPBELL	BRENDA COBB
FRED BISCI	ELLEN TART-JENSEN
GEORGE H. MALKMUS	REBECCA LINDER HINTZ
MICHAEL SAIBER	LESLIE VAN ROMER
PAUL NISON	LEONARD COLDWELL
JOHN ROBBINS	JACKIE & GIDEON GRAFF
BOB McCAULEY	LEE FREDRICKSON

THE HEALING NATURE OF JESUS

DYNAMIC HEALING PATHWAYS FOR YOU TODAY

Copyright © 2010

Published by Healing Nature Press

Springfield, MO 65807

Disclaimer: Consult a doctor if you are injured, or if you suffer from any medical conditions. This publication presents only the authors' opinions which are based on their knowledge, experiences and beliefs. The techniques and theories offered here do not represent a scientific consensus or prevention or self help. Results will be based on an individual's specific situation and will vary for each individual. You use all information and techniques published in this book at your own risk and based on your power of free will.

Requests for permissions should be addressed to:

Healing Nature Press

2131 W. Republic Rd., PMB 41

Springfield, MO 65807

ISBN 978-0-9771964-9-4

Cover: Keith Locke

Book Design: Lee Fredrickson, and Zach Dyer

HEALING NATURE
PRESS

DISCLAIMER

This book is designed to provide information about the subject matter covered. While all attempts have been made to verify information provided in this publication, neither the authors not the publisher assumes any responsibility for errors, omissions or contrary interpretation of the subject matter.

This publication is sold with the understanding that the publisher and author are not engaged in rendering medical professional services of a competent medical professional. The purchaser or reader of this publication assumes responsibility for the use of these materials and information. Adherence to all applicable laws and regulations, federal and state and local, governing professional licensing, business practices, advertising and all other aspects of doing business in the United States or any other jurisdiction is the sole responsibility or liability whatsoever on behalf of any purchaser or reader of these materials.

The purpose of this book is to educate. Any perceived slights to a specific individual or organization is unintentional.

The information in this book is not a substitute for a doctor's visit. It is not intended to treat, diagnose or prevent any illness. If you are in therapeutic care, ask your doctor or therapist first before you do any changes or use any of the techniques described in this book. This book is the way to make better-educated decisions, to find the root cause of life's challenges and shows ways to eliminate these causes. It is intended to help you to establish your personal level of optimum health in the shortest amount of time. Our desire is to Wake Up America and encourage her citizens to be responsible for their own health, and invite God back into their lives!

DEDICATION

This book is dedicated to:

YAHWEH who is also known as
ELOHIM, the Mighty One
and who is best revealed to us in Jesus Christ, whose original Name is
YESHUA!

Especially Dedicated to Jesus Christ for the Stripes He took for our healing —By His stripes we are healed!—Isaiah 53:5 And for His blood He shed on the cross to save us eternally!

And to the sick Children of the World, who are being robbed through food addictions in their generation worse than in mine!

ACKNOWLEDGEMENTS

I am deeply indebted to my friend, missionary Allen Kemper, who worked long hours with me, praying, writing, and selflessly working on this book in many capacities, especially for sharing the Word of God with me. Bob Mondy, "The Voice of the Ozarks," who prayed fervently for the production and success of this book and who worked so diligently behind the scenes to bring our message to the world!

Lee Fredrickson, co-author and co-publisher: Thank you for your wisdom, direction and guidance, and the invitation to co-create this great work.

My grandson, Joseph, who was born on 9-11, just as I was reborn on 9-11! My grandaughers, Savannah, Ja-el, and Jillyanne. I also married my beautiful wife on 9-11 on my radio show, "Vibrant Life the Hour of TRUTH."

I further desire to acknowledge the women in my life. My dear wife, Leona Totta-Freedom, who for over 25 years has taught me what Love is All About! My daughter Jincey, thank You for having the courage to live your life; you are truly a gift! Lou Ann Cassell is a care-giver and healer, you saved my life by sending me to Hippocrates where my healing journey began, and my friend, Oscar Dixon. My mother, a mother of 8, sacrificed her life, for the lives of her children. Thank You, Mom!

My Thanks, Gratitude and Special Acknowledgment goes out to all contributing authors finding common ground of TRUTH, Love and the best interests of the people and animals who share our planet. We look forward to working with you again on the next book in the series, entitled, "The Healing Nature Diet" about living food, starting with Viktoras Kulvinskas, better known as the "Grandfather of the Living Food Movement."

CONTENTS

INTERNATIONAL LIVING FOOD SUMMIT II

VIBRANT HEALTH THROUGH PLANT-BASED NUTRITION

These historic summits were held at the Hippocrates Health Institute in West Palm Beach, Florida on January 14, 2006, and April 28, 2007. The summits convened to unify the leadership in the Living Food Movement, establishing scientifically based common standards for optimum health.

Leaders from eight countries (with a combined total of 434 years following this lifestyle) agreed on the following standards:

The Optimum Diet for Health/Longevity:

- Vegan (no animal products of any kind, cooked or raw)

- Organic

- Whole Foods

- High in nutrition such as vitamins, antioxidants, and phytonutrients

- Highly mineralized

- Contains a significant quantity of chlorophyll-rich green foods

- Contains adequate complete protein from plant sources

- Contains a large proportion of high-water-content foods

- Provides excellent hydration

- Includes raw vegetable juices

- Contains all essential fatty acids, including Omega-3 fatty acids from naturally occurring plant sources

- Is at lest 80% raw (the remaining to be Vegan, whole food, and organic)

- Has moderate yet adequate caloric intake

- Contains only low to moderate sugar and exclusively from whole-food sources (fruitarianism is strongly discouraged)

- Contains adequate amounts of unprocessed salts, as needed (depending upon your constitution)

- Is nutritionally optimal for both detoxification and rebuilding

We also agree that:

- Deficiency of Vitamin B-12 is a global issue for mental and physical health, for *anyone on any* diet. Therefore, supplementation with Vitamin B-12 is advised.

- The addition of enzyme-active substances *(even in their raw form)*, such as cocoa/chocolate, coffee, caffeinated teas, and alcohol are highly discouraged.

- This way of eating can be further optimized by tailoring it based on *individual needs* (within the principles stated).

- Benefits derived by following these are proportional to how well they are followed.

- We will remain open-minded, and this information will be updated and expanded upon if necessary, as new research becomes available.

- Diet is a critical part of a healthy lifestyle, yet not the entire picture. A full-spectrum, health-supportive lifestyle is encouraged. This includes physical exercise, exposure to sunshine, as well as psychological health. Avoiding environmental toxins and toxic products is essential. Paramount is pure water (for consumption and bathing,) the use of natural fiber clothing, and non-toxic personal-care products. Also consider healthy options in home furnishings/building materials and related items.

All participating leaders agree that eating according to the International Living Food Summit Guidelines will significantly address the urgent issues of health, environmental sustainability, world hunger, and a compassionate respect for life.

The following leaders support these principles:
(listed in alphabetical order)

Fred Bisci, PhD – USA

Tamera Campbell – Vision – USA

Rajaa Chbani – Pharmacie L'Unite – Morocco

Gabriel Cousens, MD, MD(H) – Diplomat American Board of Holistic Medicine – USA

Brenda Cobb – Living Foods Institute – USA

Anna Maria Clement, CN,NMD, PhD – Hippocrates Health Institute – USA

Brian Clement, CN, NMD, PhD – Hippocrates Health Institute –USA

Carole Dougoud – Institute Haute Vitalite – Switzerland

Dorit – Serenity Spaces – USA

Kare Engstrom – Dietician – Sweden

John Eagle Freedom - Healing Nature Press, Health City USA, Vibrant Life, The Hour of Truth – USA

Viktoras Kulvinskas – "Grandfather" of the Living Foods Movement – USA

Dan Ladermann – Living Light International – USA

Marie Christine; Lhermitte Chemin du mas Magnuel – France

George Malkmus – Hallelujah Acres – USA

Rhonda Malkmus – Hallelujah Acres – USA

Paul Nison – The Raw Life – USA

Katrina Rainoshek – Juice Feasting – USA

David Rainoshek – Juice Feasting – USA

Claudine Richard – Naturopath – France

Michael Saiber – Vision – USA

Cherie Soria – Living Light International – USA

Jameth Sheridan, ND – HealthForce Nutritionals – USA

Diana Store – Raw Superfoods – UK/The Netherlands

Jill Swyers – Living Foods For Health – UK/Portugal

Walter J. Urban, PhD – USA – Costa Rica

Statement Compiled and Organized by Jameth Sheridan, N.D.

TESTIMONIES

WHAT INTERNATIONAL LEADERS ARE SAYING ABOUT THE HEALING NATURE OF JESUS

When you think of the healing nature of Jesus, what most impresses you about Jesus' healing accounts, and how is this a driving factor in your life and practice?

When I was a little girl, not more than 4 years old, my maternal grandmother, Fritzie, introduced me to Jesus, told me that he was the greatest healer who ever lived, and told me that I could have no better friend in the world. She said that whenever I needed someone to talk to about anything that Jesus was the one I could count on to always be there for me. In fact, during most of our visits until she passed away in my 20's, we talked about Jesus and how He taught (and is teaching) people how to live healthy, love-filled lives. I took her sage guidance to heart and, to this day, have always believed that Jesus was not only my best friend, but also the cornerstone of my life and my guidepost, my True North, on how to live and spread the good news that vibrant health is a choice, and that we can all embrace it in our lives.

The mission of Jesus was to bring to humanity the teachings of love and forgiveness, gentleness and compassion, vibrant health and peace. He also teaches us to take loving care of ourselves and of each other. In other words, *we are here on earth not to see through one another, but to see one another through*, as Fritzie used to tell me. His message was very simple: "Love one another" and to "love our neighbors as we love ourselves." So it begins by each of us taking good care of ourselves and making health

21

a top priority in our lives. My grandmother always impressed upon me that in order to help others, we must begin with ourselves—to be healthy and healed within – and to be a shining example of God's love for each of us. God has given us all this gift of life, and our miraculous bodies, and one of our gifts back to God is to always take loving care of ourselves so that we can inspire and uplift others simply by how we choose to live. You see, it's really quite simple, as are all of Jesus' teachings.

Jesus revealed in all its fullness is that the Divine Spirit dwells in and can illumine every human heart. Fritzie glowed with her Christ Spirit that everyone felt in her presence. She was the only one in my family who was into a healthy lifestyle, which she taught to me, and we were both considered "health nuts" or the "black sheep" by the rest of our family. She always reminded me that Jesus was the ultimate healer and we must look to Him as our example on how to heal ourselves and support others. So it was because of the healing nature of Jesus, and my grandmother's teachings of Jesus and vibrant health, that I chose my work and penchant to educate others (through my books, lectures, workshops, and other media work) on how to take better care of their God-given bodies and how to create optimum health and vitality.

Jesus refers to himself as a physician in the Bible, and responds to the Scribes of the Pharisees, as if they knew that he was a physician. Many quotations of the medical care provided by Jesus are offered in several books such as Mark 1:32, Mark 1:40-41, Mark 2:2-10 and Mark 2:15-17. The Master also once said, "Ask and ye shall receive; seek and ye shall find the truth; knock and the door of heaven shall be opened unto you." Don't forget the spirit behind these words. Seek truth in all sincerity; seek it in the quiet chambers of your own heart. Seek it in this book and these lessons of healing and vitality. Ask of that love and that power. Ask and the supply will be unfailing—the spiritual supply and the physical supply.

Always remember that health is your Divine birthright. Never doubt that you can heal your body through the loving Spirit within you and the lifestyle choices you make every day. You must keep the faith and choose the path that leads to vitality. The Master once said, "Oh ye of little faith!" "According to your faith be it unto you." With faith and commitment, along with choosing a healthy lifestyle, you will create miracles in your life. Never let anyone or anything cause you to doubt your God-given inherent power and ability to heal your body. It's a commitment that you must make and then follow through with your healthy lifestyle choices. And know that with God and Jesus as your lifeline (my heart~line), anything and everything is possible. Invite Christ to be the Light in your life to beautify and make strong every cell in your body and every human spirit.

In my following chapter, I will share with you what vibrant health means to me, how many in our country have taken the wrong path, and some of the steps you can take today, the week, this month and this year to achieve your goals and make health and healing issues a thing of the past for you and your family. I know you can do it. I believe in you and your power to dream-big and make your dreams come true. And I hope our paths cross somewhere along the way.

　　—Susan S. Jones

As I study the Gospel accounts of Jesus' earthly ministry, I find it interesting that before Jesus dealt with the spiritual needs of people, he first dealt with their physical needs. While it is abundantly clear from Scripture that Jesus' primary purpose for coming to earth was to "Seek and to save that which was lost," (Luke 19:10), and "...give himself a ransom for all" (I Timothy 2:6), it is also clearly evident that Jesus was not just concerned about man's spiritual need, but that he had great empathy for the physical needs of people as well. As a minister of the Gospel of Jesus Christ for nearly 20-years, I personally ministered solely to the spiritual needs of people. In recent years, I have had the privilege of ministering to the complete man—body, soul, and spirit, which has been most rewarding. I feel my latter years of ministry have more mirrored the ministry of Jesus than my former years. Hallelujah Acres is a ministry that ministers to the whole man!

　　—George Malkmus

Jesus' teaching reminds me that it is not just beauty that is in the eye of the beholder, but far more. I think it is true that we see the world not as it is, but as we are. The example and healing nature of Jesus humbles me and helps me to recognize that sometimes without even knowing it I tend to look at myself and at others through eyes of judgment, eyes of accusation, and eyes of distrust. When I look in this way, what kind of influence am I having? What kind of world am I creating? Jesus' example lifts me to a higher plane where I begin to experience the healing that comes from learning to see with the eyes of love.

—John Robbins

To me Jesus is a symbol of the power of unconditional love, a power that is so strong it is still radiating to every corner of the world two thousand years since he walked this earth. He is an example of how to live a perfect life, a life of peace, tolerance and forgiveness. In the face of extreme persecution from the political powers of his time, Jesus saw that his persecutors were acting out of ignorance and forgave them. When I get angry at the injustice in the world around me, the life of Jesus can remind me that love is infinitely more effective than anger and hate.

—Vicki Rae Chelf

What has always struck me most in reading about Jesus' healings was the way He conducted them: more often than not by speaking the Truth in a manner that "the Way, the Truth, and the Life" could not help but speak it. He didn't *believe* that the man with palsy could not be healed, or think that the lepers who came to him had a 50/50 prognosis, or that the Samaritan woman's faith *might* make her whole. He *knew* the Truth so thoroughly that when He spoke it, bodily conditions— organs, cells, atoms—responded just as the waves did when he stilled the sea. This inspires me in my very imperfect human way to want to try to see the Truth about myself and others, to know that all things are indeed possible, and to expect (and notice) modern-day miracles all around me.

—Victoria Moran

The title of this book says it all! All the contributing authors including myself, have been touched by the Love of Jesus! We've all experienced in our lives pain, tragedies, sickness, disease, relationship meltdown, premature loss of loved ones, missing body parts, and yet when the sky is the darkest, there's always hope and a rainbow of Love offered to us. He only asks one thing: Love Him, and Love ourself, so we can Love our neighbor as we love ourself.

All the contributing authors have come to common ground through the empowerment of the Love of Our Lord Jesus Christ! In our own way, each author has asked you our readers to wake up, be responsible for your own health and the health of our nation! We will guide you through the maze of deception on your journey to health. Come under the blood of salvation, physically as well as spiritually. Please invite your Creator back into your life and back into the U.S.A.! In this dark hour of our nation's history, His Word is the only sure foundation upon which to build our hopes and dreams! Thank you, Jesus!

—John Eagle Freedom

THE POWER OF
THE HEALING
NATURE OF JESUS

Drs. Anna Maria and Brian Clement, Ph.D., L.N.
Hippocrates Health Institute

This anthology achieves a remarkable goal by the mere fact it has gathered together experts with open hearts and minds who equally respect the power of Jesus. All too often, the words of the Savior are manipulated and adulterated so they can fit in the narrow parameters that most people harbor. There is nothing shy or wilting about the articulation from God's Son. It is clear, precise, and compassionate. Those who understand the Words will be reminded that the body is referred to as the Temple of God. Utter respect for this gift should be foremost in the minds of the believers. When abusing your biology, it is disrespectful and evidence of your own lack of self-worth. No matter how many flowery words we regurgitate about our spiritual competence, proof is in our actions.

No wonder God speaks about maintaining the body since all of its glorious chemistry creates maximum awareness when fully nourished. It is almost ironic that most people have completely lost their instinct of self-preservation and somehow have fabricated a false idea that we can replace our responsibility with haphazard neglect. Time and again, I have seen people raise themselves out of the darkness of negativity, disease, addiction, habitual problems, etc. by engaging themselves in pure living. The brain begins to function so that the mind is created which then gives birth to the consciousness that connects you with God. As you know, Jesus often fasted and prayed before speaking to His Father. Proper nutrition brings many rewards beyond sustenance. This powerful book is bold enough to tell the truth about the essential requirements of good solid nourishment as a prerequisite to spiritual awakening.

EDITOR'S NOTE

Thank you Brian, for keeping the truth of Hippocrates alive, the doctor 500 years before Christ who said, "Let food be your medicine, and medicine be your food." And he also said, "Do no harm." Brian, thank you for being there for the people of the world that have been given no hope. I owe my life to the Healing Nature of Jesus, and the Life Force He has placed in all of us, called our immune system. Choose life, or choose death. I have chosen Life. Brian, you are one of the true leaders, a great American Hero, and I encourage any and all people of the world, healthy, sick or diseased, to experience your Health Educator Program at Hippocrates to be responsible for their own health and wealth of our nation because there is no greater resource than human and the Life-force that lies within!

We can change the world by being responsible for our own health! WAKE UP AMERICA!!! The Sleeping Giant lies within all of us! The lies of deception that you can get life from dead food perpetuated by greed extending the shelf-life of our food, must be exposed! You're doing a great job educating the people of the world and I commend you most sincerely!

Your friend,

John Eagle Freedom

It is time that our ministers, priests, congregations, and churches refocus their efforts on healing the devout so they can truly become one in the spirit of Jesus. As the written Word states, we are made in the image of God. This one statement mandates that we always do our best at everything we pursue. It is false theology to believe that God will help those who do not help themselves. As you know God stated, "Help those who help themselves." What differentiates humans from all other creatures is our free will, and it is for us to use it in the way Jesus intended for us. There is never a time that you should dismiss or neglect the fundamental importance of healthy food choices. The mere act of consuming the wrong food will not only make you suffer and ultimately become sick, it will also rob your ability to be the good husband, wife, or child. Furthermore, the responsibility you have to your family, coworkers, and fellow humans, is to be strong, clear, and honest. If you do not understand these words or even worse are offended by them, you are suffering the dreaded addiction that the unconscious share today. Your path to a healthy lifestyle can begin today if you believe in the most important basics, respect the gifts that God gave us.

I congratulate all participants in this remarkable book and hope that it ignites the very soul of those who read it. Its objective is to inspire, but the result of this will be the ultimate renewal of one person at a time once again creating a capable humanity. Like you, many of the contributors, as well as I, were lost before we found our way using the basic tools that are laid out in these concise thoughtful words. You can regain the essence of God's love by accepting the bountiful harvest of the earth that Jesus Himself walked upon.

INTRODUCTION

UNDERSTANDING THE HEALING NATURE OF JESUS

Lee Fredrickson, Ph.D.

"The Spirit of the Lord is upon Me,
Because He has anointed Me
To preach the gospel to the poor;
He has sent Me to heal the brokenhearted,
To proclaim liberty to the captives
And recovery of sight to the blind,
To set at liberty those who are oppressed;
To proclaim the acceptable year of the Lord."

Jesus read this passage from the book of Isaiah to a group of people seated in the synagogue located in His hometown of Nazareth. When He closed the book, He fixed His eyes on the people as they fixed their eyes on Him and boldly proclaimed that He was the Healer sent from God as the fulfillment of this scripture.

Their response to Him among themselves was one of disbelief, "Is not this Joseph's son?"

Jesus immediately came back to them and made this statement, "You will surely say this proverb to Me, 'Physician, heal yourself! Whatever we have heard done in Capernaum, do also here in Your country'" (Luke 4:23).

Luke was called "the beloved physician" by the apostle Paul (Colossians 4:14), but unlike Luke, Jesus' healing ministry was understood by the Jews of His day as miraculous. Jesus was neither a trained physician nor was He a magician, but He healed by the power of God. It must be understood that Jesus, by His very nature, healed all who were brought to Him without thought of race, color or creed. Elmer Towns, in his book *The Son*, writes this:

Capernaum A.D. 28: Healing the Masses at Capernaum

As those inside the home of Simon Peter and Andrew enjoyed the Sabbath meal, a crowd was slowly gathering in the street out front. The lame, the injured, the sick and the demon-possessed of Capernaum lay on pallets in the street, while the whole of the city gathered around them and waited. Politely they waited, for until now they had no hope. But now there was a man in town who could help them.

After the Sabbath service, word had spread throughout the community that Jesus of Nazareth had cast an evil spirit out of a man in the synagogue. Many had heard the demon cry out in the presence of Jesus before fleeing at His word. They had seen the transformation in the once-possessed man and they were astonished. After the services, they had run to their friends and neighbors to tell what they saw.

"Come with us," they encouraged all who were sick. "Come with us, and we will take you to Jesus."

Now they waited quietly, even those who wanted to cry out in pain. Fathers, widows, wives, children, and grandparents. People who hurt, those who were depressed, those who had no hope, those who were facing death. All waited for Jesus to appear. It was a solemn crowd—hushed, awed, waiting at the front door for the meal to be over, so they could find some peace from the sickness that brought them down.

The last hints of sunset faded. Two stars could be seen high above the sycamore trees. A cool breeze off the lake brought with it the scent of coming rain. The door finally opened, and all eyes were fixed on Jesus as He stepped into the street, followed by John and James.

No one called out, and Jesus said nothing, but began going from pallet to pallet touching the sick and healing them. His voice was quiet and compassionate, and no one dared speak louder than Jesus. He cast out several demons, but would not allow any of them to speak, because they knew Him. One by one the people thanked Him, one by one they were healed; some from paralysis, some from blindness, some from afflictions that had brought them down since birth, and still He moved on. Finally, and yet without any sense of hurry in His walk, He came to the last, a blind boy clinging to His mothers garment. Jesus stooped down, looking into those blank eyes, and with love and the healing power of very God, He touched the boy and restored his sight.

He had healed them all…

Jesus' role as "physician" and healer is so a part of the gospel accounts of His life and so essential to Jesus' mission that He cannot be understood apart from it. The crowds seemed instinctively to see Jesus as a "physician." It's a title He clearly deserves. Even among unbelievers of His day and unbelievers today there is a general perception of Jesus as a healer of sick. It is closely entwined with who He is and how He acts towards needy people. Today we see Jesus as someone who is supposed to meet our deepest needs including the need for physical healing. When we read accounts of healing and see healing take place in Jesus' name it strengthens our faith in His nature and in the gospels thus enabling many to believe for salvation. Healing the sick and preaching were often associated in Jesus' ministry. But to confine healing to something that validates the gospel is to miss Christ's compassion for the sick and to turn healing into little more than an attention- gaining religious publicity stunt. The healing nature of Jesus caused Him to move out of genuine compassion for the sick. For Him healing was an essential part of His nature and ministry to hurting people and not merely an "opener" before the message.

It is important to note that the healing power from Jesus goes beyond mending broken bones and curing disease stricken bodies. The healing nature of Jesus touches every level of our existence as human beings: physical, emotional, social, as well as spiritual.

Twice, in the gospel accounts, Jesus referred to Himself as a "physician," once in the sense of "physical healer" during His encounter with His hometown of Nazareth, and once in the sense of "spiritual healer" during His encounter with the scribes and Pharisees in the city of Capernaum.

On this occasion Jesus was preaching to a crowd of people in a house. Because there was no more room to receive people in the house, four men carried their paralyzed friend to the top of the house and let him through the roof in front of Jesus. Jesus always encouraged the active involvement of the sick in their own healing; therefore faith was a necessary ingredient in the healing process. "When Jesus saw their faith, He said to the paralytic, "Son, your sins are forgiven you" (Mark 2:5). The man was healed spiritually but was not yet healed physically. Some of the scribes who heard this started to reason in their hearts and said within themselves "Why does this Man speak blasphemies like this? Who can forgive sins but God alone?" (Mark 2:7). Immediately, Jesus, who heard their thoughts, said to them, "Why do you reason about these things in your hearts? Which is easier, to say to the paralytic, 'your sins are forgiven you,' or to say, 'Arise, take up your bed and walk?'" But that you may know that the Son of Man has power on earth to forgive sins"- He said to the paralytic, "I say to you, arise, take up your bed, and go to your house" (Mark 2:8-11). This amazed everyone and they praised God, saying, "We have never seen anything like this!" (Mark 2:12). Dr. Luke's accounts are similar; "after the healing of the paralytic, the people were filled with awe and said, 'We have seen remarkable things today'" (Luke 5:26).

The scribes could take the physical healer but they had a problem with the spiritual healer who could forgive sin, so they tried to discredit this claim.

Jesus left Capernaum and went to the sea. He passed by Matthew, who was a tax collector, and said to him, "Follow Me." Matthew invited Jesus and His disciples to his house to dine with him. Matthew also invited other tax collectors and friends to dine with them. When the scribes and Pharisees saw this they said to His disciples, "How is it that He eats and drinks with tax collectors and sinners?" When Jesus heard it, He said to them "Those who are well (self-righteous) have no need of a physician, but those who are sick (spiritually). I did not come to call the righteous, but sinners to repentance" (Mark 2:16,17).

Cutting through barriers

Jesus' healing touch did more than send healing power into sick bodies. This physical contact also cut through barriers of isolation and was a sign of Jesus' compassion and solidarity with suffering people. When a leper approached Jesus asking to be healed, Jesus first touched him— an action that meant ritual impurity in Jewish Law. It was an action of extraordinary compassion putting Jesus in vital contact with this human being forced by social custom and indeed legislation to live in isolation and misery. Leprosy in those times had the kind of mark that AIDS has for many people today. Jesus broke down walls of alienation and centuries of prejudice by the simple but powerful gesture of reaching out and touching the body of the leper. Over and over again in the gospel accounts, Jesus deliberately touched sick and disabled persons.

The need for complete healing

Many have placed their hope in the numerous self-help books and seminars and infomercials that endlessly flood our bookstores and television sets. Others have turned to religious leaders that often offer expectations that they are unable to fulfill, leaving their followers discouraged, dismayed, and often even out-of-sorts with God.

This book is for people who hunger for a healing of body as well as spirit and mind they have yet to find. It's all based on the time-honored principle that it is the very nature of Jesus that wants you to be made whole. When Jesus is excluded from the mending equation, real healing just doesn't happen.

Physical ailments that have gone unhealed can fuel alcohol abuse, spousal abuse, overeating, codependency, work addiction, perfectionism, and other compulsions, causing emotional and physical breakdowns of our bodies. It eventually pollutes the very things we care about most: our loved ones, our work, our friendships, and our health and prosperity.

EDITOR'S NOTE

To enjoy the healing nature of Jesus, we must understand that healing comes first by faith and then to fulfillment by obedience to His Word. The prayer of faith comes through our ability to communicate with our creator and starts with a right relationship with His Son, Jesus, the Master Healer. My encouragement to you is to treat your body as a Temple—not a trash can and Love yourself first. How can we truly Love our neighbors if we don't follow God's plan for our self? We should see a difference between believers and non-believers!

According to Dr. T. Colin Campbell, who participated in the largest food study in the history of civilization, (I recommend everybody to read this book) "There is a cure for cancer, and all other diseases, it's called your immune system." Jesus placed the immune system in our bodies. We can enjoy the healing nature of Jesus through prayer and obedience! It's our choice, "Therefore choose Life..." (Deut. 30:19). —JEF

This book was written to let you know how much Jesus loves you and wants you to be complete, healthy, unbroken, and whole. If you want to know what made you the way you are and how to permanently improve your life, then this book is for you.

This book is a healing journal. It is intended to be an interactive guide. If you merely read it once and put it down never to refer to it again, it will not have fulfilled its purpose. You must cooperate with God in healing. Healing requires more than information: It requires transformation, and that takes effort. It takes effort to get to know the One who is in the transforming business. In this book, we will journey into Scripture and learn the healing principles God has established through His Son, Jesus Christ, for our lives. We will learn positive steps we can take to gain God's healing. You will be encouraged and uplifted with the truth of God's Word and the incredible healing nature of Jesus that is offered to each and every one of us if we only embrace His healing nature in our lives.

Living Healthy

Without Fear or Confusion

Lee Fredrickson, Ph.D.

Jesus, the Master Healer, performed miracles for humanity so they could be helped out of their physical and spiritual suffering. He did this so they would experience His presence as God. He touched them, spoke to them, and instructed them in how to live a healthy lifestyle. Some of us have given up on life because of the pain of human suffering. Our hearts cry out for help, hope, and healing.

"Where is God?" we ask.

"Can He help me?" we cry.

"Does He care?" we wonder.

These are normal questions for people in pain—whether physical, spiritual, or emotional. We all want to know if God is great enough to help us or kind enough to care about our suffering. Something deep within us cries out to God. It is as though the human heart knows that only God can help us in such times of distress. Our pain drives us to the only One who can help us. No matter what our religious background or spiritual condition, the cry of our hurting hearts is the cry for God to intervene in our lives. How many times have you heard someone cry out, "Oh, God!" in a moment of personal anguish? There are no real atheists in times of personal crises. Even the hardest hearts become tenderized by human pain and suffering.

Jesus is There When You Need Him Most

Where is Jesus when you can't take the problems of life anymore and your faith seems to be at an end? I have to admit that I've asked that question myself. Most everyone asks it sooner or later. Things can go wrong even when we are doing everything we can to live a life that is right in the sight of God. The truth is that bad things including sickness, does happen to good people. But the question is where is Jesus in the middle of your problems? The answer is in the question. Jesus is right where He said He would be—right in the middle of your problems.

Jesus' Healing Nature Shares Our Suffering with Us

No one enjoys being hurt physically or emotionally. However, no matter how much we seek to protect ourselves and our loved ones from difficult life situations, we still remain susceptible to pain. The fact that Jesus would come to this earth as the incarnate Son of God shows His willingness to share our suffering, our troubles, and our pain. God demonstrates to us, through His Son, that His love for us does not preclude disaster but instead drives Him to suffer the disaster with us. Jesus' suffering on the cross transcended human suffering—for He bore not only the physical pain but the sins of the world. This was the ultimate demonstration of His love for us—a love that would cause Him to reach out to comfort a man who was crucified alongside Him and say, "Today you will be with me in paradise" (Luke 23:43). This same love compelled Him to look down at a grieving mother and say, "'Dear woman, here is your son,' and to the disciple [the apostle John], 'Here is your mother.' From that time on, this disciple took her into his home" (John 19:26-27).

If Jesus, by His very nature, could share the suffering of others while suffering the weight of the sins of the world upon His shoulders, certainly He can share your sufferings, no matter what they may be. In fact, it is through suffering that we can truly encounter Christ. It is a great comfort to know that in our suffering, Christ also suffers with us. Suffering affords possibilities for growth that better times do not. As you come to see hurt as a unique opportunity to encounter the healing touch of grace from Jesus, you are able to move from a position of distress and depression to one of acceptance and victory.

Jesus Gives Us Hope in Our Suffering

Jesus left there and went along the Sea of Galilee. Then He went up on a mountainside and sat down. Great crowds came to Him, bringing the lame, the blind, the crippled, the mute and many others, and laid them at His feet; and He healed them. The people were amazed when they saw the mute speaking; the crippled made well, the lame walking and the blind seeing. And they praised the God of Israel (Matthew 15:29-31).

In this passage Jesus did a lot more than physical healing—He brought hope. A father whose daughter had just died had no hope. A woman who had been bleeding for twelve long years had no hope. Men who were blind and couldn't work or be independent had no hope. A person who couldn't communicate through speech knew only frustration, not hope.

But Jesus brought hope. He raised the dead and stopped the bleeding; He gave sight to the blind and voice to the mute. And Jesus brings us hope too. We know that we can't do what we need to do to please God. Even the apostle Paul writes about his frustration and hopelessness before his own sin (see Romans 7:15-24). But into the picture of hopelessness, Jesus brings hope. He brings hope through His sacrifice for our sins. He brings hope by sharing eternal life with His followers. He gives us hope by personally bringing us the promises of God.

Jesus says something very important to us through His healing miracles. He reminds us that when He is with us, we always have hope. And we do.

God Provides Answers in His Word

If you really want to find God's answers to your troubles, turn to His Word. The Bible is filled with principles for living, and in it we find the answers to the questions that so often trouble our souls. Finding the healing nature of Jesus is not a vague, mystical experience. Rather, it is the result of a deliberate search for truth in His revealed Word.

Jesus is always with us. Even in our darkest hour, He is at work in our lives. We simply need to learn to discern His healing nature.

Why Can't I Find God's Healing?

In the Gospel of Mark, we see an interesting picture. Jesus has just called Matthew, a Jewish tax collector, to be His disciple. Now, Matthew was not at all popular among the Jews. He was, in fact, seen as a traitor. He served the Romans and collected money from his own people (while extorting money from them as well). After Jesus called Matthew, Jesus went to his house and had a meal with none other than tax collectors, publicans, and sinners. When the scribes and Pharisees saw this, they began to complain, "How can Jesus eat with these sinners?" Jesus' response was not what they expected. "It is not the healthy who need a doctor, but the sick. I have not come to call the righteous, but sinners" (Mark 2:17).

Time after time we see in the Bible that Jesus desires for all to be made whole. Being whole means to be complete, to be full of health, to live a life of full abundance in our whole being. This includes our body, our soul, and our spirit. In fact, Jesus said that the reason He came to this earth was "to seek and to save what was lost" (Luke 19:10) and that we "may have life, and have it to the full" (John 10:10). His plan and purpose for us is that we be complete, undiminished, unbroken, and whole.

Throughout His ministry, we see Him healing the sick and hurting. He had compassion on those who were not whole, and with His mighty touch, He restored them.

While in Jerusalem, Jesus came to the pool of Bethesda (incidentally, Bethesda means "House of Grace"), where many were waiting to be healed. "At certain seasons" (John 5:4 NASB), an angel would stir the waters, and the first to enter the waters would be healed of his or her disease, no matter what it was. One man had been there for thirty-eight years—since before Christ had been born.

Jesus came to him and asked him a simple question: "Do you desire to be made whole?" (John 5:6 NKJV). The man answered that he had no one to help him into the water and that others always entered before him so he could not be healed. Jesus said to him, "Get up! Pick up your mat and walk."

Jesus approaches us today and asks us the same simple question: "Do you want to be made whole?" If it's true that He desires wholeness for us, then why are so many not whole?

If there is one thing that is certain, it is the fact that God desires His children to be whole, complete, and fulfilled. But first, we must rid ourselves of those hindrances that keep us from these blessings. Simply put, only when we cooperate with God and by faith position ourselves in a right relationship with Him are we able to find the healing touch we so desire and He desires to give us. The principle taught by the psalmist is still true today: "No good thing does He withhold from those whose walk is blameless" (Psalm 84:11).

Before we get into the details of the healing nature of Jesus, we need to clearly understand that complete healing is possible. Often we see Christ's work of salvation only in terms of forgiveness from our sins. But salvation is much more than this. Jesus came to heal us from all our wounds and set us free from all that binds us. Yes, hurt is inevitable, but healing is possible. Jesus Christ calls us to be whole and makes this possible through His willingness to be broken for us.

Too often we take a fatalistic view about the damaging effects of tragedy. We may feel bitterness and anger as a result of tragedy but at the same time feel, "I am what I am because of what has happened to me, and there is nothing I can do about it now." Just because I experience hurt from the hands of others or natural causes doesn't mean I have to go through life an emotional cripple in bondage to the pain and anger associated with those hurts.

Many people continue to live in slavery to the past. Some lack the faith to believe that Jesus can set them free from the gripping effects of their hurts. Some are not ready to forgive those who hurt them and are resolved to cling to their anger and the pain that is associated with it. Others give, but they can't get any relief from the anger and pain. Still others are simply afraid of experiencing more pain and, knowing that healing will involve more pain, would rather remain stuck in park.

Three steps are necessary for emotional healing:
1.   Accept the gain that comes from pain.
2.   Allow the healing nature of Christ to share your burden.
3.   Anger is released through forgiveness.

Step One: Accept the Gain That Comes From Pain
God often uses the worst circumstances to bring about the best results in our lives. He allows us to experience pain, sorrow, anguish, and disappointment so that we might reach out to Him and find His grace sufficient to our needs. When everything is going well in our lives, it is easy to forget God. Pain is the great reminder that we can't make it without Him.

Most of all, God uses pain and suffering to display His power and grace. When we struggle with the difficulties in life, we recognize afresh how great His provisions really are on our behalf. Most of our problems, difficulties, and pains are only temporary. They get our attention focused on God so that He can heal us, strengthen our faith, and restore us to even more effective lives in serving Him.

Everyone has his or her own way of coping with pain. Some go to a friend, some use spiritual resources such as prayer and Bible reading, some lose themselves in their work, while others cope with the hurt through some form of entertainment. While these are good ways to deal with the pain, there is a danger in immersing yourself in them in order to hide the hurt and not deal with it.

All hurt involves loss, and for emotional healing to take place, we must often allow ourselves to face again all the feelings associated with that loss, uproot these hidden hurts, see them in the light of God's mercy toward us, release them to Him, and go on with living.

When you allow yourself to experience the pain again and allow Jesus to share your burden, then you are ready to take your next step toward total healing.

Step Two: Allow the Healing Nature of Christ to Share Your Burden

Although the hurt you feel inside will often cause you to want to go into a corner and hide, there is something inside that cries out for love. It is within our human nature to want to share our hurt with someone who can care for, support, and love us. Sometimes sharing our burdens with Jesus is God's way of preparing us to share them with others. God often shows His love to us through the compassion of others. Sometimes, all that is needed is a listener with a face and gentle arms to hug.

The healing nature of Jesus caused Him to want to be our burden bearer. Isaiah described this attribute of Christ when he penned these words: "Surely He took up our infirmities and carried our sorrows, yet we considered Him stricken by God, smitten by Him, and afflicted. But He was pierced for our transgressions, He was crushed for our iniquities; the punishment that brought us peace was upon Him, and by His wounds we are healed" (Isaiah 53:4-5). God became personally involved with our hurts when He sent His Son to be the One who would bear our burdens, carry our sorrows, take upon Himself our sickness and infirmities, and heal us.

Because Jesus came to this earth and suffered with us and for us, He understands our suffering and is able to share our burdens. This suffering qualifies Him to help us when we can't take the hurt anymore. When we feel like throwing in the towel because of hurts, disappointments, or losses, we need to remember that Jesus is always available to share these burdens, and He shares them with compassion.

The Feeding of the Four Thousand

Three days came and went while Jesus healed the sick brought to Him on that hillside in Galilee. A crowd of four thousand men, not counting women and children, had followed Jesus to a lonely place away from the towns. Jesus had compassion on the crowd, called His disciples together, and said, "I do not want to send [the people] away hungry, or they may collapse on the way" (Matthew 15:32). He then proceeded to feed the entire crowd with only seven loaves of bread and a few fish.

In itself, this is an amazing story—a miracle! But we would be wrong to see it as the whole story. If today, two thousand years after the event, we were to read this story out of context, it would be of little or no significance. The full story is not the story of the God-man named Jesus who miraculously fed thousands of people many centuries ago. The real story—the "story behind the story," as the journalists say—is about a man who healed lepers, a man who caused the blind to see and the deaf to hear, a man who brought dead people back to life, a man who welcomed sinners into His company and forgave them their sins, a man who suffered and died for us human beings, a man with total respect and reverence for all people as God's supreme miracle of creation. The real story in this miracle and in all the miracle stories about Jesus is that He cared enough to do what He did for other people. He cared for them one person at a time; each with special needs for healing. He listened to them and by His very nature He healed them.

Step Three: Anger is Released Through Forgiveness

In the sixth chapter of Matthew, Jesus taught His disciples how to pray through what is commonly known as "The Lord's Prayer." This is perhaps the most important prayer recorded in all of Scripture, because it serves as a model prayer for all Christians. There are six petitions within this prayer, but Jesus elaborates on only one of them. It is not the petition for the kingdom of God to come to earth or the request for daily bread, but His plea that God forgive us our debts as we forgive our debtors. Perhaps He returned to this petition because it is so foreign to human nature to forgive. Without a doubt He felt that it needed an explanation and even a warning to those who chose to neglect it.

Jesus expounded on this petition in verse 14 and 15 when He said, "For if you forgive men when they sin against you, your heavenly Father will also forgive you. But if you do not forgive men their sins, your Father will not forgive your sins."

We read a similar statement in Mark 11:26, "If you do not forgive, neither will your Father . . . forgive your sins." Christ tells us that if we do not exercise forgiveness toward others, our own sins will not be forgiven us. Not that God forgives only on an exchange basis, but this teaching clearly indicates that God has a great flood tide of forgiveness for us, and He is bound to restrain it until we ourselves forgive those who have wronged us. He will forgive all our sins, mistakes, and blunders by the power of the blood of Christ, but we will never know that true forgiveness until we are willing to forgive others.

Christ—Our Great Example

Christ is our prime example for forgiving others. It was a horrible, yet glorious day in history. So much had happened in the previous twenty-four hours that we cannot begin to comprehend. Less than a day before, Christ had been spending time with His disciples in prayer at the Garden of Gethsemane. Gethsemane was the place where olives were pressed into oil with the millstones. The crushing weight of the huge stones would squeeze the very juices out of the fruit until it was a lifeless pulp. Christ felt a similar weight upon Himself that night, knowing that He would offer up His life for humankind.

Imagine the dusky sky illuminating the city below as He prayed in the garden. Visualize a line of torches moving up the mountain like glowing ants. Imagine the feelings Christ must have experienced, knowing that those lights were carried by soldiers coming to arrest Him. Imagine the thoughts that ran through His mind since He knew that Judas, one of the twelve, was leading the way.

Judas was the one whom most of his contemporaries viewed as successful. He was a go-getter and a manager of money. He was known for his business ability and had been given great responsibility. Even those close to him trusted him and gave him charge of the books. But his strength was also his weakness. He was trusted by the other disciples to the very end, to the extent that they thought he left the Passover meal to make payments for the food or to the charities. That departure was instead his dismissal by Christ to do what he was to do, namely to betray Christ. Scripture tells us that he was a thief and stole from the money bag (see John 12:6). His greed for money led him to the priests that night. Have you ever had anyone betray you?

Another man who deeply hurt Jesus was Simon Peter. Peter was one of the inner circle of the disciples. Whenever Jesus drew His intimate circle to Him, Peter was there. Peter was a man of common interests and upbringing. He was also a tradesman, a fisherman. Unlike Judas, his interests were spending time with a select few, building relationships, and sharing dreams. His love for Jesus was incomparable. Many events prove this: walking on the water to meet Jesus, declaring his desire to build him a shelter, proclaiming undying devotion, and even jeopardizing his own life by attacking one of the Roman guards who came to take Christ away. Peter's devotion was so strong that he and John were the only disciples (as far as Scripture says) who followed Christ and His captors to the house of the high priest.

But we also read that on the night of Jesus' trial, when observers asked Peter if he was one of Jesus' followers, he quickly denied his association three separate times (see Luke 22). Upon the third denial, Christ looked at Peter with knowing eyes and all could hear the cock crow, according to prophecy. This same man who declared undying allegiance to Christ had denied Him.

As Christ was hanging on the cross just a few hours later, He said some of the most profound and convicting words of exhortation. He had been beaten, He was bleeding, and He had a crown of thorns on His head. He had been mocked and spit upon. His closest friends had deserted Him, betrayed Him, and hid from Him. With these events in the forefront of His mind, yet having a heart of compassion, He cried out, "Father, forgive them, for they do not know what they are doing" (Luke 22:34).

If Jesus could forgive us, how can we not forgive those who have wronged us? The real heart of the matter of forgiveness is realizing that God is greater than all our hurts. He can deal with those who wrong us if we are willing to forgive them. Who has hurt you? Your wife, your husband, your parents, an ex-wife, an ex-husband, a former business partner, your boss, or your friend? Whoever they may be, God can enable you to fully and completely forgive them.

In Matthew 18:21, Peter asked Jesus about the law of forgiveness: "Lord, how many times shall I forgive my brother when he sins against me?" Then Peter, thinking he had prescribed and added one: "Seven times?" Peter's generosity paled in comparison to Christ's response of "seventy times seven times." This was not intended to be a specific number but an exaggerated hyperbole meaning infinite and without end.

Why? Because it's the character of God to have complete, total, everlasting forgiveness. We must be willing to admit that we have feelings against someone and confess them before God. If we do that, God is willing and waiting to forgive us. Only we and our attitudes of unforgiveness stand in the way of God's healing in our lives. Christ's words ring just as true today as they did two thousand years ago when He said, "If you forgive men when they sin against you, your heavenly Father will also forgive you" (Matthew 6:14).

Blessings are Unleashed Through Forgiveness!

When we forgive, we unleash the dynamic and powerful blessings of God upon our lives. First Peter 3:8-9 states it clearly: "Finally, all of you, live in harmony with one another; be sympathetic, love as brothers, be compassionate and humble. Do not repay evil with evil or insult with insult, but with blessing, because to this you were called so that you may inherit a blessing." This verse shows us that if we live in a spirit of compassion and love, caring for one another, not bearing a grudge, but forgiving one another, we will inherit untold blessings from God. These blessings include mercy shown to us by God and others, a restoration of joy in our lives, and a spirit of love and peace toward others.

Simply put, in our search for healing, forgiveness is a vital key. Without it, we will do no more than what we can do in our own flesh. But with forgiveness playing out its divine role in our minds and hearts, God's power will be released in our behalf and the healing nature of Jesus will have already begun!

DEALING WITH
PAIN AND SUFFERING

Lee Fredrickson, Ph.D.

Pain and suffering: Without a doubt these are two of the hardest subjects to deal with. We consistently ask, "Why do Christians suffer? Christians are supposed to have joy and peace and prosperity; so why do we suffer?" That question is not so easily answered—especially when a Christian is struggling with personal or family illness.

Part of the problem is that many misunderstand what it means to be a Christian. Being a Christian does not mean we will never have pain or sickness or suffering. But it does mean that we will have enough strength and peace and joy to make it through. In 2 Corinthians, Paul identifies why we, as Christians, sometimes have to suffer. In fact, even Christ speaks of the fact that we will be persecuted and endure suffering for His sake. I believe that this sometimes includes personal illness, no matter how close we are to God. Why? So that God can receive glory when our healing comes. Elmer Towns, in his book *The Son*, writes this:

Jerusalem A.D. 28: Jesus heals the blind man

As Jesus left the Temple, John and the other apostles quickly ran to catch up with Him. The apostles tried to hurry Jesus along, but the Messiah's attention was drawn to a blind man sitting outside the Temple begging for alms. His soiled tunic was stretched out in the street. Bugs and ants were eating the few remains of bread that had fallen into his lap. The blind man was propped against a stone wall, his vacant eyes wide open, staring into the space, seeing nothing. The sun shone directly in his eyes, but he knew it not.

Jesus knelt and said to the man, "Be of good cheer, my son. Salvation has come to you this day."

The man smiled and said, "I will gladly accept it. I have been blind since birth these forty years."

John expected Jesus to touch the man's eyes to heal him, and on many occasions Jesus had simply spoken and the blind saw. But Jesus did neither this time.

"I am the light of the world to the woman caught in adultery," Jesus explained to His apostles, "but I am also the light of the world to this man born in blindness."

The shadow of Jesus fell across the blind man's face, blocking out the glaring sun, but still the man did not blink. He couldn't discern the difference between light and darkness.

Jesus spat on the ground. Then He stooped to make mud with the saliva and clay from the ground. In the palm of His hands, He formed the clay into a thick paste. Then Jesus dipped the tip of His finger into the clay and rubbed the mixture into the man's eyes—not on his eyelids, but right into the eyes.

Jesus said to him, "Go wash in the pool of Siloam." John looked down the street, past the shops and tables, past the commotion of shoppers and businessmen in the bazaars in the direction of Siloam. He knew it was a long walk.

Then Jesus turned, saying to the apostles, "Let us go."

And they walked away in the other direction, knowing this

task was done. Jesus had left the responsibility for the miracle with the one in need. It was now the blind man's responsibility to obey and be healed.

John was puzzled by the instructions of Jesus. The pool of Bethesda was only a half a block away. Why hadn't he sent the blind man to wash in Bethesda? Across the street, a donkey drank from a feed trough; it had water with which the blind man could wash the clay from his eyes. But the pool of Siloam was all the way down the Tyropoeon Valley on the other end of Jerusalem. It was a long, tedious walk through many narrow arches, across shopping bazaars and down terraced steps.

John was concerned for the ragged man, and yet the blind man seemed to know the way. He had not hesitated, but at Jesus' command had struggled to his feet, propping himself on a gnarled walking cane, and immediately set out for the pool as Jesus had instructed him. In fact, it was a trip the blind man had taken many times. *Tap . . . tap . . . tap . . .*, he instinctively began tapping his cane on the cobblestones, searching for a passage through the crowds. His steps were unsure on the uneven pavement, yet his feet had direction. He began walking toward Siloam. John turned and set off after the apostles, convinced that the old man knew where he was going.

The blind man picked his way through the crowds, passing tables and stacks of pottery. He was not distracted or detoured. Near the pool of Siloam, the steps narrowed and descended steeply. The flow of water emerged from Hezekiah's Tunnel and, with a friendly gurgle, emptied into a larger pool. Palms and a large eucalyptus shaded the garden like setting tucked away under the shadow of the outer wall of Jerusalem. The freshwater usually attracted a large crowd, most of who came to fill their water pots. But on the Sabbath, only a few moved about the pool enjoying a relatively cool autumn day. Slowly, step by step, the blind man descended. He instinctively reached out for a handhold that was not there.

Tap, tap, tap, the blind man stumbled toward the edge of the pool. *Tap . . . tap . . . SPLASH.* He found the water's edge. Dropping his walking stick to the ground, he bent over to lie flat on his belly at the pool's edge. Dipping his hands into the water, he splashed clear liquid into his muddied eyes. Then he splashed another handful of water into his face. Then he repeated the process again . . . and again.

Finally, he dried his eyes with the sleeve of his robe, and then stopped suddenly, realizing he could see the fibers of his tunic. He jerked his head backward when he spotted his reflection in the water for the first time. He stared steadfastly at his face in the water, puzzled every time the waves of the pool distorted his vision. He lay on his stomach for a long time trying to match the image he saw in the pool with his previous self-perception.

Then rolling over onto his back, he gazed up into the blue skies. "Look!" he said to no one in particular, pointing at the white clouds. Then he stared into the sun and for the first time in his life, he blinked, putting up his hands to shield his tender eyes from the sun's piercing rays. This man, who was born blind, could now see.

What can we learn from the healing of the blind man?

One day, while Jesus and His disciples were walking through Jerusalem, they saw a man who had been born blind (see John 9). The disciples asked Jesus whose sin had caused this man's condition—his own or his parents'. They assumed that suffering is always the result of someone's personal sin. Christ responded that the man's condition was not caused by sin at all: "But this happened so that the work of God might be displayed in his life" (v. 3). Jesus then used this opportunity not only to perform a miracle but also to bring God glory.

As the Son of God, Jesus made new eyes for this man out of the dust of the earth (clay) and spittle. How curious that He did this. Today with laser surgical techniques, corneal transplants and other techniques, the physical accuracy of vision correction can be understood by today's science. However, Jesus did this as an example of His position as God and not just as the "sinner" like the rest of the authorities who questioned the truth of the blind man's claims. What is also interesting is that this was a test for the blind man. He was told to go wash his eyes at the pool of Siloam, which was across town several miles away. Jesus could have told the blind man to wash his eyes in the pool at Bethesda. But He told him to walk to the pool across town. We can learn several things from this healing. One is obedience to the Word. When we are told to do something as a request by those trying to help us, we should consider following the set of instructions. Humility as a virtue is falling by the wayside today. Being humble to take instructions is an important aspect to our healthy lifestyle. Another thing to consider is the fact that Jesus was compassionate towards this blind man. While this was an extraordinary example of healing, our tendency may be to overlook the simple things that we can do to change our lifestyle into one that is not only appealing to God, but will allow us to reap the benefits of good health today.

Those who had known the blind man all his life were incredulous! "Isn't this the same man who used to sit and beg?" (v. 8). When they took him to be examined by the Pharisees, they wouldn't believe he'd been born blind until they interrogated his parents. As much as they didn't want to believe that this man had been healed, they could not argue the fact that he had gained his sight.

How did God receive glory in this? First, the event increased the disciples' faith. During these first months of Christ's ministry, His disciples were still fluctuating in their faith that He was the Messiah. Each miracle brought them closer to a deeper knowledge that Jesus was the Christ. This should be the same in our lives.

Second, the man declared his faith in Jesus when Jesus found him in the temple court. What better reward can there be for our sufferings than to see a person, possibly a loved one, come to salvation through the testimony of our experiences?

Unless the physical body, including the emotional and mental processes, is prepared for healing than we cannot realize the full healing that is available to us through Jesus. The rules of a healing nature lifestyle including those expressed about diet, proper work ethic and activities, prayer, fasting and balancing activity with rest are talked about in this book. There are rules for a healing nature lifestyle that are clear and accessible for man, woman and child. Following these rules can help re-establish health. It was Christ's way, to minister to the people in all walks of life regardless of status, and to instruct them how to care for themselves. This is truly health freedom. This lifestyle is a system of restoring health that develops personal independence and freedom. To-day's healthy lifestyle uses natural things for curing disease and restoring health.

EDITOR'S NOTE

"Pain is the number one reason why people go to doctors." Dr. George Malkmus, wrote a book, *Why Christians are Sick.* He asks a question: "What does a Christian, and a non-christian do when they get sick? When a non-christian gets sick, he runs as fast as he can to a doctor, and if he doesn't like the diagnosis, he goes to another to get a second opinion...when a Christian is diagnosed, he prays first, and then runs as fast as he can to a doctor, and if he doesn't like the diagnosis, he runs to get a second opinion from another doctor!"

God made the statement that He would be our Master Healer, "I am the Lord that Healeth thee" (Exodus 15:26).

We need to go back to the Word! The Word is Love! Love yourself, educate and put into practice the Word. Five years from today, you will be the same, except for the books you read, the people you associate with, and the "food" you put in your mouth. Vibrant Life, and Wholeness can be yours! "Choose life, that both you and your seed [children] may live...that you may obey Him..." (Deut. 29:19,20). —JEF

STEPS TOWARD WHOLENESS

Lee Fredrickson, Ph.D.

Let's look at the story found in Matthew 8:5-13 about the miracle of the healing of the servant of a Roman centurion to see if we can better understand how to appropriate healing in our lives.

The story opens when Jesus entered Capernaum, on the northwest shore of Galilee. Jesus was frequently seen here with His disciples or with a crowd. Capernaum is believed to have been His primary resting-place during His Galilean ministry. Jesus had been speaking to a crowd, expounding on doctrines and teaching the people.

While there, a centurion approached Him and caught His attention. Roman soldiers were commonplace in Capernaum at this time. The city was a seaport and customs station. Many affluent officers of the Roman government lived there. It was also occupied by the Roman soldiers whose job was to keep the Jews content by erecting a synagogue in the city.

This particular centurion frantically came to Jesus, begging Him, "Lord, my servant lies at home paralyzed and in terrible suffering" (v. 6). Jesus responded by simply saying to the man, "I will go and heal him"

(v. 7). To this, the centurion responded that he was not worthy to have Jesus in his home and that if Jesus would just say the words, his servant would be healed. He then explained that he understood the principles of authority. Just as a commander in the Roman army, all Jesus had to do was speak and the instruction would be carried out. The centurion believed that Jesus' authority over the created universe included the ability to heal people of any disease, and any abnormality, both physically and emotionally. Jesus was amazed at this man's faith, and He looked to the disciples and said, "I tell you the truth, I have not found anyone in Israel with such great faith" (v. 10).

Seven Steps To Follow When Seeking Healing

If you are presently suffering from physical illness in your life, let me suggest seven steps for dealing with that sickness. To aid our discussion, we'll further examine the story of healing we just discussed.

Step #1: Come To Jesus with Your Need

This first point may seem obvious, but many overlook it. If we need healing, we must come to Jesus with our need. The Roman centurion's first step was coming to Jesus; this showed that he believed Jesus could meet his need. We see over and over in the Bible that we need to come to Jesus in order to receive help. Jesus himself said, "Come to me, all you who are weary and burdened, and I will give you rest" (Matthew 11:28) and "Whoever comes to me I will never drive away" (John 6:37). In other instances of healing, people came to Jesus with their needs, and He healed them. In fact, most instances of healing occurred when people *came to Jesus* and *sought Him out* with their needs. We should not ignore this precedent; we, also, should approach Him with our needs. Hebrews 4:16 specifically instructs us to come boldly to God's throne of grace so that we can obtain help in our times of need. When we come to Jesus with our needs, we demonstrate our trust and our faith in His ability to meet that need.

Step #2: Request—Don't Demand

Next, we notice that the centurion came with a *request* for Christ to heal his servant, not with a demand. He approached with a humble attitude, aware of the fact that Jesus' authority gave Him the right to deny the request. We need to understand that God's sovereignty gives Him the right to choose how He will respond. We cannot manipulate God; we can only come to Him with a humble attitude and believe that He can overcome our situation. Respecting His sovereignty should also make us mindful that our demands cannot accomplish anything. And just as the centurion humbled himself to beg Jesus' assistance on behalf of his servant, so should we humble ourselves.

Now you may say, "I would never demand anything from Jesus." But so often we do. We know what our problem is and have even figured out how God should fix it. We pray, saying, "God, I have this problem. Now if you will do things this way, I won't have this problem." Does that sound familiar? We do this so often and never realize how demanding we are of God.

The major problem with this technique is that it does not work! Why? Because we ignore that the will of God is to do what is best for His children. God knows more than we do, and He understands what we need, even before we need it. Jesus lovingly calls us to cast our cares upon Him, for He cares for us. He simply says, "Let me have them; I know what is best for you." The centurion came to Christ demanding nothing; rather, he simply trusted that the God who made his servant could heal his servant if He wished.

Step #3: Submit to God's Authority

When we bring our requests to Jesus, we come in obedience to His authority. The centurion demonstrated this obedience when he responded, "Lord, I do not deserve to have you come under my roof. But just say the word, and my servant will be healed. For I myself am a man under authority, with soldiers under me. I tell this one, 'Go,' and he goes; and that one, 'Come,' and he comes. I say to my servant, 'Do this,' and he does it" (Matthew 8:8-9).

This soldier was a man of authority! He was a Roman centurion, given charge of one hundred fighting soldiers. He would have been one of sixty men in charge of a Roman legion. His responsibilities would have included drilling his men; inspecting their weapons, food, and clothing; and commanding them in battle. If men did not obey his orders, they could be killed on the spot. A centurion held complete authority over the soldiers. This man knew well the power of the spoken word. When he spoke, it was with the authority and power of Rome behind him. His explanation of authority was to show Jesus that he understood His power. He recognized that Jesus was Creator and under the authority of heaven itself.

It is useless to ask God for anything unless we are willing to live under His authority. We must do what He tells us to do—without compromise—when He tells us to do it, no matter what it may be! This is the only way to truly live under the authority of God. If we do not submit ourselves, we might as well not ask.

I believe that one of the reasons few people are healed today is that few are willing to submit to God's authority. They want the blessings of God but do not want the responsibility of walking closely with Him and living in total obedience to His will.

The old hymn "Trust and Obey" describes it so aptly:

Then in fellowship sweet, we will sit at His feet,

Or we'll walk by His side in the way;

What He says we will do, where He sends we will go.

Never fear, only trust and obey.

Trust and obey, for there's no other way

To be happy in Jesus, but to trust and obey.

Step #4: Believe That It Can Be Done!

The last principle that we see in this story is that we need to have the faith that God *can* work and *will* work in our situation. What impressed Jesus about the centurion was his faith: "He was astonished and said. . ., 'I have not found anyone in Israel with such great faith'" (v. 10). Jesus went on to say that many "from the east and the west" would take their places in the kingdom of God. This man would be one of those men of faith. And true to the man's faith, Jesus simply spoke the words and Scripture tells us that the servant was healed at that very same moment. " 'Go! It will be done just as you believed it would.' And his servant was healed at that very hour" (v. 13).

Just as this man believed and asked God, we must do the same. Although we do not have the opportunity to find Jesus walking along our streets, He has provided a means to communicate with Him. Philippians 4:6 tells us that through our prayers, we need to make our requests known to God, not being anxious or fearful. We should not be surprised when God answers our prayers, as long as we approach Him with a pure heart and have the faith to believe that He can work miraculously in our lives. So often we pray but do not believe that God wants to answer our prayers or is capable of answering our prayers. This man staked it all on Jesus and wasn't surprised when the answer came.

A Biblical Example of Faith in Action

In Acts 12, we see a different picture of prayer and a lack of belief that God is listening and actively working. Peter has been thrown into prison during the Passover season because Herod became hostile toward the church in Jerusalem. Herod had recently murdered James, the brother of John the apostle. Peter's life was spared for the moment because it was Passover time. Herod intended to bring Peter before the Jews, most likely to be killed like James, because it would please them. Peter was under heavy guard and bound hand and foot. He slept between soldiers, and a guard was at the door. This would have weighed heavily on Peter's mind as he sat in the prison, even as he prayed for deliverance.

Several believers from the church had gathered in prayer for Peter at the house of John Mark's mother—and God responded. He sent an angel to Peter's cell during the night. The angelic visitor awakened Peter and removed his chains. He then told Peter to put on his clothes and shoes and to follow him. The angel led him into the city, down the streets, right to Mary's door. All this time, Peter "had no idea that what the angel was doing was really happening" (v. 9). But when the angel left him, he knew that God had delivered him out of the hands of Herod and the Jews. When he realized that he was standing in front of Mary's house, he knocked on the door and a young girl named Rhoda came and asked who it was. Peter responded, and Rhoda, recognizing his voice, turned and ran to tell the others that Peter was standing at the door! Instead of believing that God had done what they were asking, they told her to be quiet and would not believe her. When she kept insisting, they suggested that it was his angel at the door. But this did not stop Rhoda, who knew for a fact that God answered their prayers. The Bible says that Peter continued to knock, and when they finally opened the door, they were "astonished" to see Peter. Astonished at answered prayer! If God miraculously answered our prayers, would we be surprised? How often do we pray and not truly expect a response? There is no doubt that God calls us to pray with faith. If we pray without faith, we seldom see the results.

Why Is Faith So Important?

The Scripture clearly teaches that we can come to God by faith and request physical healing. We must not demand it from God, but we can come boldly before the throne of grace and call upon Jesus for His healing touch.

But what is so special about faith? It permeates the pages of the Word of God from Genesis to Revelation. It is the essential ingredient in any exchange between God and man. In fact, Scripture says that we cannot please God without it: "Without faith it is impossible to please God, because anyone who comes to Him must believe that He exists and that He rewards those who earnestly seek Him" (Hebrews 11:6). By our faith we gain access into the "grace in which we now stand" (Romans 5:2). Deliverance from sin and sickness and all the power of the enemy is by faith.

Faith is equivalent to obedience and righteousness: "To the man who does not work but trusts God who justifies the wicked, his faith is credited as righteousness" (Romans 4:5).

What Is Healing Faith?

Faith is the heart cry of the child of God. It penetrates the heavens, parting the veil, allowing us to obtain all the will of the Father. It is a light the darkness cannot extinguish, an anchor the storm has no power to uproot.

Faith sees the invisible, believes the unthinkable, and does the impossible. Faith is the life of the righteous, the substance of intangible hope, the assurance of possession in the absence of perception. Faith precedes seeing, hearing, touching. Believing is seeing! The writer of Hebrews says, "Now faith is being sure of what we hope for and certain of what we do not see" (Hebrews 11:1).

Faith is fully persuaded. Speaking of Abraham, the Scripture says, "He did not waiver through unbelief regarding the promise of God, but was strengthened in his faith and gave glory to God, being fully persuaded that God had power to do what He had promised" (Romans 4:20-21). The Book of James says we must not doubt: "When he asks, he must believe and not doubt, because he who doubts is like a wave of the sea, blown and tossed by the wind. That man should not think he will receive anything from the Lord; he is a double-minded man, unstable in all he does" (James 1:6-8).

Faith trusts in the character of our God and in the veracity of His Word. Faith defines truth by eternal standards. It is a gift from the Father to the heart of the believer. The psalmist knew what it meant to trust in the unfailing character of God: "But I trust in your unfailing love; my heart rejoices in your salvation" (Psalm 13:5).

Faith is never stagnant; it should be ever increasing, fed on the Holy Scriptures and exercised in the trials of life. Paul praised the Thessalonians for their increasing faith: "We ought always to thank God for you, brothers, and rightly so, because your faith is growing more and more, and the love every one of you has for each other is increasing" (2 Thessalonians 1:3).

Faith gives glory to God in advance of evidence. Like Paul in prison, it sings praises at midnight, ignoring the chains that bind and worships in the day of adversity. It looks beyond the storm-swept sea to meet the Master's eyes, and it walks upon the living rock of His Word.

Faith has a voice! "'The word is near you; it is in your mouth and in your heart,' that is, the word of faith we are proclaiming" (Romans 10:8). Faith flows from the heart through the mouth and frames new worlds of beauty conceived in heaven. It calls things that are not as though they were, and they become. It calls defeat victory and weakness strength.

David believed and spoke, and the giant perished. Joshua believed and spoke, and the walls crumbled. Abel believed, and now by faith, though he is dead, he still speaks. If you have ears to hear, you can yet hear his words echoing through the ages. Faith has the ring of immortality to it. It speaks of higher thoughts and higher ways. Through us, Abraham's faith is still reaping the promise.

Faith's voice speaks the language of truth, the vocabulary of blessing, the dialect of peace. No lie is found on its holy lips.

Faith combs God's Word for the promises of God. Then with the lips it turns the key; with the tongue of thanksgiving, it slides the bolt; and with actions in harmony with its words, it opens the door. What faith has opened, no man can shut.

Faith demands action. Noah built the ark. Abraham offered Isaac. David ran to meet the giant. Their faith and their actions were working together. Their actions quickened their faith. The Roman centurion we discussed earlier had a great faith mixed with a great obedience, and that brought great power with God. And Jesus rewarded his display of faith by answering his request to heal his servant.

Faith must be exercised. James 2:14 says, "What good is it, my brothers, if a man claims to have faith but has no deeds?" Use your faith or lose your faith! Feed it with the Word. Water it with the Spirit. Exercise it, embrace it, and protect it—for your faith is your victory!

God wants us to come to Him in faith and ask for His intervention on our behalf. But He doesn't guarantee healing based upon the degree of our faith. The healing response of God is conditional upon two factors: our faith and His will.

Step #5: Add Patience to Your Faith

Through faith and patience, you inherit the promises. Make up your mind never to quit! The darker it gets, the more you confess. The longer it takes, the stronger you become. How long do you have to do it? For as long as it takes. Every case is different. Healing can take ten days, six weeks, three years, or longer. In some cases, it may not come this side of heaven, but rest assured, healing will come. Just decide in your heart right now that you're in it for the long haul, and come hell or high water, you will never quit. Once you are locked in to faith, your victory is assured. The only way you can lose is by agreeing to be defeated, so refuse to agree!

Step #6: Confess and Forsake All Known Sin

As we have seen, there are many reasons why people are sick. In some cases, it is merely a result of the frailty of our bodies and the aging process. For others, sickness is an attack of Satan. (But in every "attack" case, God, in His goodness, sets a limit on that suffering and overrules it for His own good purpose.) And sometimes, God allows sickness to bring about His divine purpose. But for some, sickness is a direct result of a sinful lifestyle.

If you are in need of healing, examine your heart to make sure that your suffering is not a result of some deliberate sin in your life. If you do have such sin in your life, confess it to God and forsake it. If you are ill because of a destructive habit that is destroying your physical body, you may not be able to undo all of the damage that has been done, but the sooner you quit, the better. Without making a complete break from that habit, you may never know the kind of health that you could have known had you quit.

You can continue to go through the routine of life pretending that your illness is not all that serious. But chances are that it will eventually take you. There is nothing more tragic than a premature death caused by a sinful habit that was known to be harmful but was never dealt with. The psalmist put it like this, "Before I was afflicted I went astray, but now I obey your word" (Psalm 119:67). The writer acknowledged that his sinful lifestyle had led him astray and resulted in physical illness. But he had now come to a point of physical repentance and had returned to the Lord and was keeping His commandments.

The longer you indulge in sinful habits, the more you will accelerate the process of sickness and death in your own body. The sooner you turn away from those habits, the more quickly you can hope to return to health.

Step #7: Trust God To Do What Is Best For You

There is a vast difference between trusting the sovereignty of God and fatalistically resigning oneself to sickness without hope of change. For example, if you have been told that you have cancer, you can resign yourself to the consequences and sit there and die or you can make use of every possible medical procedure to help cure the cancer and pray in faith asking God to heal you. I believe the latter option is the correct one.

All of us have seen many who received healing through prayer and medicine working hand in hand. With that in mind, the essence of the prayer of the believer should be something like this:

Dear Lord, I know that you love me more than I love myself. I believe that your purposes for my life are greater than my own could ever be. Therefore, I believe you will answer my prayer in the greatest way possible. I am asking you to heal me of this sickness. By faith, I thank you in advance for hearing my prayer and bringing me the answer. I receive my healing in accordance to your will. In the mighty name of Jesus Christ, I pray. Amen.

When you pray like that, you will have come to a point of spiritual maturity where you are able to trust the sovereign purpose of God, while at the same time believing that He can move miraculously on your behalf. By taking these seven steps toward healing, the outcome will always be the very best God has for you. And you can firmly place your trust in that unfailing truth!

COMMITMENT IS EVERYTHING

Simple Ways to Be Healthy, Stay Balanced & Experience Health Bliss

Susan Smith Jones, Ph.D. ©

Many years ago, my doctor told me that because I fractured my back in a terrible auto accident, I should get used to a life of pain, inactivity, and difficulty, and I would never be able to carry anything heavier than a light purse. I felt quite upset when hearing the doctor's prognosis. The accident was the *impetus* to change my life. I refused to believe the doctor's prognosis and turned inward, to God. As I began to read books and attend lectures on the power of commitment and of the Lord in physical healing, I got the courage and the passion to prove my doctor wrong. Within six months, I had no more pain, and the doctor said it was a miracle. My recovery proved to me that we have within ourselves everything we need to live our lives to the fullest.

Today, my health and my life has become the antithesis of that diagnosis. How did I get from the hospital bed to a life of health, peace, and success? Well, this chapter, along with my books *Be Healthy~Stay Balanced, Health Bliss, The Healing Power of NatureFoods Renew Your Life, Choose to Live Peacefully*, and *Recipes for Health Bliss* provide you with the roadmap and all of the tools you need to disease-proof your body and create vibrant health.

Helen Keller once communicated the following: *When one door closes, another opens; but often we look so long at the closed door that we do not see the one which has opened for us.* After the accident, all I could see was a closed door. I was filled with depression, self-pity, confusion, and feelings of being victimized. After a couple of weeks, I went to a favorite spot overlooking the Santa Monica Bay where I often go when I am in need of inspiration. I had a heart-to-heart talk with Jesus, who has always been my constant companion, ever since I was a little girl.

On the one hand, I was convinced that life was meant to be a magnificent adventure—to be lived fully, which to me means to be lived joyfully, passionately, healthfully, and peacefully. Yet it was clear that the life the doctor had described didn't align with my beliefs and desires; I just couldn't accept it. I knew I had a choice to make—and I made it. While I didn't know exactly how I could change my physical condition, I recognized that my best friend and confidant, Jesus, had the answers. So I simply made a deep commitment to let go, to live more from His guidance, and to accept only vibrant, radiant health.

Of course, it hasn't always been an easy road, and I have made many mistakes. That's just part of living and learning. Nonetheless, in retrospect, I can see that the car accident was a valuable experience, for it was out of hitting a real low spot that my life turned around. Someone once said, "The darker the sky, the brighter the stars." It wasn't until I made a real commitment that amazing—and what some people would call miraculous—things began to come my way. I discovered the power of belief and faith—faith meaning sometimes having to believe in things when appearances and common sense tell you not to. I also discovered the power in commitment.

Here's my favorite quote on commitment.

"*Until one is committed there is hesitancy, the chance to draw back, always ineffectiveness. Concerning all acts of initiative (and creation) there is one elementary truth, the ignorance of which kills countless ideas and splendid plans: that the moment one definitely commits oneself, then Providence moves too. All sorts of things occur to help one that would never otherwise have occurred. A whole stream of events issues from the decision, raising in one's favor all manner of unforeseen incidents and meetings and material assistance, which no man could have dreamt would have come his way.* I have learned a deep respect for one of Goethe's couplets: '*Whatever you can do, or dream you can, begin it. Boldness has genius, power, and magic in it.*'"* W. H. Murray, *The Scottish Himalayan Expedition* (J. M. Dent & Sons Ltd., 1951).

After my experience by the ocean, a stream of events began that assisted me in healing my condition: from finding the perfect books and audio programs, to hearing a certain lecture, to meeting people who told me about healing and salutary foods, visualization, and silence—much of which sounded weird to me at the time. One of those books that a dear friend gave me immediately following the accident changed my life for the better, and I've read it countless times since then. It's entitled *Practicing His Presence* by Frank Laubach about the life of Brother Lawrence and his devotion to God in everything he does during his days. This gem-of-a-book is truly one of Christendom's greatest literary treasures, as it says on the book's jacket. After the first reading of that book, I aspired to make my life—every thought, every word and every action—a loving gift to the Lord.

She also gave me another special book *Love You Forever* by Robert Munsch. Even though it's a book for children, everyone should read this book. I guarantee that you'll not be able to finish it (it takes less than 5 minutes to read) without shedding some tears. It's about a mother's love for her child, but it also reminds me of God's love for me.

During the months following the accident (and to this day), I have made several changes in my lifestyle, behavior, thoughts, and attitude.

After examining me at my six-month checkup following the accident, the doctor just shook his head in bewilderment and said, "This just can't be. There is no sign of a fracture, and you seem to be in perfect health, free of pain. There must be some mistake. It's just miraculous." Perhaps it was. Yet, I've since discovered that miracles are a natural part of committing to being healthy and living peacefully and, most importantly, living a God-centered life.

It doesn't matter where your level of health is at this moment. Regardless of the lifestyle you've lived until now, or perhaps how contrary to living a wellness lifestyle you've chosen up to now, you can, at any moment, choose differently. Surely, you can use your past mistakes or poor choices and learn from them and yes, for some people it sometimes takes being at the bottom before you awaken to the fact that you can choose something else.

Commitment is the Key

What about you? Have you made a commitment to being healthy and living peacefully? Your level of health, right this moment, is a result of the countless choices you have made regarding the foods you eat, the exercise you get, the thoughts you think, what you believe and expect —simply how you choose to live your life.

A commitment to choose health begins with appreciating, respecting and loving your magnificent body. One of the most important things you can learn in life is to appreciate yourself. As you open your heart to your own self-worth and to the divine essence of all humanity, you access the most powerful healer of all—the healing power of love or of God. The human body is indeed a miracle of God's creation. The more I study the body, the more I am amazed and in awe at how beautifully it is designed. Clearly, the body is fantastic and deserves reverence.

Start today and tune in more to your body. It is a remarkable feedback machine. If you listen, you will discover that it actually talks to you. When you get a headache, for instance, your body is trying to tell you something. Listen to your body's signals with health and peace as your goals. The key here is your willingness to listen and act.

Many people think that the way to handle a headache is just to reach for a bottle of aspirin because it's normal to have a headache. One of my clients, Steve, had headaches every day, usually around the same time of the day. Before he adopted a wellness lifestyle, he would simply pop a couple of aspirin, drink a few cups of coffee, and he would soon feel his normal self again—wired and stressed.

Collectively, this country has been making some poor choices. Just look at all the commercials on television and advertisements in magazines. Here's what you can do for a headache, constipation, sleepless nights, diarrhea, indigestion, foot odor, underarm odor. (My gosh, take a shower!) We've come to depend on things outside us for the treatment. We've become a self-medicating society because we don't really understand how beautifully robust the human body is, or how efficiently and effectively equipped we are to meet our problems. (I have never taken medication in my life and feel deeply blessed that I know the best foods to eat, and the other important lifestyle choices, so that I will continue to be vibrantly healthy well into my late senior years.)

Choose to Make a Positive Difference

I have some astonishing news for you. It's normal to be able to go to sleep at night without taking a pill. It's normal *not* to have headaches, sinus problems, hemorrhoids, constipation, and shaky hands. It's normal to be well. We just have to "get out of our own way." By getting out of our own way and living more from inner guidance, the power of the Lord within each of us, we can enrich the quality of life on this planet.

I love what Erich Fromm once said: *Our highest calling in life is precisely to take loving care of ourselves.* In simply doing this, we can make a difference in our world. *You* make a difference. You see, our bodies are made up of trillions of cells. In order to maintain optimum health, each of these cells must operate at peak performance. When we have sick or weak cells, our healthy or stronger cells must work harder so that our body as a whole will be healthy.

There is no room for negative thinking, unforgiveness, bitterness toward others, or selfishness. It is our responsibility to this body that we call our country and this world to be a healthy, happy, peaceful, loving place that radiates only goodness, positiveness, and joy. In this way, we can help make our world a better place to live.

The separation and division that has so long colored our thoughts and beliefs regarding our lives on this planet, that God placed us on, must now be examined and corrected. To create peace on earth, we must stop dividing the world, and know that it's time to come together and live in harmony, forgiveness, and love. The awareness of our place on this earth must precede our thoughts and actions as a part of our belief system. It's your choice. You can choose to make a difference with the way you live your life.

In his book *The Hundredth Monkey*, Ken Keyes, Jr., tells of a phenomenon observed by scientists. The eating habits of macaque monkeys were studied. One monkey discovered that by washing sweet potatoes before eating them, they tasted better. She taught her mother and friends until one day a certain number (say 99) of the monkeys knew how to wash their sweet potatoes. The next day, when the hundredth monkey learned how to wash sweet potatoes, an amazing thing happened: the rest of the colony miraculously knew how to wash their potatoes too! Not only that, but the monkeys on other islands started washing their potatoes. Keyes applies this "Hundredth Monkey" phenomenon to humanity. When more of us individually choose to make a difference with our lives—when we realize we do make a difference and start acting like it, more and more of us will hop the bandwagon until we reach the "Millionth Person" and peace spreads across the globe.

Wherever You Go, There You Are

Where it starts is right here where we are. I believe that while we may not be able to change the world, we can choose to change ourselves and, as we do that, the world will be different. We can create a magnificent, glorious world. I see it changing now. My vision is clear and fantastic. But it takes all of us together, committing to being healthy and peaceful, choosing to do the things that make a difference—things that support wellness, that embrace humanity, and that serve all creation. Let's all remember that we're here on earth not to see through one another, rather we are here to see one another through.

It's simply a matter of choice. Radiant health, peace, and living your highest vision come from making a commitment and choosing to live more from inner guidance, the love of the Lord dwelling within you, and assisting others in their journey. When you choose to live and be this way, life will take on new meaning. You will not only understand what it means to celebrate yourself and life, you will enrich the quality of life on this magnificent, wondrous planet. I salute your great adventure.

Do not be conformed to this world, but continually be transformed by the renewing of your minds so that you may be able to determine what God's will is—what is proper, pleasing, and perfect (Romans 12:2).

Twenty Sure-Fire Tips to Create More Joy & Less Stress

It is within our power to live a healthy, halcyon life filled with vitality and ongoing rejuvenation. This second half of the chapter will show you how in 20 simple steps. I encourage you to read this section through once in its entirety and then read it a second time more slowly and see which of these following tips you can adopt in your life right away. Remember, it's not what you read that makes the difference; it is what you assimilate and put into practice in your life. And it is simply a matter of choice. Choose to create your best life, and start to live with balance and radiant health today!

1. Make fitness the mainspring of everyday life.

Develop a well-rounded fitness program that includes strength training (weights), aerobics, and some kind of stretching for flexibility. Make it a top priority. Nothing can do more to make you vibrantly healthy, energetic, and youthful than a regular fitness program. An impressive study at Tufts University found that after one year of twice-a-week strength training, women's bodies were 15 to 20 years more youthful. (I bet I now have your full attention!) Here's what they discovered: The subjects had less fat and more muscle; their bone loss was prevented or reversed; their strength and energy had increased dramatically; and they all showed surprising gains in balance and flexibility. Wow! No other program, including diet or aerobic exercise, has ever achieved comparable results. You can learn more about this study (published in *JAMA*, 1994, Miriam E. Nelson et al., "Effect of High-Intensity Strength Training on Multiple Risk Factors: A Randomized Controlled Trial," volume 272, pages 1909-14.) and the program in the book, *Strong Women Stay Young*, by Miriam E. Nelson, Ph.D. Men, although they are generally more attuned to the benefits of strength training, should be aware of these results, too.

Make sure to get enough water and wholesome foods, too. Always try to eat your foods close to the way nature produced them, rich in color and with emphasis on diversity. (Please refer to my 3-book series *THE HEALING POWER OF NATUREFOODS, HEALTH BLISS*, and *RECIPES FOR HEALTH BLISS* to learn more about the 100 healthiest foods you can eat and the best recipes for meals you and your family will love.) I choose to eat a plant-based diet because after 35 years of research, I know this to be the healthiest way to eat. In Genesis 1:29, we read: *And God said, Behold, I have given you every herb bearing seed, which is upon the face of all the earth, and every tree, which is the fruit of the tree yielding seed; to you it shall be for meat.*

Nothing will benefit human health and increase the chances for survival of life on earth as much as the evolution to a vegetarian diet.
—Albert Einstein

Take top-quality, all-natural nutritional supplements, which you'll learn about on my website, www.SusanSmithJones.com when you click on *Maximize Health*. These are stellar supplements that I recommend to everyone and they are an integral part of my nourishing lifestyle. You will also want to click *Susan's Favorite Products* to find out about some of my other favorite healthful, must-have products.

If you want to find out about the most important antioxidant, the body's master antioxidant, and an easy way to accelerate fat loss so that you can reach your ideal healthy weight once and for all, please visit my website above and read the articles posted under the heading *Maximize Health.* (To order these supplements now, simply visit: www.4HealthBliss.com and click on *Products* to learn more about each one or on *Preferred Customer* to order at wholesale prices, as I do.

Additionally, I take several products by one of the other authors in this book, Dr. Ellen Tart-Jensen, including her *Internal Cleanse Kit, Sun Cleanse, Organic Rainbow Salad, Bone Knitter,* and *Super Circulation.*

Also, make sure to get plenty of fresh air and healthful amounts of sunshine, and drink fresh vegetable juices to help rejuvenate and nourish your more than 70 trillion cells. Avoid dependence on caffeine, nicotine, alcohol, and drugs that interfere with your immune system's functioning. The only person's health and fitness you can change is your own, so if you want to have a good influence on the health and fitness of those you love, take care of yourself. There is nothing stronger than the ripple effect of personal example. I love George Bernard Shaw's comment, "*If you must hold yourself up to your children as an object lesson, hold yourself up as an example and not as a warning.*" By the way, he was a vegan and was still climbing trees at 87 years young.

2.   Get enough sleep.

Even though 98 percent of us know that sleep is just as important to our health as nutrition and exercise, most adults fail to get sufficient sleep. Americans average 6 to 7 ½ hours of sleep a night, whereas the ideal is between 8 and 10 hours. In his book, *Power Sleep*, Dr. James Maas points out that half the population of the United States is sleep-deprived. He also maintains that many Americans do not know what it's like to be fully alert and have become habituated to low levels of alertness. If you need an alarm clock to wake up, or if it is a struggle to get out of bed in the morning, or if you fall asleep in meetings or watching television or reading an enthralling book as you're doing right now, you are sleep-deprived.

Even minor sleep deprivation causes mood changes. People get angry and upset more easily, lose patience, and snap at one another. One of the first things to go when one is sleep-deprived is communication skills. Maas recommends taking 10 to 20-minute "power naps." Any longer than 20 minutes sends you into delta or deep sleep, and you wake up groggy. Also, if you nap too long in the afternoon, it will cause insomnia at night. Power naps pay back on the installment plan the debt we carry in our sleep-deficit banking account.

Never underestimate the importance of getting enough sleep. It is clearly an essential part of living a balanced life.

3.   Learn to elicit a relaxation response.

With practice, anyone can become deeply relaxed in mind and body. Our nervous systems are bombarded every day by excessive environmental stimulation. Learn deep relaxation techniques such as deep breathing exercises in order to keep stress levels under control.

When several hundred participants in a stress reduction seminar I gave in Los Angeles were asked what was the most important aspect of what they learned, the majority named breathing. This may sound odd, since we all know how to breathe or we would not be living. Yet in reality, these people did not breathe efficiently and found that when they did, the impact of stress was noticeably reduced. Also, paying attention to breathing, and becoming more mindful, got them back in touch with the most basic of bodily functions. Disciplined, deep diaphragmatic breathing, along with prayer and meditating on the things of God, helps bring you toward a state of perfect stillness and tranquility. (Refer to my audiobook *Choose to Live Peacefully* for more detailed information on prayer, how to breathe properly and using prayer to quell stress and promote calmness and serenity.)

Every hour, except when you're sleeping, of course, take a deep breathing break for one to five minutes, instead of a coffee or snack break. This simple action will do wonders to relieve stress, foster calmness, clear your mind, and help you to see your life from a higher, more positive perspective.

4. Free yourself from anger and depression.

Beware of unexpressed feelings, especially negative ones. People who do not express their feelings get sick more often, stay sick longer, and die sooner than expressive people. Non-expression of emotion and denial of hostility or anger are two of the factors most related to an unfavorable prognosis in cancer patients. Unexpressed negative feelings feed on themselves: anger, for instance, can turn against the self and emerge as depression or severe anxiety. Negative emotions, as we have just seen, also trigger the release of substances that can suppress immune function.

Deal with problems in a way that lets you clear up your negative feelings as thoroughly and quickly as possible. Remember that feelings aren't all good or all bad; they just are. Sharing them with a trusted friend or other support person is healing. Personally, I always talk to Jesus about everything going on in my life and seek His guidance.

Teach yourself to have positive expectations about everything in your life, including your wellness. In his lectures on psychoneuroimmunology at UCLA, I often heard Norman Cousins talk about two groups of people about to have surgery. The first group of patients dreaded surgery and attempted to postpone or avoid it. The second group, with the same medical problems, regarded the surgery as an opportunity to rid themselves of their illnesses. After surgery, those who had positive expectations had much better post-operative experiences. Such outcomes have been documented repeatedly and can be perused in any of my books.

The loss of a loved one tests our emotional balance severely. If a person is able to integrate loss into a broader texture and meaning of life, and feel grief and depression without losing the inner sense of safety, those feelings will be relatively temporary. But if someone responds to loss with prolonged depression, the body will also be in a state of depression, making that person susceptible and vulnerable to many things. When we can see ourselves as participants in life, rather than as victims of unfortunate circumstances, our lives automatically become less stressful and more wholesome.

5.   Be aware of your words and thoughts.

What we think determines what we experience. Each of us has the freedom to accept and embrace whatever thoughts we choose. We possess within the silence of our being the ability to decide, create, and become whatever we want to become. Monitor what you're thinking and don't allow yourself to think negatively. Instead, think only about things you want to be part of your life.

Control of the mind is essential if we are going to live peacefully, joyfully, and healthfully. Be firm but loving, for the mind is the rein that controls the horses—the emotions and the body—and guides them to safety along the road of life. Train the mind always to be loving and kind and to see the best in others and in everything. When the road of life is steep, keep your mind even and your attitude high. *Attitude is the mind's paintbrush; it can color anything.*

Keep your words sweet, loving, true, kind and helpful, in case you have to eat them, as the folk wisdom admonishes. Words have power. As Ralph Waldo Emerson advises: *"When you unlock the human door, you are caught up in the life of the universe where your speech is thunder, your thought is Law, and your words are universally intelligible."*

6.   Substitute forgiveness for judgment.

The strongest poison to the human spirit is the inability to forgive oneself or another person. Forgiveness unlocks the gate to healing and health, prosperity and abundance, joy and happiness and inner peace. While you can't control another person's feelings, you can choose what you want to experience. Let kindness and tenderheartedness be your goal.

When your mind starts trotting along the judgment path, pull back the reins. Pay attention because you cannot change what you do not recognize and acknowledge. Take charge of your thoughts before they pick up speed and increase to a gallop. It is easier to nip your judgmental thoughts in the bud before they take over and muddle your higher perspective of life. *Keep the golden rule close to your heart. Treat others, the way you would like to be treated.* Civility and comity go hand in hand with respect and kindness. And never forget, you attract back to yourself those things you think, feel, say, and do. As it is proclaimed in the Bible, *"as you sow, so shall you reap"* (Gal. 6:7). Walt Whitman expressed it well in this succinct sentence: *"When I give, I give to myself."* So today, and always, find ways to give others your kindness, compassion, respect, and forgiving heart rather than negative judgments.

7. Feel the fear and let it go.

Fear is such a significant, powerful force that it always seems to come from outside. We feel it on many levels—physically, mentally, and emotionally. Often, we don't begin the one thing we really want to do in life because of fear. Yet the greatest possible growth and personal development comes from facing our pain and fear. I like what Jack Kornfield says in his book, *A Path with Heart*: "The compartments we create to shield us from what we fear, ignore, and exclude exact their toll later in life. Periods of holiness and spiritual fervor later can alternate with opposite extremes—binging on food, sex, and other things—becoming a kind of spiritual bulimia. Spiritual practice will not save us from suffering and confusion; it only allows us to understand that avoidance of pain does not help."

Recognize that your fears are just like other feelings—not all good, not all bad. They just are, and all you risk by uncovering them is the amazing surprise that by acknowledging fear and moving on, you become healthier and more fully human.

On the other side of fear—if you are willing to pull back the veil and examine what's there—is faith and hope. For me, faith is believing in things when common sense and appearances may cause you to doubt and lose hope. Hope is the loving energy behind faith that keeps the faith-fire lit. To create your best life, you must keep faith and hope alive—always. Here is one of my favorite poems about hope from the inspiring, prolific writer Emily Dickinson:

> *Hope is the thing with feathers*
> *That perches in the soul*
> *And sings the tune without the words*
> *And never stops at all.*

8. Visualize your goals and dreams every day.

In the mid 1800s, Henry David Thoreau wrote these words in his illustrious essay, *Civil Disobedience*, and they are just as true today: *"If one advances confidently in the direction of his dreams, and endeavors to live the life which he has imagined, he will meet with a success unexpected in common hours.... If you have built castles in the air, your work need not be lost; that is where they should be. Now put foundations under them."* He reminds us how creative we really are. Every day, spend a few minutes visualizing with your mind's eye not only your goals, but also how you would like your life to be in every detail.

In addition to visualizing, assume the feeling of the wish fulfilled. What you put your attention and feelings on in life will expand and grow. Choose to think and visualize only thoughts of how you want to live and be rather than on what you don't want to occur in your life. Thoughts are powerful! Pay attention to your thoughts and dream big! Never let anyone or anything cause you to doubt your power and ability to make your dreams a reality.

I spend approximately 5-10 minutes daily visualizing my goals and dreams, and I always end these respites of visualization with a prayer and the affirmation, *This, or something better, I now accept in my life.* You see, I do this because I choose to live a God-surrendered and God-centered life. Only God knows what's for my highest good. In other words, *Thy will be done. . .* My job is to keep my focus on the positive and what I want to achieve and create in my life and I leave the rest up to God's will for me.

9. Find time each day to be alone.

It is by spending time alone, breathing deeply, and quieting everyday thoughts that we can do the most for our happiness and peace of mind. Mother Teresa wrote, *"We need to find God, and He cannot be found in noise and restlessness. God is the friend of silence."* In solitude and silence, I see most clearly what is out of balance in my life, and the inherent power that sustains me. However brief it may be, find some time each day to enjoy the peace of your own company. Remember, the word "alone" is derived from the Middle English phrase "all one."

Even if you're married, you need times of privacy and solitude. In my counseling, I always encourage couples to spend occasional time alone, not only daily, but at regular intervals during the week, month, and year. In this way, you regain your identity as an individual. It was William Wordsworth who gave us these simple, yet profound, words:

> When from our better selves we have too long
> Been parted by the hurrying world, and droop,
> Sick of its business, of its pleasures tired,
> How gracious, how benign is
> Solitude.

Solitude is not a luxury. It's a necessity and an essential component for rejuvenation of body, mind, and spirit.

10. Embrace a daily spiritual practice.

Meditation goes hand in hand with spending time alone each day. Please don't let this energy-charged word, *meditation*, close your mind to what I'm about to share with you. I first learned about meditation in the 70's from Brother Lawrence, in the book about his life, *Practicing His Presence.*

In my personal life, I have a rich prayer-life. In fact, I take several breaks during the day and spend time in quiet communion with God/ Jesus where I talk to Him and share my heart's concerns and wishes. This kind of communication with my loving Source, where *I talk to God*, is my prayer-time. I also take a couple breaks during the day from the "busyness" of life when I turn within, quiet my chattering mind, and pay attention to the quiet whisperings of *God speaking to me.* That's what meditation is for me and for most people I know who meditate; a turning away from life's stresses and complications to dwell in the beauty, magnificence, Light, and loving Presence of the Lord. God comes to us when we quiet our minds and open to His loving guidance.

My spiritual life and my relationship with the Lord are paramount in my life; you could say that it's the hub of the wheel for me. In fact, I get up early each morning, before sunrise, simply to spend quality time in quiet meditation and prayer so that I can open to God's will for me each day and, as my diurnal practice, surrender my day to the Lord and nourish my spiritual life. I also repeat this, time-permitting, for a few minutes every night. This way, I bookend my day in quiet reflection with God, my personal and private time with the Lord, so that I strengthen my relationship daily and dwell more deeply in God's love. So please keep an open mind to the word meditation. If you would like to learn more about this gentle practice, please refer to my audiobook, *Wired to Meditate*, which is available on my website www.SusanSmithJones.com.

Meditation nourishes faith and connects us to the fountain of Love and Light that's within each of us and connects us to everyone. The most important thing in human life is to turn within so you can stay connected to this loving presence. What you will discover, if you practice a few minutes of meditation daily, is that you don't have to run around looking for faith; it springs from within. When you stay centered in the Lord, faith will find you.

But there's so much more to meditation than the spiritual benefits. The physical benefits of meditation are as well documented as the mental and spiritual rewards. Research by Herbert Benson, M.D., of Harvard University, author of *Beyond the Relaxation Response*, has shown that meditation not only improves immune function, but also is associated with a host of positive physiological effects such as altered brain states, decreased heart rate, lower blood pressure, a relaxed body, and a more youthful appearance. In fact, scientific studies indicate that those people who meditate regularly look 12-15 years younger than non-meditators of the same age. Now I probably have your full attention!

Consider carving out time every day to turn within. Perhaps you can bookend your day with a few minutes of quiet reflective/meditative time first thing in the morning and some time before you go to sleep at night. You will discover, as I have, that this simple practice will have a positive effect on your life and bring you closer to your goal of being radiantly healthy, happy, energetic, and peaceful, and living a God-surrendered life. Before and after my time of quiet meditation, I focus on prayer and reading a few passages from the Bible. This simple practice helps me live a God-centered life and keeps Jesus front and center in my life, too.

I call to remembrance my song in the night; I meditate within my heart, And my spirit makes diligent search (Psalms 77:6).

This Book of the Law shall not depart from your mouth, but you shall meditate in it day and night, that you may observe to do according to all that is written in it. For then you will make your way prosperous, and then you will have good success (Joshua 1:8).

Finally, brethren, whatever things are true, whatever things are noble, whatever things are just, whatever things are pure, whatever things are lovely, whatever things are of good report, if there is any virtue and if there is anything praiseworthy—meditate on these things (Philippians 4:8).

Meditate within your heart on your bed, and be still (Psalms 4:4).

11. Simplify life.

Simplify! What a wonderful word and a powerful process. Simplifying doesn't necessarily mean we have to restrict our activities, but it does mean uncluttering our lives so that we can put all our energy into activities we really care about. Activities, material things, and relationships are all time and energy consumers. Maybe it's time to take inventory of your life and weed out the superfluous. Being simple with life—not naive, but clear—allows us to experience the present fully and deeply.

Plato wrote, *"In order to seek one's own direction, one must simplify the mechanics of ordinary, everyday life."* Contrary to popular belief, we are not mere victims of our environment. When we yield to the pressure, we go faster and push harder without keeping life in perspective, growing more and more insensitive to our own personal needs and the needs of those around us. It requires effort, but you can slow down. Discover the joy in simple pleasures. Breathe deeply, smell the flowers, talk to the animals, sing to the birds, be with friends, greet the sun, seek out shooting stars, scratch behind a cat's or dog's ear, make someone smile, marvel at the miracle you are, tell someone you love them, laugh out loud and often, and spend quality time out in nature.

Take time to breathe deeply and simply "be," without a cell phone, TV, radio, noise, or traffic. In *Walking with the Angels*, White Eagle shares his love of the trees—and how healing they can be—in this passage: *"The trees enfold humanity as a mother; the trees are symbolic of the Great Mother. Realize this, we can walk in the groves, sit beneath the great oaks, or an ancient banyan, or the majesty of the cedar, and become conscious of this mother-love enfolding us."*

White Eagle whose book *Jesus Teacher and Healer* touched my life, and who looked to Jesus as his greatest teacher, encourages us to spend quality time out in Nature. He goes on to say, *"In some quiet woodland— veritably a natural cathedral—have you not felt the sense of love and peace, and registered the blessing of those natural sanctuaries? There are many such cathedrals...where weary souls can find refreshment and worship, not by word, but through the adoration and thankfulness of their hearts."*

That's one of the reasons why I'm an avid hiker. Most mornings, when I'm not traveling, you can find me beginning the day hiking in my local Santa Monica Mountains. I enjoy the workout, that's for sure; but I also feel deeply connected with God, my angels, and the oneness of all life when I am surrounded by God's radiant beauty surrounding me and magnificence of nature.

Find ways to let nature nourish your body, mind, and spirit and teach you the value of simplifying your life.

12. Nourish your sense of humor.

Yes, laughter is good for everybody. A bit of emotional detachment and hearty laughter every day really does stimulate the immune system. In fact, in a recent study it was found that those people who laugh several times a day and maintain a positive attitude will *add eight years to their life*—eight happy hears I might add! Laughter aids most—and probably all—major systems of the body. A good laugh gives the heart muscles a healthy workout; improves circulation; fills the lungs with oxygen-rich air; clears the respiratory passages; acts on alertness hormones that stimulate various tissues; alters the brain by diminishing tension in the central nervous system; helps relieve pain; and counteracts fear, anger, and depression, all of which are linked to physical illness.

Laughter is the best demonstration that creating vibrant health can be fun. Try to move gracefully among all the activities of daily life without being ensnared by either outer demands or inner desires. Don't take life so seriously.

13. Nurture and develop your intuition.

Intuition is sometimes called a sixth sense, a hunch, a gut feeling, going on instinct, or just knowing deep inside. Psychologists consider it an obscure mental function that provides us with information, so that we know without knowing how we know. Intuition can be nurtured in a variety of ways that quiet the conscious mind—through meditating, gazing out a window, relaxing, or taking silent walks in nature. However you do it, the best way is to be still and listen. The more you trust and act on your intuitive hunches, the stronger and more readily available they become.

In my workshops on "Nurturing Your Intuition & Living Peacefully," I recommend taking brief (3-5 minutes) mini-meditation breaks a few times each day to effectively center and balance yourself, and to feel God's loving Presence. During this time, breathe slowly and deeply, get very quiet, and tune into your wellspring of Love and Light. As you do this, your energy begins to rise and you feel relaxed, focused, and vibrant. Focus on your deep feelings of gratitude for health, life, and all of the blessings you experience every day.

14. Be grateful.

Poet, writer, and Nobel Peace Prize winner, Maya Angelou, author of *A Song Flung Up to Heaven*, says that a joyful spirit is the best evidence of a grateful heart. Be grateful for everything that's going on in your life, whatever the circumstances, for this attitude can foster happiness and peace of mind, assisting you to live more fully. Remember that there is power in difficulty and challenge because they force you to tap reserves of courage, hope, faith, surrender, and love you weren't aware you possessed.

In the past I have found discouragement in particular situations until I compared the condition of my life to others less fortunate. Just as a fresh breeze cleans smoke from the air, so a grateful spirit removes the cloud of despair. With a joyful, thankful heart, you will discover that it is virtually impossible for the seeds of depression and negativity to take root.

I like this quote by Meister Eckhart, the renowned philosopher in the 13th century, who wrote: *"If the only prayer you ever say in your life is 'thank you!,' this would suffice."*

When you live with gratitude, it is easy to bring happiness and reverence for life into your daily experiences. Give thanks for the "small" things, such as healthful, colorful fruits and vegetables, the beautiful clouds, some pure water after a vigorous workout, the friends in your life, and the comfort of your bed after a long day's work. Take notice and enjoy the sacredness of every moment. Most importantly, be forever grateful for God's loving guidance in your life.

15. Encourage the child in you.

So many of us are searching for the "fountain of youth," the secret that will enable us to live long and healthy lives. Although special diets, supplements, and exercise are important and have their place in rejuvenating body, mind, and spirit, it is my belief that the real secret to living a quality life, full of vitality and aliveness, comes from within—from our attitudes, our expressions, our thoughts, and how we view ourselves and the world around us.

Young children seem to know how to make life a celebration and create magical moments. They see the everyday world as full of wonder and mystery, and with this perception, they infuse the most ordinary things with excitement. Children know how to open the door to the kingdom of wonder. Take their example: Don't plan your calendar down to the last minute. Be flexible and leave time for spontaneity in daily activities. Let your inner child come out and play.

Carpe diem. That's Latin for "seize the day." Moment by moment, choose to be aware of everything around you. Pay attention. Participate fully in life. Maintain a childlike enthusiasm, even for everyday chores. Think about your attitude when taking out the trash, dusting, or weeding the garden. You probably find these activities boring. Have you ever seen a young child help with these activities? Quite often, a young child can't wait to participate, and acts as though it's just about the most exciting thing he or she has ever done. What a magnificent quality that is! To be excited about every part of life as though it's always fresh and new. Actually, it is. It's only old thoughts and distorted attitudes that get in the way of celebrating each moment.

When you embrace this sacred attitude, like Brother Lawrence did in *Practicing His Presence,* that you are doing everything for God, then it's much easier to be positive and joyful—no matter what you are doing.

16. Live in the present.

Don't spend time comparing the present with the past. Every new step you take is upon sacred ground. Every moment is imbued with wonder and miracles. When you're trapped in the past, it's impossible to be fully present and pay attention to what's happening around you. Ralph Waldo Emerson reminded us:

> *Be not the slave of your own past—plunge into the sublime seas, dive deep, and swim far, so you shall come back with self-respect, with new power, with an advanced experience, that shall explain and overlook the old.*

Rather than living with continual five- or ten-year plans, concentrate on living one day at a time, continuing to strengthen your relationship with God, and look for miracles each day. Don't look back in anger or regret, or forward in fear or worry, but look around with conscious awareness.

17. Show kindness, honor, and respect.

To be loving and kind with other people, you must first be loving and kind towards yourself. Honor the precious person inside of you. Take time to slow down, breathe, and simply be in the moment. Each one of us is a sacred being and deserves loving kindness.

In the practical book, *Inner Peace for Busy People: 52 Simple Strategies for Transforming Your Life*, author Joan Borysenko, Ph.D., suggests an effective way to promote loving kindness. She recommends that you think of a person whom you love and respect. (I usually think of Jesus or my mom or grandmother.) For the next month, each time you forget how to care for yourself, pretend that someone wonderful lives inside you. Honor that person and treat him or her with all the respect you really need to begin giving to yourself. If you adopt this as a daily practice, little by little a strange and wonderful transformation will occur. You will remember how to be good to yourself. "You will experience how much more creative and productive you are when you know that you're worthy of your own care and love," explains Borysenko.

Whether we are at work or at play, with friends or with strangers, a friendly smile and a kind word can brighten someone's day and bring us rewards of health and happiness at the same time. Every day we also have opportunities to be kind and loving toward our environment by taking care of our home, planet Earth. As Mother Teresa said, *"Do ordinary things with extraordinary love."* Jesus told us to love our neighbor as we love ourselves. So you see, it really begins with how you feel about yourself, your relationship with yourself, and what you feel you deserve in life. Support high self-esteem with every thought, word, and action and your life will change for the better in just 24 hours.

18. Live with integrity.

Living with integrity means that who we appear to be is who we really are. All of our inner realities—our beliefs, our commitments, our values—are reflected on the outside in the way we live our lives from day to day. It takes a lot of energy to live without integrity, because it is emotionally and intellectually exhausting when the way we behave is not aligned with the way we are on the inside. Simply put, dishonesty is enervating. Every time you don't tell the truth—even if it is a little, white, I-don't-want-to-hurt-their-feelings lie, you lower your self-esteem and self-empowerment. Choose self-respect and elect to be honest in a kind and loving way. The more you live with synchronicity in what you believe, think, feel, say, and do, the more peace and happiness you will invite into your life. Your self-esteem will soar when you start keeping your word with yourself and others.

Every time my dear late friend Lynn Carroll, who was almost 94 when she died in 2008, made a promise, no matter how small or seemingly insignificant, she kept her word. If she made plans with someone and then was offered the opportunity to do something more exciting or interesting, she never hesitated, saying, "Thank you, I would love to do it, but I already have a commitment." The first friend was pleased because she and Lynn stuck to their plan, and the second friend was also impressed. Lynn was not only well liked, she was also very healthy, happy, and peaceful until the day she passed away in her sleep. Lynn was as good as her word, friends always said of her. To me, there can be no higher praise than that. Make a habit of speaking from truth and kindness. Make your word count all the time. It is a gift you give to your family, friends, business associates, community, and the world.

19. Develop high self-esteem and self-love.

High self-esteem is important for our own well-being and the well-being of everybody around us. Your life is a reflection of how you feel about yourself. Oliver Goldsmith, the English poet, novelist, and dramatist, wrote, *"You can preach a better sermon with your life than with your lips."*

Of course, we all have days when nothing seems to go right and we feel all bent out of shape. During these times, it's helpful to remind ourselves that life ebbs and flows. Henry Wadsworth Longfellow reminds us that: *"The lowest ebb is the turn of the tide,"* while the talented and gifted Benjamin Franklin wrote: *"Anything that hurts, instructs."* When you are hurting, know that these are growing pains necessary to learn some lessons and to develop. Continue to champion your needs, desires, and healthy self-boundaries. Connect with the wisdom of the situation, challenge, or moment. *"I am in the habit of looking not so much to the nature of a gift,"* writes Robert Louis Stevenson, *"as to the spirit in which it is offered."* Changes that are loved into existence are permanent while changes that come about through self-denial and abuse often will be fleeting.

To find out if you are being true to yourself, ask yourself these questions: If I weren't getting paid for what I'm doing, would I do it anyway? If I knew I had only one year to live, would I continue to do what I'm doing? If your answers are no, carefully consider how you can make different choices that will change your answers to yes! Self-love and self-esteem will shine in all the actions that come from your heart.

20. Live peacefully and lovingly.

There can be no greater goal in life than peace. What asset could be of more value to us than unshakable calmness and tranquillity? What better evidence of spiritual strength could we have than a peaceful mind and heart?

Peace of mind comes from accepting what you can't control and taking responsibility for what you can. It grows out of faith in your higher power and your spiritual nature. It comes when you let go of guilt, fear, and doubt. It is the result of forgiving yourself and others for all human imperfections. When you let go of the delusion that something, someday, will make you happy, you can concentrate on finding peace and contentment in the present moment. At the most fundamental level, being loving and kind improves health. That warm feeling we get from hugging a child, cheering a friend, being a good listener, or even treating ourselves to some little luxury boosts the immune system. Even petting a dog or admiring fish in a tank lowers the blood pressure.

"If scientists suddenly discovered a drug that was as powerful as love in creating health, it would be heralded as a medical breakthrough and marketed overnight—especially if it had as few side effects and was as inexpensive as love," writes Larry Dossey, M.D., in his heartwarming book *Healing Words: The Power of Prayer and The Practice of Medicine.* Throughout history, "loving care" has been recognized as a valuable element in healing. This tenet was brought to life by David McClelland, Ph.D., of Harvard Medical School, who demonstrated the power of love to make the body healthier through what he refers to as the "Mother Teresa Effect."

McClelland showed a group of Harvard students a documentary of Mother Teresa ministering lovingly to the sick, and measured the levels of immunoglobulin A (IgA) in their saliva before and after seeing the film. (IgA is an antibody active against viral infections such as colds.) IgA levels rose significantly in the students, even in many of those who considered Mother Teresa "too religious" or a fake. A similar effect resulted when McClelland later asked his graduate students to simply think about two things: past moments when they felt deeply loved and cared for by someone else, and a time when they loved another person. McClelland discovered that he even could abort colds with this technique. As a result of his personal experiences and research, he became an advocate for the role of love in modern health (Joan Borysenko, "Healing Motives: An Interview with David McClelland," Advances 2 (1985): 29-41).

McClelland explained to a group of his medical colleagues, "I can dream a little about changing hospital environments, one that relaxes you, gives you loving care, and relieves you of the incessant desire to control and run everything; a healthful environment. Certain doctors, nurses, social workers—all of us—can learn...that being loving to people is really good for their health. And probably good for yours, too." (Steven Locke and Douglas Colligan, *The Healer Within: The New Medicine of Mind and Body*, New York: E.P. Dutton, 1986, 211.)

Peace and love go together. Without love, it's difficult to feel peaceful. And without a peaceful mind and heart, love is fleeting.

Each of us, in our own personal way, can make a positive difference on our magnificent Spaceship Earth by simply choosing to be loving and peaceful. I strive to live by this wise adage often told to me by my mom: "The more you love, the more you're loved, and the lovelier you are."

But let all those that put their trust in thee rejoice: let them ever shout for joy, because thou defendest them: let them also that love thy name be joyful in thee (Psalms 5:11).

See how many of these 20 tips you can incorporate into your life today, this week, and this month. Just the physical act of beginning creates the momentum and energy that will allow you to travel beyond the fear and toward your greatest accomplishments.

A healing nature lifestyle is more than eating right and exercising regularly. Make a commitment to yourself to enrich each day physically, emotionally, and spiritually. By putting this splendid balance into your life, you'll reap the rewards of living—healthfully, vibrantly, and joyfully.

I would like to end this chapter with one of my favorite poems by Rudyard Kipling titled *IF*.

EDITOR'S NOTE

There is an order to commitment. The highest level of commitment is to yourself. God instructed us to Love Him, to Love ourself, and to Love our neighbor as ourself.

How can we Love our God, and Love our neighbor if we do not Love ourself? Jesus summed up The 10 Commandments when He said, "Love God, and Love your Neighbor as yourself."

I encourage you to raise your level of commitment to yourself and follow God's direction to: Treat your body as a Temple—not a trash can which was also voiced by Hippocrates, the Father of "Modern" Medicine when he said, "Do no harm."

Everything has a gestation period. A baby takes nine months. Start your journey to health with a commitment to yourself, and learn from Susan Smith Jones. She is truly a leader of leaders! —JEF

If

If you can keep your head when all about you
Are losing theirs and blaming it on you;
If you can trust yourself when all men doubt you,
But make allowance for their doubting too;
If you can wait and not be tired by waiting,
Or, being lied about, don't deal in lies,
Or, being hated, don't give way to hating,
And yet don't look too good, nor talk too wise;
If you can dream – and not make dreams your master;
If you can think – and not make thoughts your aim;
If you can meet with triumph and disaster
And treat those two imposters just the same;
If you can bear to hear the truth you've spoken
Twisted by knaves to make a trap for fools,
Or watch the things you gave your life to broken,
And stoop and build 'em up with wornout tools;
If you can make one heap of all your winnings
And risk it on one turn of pitch-and-toss,
And lose, and start again at your beginnings
And never breath a word about your loss;
If you can force your heart and nerve and sinew
To serve your turn long after they are gone,
And so hold on when there is nothing in you
Except the Will which says to them: "Hold on";
If you can talk with crowds and keep your virtue,
Or walk with kings – nor lose the common touch;
If neither foes nor loving friends can hurt you;
If all men count with you, but none too much;
If you can fill the unforgiving minute
With sixty seconds' worth of distance run –
Yours is the Earth and everything that's in it,
And – which is more – you'll be a Man my son.
        —*Rudyard Kipling*

INFLAMMATION

Adding Years to Your Life & Life to Your Years

Why You May Be Losing Your Health to Inflammation

Susan Smith Jones, PhD ©

Most of us never give a second thought to inflammation unless we get a bee sting, experience a physical injury such as stubbing our bare toe on a piece of furniture, or injure our back. As soon as one of these events takes place, we experience an immediate sensation of pain that tells us something is definitely wrong. Redness, heat, and swelling usually follow almost immediately. This immediate reaction is a result of inflammation.

Unfortunately, the most devastating diseases known to human-kind—cancer, heart disease, diabetes, asthma, Parkinson's, Alzheimer's, and the list goes on—are almost always preceded by months and years of very subtle, unnoticed inflammation. Inflammation is good when an injury is experienced in that often the swelling and pain limit the range of motion, allowing the body to heal. However, when subtle inflammation continues for too long, it becomes destructive and may lead to manifestation of various diseases. Almost all diseases are preceded by and accompanied with inflammation. In this chapter, I'll explore what is involved with inflammation, its impact on the body, what we can do to reduce uncontrolled inflammation and its damaging effects on our health, and how to preclude falling prey to nutritional flap doodle.

In his book *Inflammation Nation* (2006, Fireside, New York, NY), Floyd H. Chilton, Ph.D., provides us with some interesting insights into inflammation. He discusses inflammation in the sense of it being a "double-edged sword"—both a helper and a villain. While inflammation is great when it serves as a warning signal as in the stubbed toe illustration, it becomes a villain when initiated by diet and lifestyle, subtly beginning an uncontrolled destructive process in the body that goes unnoticed for decades until a disease of inflammation is manifested. Dr. Chilton states, "We are unquestionably facing an epidemic in inflammatory disease. By my estimate, approximately half of all Americans suffer from an inflammatory disorder, and even more of us are at risk.

"By contrast (contrasting the infectious diseases of the previous century that have been almost entirely eradicated with inflammatory diseases of today), noninfectious inflammatory diseases have gotten worse in each of the last three decades. A physician friend of mine jokes that Celebrex has replaced Prozac as the 'must-have' drug of the decade.

"A silent plague is sweeping America, and the vast majority of us are at risk."

Dan Chesnut, M.D., in his book *Lying with Authority* (2008, Restoration Health Publishing, Oklahoma City, OK), states, "Inflammation results when cells are sick, traumatized, chemically irritated, infected, etc. Sick zones always signal the immune system for assistance. It is important to realize that inflammation can occur in a low-grade, barely noticeable way, especially in the brain. Almost all vaccines can cause brain inflammation, which may last for as long as a year. Even stress and depression can cause a low-grade, unnoticed inflammation and signals are sent to the immune system for help.

"When immune cells or other immune components rush into sick or 'hot' zones, *free radicals* are formed during the heat of battle. . . . Free radicals can be released and always have the potential of cell and DNA damage, which can lead to disease." Left unchecked, these free radicals can damage a cell membrane or, when created within a cell, damage the DNA. The body has a built-in system for dealing with and preventing free radical damage when all cells are functioning optimally. But when they are not, problems arise.

Those Pesky Free Radicals

A diet rich in antioxidants provides "free radical scavengers" that neutralize free radicals before damage occurs and, ideally, also should supply raw materials from which each individual cell can produce its own master antioxidant, glutathione (also known as GSH), which I will discuss later. Unfortunately, today our diet of nutritionally deficient foods does not support our bodies' efforts to prevent free radical damage. Our cells are malnourished and toxins are not eliminated efficiently. As a result, our cells are becoming sicker by the day.

Prolonged inflammation of a tissue caused by tobacco smoke, alcohol abuse, chemical exposure, exposure to electromagnetic radiation, and improper diet produces a continuous onslaught of free radical damage that, left unchecked for years, often leads to various types of cancers. *The Blaylock Wellness Report,* Vol. 2 No. 2, Jan/Feb 2005 (edited by Russell L. Blaylock, M.D., published by Newsmax Media, Inc.) states, "A recent study found that one central event is most closely associated with cancer development—chronic inflammation. In the study, researchers looked at a large number of cancer patients and found that almost 70 percent had pre-existing chronic inflammatory diseases for 10–17 years *before* they developed cancer.

"We know that people with chronic inflammatory diseases like lupus and rheumatoid arthritis, as well as those with inflammatory bowel disease (Crohn's and ulcerative colitis) and certain parasitic diseases, have substantially higher cancer rates than that of normal people. If we include diabetes (also an inflammatory disease), we see that a great number of people are at risk."

In the June, 2008 issue of *The Blaylock Wellness Report,* Dr. Blaylock states, "It turns out that two physiological processes play a major role in inflammation: the immune system and the prostaglandin system. They interact with each other and either enhance inflammation—or reduce it.

"Now there is growing evidence that one or both of these systems stop functioning correctly in many people and get stuck in the inflammation mode. A process meant to speed recovery, in fact, goes into overdrive, causing potentially far greater problems."

Dr. Blaylock goes on to state that the key players that influence this process are toxins, infections, injury, and heredity, and that our diet has a major influence on all of these factors. Dr. Chilton is in full agreement as he states, "I believe that our diet is a major—if not the most important—external factor behind the inflammation epidemic."

For over a century, science has thought that certain chemical exposures, viruses, and even parasites can cause cancer and other chronic diseases. But are these the actual causes? Growing evidence seems to suggest that it is our body's natural *reactions* to these exposures that are the actual causes.

Inflammation & Cancer

A wide variety of exposures have for years been thought to be carcinogenic. Those suffering with diabetes, depression, and cardiovascular and autoimmune diseases generally have a higher risk of developing cancer. All of these conditions have one significant thing in common—they all cause inflammation, which itself may be a cause of subsequent disease. In this model, the inflammatory process may be a vicious cycle that is out of control!

Researchers are finding that cancer often appears 15–17 years after the onset of inflammatory disease. One study found that 65 percent of whites and 70 percent of blacks suffered from prolonged inflammatory disease before developing cancer (Blaylock, June 2008). Ongoing inflammation also makes the cancers grow faster and spread more readily.

Since many processed foods are sources of inflammatory agents found in food additives, it is imperative that you avoid processed foods as much as possible. A diet of primarily plant-based foods, with an emphasis on raw foods is most ideal and is anti-inflammatory.

Your diet and lifestyle are foundational in supporting your body's efforts to maintain optimal health. The standard American diet (SAD) is rich in foods such as trans fats from partially hydrogenated oils, sugars, and animal foods that promote inflammation. The SAD of today has about 50 times as much omega-6 fat as the diet of our ancestors a century ago and is radically deficient in omega-3 fats. Omega-6 in excess promotes inflammation while omega-3 is anti-inflammatory. A plant-based diet with a high percentage of raw foods with a heavy emphasis on leafy green vegetables and omega-3-rich foods (such as flaxseed, walnuts, and flax oil) is anti-inflammatory and supports optimal health at the cellular level.

Life at the Cellular Level

Health is maintained at the cellular level. The health of each individual cell is critical in maintaining optimal health and a body that is free of inflammation and disease. Each cell must be able to take in nutrition, eliminate toxins efficiently, and replicate new healthy cells, if our organs, tissues, and body are to maintain the highest level of health.

The normal processes of metabolism that take place on a daily basis, as we saw earlier, produce free radicals (oxidative stress) that the body must be able to deal with. Each individual cell is a small factory that carries out a multitude of functions on a continuous basis. One of those very important functions is for the mitochondria to produce energy by way of the production of adenosine triphosphate (ATP). This process of energy production also creates free radicals that, if not neutralized, may damage the cell membrane, the cellular DNA, or other areas of the cell. Fortunately, the body has a built-in mechanism to handle this free radical damage when all is functioning optimally.

The Master Antioxidant—Glutathione

Unfortunately, however, all is not functioning optimally for most people, and their level of health is on a gradual decline. Each cell produces glutathione (GSH)—the "master antioxidant"—when it has the necessary raw materials. The intracellular glutathione has the ability to neutralize the free radical damage that results from the mitochondria's production of ATP (energy). Glutathione is capable of neutralizing thousands of free radicals while antioxidants such as vitamin C and vitamin E only neutralize a very limited number of free radicals. The antioxidant activity of vitamin E is supported by glutathione in much the same way that vitamin C is supported by glutathione.

Jimmy Gutman, M.D, FACEP, in discussing vitamin C's role as an antioxidant states, "When a vitamin C molecule mops up a free radical, it effectively neutralizes it. However, the vitamin C complex is now tied up. It is either ejected from the cell and eliminated by the body, or it is recycled to go back and do more work. In the latter case, glutathione is the recycling agent; GSH and GSH enzymes accept the free radical from the vitamin C complex and free it up to get back to work. This cycle drives antioxidant function in our bodies" (*GSH Your Body's Most Powerful Protector Glutathione*, Jimmy Gutman, M.D., FACEP, 2002, Kudo.ca Communications, Montreal, Canada).

Researchers have learned that beyond the age of 20, the body's ability to produce glutathione declines by 10–12 percent per decade. It is thought that this decline is related to poor diet and lifestyle, as well as other external influences on the body. The raw materials necessary for the production of glutathione are often lacking in the diet. And, unfortunately, glutathione is not a supplement that can be taken with any significant benefit, as orally ingested glutathione is degraded in the stomach environment and never reaches the cellular level where it is critically needed.

Dr. Gutman states, "Blood-GSH concentrations in younger people (20–40 years) have been shown to be some 20–40 percent higher than in older people (60–80 years). Studies by some of the world's leading experts on aging suggest that elderly individuals with elevated GSH levels have a physical advantage over those with lower levels. Those with 20 percent higher blood levels have been found to experience approximately one-third the rate of arthritis, high blood pressure, heart disease, circulatory difficulties, and other various maladies than others."

Glutathione & Vibrant Health

One common characteristic seen in patients diagnosed with asthma, Parkinson's, Alzheimer's, AIDS, multiple sclerosis, cancer, and a host of other diseases is that they are all usually dramatically low in glutathione. Low levels of intracellular glutathione means free radicals are neutralized less efficiently, and inflammation goes on uncontrolled.

In speaking of glutathione's role as a master antioxidant and detoxifier, author and nutrition researcher Michael Murray, N.D., states, "This combination of detoxification and protection from free radicals results in glutathione being one of the most important anticarcinogens and antioxidants in our cells, which means a deficiency is devastating. When we are exposed to high levels of toxins, glutathione is used up faster than it can be produced or absorbed from the diet. We then become much more susceptible to toxin-induced diseases such as cancer, especially if our phase one detoxification system is highly active. Diseases that result from glutathione deficiency are not uncommon. A deficiency can be induced by diseases that increase the need for glutathione, deficiencies of the nutrients needed for glutathione synthesis, or diseases that inhibit the formation of glutathione" (*Encyclopedia of Natural Medicine*, Michael Murray, N.D., and Joseph Pizzorno, N.D., 1997, Prima Health Publishing, Rocklin, CA).

Dr. Robert Keller, M.D., Chairman, CEO & CSO of Phoenix Bio-Sciences and practicing physician, is considered to be one of the greatest scholars of the 21st century. Dr. Keller believes the decrease in production of glutathione is much more rapid than stated in scientific literature. He contributes much of this decline to the diets lack of nutrition and the extensive load of toxins our body is subjected to from our environment, our water, our food, and our lifestyle.

These factors have an impact on the ability of each individual cell to produce energy, eliminate waste, and function optimally. The immune system is then impaired, and the body's innate ability to self-heal cannot function as designed. "The protective activity of GSH is twofold: It enhances the activity of the immune cells and also functions as an antioxidant within them," opines Dr. Gutman.

In his medical practice, Dr. Keller has found that almost all of his critically ill patients have had one thing in common—they were dramatically low in glutathione. During more than a decade of intensive research on glutathione's role in the body, he has found a way to increase the glutathione levels in his patients so that they could enjoy a greater quality of life. Interestingly, Dr. Keller notes that individuals who live to the age of 100 have GSH levels of a 40-year old. This is indicative of the protection that higher levels of glutathione afford an individual as he or she ages!

The Best Form of Glutathione

If you think that all you need to do is visit your local pharmacy or natural food store to purchase a bottle of glutathione, think again. Glutathione cannot be used in supplemental form with any significant benefit; when the protein molecule is broken down in the stomach, it is degraded so much that it is no longer GSH. Until Dr. Keller's recent, cutting-edge discovery, the most efficient way of increasing glutathione levels was by injection. Not only is this a short-term solution, but it also is quite expensive.

After more than ten years of trial and error with his patients, he learned how to combine the building blocks of GSH in such a way that they could help make it much easier for the body to produce more optimal intracellular levels of GSH.

Now, thanks to Dr. Keller, we have available a simple, inexpensive, and scientifically proven way to improve our body's ability to produce glutathione (GSH) at the cellular level by *300 percent and more over a three-month period of time*. In speaking of Dr. Keller's discovery, John Nelson, M.D., MPH, FACOG, Past President of the American Medical Association states, "This product, in my opinion, represents the single most important breakthrough in health that I will witness in my lifetime. I believe it will revolutionize, change, and transform the practice of medicine worldwide and make Dr. Robert Keller more famous than Jonas Salk, who created the polio vaccine."

To learn more about Dr. Keller and his glutathione accelerator

(MaxGXL), please visit: www.911yourhealth.com, click on the picture of Dr. Keller and listen to his interview. Additionally, you'll also enjoy listening to another interview on glutathione and vibrant health at this site: weeu.com/mp3/idol51208.mp3. Finally, you also may want to visit SusanSmithJones.com, click on *Maximize Health*, and peruse the variety of information I've included on glutathione and why it's such a stellar supplement.

Susan's Personal Favorite

On a personal note, I've been taking Dr. Keller's nutritional supplement for some time now, and it has made a profound difference in how I feel and look. I now have more energy, recover faster after workouts, sleep more easily and deeply, and even experience better concentration, focus, and mental alertness from taking this supplement.

Some of the clients in my private practice have experienced much easier weight loss and a noticeable relief from PMS, menopause symptoms, muscle and joint pain, fibromyalgia, fatigue, diabetes, colds and flu, cellular inflammation, accelerated aging, cardiovascular disease, and so much more. I encourage you to try it for three months and see how much better you will look and feel. When optimal levels of GSH are available, a person often experiences renewed energy as well as vibrant health and youthful vitality. Because most of us live in an environment where not only are many of our foods toxic from chemicals and environmental pollution, but our water and air is also polluted. It has become increasingly important to supplement our diet with nutrients that support optimum health. MaxGXL is that supplement. Please visit www.911yourhealth.com. If you would like to get wholesale pricing, as I do, then click on Preferred Customer to order easily and quickly as you also register for regular monthly shipments to keep you continuously supplied with this remarkable supplement that you will not want to be without. You will thank your lucky stars that you found out about this cutting edge, breakthrough supplement and are making it part of your daily health regimen. I would not be without this salubrious supplement.

In addition to taking this supplement, you can even start today by eating some of the best glutathione-rich foods such as asparagus, avocado, okra, cauliflower, broccoli, squash, tumeric and raw tomatoes. You'll also find more foods teaming with glutathione recommended in my book series *HEALTH BLISS, RECIPES FOR HEALTH BLISS, THE HEALING POWER OF NATUREFOODS* and *BE HEALTHY~STAY BALANCED*. These are all available at your local bookstore, at Amazon.com, through my website, or by calling: 1-800-843-5743.

Wishing you a balanced life filled with love, peace, and vibrant health. Don't forget to celebrate yourself and life today, and remember to always put God first in your life.

EDITOR'S NOTE

It is not only the food you put in your mouth. It is the life in your food and what you assimilate that adds years to your life! Between the ages of 25-35, our enzyme bank account begins to deplete because of our addictive, over-processed foods.

Inflammation can be reduced with living food and proper supplementation of enzymes and glutathione.

When we're born we have over 5,000 enzymes in every cell in our body. Adding minerals and vitamins, we have over 10,000 enzymatic reactions. You pick an orange from the tree, you have 100% of the enzymes necessary to digest it. You set it on the counter, 30 minutes later, you have 50% of the enzymes in the orange.

A lot of the produce we consume is harvested unripe which aids in depleting the body of minerals. Eat locally-produced fruits and vegetables in season as often as possible nearest harvest time. Inflammation is your body's friend, out of control it will destroy! —JEF

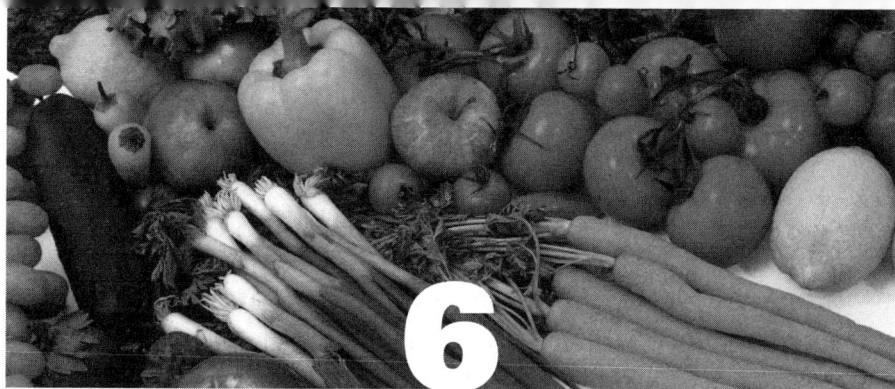

THE HEALING NATURE OF HIGH SELF-ESTEEM

LET'S MAKE WEIGHTY ISSUES A THING OF THE PAST

Susan Smith Jones, PhD ©

No one can make you feel inferior without your consent.
—Eleanor Roosevelt

While millions are starving to death around the world, Americans have the dubious honor of being the fattest people on the globe. Is it any wonder that we are preoccupied with our waistlines? U.S. residents spend more than $40 billion a year on diet foods, programs, pills, and other "guaranteed" weight-loss regimens and products. Yet, according to the National Center of Health Statistics, we're getting fatter all of the time.

Our miraculous bodies have been designed by God, in all His glory, to be self-healing, self-renewing, and self-rejuvenating. They are often referred to as the temple of the Spirit. Unfortunately, for too many us, our bodies have upsized from temples to cathedrals.

Experts call obesity an American epidemic—one that brings with it major health problems. Heart disease, endometrial (uterine) and breast cancer, high cholesterol, high blood pressure, immune dysfunction, osteoarthritis, stroke, gout, sleep disorders, gallstones, and diabetes are all associated with obesity. Since I am always looking at the glass half-full and choose to discern things from an optimistic point of view (that is why I got my nickname, Sunny), let's put this in a more positive way: *Losing even a little weight will improve your health and well-being significantly—and help prevent those very same diseases.*

Undereating also is a problem, and disorders such as anorexia and bulimia are on the rise. Advertising for women's clothing contributes to the problem by using models who look like waifs. Consider Barbie, a doll that is part of most little girls' upbringing. This model of good looks and the perfect body is giving the wrong message about what a healthy woman should look like. Were Barbie an actual person, her body fat would be so low that she probably would not even menstruate. As little girls treasure the doll and teens try to emulate her, she has one accessory that is consistently missing—food.

Surveys indicate that most people are unhappy with their weight or the shape of their bodies. Currently, half of the women and a quarter of the men in the United States are trying to lose weight and reshape themselves. The sad thing is that the majority are going about it in the wrong way, by dieting, which doesn't work! Throw away books that tell you that you can eat whatever you want and still lose weight, and keep it off, or that you can expect long-lasting success without exercising. Dieting is not the cure for excess fat. After you finish such a program, you may have lost some fat, but *you have not lost the tendency to get fat.*

Obesity, Diabetes & Insalubrity

Obesity and Type II diabetes are near epidemic levels, as nearly two-thirds of the adult population is overweight. The 2003-2004 National Health and Nutrition Examination Survey (NHANES) data on the prevalence of overweight and obesity among adults reveals to us that noninstitutionalized adults age 20 years and over who are overweight and/or obese is at 66.3 percent of the U.S. population. The percentage of adults age 20 years and over who are obese is 32 percent.

Seventeen percent of adolescents ages 12-19 years are overweight, and 19 percent of children ages 6-11 are overweight. Joel Furhman, M.D., in his book, *Eat to Live* (2003, Little, Brown and Company, Boston, New York, London) states, "The number one health problem in the United States is obesity, and if the current trend continues, by the year 2030 all adults in the United States will be obese."

A study in the July 2008 issue of *American Journal of Epidemiology* found that people who were obese or overweight in adolescence were three to four times as likely to have died of heart disease by middle age as compared with other thinner peers. (Bjorge T, Engeland A, Tverdal A, Smith GD. Body mass index in adolescence in relation to cause-specific mortality: a follow-up of 230,000 Norwegian adolescents. *Am J Epidemiol.* 2008;168:30-37.)

What does the future hold in terms of health and quality of life if this epidemic is not halted? Is there a way for individuals struggling with weight issues to take control of their health and permanently shed those unwanted, life-threatening pounds? The answer is a resounding yes! In these pages, we will look at some of the causes and the consequences of the current obesity epidemic, and how each individual who chooses to do so can take control and win the battle of the bulge and declining health. So please stay with me; you'll be glad you did.

A recent article in *USA Today* (January 24, 2008) stated, "Uncontrolled diabetes wreaks havoc on the body, often leading to kidney failure, blindness, and death. A new study shows that the nation's unchecked diabetes epidemic exacts a heavy financial toll as well: $174 billion a year. That is about as much as the conflicts in Iraq, Afghanistan, and the global war on terrorism combined. It is more than the $150 billion in damages caused by Hurricane Katrina.

"The incidence of diabetes has ballooned—there are one million new cases a year—as more Americans become overweight or obese. The cost of diabetes—both in direct medical care and lost productivity—has swelled 32 percent since 2002. And, diabetes killed more than 284,000 Americans last year."

What Causes This Weighty Issue?

Over the last few decades, the population in general has moved further and further away from a diet rich in plant-based foods to a diet centered around commercially produced animal products and low- to no-fiber sugar-enhanced processed foods, refined grains, and fast foods that provide little nutritional value and an excess of calories. Not only do these caloric-rich, nutrient-poor foods contribute to excess weight, but they also contribute to insulin resistance and other hormonally related issues.

Americans as well as most of the industrialized world have a "love affair" with rich foods that are nutrient-deficient and disease-causing. Even in biblical days, here is how God's people were instructed regarding the consumption of a diet that was filled with rich foods. In Proverbs 23:1-3, it says, "When you sit to dine with a ruler, note well what is before you, and put a knife to your throat if you are given to gluttony. Do not crave his delicacies, for that food is deceptive." *(Holy Bible, New International Version)* Wow. There is no mincing of words there. And, in the days of Solomon, author of Proverbs, only rulers could afford the luxuries of rich foods. The common man only could partake of these foods on special occasions. I find it remarkable that even thousands of years ago, there is a warning to be careful with rich foods because they are "deceptive." They satisfy the taste buds, become addictive, and do not support optimal health. Most Americans today eat like kings three times each day or more, 365 days of the year, and are reaping the consequences of their poor choices.

Floyd H. Chilton, Ph.D., in his book *Inflammation Nation* (2005, Fireside, New York, NY), when discussing the obesity connection to inflammation and other diseases states: "Inflammatory disease and obesity are not simply maladies running on parallel tracks, but are intrinsically intertwined for a number of reasons. There are a number of straightforward connections between those excess pounds and inflammatory disease.

"One of those commonalities is what I call 'foods of affluence' and the overwhelming quantities of some of those foods in the typical Western diet. For instance, early humans obtained more than half of their calories from carbohydrates, but most of these carbohydrates came from vegetables and fruit, with a smattering of beans and whole grains thrown in. In affluent societies, carbohydrates take the form of refined, added sugars and highly processed grain flours, highly caloric foods that provide us none of the nutrients necessary for optimal health. The ready availability of eggs, meat, and poultry is another function of our affluence."

When we look around us, almost all social events are centered around food—food that has little if any nutritional value, but that appeals to the taste buds. If we ever are to overcome the epidemic of overweight and obesity, we must change the way we look at food. We should be making wise choices that support optimal health, eating to live and not living to eat.

Maybe It's Not All in Your Genes

Children whose parents are obese have a tenfold increased risk of being obese. While obesity in the parents sets a predisposition for obesity, it is the combination of food choices, inactivity, and genetic tendencies that determine obesity. Can we blame genetics for the problem? On June 16, 2008, *Reuters News* published an article titled "Healthy Lifestyle Triggers Genetic Changes," which described a three-month, groundbreaking study led by Dean Ornish, M.D., that demonstrated that the subjects affected changes in activity in about 500 genes—including 48 that were turned on and 453 genes that were turned off—as a result of eating more healthful foods, keeping stress levels down, practicing relaxation techniques such as meditation, and exercising regularly. Regarding the study, Dr. Ornish states: "It's an exciting finding because so often people say, 'Oh, it's all in my genes, what can I do?' Well, it turns out you may be able to do a lot. In just three months, I can change hundreds of my genes simply by changing what I eat and how I live. That's pretty exciting."

Dr. Ornish's study demonstrates that we do indeed have control over our health by the choices we make. We just need to be better informed so we can make those better choices. The present epidemic of overweight and obesity for most people is a result of a few choices made daily that, over time, have led to what is now the number one health crisis in this country. Optimal health is built on the *foundations* of health, and optimal health is the result of hundreds of choices you may make that gradually turn your health, at any given moment, toward optimal health or toward disease. If that decision-making process is not present, you'll still have some level of health—you will still be alive, but you may be moving toward a disease state rather than moving toward optimal health.

Remember that being vibrantly healthy results from decisions you—and only you—can make. No one shoves unhealthful food down your throat; you decide what to eat and how to live. Put another way, health is not something you were born with that can't change, like your fingerprints. We all must take greater responsibility for our health. You can tell by your daily actions what you are committed to, what is a priority in your life. For example, do you say that you are committed to being healthy, but do not take time out to exercise and choose to eat healthful foods? Make your word count, and make vibrant health a top priority. Ralph Waldo Emerson would probably agree, since he said: "Health is our greatest wealth." How true that is!

Dan Chesnut, M.D., author of *Lying with Authority* (2008, Restoration Health Publishing, Oklahoma City, OK), reinforces what Dr. Ornish's study shows. Dr. Chesnut states, "Genes control everything in our body and they can cause disease when abnormal, but not always! So who controls genes? Nutrition can control genes. Genes can be silent and do nothing. Most are like that. For most genes to become active (to be expressed) something in nutrition triggers it, bad or good... Good genes that can boost immune activity can be expressed by good nutrition and that is good news. We know for sure that harmful genes can also be activated by animal products, especially cancer. That could be bad. . . . Weight gain may be influenced by 400 or more genes in worms! Probably in man, too. Plant-based nutrition beneficially affects gene activity. It can shut off or suppress 'bad' genes. Animal-based food adversely affects gene activity. It can activate 'bad' genes."

Consequences of Overweight and Obesity

Why does Dr. Fuhrman call obesity the number one health problem in America? Obesity and excess body weight is an underlying factor in a host of other disease conditions that significantly increase overall premature mortality. He states, "Obesity is not just a cosmetic issue—extra weight leads to an earlier death, as many studies confirm. Overweight individuals are more likely to die from all causes, including heart disease and cancer. Two thirds of those with weight problems also have hypertension, diabetes, heart disease, or another obesity-related condition."

In the article, "The Hidden Dangers of Your Excess Abdominal Fat—More Than Just Vanity," that appeared on IronMagazineForums. com, Mike Geary, Certified Nutrition Specialist, Certified Personal Trainer, states, "What most people do not realize is that excess abdominal fat, in particular, is not only ugly, but is also a *dangerous risk factor to your health*. Scientific research has clearly demonstrated that although it is unhealthful in general to have excess body fat throughout your body, it is also particularly dangerous to have excess abdominal fat.

"There are two types of fat that you have in your abdominal area. The first type that covers up your abs from being visible is called subcutaneous fat and lies directly beneath the skin and on top of the abdominal muscles. The second type of fat that you have in your abdominal area is called visceral fat, and that lies deeper in the abdomen beneath your muscle and surrounding your organs. . .

"Both subcutaneous fat and visceral fat in the abdominal area are serious health risk factors, but science has shown that having excessive visceral fat is even more dangerous than subcutaneous fat. Both of them greatly increase your risk of developing heart disease, diabetes, high blood pressure, stroke, sleep apnea, various forms of cancer, and other degenerative diseases."

Research indicates that the entry of fats into the liver from abdominal stores may trigger increased insulin resistance which, in turn, may lead to diabetes. Our body uses insulin to "open the door to the cells" to allow the sugars circulating in the blood to be escorted into the cells to be used as energy. Circulating fats (especially animal fats and excess omega-6 fats) often cause the cells to be "resistant" to the efforts of insulin to escort the sugars into the cells. This "insulin resistance" signals the pancreas to produce more insulin in an effort to force the sugars into the cells. This becomes a vicious cycle that often leads to the use of drugs to help supply additional insulin. Unfortunately, all of the excess insulin leads to other problems, and the pancreas may become exhausted, leading to Type 1 diabetes.

Fat tissue also is the storage site of many of the toxins the body is unable to eliminate. We live in an extremely toxic environment today. Our body is continually subjected to chemicals in our food, water, and air as well as from drugs that create a toxic load that often cannot be eliminated timely and efficiently. These toxins are stored in fat tissue until such a time that the body is equipped to deal with them. Our liver is designed to be a manufacturing and conversion facility as well as a detoxifier. It was not designed to deal with the onslaught of such a heavy load of toxins we subject it to daily. Its ability to perform all of these tasks is limited. It is also called upon to deal with free radical damage and the production of and recycling of glutathione. This vital function is often hindered as the increasing toxic load takes precedence over this important task.

Leptin—An Essential Key in the Weight Loss Struggle

In 1994, a key factor in weight loss was discovered. Jeffrey Friedman and colleagues at the Rockefeller University discovered the hormone leptin that is produced by fat cells. Understanding the role of leptin in the body helps us understand why so many people struggle with weight loss and the inability to lose weight and keep it off long-term.

Leptin is produced by fat cells, interacts with six types of receptors, and helps regulate energy intake, energy expenditure, fat storage, and reproduction. The amount of fat determines, to a great extent, the amount of leptin that is produced.

At one time, scientists thought it was a deficiency of leptin that contributed to excess body weight, but now they have learned that it really is not a deficiency but rather an excess of leptin that is compounding the problems in weight loss. Due to the excessive amount of leptin produced by the fat cells, the neuron receptors have become insensitive to the leptin signals. With so much leptin circulating, it is likened to being in a room where there is so much noise that you cannot understand the words of someone trying to communicate with you. With so much leptin circulating, the brain doesn't understand the signals to turn off the appetite, quit storing fat, and burn the fat for energy.

Scientists at the University of Minnesota have invested seven years of research into a remarkable discovery about leptin. They have learned that by reducing the amount of circulating leptin that leptin sensitivity can be restored. With restored leptin sensitivity, the brain hears the signal to turn off the appetite and discontinue storing fat. As a result of this research, a composition supplement of polysaccharides was developed that helps reduce the production of leptin and restores leptin sensitivity.

In an eight-week, double-blind, placebo-controlled study, scientists at the University of Connecticut Human Performance laboratory demonstrated that when a sensible diet and moderate exercise were used along with a supplement known as MaxWLX—weight loss accelerator, the following results occurred. In 8 weeks, the MaxWLX group lost 21.5 lbs. of body fat. 3.96 inches off their waist, 3.28 inches off their hips, and 1.20 inches off each thigh. They achieved a 90 percent greater fat loss than the placebo group! (If you would like to peruse the details of this exciting study, please go to: WLXmovie.com, WLXvideo.com, or WLXstudy.com.)

Time to Take Control

As mentioned previously, excess weight carries many harmful implications and increases risks of diabetes. The hormones insulin and leptin may play critical roles in the inability of many people to shed the excess pounds and keep them off. While they truly may desire to take control of their health by adopting a healthful diet and lifestyle, the effect of a diet rich in refined sugar, refined grains, and processed foods can impair frontal lobe function and the ability to make and follow wise choices long-term without some supplemental help.

In his book *Proof Positive* (1991, Neil Nedley, M.D., Ardmore, OK), Dr. Nedley explains the role of glucose as almost the exclusive source of energy for the brain. While our brain makes up about 2 percent of our body's mass, it accounts for about 15 percent of our total metabolism. When poor dietary factors require our body to produce an excess of insulin to deal with high levels of blood sugar, the excess insulin often causes too rapid of a drop in blood sugar (a hypoglycemic response). This hypoglycemic response deprives the brain of the necessary glucose for normal mental function. Dr. Nedley tells us that it takes 45–75 minutes to regain normal intellectual function after the blood sugar returns to normal. With the reactive eating patterns of most people, it is easy to see how they may lack the ability to make appropriate choices that would allow them to follow an optimal weight loss program, especially when you factor in the role of leptin.

By following a well-balanced, natural foods, plant-based diet (described in this book) coupled with the stimulant-free, all natural Max-WLX supplementation, we can control the production of leptin and restore vital leptin sensitivity. Other beneficial factors include engaging in moderate exercise, keeping the body hydrated with an optimal intake of purified water, managing stress, and practicing relaxation techniques such as meditation or deep breathing. These lifestyle choices will enable most people to get the leptin production under control so their body is not constantly being signaled to eat and store fats. An empasis on plant-based foods will provide an abundance of nutrients with a lower caloric intake that promotes optimal insulin production and utilization. This, in turn, will allow for optimal mental function so that this can be a permanent lifestyle change and not a temporary weight-loss program.

By achieving an optimal body weight through healthful diet and lifestyle changes, the likelihood of developing diabetes and other chronic disease conditions is dramatically reduced. I would like to challenge you today to take the necessary steps that will allow you to take control of your health as well as your weight and this also includes keeping your body detoxified, as you'll read about in a moment.

For more information on MaxWLX as well as upgrading body image and self-esteem, accelerating fat loss, supercharging energy, and shaving years off your looks and attitude, please visit my new website: SusanSmithJones.com and click on *Maximize Health*. There you will find a wealth of information and will also learn more about this revolutionary weight loss accelerator (MaxWLX) and can order it for yourself and your loved ones. I encourage you to try it for three months. I have seen positive weight loss results from client's using it in my private practice as well as hearing weight loss success stories from countless others. If you would like to order MaxWLX today, along with one of my other favorite nutritional supplements, the anti-aging, anti-inflammatory, immune-boosting, detoxifying glutathione accelator—MaxGXL, please visit: 4HealthBliss.com and click on *Products* for more information and *Preferred Customer* to receive wholesale pricing, as I do.

Internal Cleansing—Another Essential Key to Healing Your Body

I want to ask you some questions and encourage you to be honest with yourself in your answers. When you look in the mirror, sans clothes (in your birthday suit), are you feeling and looking your very best? Do you ever feel powerless to improve your body image and feel your best? Do you wish you could look years younger than your age? If you are like most people, your answers will not be positive. It's been my experience—from having a private practice for almost 30 years, and working with clients worldwide on healing the body, losing weight, looking years younger, and living a sacred, balanced life—that everyone needs to upgrade their healthy living program and keep their body temples cleansed and detoxified. If you don't take time to embark on an internal cleanse program from time to time, you will be sabotaging your weight loss and optimum health goals. So for the rest of this chapter, I will share with you the importance of keeping your God-given body temple cleansed and rejuvenated and worthy of the indwelling Spirit. I will start with the basics of internal cleansing (Detoxification & Rejuvenation 101), so you will know of its importance and will, hopefully, delay no longer in taking better care of your magnificent body. So let's get started.

In case you're not aware, there is an epidemic sweeping America that I refer to it as "internal toxic pollution." Many people suffer from chronic disease and loss of health not only as a direct result of unhealthy conditions environmentally, but internally as well—within the human body. We often think of health as the absence of disease. But, is this truly health? Are we healthy one day and then all of a sudden sick the next? There's a plethora of evidence that demonstrates to us that health or sickness is a process that develops over a period of time (often years) and is based at the cellular level.

Whether you're embarking on an annual New Year's Day fresh start health regimen, or a spring cleanse, or a quarterly change-of-season detox program or, perhaps, a one-day-a-week energy and vitality booster, here are the basics and some simple tips to give you the very best results. It's not difficult to look and feel years younger than your age. It's simply a matter of choice.

Our bodies are made of over 70 trillion cells. Cells of the same ilk join together to form organs, tissue, bones, blood, etc. Each cell is constantly in the process of dying and being replaced. Each cell receives nutrition and also expels waste and toxins, which must be eliminated from the body in a timely manner. When the cells are deficient in nutrients or are overpowered with toxins and waste, cellular malfunction begins and thus the slow decline in the level of health until one day a disease state is recognized by the manifestation of symptoms.

There are thousands of toxic chemicals all around us. There are pesticides in our foods, chemicals in our water and pollutants in the air we breathe. Even common cosmetics are full of chemicals. We drink, eat, breathe and live in a soup of quotidian, toxic chemicals. One of the greatest health secrets is that you have control over the pollution in your body. If you keep a balanced and clean internal environment, you won't succumb to the toxic build-up so prevalent in most people's bodies. Those who cleanse regularly look and feel younger, are much healthier, and live a longer life than those who ignore the need to internally cleanse.

Are You Toxic?

The following are some of the possible symptoms of toxic build-up in the body: constipation; chronic yeast infections; brittle hand and toe nails; frequent colds; weight gain; acne, dry or pale skin; mood swings or depression; low sex drive; lack of concentration; impaired short term memory; sleeping problems; frequent headaches; chronic urinary tract infections; arthritic bone pains or rheumatism; allergies, gas, bloating, flatulence; general weakness; and frequent/chronic fatigue or lack of energy, just to name a few.

Our modern diets are to blame for many of our most common ailments. Many people are digging their graves with their knives and forks and are making life and death decisions every time they sit down to a meal or snack. Disease often occurs as a result of an unhealthy lifestyle, which causes the body to become sluggish, congested, acidic and polluted. Antibiotics, excess sugar, carbonated beverages, chemical food additives and over-the-counter drugs can alter the acid/alkaline balance of the intestinal tract, often killing beneficial bacteria and creating the perfect environment for harmful microbes to grow. Without the "good" or "friendly" bacteria to keep them in check, these "bad" bacteria can eventually overrun our body and severely depress our immune system.

Mucoid plaque is a slimy gel-like substance that covers the inner lining of the intestines and bowel. Plaque harbors toxins and interferes with nutrient absorption. The colon is known to hold up to 30 or more pounds of old matter and can be packed with undigested foods and disease promoting bacteria.

Additionally, parasites are a toxic menace and can wreak havoc in your body. When faulty digestion keeps food from being properly processed and sent out of the body, undigested food can remain in the body and create fermentation and putrefaction. This can cause parasites and germ life to develop. Parasites thrive in an unhealthy, unclean colon. If the bowel contains partially digested proteins, sugars or starches, it can harbor an alarming variety of parasites. These parasites can range from microscopic organisms to tapeworms 15 inches long.

Benefits of Cleansing

So what can internal cleansing do for you? Here are some of the most commonly reported benefits of cleansing and detoxifying the body: flatter abdominal area; relief from bloating and constipation; clearer thinking; greater sense of well being; stronger immune system; improved digestion; better sleep; youthful appearance and healthier skin; more energy and confidence! Simply put, internal cleansing can dramatically improve the quality of your overall health. It's also one of the best ways to break any bad food habits you might have such as always salting foods, being addicted to white sugar/white flour products and sodas, etc.

When the colon and liver are clear of excess toxins and waste, it frees up energy to be used by the rest of the body. It also helps the liver and intestinal tract to manufacture nutrients as well as absorb them from your food much more efficiently. This supports the healing, repair and maintenance of your entire body.

The late Dr. Bernard Jensen, who was the father-in-law of one of this book's authors, Dr. Ellen Tart-Jensen, was considered a worldwide authority on colon, tissue and whole body cleansing. You can find his entire program in his bestselling book *Tissue Cleansing Through Bowel Management*. This book has guided millions of people through cleanses and brought remarkable healing results. Everyone should read this book; you'll be inspired to embark on a personal cleanse program after you see the photographs in this book of what comes out of the body (and into the toilet) as the result of embarking on a whole-body cleanse.

When to Cleanse and What to Expect

Almost 40 years ago, I met and began studying with Dr. Jensen and living a natural lifestyle. During these past four decades, I have embraced the regular cleansing schedule. One day a week, 2-3 days monthly, 7-10 days with each change of season, and 30-40 days every two to three years, I engage in some kind of detox/cleanse program to preclude a toxic build-up in my body and to keep me vibrantly healthy. In addition, for over 30 years I have also created custom-tailored cleanses and health programs for my clients worldwide, designed for their personal needs. In other words, I'm passionate about the healing power of whole-body cleansing.

Depending on how toxic your body may be, and how long you choose to cleanse, during your detox, you may feel a bit more tired than usual. If that's the case, just make sure to get more rest. Some people report feeling more energy; others have broken out with rashes on the skin, but these go away in a few days; some experience a slight fever or headaches (that's a sign that your body is house-cleaning); most people release lots of mucus during the cleanse; others experience mood swings or depression. At the end of a detox program, most will feel "lighter" and more peaceful; certainly you'll feel in more control over your body and experience an increase in self-esteem and confidence.

The Body's Largest Organ—Your Skin

Weighing in at approximately six pounds and covering an area of about two square yards, your skin is the largest organ of the body. Not only is it an organ, but the skin is also a major area for the elimination of toxic wastes from our systems. It has been called our third kidney because it works closely with the kidneys to help release uric acid. Our body must eliminate large amounts of waste products from our systems daily or we will die. The bowel, lungs, kidneys and skin are our four channels of elimination. Each of these organs ideally should release two pounds of toxins per day. Therefore, our skin is responsible for getting rid of nearly a fourth of our bodily toxins every day. If the skin is not doing its job, the kidneys, lungs and bowel will have an extra load to deal with.

Skin brushing is one of the finest ways to detoxify the skin and promote good circulation. While I discuss the healing power of dry skin brushing (as well as restoring youthful, joy-filled vitality) in my books *THE HEALING POWER OF NATUREFOODS, HEALTH BLISS, RECIPES FOR HEALTH BLISS* and *BE HEALTHY~STAY BALANCED*, here's a brief summary. Make a commitment for 30 days of skin brushing. After one month, your skin will feel and look about 10 years younger with daily dry skin brushing. Your brush should be made from natural vegetable fibers, not nylon or other synthetic material. Brush your entire body (except your face and private areas) *before* you shower or bathe. Brushing the skin dry rather than wet is very important because it does a much better job of removing dead skin cells and toxins. I use a special smaller, softer brush for my face and neck. My favorite skin brushes, and the only ones that I use, are available through Bernard Jensen International, bernardjensen.com, 1.888.743.1790, 1.760.471.9977. I also highly recommend the book *Health is Your Birthright* by Dr. Ellen Tart-Jensen.

Your Personal Cleanse

There are many aspects to internal cleansing that are too numerous to mention in this short section. For the detailed program, you will want to get a copy of Dr. Ellen's *free* 21-page stellar E-Book entitled *The Simplified Guide to Internal Cleansing*, which is available on bernardjensen. com. Just click on the e-book cover to download. It offers her worldrenowned, time-tested program that I personally use and recommend in all of my media work.

But as a brief summary, here is what I incorporate personally and with my clients, whether it's a 1-Day or 30-Day Cleanse. See how many of these eleven steps you can incorporate into your next cleansing program. If you visit my website and click on *Susan's Favorite Products*, you will learn more about my favorite juicer, blender, sauna, water purifier, nasal cleansing pot, and other healthy living products.

1. **Plant-Based Food & Fresh Juices:** While on a cleanse, adopt a plant-based diet with as many raw or "living" foods as possible. I also drink organic detox teas that I purchase from my local health food store. High water content foods—especially fresh fruit and vegetables—are easy to digest. Emphasize any leafy greens because the greens are very detoxifying and rejuvenating. These fresh, colorful foods take stress off of your digestive system. For short cleansing programs, you may want to consume only raw food or just drink fresh vegetable juices. Everyone should have a good home juicer so you can make fresh juices.

2. **Neti Nasal Cleansing:** The practice of nasal irrigation, known as Neti, has been used by health practioners for thousands of years worldwide. Many people in America practice Neti cleansing on a daily basis to keep their sinuses clean and improve their ability to breathe freely. Most find it a soothing and pleasant practice once they try it. Dr. Oz has discussed the benefits of nasal cleansing on the Oprah Show a few times. Why cleanse your body and ignore your nasal passages? I highly recommend this practice daily, whether cleansing or not. I have been practicing nasal cleansing since my grandmother taught it to me as a teenager (just a few years ago).

3. **Sunshine & Air:** Enjoy approximately 10-20 minutes of healing sunshine on as much of your body's skin as possible; avoid the midday sun. During your cleanse, breathe in fresh, clean air. This is the perfect time to do your deep breathing practice several times each day.

4. **Water:** Drink at least 8 glasses of purified water daily, in-between meals. When your body is fully hydrated, you can more easily flush toxins out of your system.

5. **Rest & Breath Deeply:** Find time for quiet reflection and relaxation during your detoxification program. This is not the time to fill your life with unlimited activity. Instead, choose to slow down, smell the flowers, keep a gratitude journal, and breathe deeply throughout the day.

6. **Simplify & Read:** When I'm doing a cleanse, long or short, I will often find simple ways to de-clutter my surroundings. In other words, I cleanse my body, soul and environment. This is also an excellent time to read books on how to take better care of your body. Any of my books or Dr. Ellen's are perfect to read to inspire and motivate you to live your very best life. In fact, you'll find more rejuvenation, cleansing, weight loss, anti-aging and balanced living tips in

BE HEALTHY~STAY BALANCED: 21 Simple Choices to Create More Joy & Less Stress. To order copies for you and your friends, please call: 1.800.843.5743.

7. **Exercise:** It's important to workout during a cleanse. If you're feeling tired, do some stretches or other simple movements. Make sure to include aerobic activity such as walking to help with your circulation.

8. **Hot Baths, Sauna & Massage:** A hot bath or sauna is also an excellent way to facilitate the removal of toxins through the skin. Also, during a cleanse, schedule in time to get a massage. Find a massage therapist who knows how to do a lymph massage, which will also help flush the toxins out of your body.

9. **Buddy Cleanse:** Sometimes I'll find a friend who will do the cleanse with me. Even though you might both live in different homes, or even across the country, it is still comforting to know that there's someone else (friend or family) joining you on the cleanse. Each day, visit with that person, even if it's over the telephone or by email, and compare notes and encourage each other on.

10. **Internal Cleansing Products:** Whether you cleanse for 1, 3, 7, 10 or 40 days, I encourage you to supplement your program with the best internal cleansing products. The one I always use and highly recommend is called *The Internal Cleanse Tool Kit*. This tool kit, created by Dr. Ellen, is the result of years of experience working with Dr. Bernard Jensen, and it includes five different bottles containing only the most effective and pure ingredients that you'll want to take each day of your cleanse. In addition to the Internal Cleansing Tool Kit, I also recommend Ellen's *Super Organic Rainbow Salad, Sun Cleanse, Super Circulation* and *Bone Knitter* and her must-have *free* e-book. All of her products and books are simply the best. For more information or to order Dr. Ellen's products, please contact: www. bernardjensen.com, 1.888.743.1790.

11. **The Master Antioxidant:** As mentioned above in this chapter, glutathione (GSH) is a tri-peptide (three amino acids in one molecule) that's critical to our 70+ trillion cells. As the body's premier antioxidant, it functions as an immune booster and a detoxifier of numerous toxic chemicals and heavy metals like mercury. It helps your body repair damage caused by stress, pollution, radiation, infection, drugs, poor diet, aging, injury, trauma and more. I take Max GXL daily to keep my body energized, detoxified, and rejuvenated; I would not be without Max GXL or Max WLX (For more information or to order this salubrious supplement, please visit: www.911yourhealth.com.

Keep in mind that the secret to vibrant health, youthful vitality, and a rejuvenated body is in cleansing the body and mind and then adopting a lifestyle that includes positive, grateful thoughts, natural foods, pure water, fresh air, sunshine and exercise. Learning to cleanse the body and mind is an essential part of healing, healthy weight loss and staying lean and fit. When the body is burdened with toxic waste material, it will be tired and have low immune function. When the body is clean, it can absorb more efficiently the essential nutrients it needs to heal, repair and maintain good health.

So the next time you hear the expression, "Cleanliness is next to Godliness," you may understand better that it conveys an extremely important aspect of health and rejuvenation: The more cleansed you keep your miraculous body, the more room you'll have to be filled with God's Light and Love. I wish you vibrant health and a life free from weighty concerns forevermore.

Regardless of your body size, self-respect and self-acceptance are the starting points for making peace with our size. We must know that we have the power to get off the weight treadmill and start enjoying our life, no matter where we are.
—Christiane Northrup, M.D.

As believers we are all God's children. We get an owner's manual when we purchase a cell-phone, toaster, car, jet airplane, etc. We're given one of the greatest gifts of all, it's called our body. All the money in the world can not purchase a new vehicle for you to reside in! God gave us an owner's manual—it's called the Bible. Very few people obey the Owner's Manual for a lack of understanding because of our society driven by greed and media brainwashing. How far do you think your car, or airplane would travel with improper fuel? Put soda pop, sugar, in your fuel tanks. Refusing to put water in your radiator, or oil in your engine results in a penalty called vehicle breakdown. Disease, sickness, and obesity are symptoms of improper fuel and disobedience, and/or lack of understanding. We see the results in prayer requests for our loved-ones in hospitals, churches, homes, etc. This is not our Creator's desire or design! These are indications of our vehicle breakdown where our spirit and soul reside. You can return to the vibrant life of your youth! Make the decision to allow your Creator to forgive your iniquities, and be obedient to His temple!—JEF

THE LOVE-POWERED DIET

Adapted from
The Love-Powered Diet: Eating for Freedom, Health & Joy
Published by Lantern Books, 2009

© Victoria Moran

Most people who have battled food have done exactly that: battled. I did it for thirty years. It started in childhood with a father who was a diet doctor and a mother who worked in "reducing salons." It continued in adolescence when I put myself on diets in attempt to meet the cultural standards of teen perfection, and went on into adulthood as I lost and gained weight over and over again. The beginning of the end of my personal battle was the day I gave up. I hoisted an invisible white flag in the kitchen and gave the whole thing to God: the food I depended on, the fat I despised, the thinness I craved. For the first time, my prayer was not to lose weight: it was to be at peace.

For a fleeting instant, it didn't matter to me if I weighed 120 pounds or 210. I just wanted out from under. In that moment of willingness, God took my hand and lifted me up. It was difficult in the beginning:

sometimes I had to take it an hour at a time, staying close to God and supportive friends who had taken this path before me. It's been nearly twenty-five years now, one day at a time. I am sixty-five pounds below the weight I once was and far more important, I am not a slave to food or to the bathroom scale. Most of the time, I even seem "normal" to myself.

When a craving does surface, I look at my spiritual life: do I need more prayer and meditation time? Have I been reading scripture and other inspiring books? Am I keeping the "wills" in order—God's first, not mine? When my connection to God is strong, my need for food is what anyone else's is: nourishment. This is what happened for me. For anyone who has never seen a quart of ice cream as a modern-day Goliath, it might not seem like much of a miracle, but I lived it and I know that what happened for me is a tremendous grace, one that can also happen for you.

Once you've given God—*without reservation*—your food and your body, you can ask to be shown a way of eating that mirrors spiritual maturity and emotional stability, one that truly "does a body good" and sends feelings of deprivation packing. I have found this in what I call a *Love-Powered Diet.*

Expecting food, even the best food, to cure a food addict would be like expecting a drug to cure a drug addict. It will take more than an eating plan, however enlightened, to heal the emotional wounds that you may have tried to salve with food. Your conscious contact with the love of the Lord comes first. This will give you the emotional strength that no food can provide.

Then and only then will you be ready to make food choices that will help you get your weight where you want it, nourish your body temple, and keep cravings at bay. It is important to realize that when God's power touches you anywhere, it touches you everywhere. When this happens, wanting to have it all—peace with food, peace with your body, peace within—isn't greed; it's good sense.

Surely a loving God does not want you tormented by food cravings, subject to depressing and even dangerous diets, or risking your life with morbid obesity or a binge/purge merry go-round that ceases to be merry long before the ride is over. It also stands to reason that He would be interested in your overall welfare and the welfare of all people, all forms of life, and this planet he created.

Nothing about your life is unimportant to God, including, tonight's dinner menu. Ponder this for a minute. What would pure Love, the loving parent of all life, want people to eat? I think it would be a way that:

- Is generous, delicious, and aesthetically pleasing
- Promotes high-level health as well as normal weight
- Is economical and provides plenty for everybody
- Respects all life, and
- Is environmentally sustainable.

This way of eating is what I call a *Love-Powered Diet*: whole foods, predominantly (or even exclusively) from the plant kingdom. This is a vegetarian diet—vegan, even, meaning that, if you do this completely, you will be creating your meals with no products of animal origin. Let me reassure you that eating solely from the plant kingdom—most of the time or even all of the time—need not change your politics, your religion, or any other part of yourself that the label *vegetarian* or *vegan* doesn't seem to fit. You never need to use these words if you're uncomfortable with them ("plant-based diet" works well instead).

Some historic Christian luminaries who didn't shy away from the "vegetarian" label include: General William Booth and his wife Catherine, founders of the Salvation Army; John Harvey Kellogg, health reformer and cereal magnate; Rev. Fred Rogers of the *Mr. Rogers* children's show; Rev. Dr. Albert Schweitzer, medical missionary to Africa; *War and Peace* author Leo Tolstoy; and John Wesley, founder of the Methodist Church. Should you decide to join them, you'll be in good company, but because the love-powered diet does not require absolute adherence, you can start to make progress even before you've gone "all the way."

It starts with the love that God has for you, and follows through with your making food choices that honor God, yourself, and all creation. Interestingly, this way of eating is very much akin to God's original diet for man set forth in Genesis 1:29 when He said, "Behold! I have given you every herb bearing seed, which is upon the face of all the earth, and every tree, in the which is the fruit of a tree yielding seed; to you it shall be for meat."

Even after the Fall when the Edenic state was no longer the lot of mankind and we first needed (as we still do) the salubrious and curative properties of leafy greens, God said in Genesis 3:18: "...and thou shalt eat the herb of the field." We were allowed animal foods after the flood when there was no vegetation (Genesis 9:3: "Every moving thing that liveth shall be meat for you; even as the green herb have I give you all things"), and yet our bodies were *designed* to live and thrive on foods that grow up out of the ground. As Paul would write so many years later in 1 Corinthians 10:23: "All things are lawful for me, but all things are not expedient..." The context was different, but the truth applies.

The love-powered diet celebrates the abundance of nature. Its basic food groups are:

• Fruits, preferably fresh but also frozen, unsweetened

• Vegetables (salads, crudités, and steamed, sautéed, and baked veggies, with an emphasis on super-nutritious leafy greens); The starchy vegetables including potatoes, yams, and corn belong here nutritionally as well, although in terms of meal-planning, you'll often be using them the way you'd use grains

• Whole grains, including whole wheat (bread, bulghur, pasta, etc.), brown rice, oats, cornmeal (cornbread, polenta), buckwheat (pancakes, noodles), and gourmet grains such as millet, quinoa, and amaranth

• Legumes, such as dried beans (navy, kidney, red, pink, lima, garbanzo), peas, lentils, and soybeans (i.e., edamame) and soy foods such as tofu and tempeh

• Oil-rich foods including nuts, seeds, coconut, and avocado. These are rich foods (fats and oils have twice the calories per gram as either protein or carbohydrate) to used sparingly, especially for anyone wishing to release weight

This translates into meals such as fruit plates and fruit smoothies; crisp salads and vegetable stir-fries; casseroles and chowders; sandwiches on hearty whole-wheat bread and quick loaves like cornbread and banana bread served with satisfying soups such as lentil and split pea; an assortment of rice and noodle dishes; beans and rice, beans on toast, and Boston baked beans; veggie-burgers, veggie wraps, or a breakfast-style supper of scrambled tofu, grilled onions and tomatoes. The world of ethnic cooking comes alive for love-powered chefs, too. You can experiment with dishes from:

- The Middle East: pita sandwiches with hummus (chick-pea spread) or baba ghannouj (eggplant dip), tabbouleh (cracked-wheat salad), rice pilafs

- Italy: eggplant dishes, gnocchi, and an endless array of pasta with vegetables and tomato or wine-based sauces

- India: a variety of vegetable curries with tantalizing complementary chutneys, dahl (spicy sauces made from lentils or split peas), pungent rice dishes

- Mexico: chili sans carne, avocado tostadas, bean burritos, vegetable fajitas

- Asia: vegetable sushi with miso soup and seaweed salad at the Japanese place; steamed veggies and brown rice with garlic sauce on the side from the Chinese delivery guy; the potato, cabbage, and tofu dish from the Vietnamese restaurant; and the cellophane noodles with lotus root and exotic vegetables from the Thai café

Even in traditional American fare you can make easy shifts, such as a veggie-burger for hamburger. You can customize what you eat to the way you live.

A gradual change works best. Get yourself a good, basic plant-based cookbook such as *Ten Talents*, by Rosalie Hurd and Dr. Frank Hurd (www.tentalents.net), and commit to eating vegetarian meals three days a week. Once this feels right, go to four or five days. Or eat all plant-based meals for breakfast and lunch and continue to have meat with your family a few evenings a week. This isn't a race or a content. You can take your time to adjust, going as far as you, with prayerful consideration, are willing to take this.

A Taste For Quality

Love-powered dining doesn't just bypass animal foods, however. It also gives short shrift to the highly refined, overly processed, phony foods that we're fond of calling *junk*.

Although we're making progress and real food is showing up where it never did before, the majority of items found in convenience stores and gas stations, much of what's in an ordinary bakery, and just about all the offerings at the movie theater are still likely to be junk food. The supermarket has its share of nutritionally vacant items, and some of them even creep into health food stores. Reading labels is a good practice, but the best food is fresh food—fruits and vegetables from the orchard and garden that have no packaging and no label.

For a love-powered diet to give you all it can, you'll want to avoid any food that isn't good enough for you—just the way your mother may have told you not to date a particular boy (or girl) for that very reason. If it's high in sugar (when sugar is near the top of an ingredients list, it's high), high in salt (enough to make you thirsty), or very fatty (if it's fried, "melts in your mouth," or leaves a shine on your napkin), it's not up to your standards.

Everyone knows that junk food is a nutritional disaster, packs in the calories, and causes a yen for more of the same. In addition, it simply isn't becoming to people who are out to love themselves more. You can go to an elegant restaurant and consume a thousand calories in a special dinner with a special person and leave there feeling terrific about the world and everything that's in it, yourself included. Or you could go to some fast-food place, gobble up a thousand calories in 4.2 minutes, and feel fat and guilty as you toss the wrappers. Cultivate your taste for quality food and select the best food that you can afford.

Go for quality drinks, too, since many are questionable. Alcohol, with its empty calories and mood-altering potential, should be limited to moderate consumption, if you choose to drink at all. A typical soda contains some 9 teaspoons of sugar in a 12-ounce can, and no artificial sweetener has been proven unequivocally safe.

The caffeine in cola as well as in coffee and black tea can also be a problem. Caffeine is a stimulant, sending stress hormones coursing through the body. The easiest way to modify a caffeine-induced buzz is to eat, and many people do this unconsciously. Caffeine can also suppress the appetite temporarily, but it comes back like gangbusters. Dieters usually drink lots of coffee, tea, and cola, and dieters usually relapse. It's possible that there is a caffeine connection. According to Agatha Thrash, M.D., in her book *Nutrition for Vegetarians*, "Any drug that will stimulate the nerves will stimulate the appetite in susceptible people. This includes coffee, tea, colas, and chocolate. These beverages stimulate cravings."

If you consume beverages that contain caffeine, pay attention to the ways they affect your attitude and your appetite. Discontinue or moderate your use and try herbal teas, sparkling mineral water, and natural spritzers (mineral water and fruit juice) instead. The drink that helped get a diet-cola hankering the size of Texas off my back is licorice tea. Hot or iced, this herbal drink is naturally sweet but calorically negligible. And if you love the taste and ritual of coffee, look into the herbal coffee replacement Teeccino (www.teeccino.com). You brew it in your regular drip coffeemaker (use an inexpensive, reuasable "gold" filter instead of paper filters), French press, or espresso machine: it has the aroma and full body of the finest java with not a hint of caffeine.

With animal products, junk foods, and iffy drinks out of your diet, you will also have inadvertently eliminated all or most of your personal binge foods. You may, however, have others, and it's important that you come to terms with them. Not everyone who wants to lose a few pounds has binge foods, but if you've ever been on an eating binge—that's an all-out food frenzy that leaves you feeling intoxicated—you're probably intimately acquainted with them. When it comes to binge-inciting foods, people say that "one bite is too many and a thousand aren't enough." These are the foods that encourage appetite instead of extinguishing it. You really can't eat just one. If you have some today, you'll need more tomorrow. In other words, binge foods are addictive.

The usual recipe for a binge food is fat plus sugar or fat plus salt. Common culprits, then, are what you'd expect: ice cream, chips, chocolate, pastries, and cheese. But even something as subtle as combining nuts and raisins for trail mix can turn two otherwise innocuous foods into the makings of some overeater's lost weekend. Besides, binge foods are intensely personal. For a given individual, something about the taste or texture of almost any food, or past associations with it, can make it far more than just something to eat. You may have trouble with a broad category of foods—sugar, meat, flour, or anything at your mom's house—or specific items such as granola, yogurt, dates, peanut butter, or white bread.

If you can be really honest with yourself, you'll probably realize that you already know your own red-light foods. You may not want to claim them, but you may as well—they've already claimed you. If you're unsure about a specific suspect, try to eat a little and save the rest for next week. If you can't do it, or if you think incessantly about it while it sits in the cupboard or fridge, you have yourself a binge food.

The point in identifying these is to protect yourself from infiltrators out to sabotage your victory. If there was a stalker set on harming you, you would notify the police do everything in your power to protect yourself. Understand that any food you haven't been able to eat reasonably since you cut teeth is as threatening to you as that stalker. The safest path to tread with a binge food is the one that leads away from it. In other words, don't eat it—not because I said so, but because you would rather not socialize with a dietary hit man.

The prospect of living without some food you've depended on may seem unbearable, but you can do it. The secret is to think in terms of *today* instead of the rest of your life. There is disagreement among eating-disorders experts and recovering overeaters (who are also experts, in my opinion) on whether or not these dynamite foods can ever be defused.

That is to say, can the allure of carrot cake come down to that of carrot sticks? I've found that I'm able to eat anything that I choose to eat today providing my spiritual life is in order. Other overeaters in recovery—people every bit as attentive to their spiritual lives as I am—assiduously avoid certain foods, usually sweets.

With sufficient self-honesty, you'll find your own way with binge foods. They are potentially loaded weapons, but they will in time lose much of their attractiveness. Snacking—with wild abandon at least—can meet a similar fate. With the love-powered diet, you can elect to snack on something that will support your health, or you may decide not to snack at all. There are magazine articles all the time claiming that eating small, frequent meals ("grazing") keeps blood sugar steady and is therefore superior to having three regular meals. This works for certain people and there are, in fact, medical conditions that require it. For most of us, though, the sanest approach is also the simplest: three reasonable meals a day, eaten on a fairly predictable schedule. As I write in my book *Fit from Within*: "If you start to eat only three times, you have to stop only three times, and stopping has been the problem."

In the earliest stages of your lifestyle change, you may need large meals to bridge the gap between binge eating and moderation. That's fine. Begin wherever you can. With a commitment to three meals, you'll find that, in starting to eat only three times, you'll have to stop only three times. For anyone with a food problem, stopping is the hard part. Moreover, society is set up for three meals a day. You go on vacation and stay at a bed-and-breakfast. Your workday is punctuated with a lunch hour. You're invited out for dinner.

As you embark on this adventure, you'll be enjoying bountiful meals and may well find that eating three of these a day with nothing but living in between is fully adequate. On the other hand, this is a low-fat food plan that includes lots of water-rich fruits and vegetables that are efficiently processed by your digestive apparatus. They don't stay with you like heavy, fatty foods that must be laboriously digested. Therefore, you may feel the need for something to eat at morning break time, or in the middle of the afternoon, or before bed.

The best snack is a piece of fruit. This is the original, portable fast food. The natural sugars in fruit will pick up your energy, and it's as close to fat-free as you're going to get. Have fruit between meals if you want it. Raw vegetables make good snacks, too, and it's good to keep them washed, chopped, and ready. Freshly extracted vegetable juices, especially those that include the nutrient superstars, dark, leafy greens, may well be the best snack going. They flood your system with needed nutrition and lasting satisfaction in liquid form, so the noshing reflex—a nibble here, a nibble there—isn't activated. (They make a terrific beverage with meals as well.)

Another bonus to sticking with three meals a day for the most part, however, is that the time in between meals is a small period of fasting that benefits us physically by giving the digestive process a chance to proceed unimpaired, but it also benefits us spiritually. When you wait for the next meal, you're also "waiting on the Lord." When you go about your business without something to munch on and feelings come up, you have to take them to God because you're not indulging in a "fix" from food. Remember when the disciples asked Jesus why they could not cast out a demon? Jesus' reply in Matthew 17:21 was: "Howbeit this kind goeth not out but by prayer and fasting." Compulsive overeating, once it crosses the line from bad habit to genuine addiction, is in the same category.

Generous, Delicious, and Aesthetically Pleasing

As important as periods without food are, eating, when it's time to eat, should be a joy. One downside of conventional dieting is lack of food. You're told to compensate by using a smaller plate. With a whole foods, plant-based way of eating, you can use a standard plate and a big salad bowl. If a substantial salad with a light dressing is the center of your meal, ordinary salad bowls are a joke. Uncooked vegetables as well as fruits are both low in fat and high in water; therefore they are low in calories. The filling starches from which you'll make many of your entrees—rice, pasta, beans, potatoes (yes, plural!)—are low-fat foods as well, so they're lower in calories than traditional main dishes.

Even the leaner animal foods are generally higher in fat than grains, vegetables, and most beans. In addition, some evidence suggests that calories from fat are more fattening than the same number of calories from carbohydrates because the body has to work to turn carbs into storable fat while dietary fat can be stored as is.

I'm not suggesting that because most love-powered foods won't put you at odds with the bathroom scale, you should overeat. I am saying, however, that the concept of a moderate portion has to be redefined when you adopt a low-fat diet. If you're having salad, steamed asparagus, and corn on the cob for dinner, don't have one ear of corn: have a couple, and a whole wheat roll, too, if you want it (just spread on some all-fruit jam and bypass the margarine or butter). You'll need to rethink portion sizes on the side dishes that, in this way of eating, become entrees. Those boxes of rice pilaf, for example, don't serve six anymore. They served six with roast beef. As a main course, they'll serve two or three.

Not only are love-powered portions generous, the variety of foods from which you'll choose is enormous. When people find out that you're doing this, they'll say, "But what do you eat?" Take it from me: they wouldn't stand still long enough to hear the names of all the tasty foods on nature's table.

When you're eating natural foods and concentrating on those from the plant kingdom, you'll become more aware of seasonal fruits and vegetables. When you travel, you'll find regional delights that are lost to people on the burger-and-fries circuit. There are hundreds of varieties of vegetables and fruits, dozens of kinds of grains and legumes, and plenty of interesting specialty and convenience foods made from them.

From this abundance, you can select what you like. You don't have to eat any specific food—not grapefruit, not spinach, not soybeans. You build your eating plan around foods you already like, and with a little daring you can discover both delicious new foods and tasty new ways to fix old favorites.

Either way, what you'll offer yourself and others to eat will look beautiful. A supermarket checker once bagged my week's provisions and said, "I've had this job for 15 years and I've never seen such pretty groceries!"

That's because fruits and vegetables really are edible works of art, and whether in a shopping cart or on a serving tray, they are very appealing to people. Natural foods from the plant kingdom entice the eye and have wonderful fragrances and distinctive flavors. They tantalize several senses, and meals based on them invite appreciation and the slower pace that's essential in retraining eating habits.

It's also pleasant to be in the company of these foods. If you were going to meet a friend in the city, wouldn't you rather rendezvous at a fruit stand than at a butcher shop or fish market? And if you went back to your place for the kind of simple but elegant dinner you will soon be adept at preparing, cleanup would be a breeze. Greasy pots do not exist when you don't fix greasy foods, and that counts as aesthetically pleasing, too.

Eating for High-Level Health and Normal Weight.

"I have lived quite long enough and am trying to die," wrote witty vegetarian George Bernard Shaw at eighty-four, "but I simply cannot do it. A single beefsteak would finish me, but I cannot bring myself to swallow it. I am oppressed with a dread of living forever. That is the only disadvantage of vegetarianism."

We know, in any case, that a poor diet can keep you from reaching your health potential. In replacing animal foods and processed foods with unrefined grains, fruits, vegetables, and legumes, a dietary program results that is:

- Cholesterol-free (cholesterol in our diets comes only from foods of animal origin)

- Low in fats, especially saturated fats

- High in natural carbohydrates (Don't panic: these are whole, natural carbs that will keep you going, not fatten you up)

- Rich in fiber

- Abundant in vitamins A and C, which some research indicates may protect against certain cancers, and other possible anti-carcinogens

such as indoles in cruciferous (cabbage family) vegetables and protease inhibitors in legumes

- Adequate but not excessive in protein (too much protein has been
  linked with osteoporosis, kidney stones, and deterioration of kidney
  function)

- Markedly lower in pesticide residues, particularly chlorinated hy-
  drocarbons, than are animal foods (these residues concentrate in the
  fatty tissues of animals)

- Bulky and satisfying to assuage hunger without excess calories

It is, therefore, widely accepted in medical literature that vegans, people who eat only plant foods and no meat, fish, eggs, or dairy products,
typically weigh 8 to 20 pounds less than comparable omnivores who
average 17 to 22 pounds over ideal weight. The serendipitous thing about
vegans and weight is that their slimness is not something they work at. It
happens naturally—without hunger, suffering, or willpower. That's precisely how it will happen for you, provided that you practice the spiritual
principles that will keep you from needing to eat for a fix, and that you
build your diet predominantly from the love-powered food groups.

Economical Eating with Plenty for All

You can afford a love-powered diet, even if you're a full-time student, a
retired person on a fixed income, or a food-stamp recipient. The staples
for this eating style are among the most inexpensive foods in the mar-
ketplace: brown rice, beans, whole-wheat flour and bread, potatoes, carrots, greens and other seasonal vegetables, apples, oranges, bananas, and
other fruits selected when they're most abundant and least costly. And
you can grow nutritious sprouts on a kitchen counter—alfalfa, mung
bean, sunflower…the list is endless—for mere pennies. You'll be saving
cash by skipping the high-ticket items like meat and cheese—as well as
the junk foods, which may sometimes be bargains until you consider the
physiological price you pay for them.

You certainly can spend money on rare, tropical fruits, exotic vegetables (I'm astounded by how many vegetables come in purple), health food store convenience items, and gourmet specialties. You don't need these, though, to design love-powered menus that are nutritious and conducive to bringing your best body into being. Simple foods—those that the planet provides generously for all—can be the makings of elegant repasts, celebrations of life and health in good taste and good conscience.

A Way of Eating that Respects All Life

In summer and fall, the classifieds are filled with ads for "pick-your-own" places, inviting city folks on country outings that will bring in a miniature harvest of apples or berries. That's the same time of year that the gardeners are out in force, turning suburban yards into small truck farms or greening midtown balconies with lettuce and radish and to-mato plants. People delight in these pursuits, even before the fruits of their labors reach the dinner table.

Throughout the year, however, something else is going on. Animals are being slaughtered for us to eat—an astronomical nine-billion-plus every year, something like one million per hour, according to Physicians Committee for Responsible Medicine. The Bible rightfully states that man was given dominion over nature, and others would say it's survival of the fittest and we're at the top of the food chain. I believe that God means in the Bible that I have dominion over animals the way a parent has dominion over children: to care for them. As we said before, you are *allowed* to eat meat, but you have the *choice* whether or not to do so.

Animals in modern, corporate agriculture are more production units than they are God's creatures, and the slaughter process is a horrific one. I know. I spent a day in a slaughterhouse. While the entire experience lives in my brain as a real-life horror movie complete with the cold, the blood, the screams, the stench, and deplorable conditions for the work-ers, there was one cow whose face, and fate, will be etched in my memory until I take my last breath. She was old, a reject from a dairy herd— "used up," the man said. She seemed comfortable with people and trusting, so she didn't require the cattle prod—an instrument capable of producing first-degree burns—to walk the ramp to the metal enclosure where she would be stunned with the captive bolt pistol. When the worker came at her with the stunner, she crouched to avoid it. He whistled at her, the way I imagined he might whistle at his dog when he got home that evening. She raised her head in response and was shot with the captive bolt.

She dropped to the floor, was immediately hoisted up by one leg, her throat slit, and as the blood gushed from her body, she was efficiently skinned before my eyes. She was turned within a minute, maybe two, from *being* to *beef*. "You have just dined," wrote Ralph Waldo Emerson, "and however scrupulously the slaughterhouse is concealed in the distance of miles, there is complicity." Emerson was a vegetarian.

Today there are problems in the barnyard as well as at the slaughterhouse. Most of the animals raised for food today come from factory farms where they may be confined to small cages or stalls, and without anesthesia are dehorned, detailed, debeaked, and mutilated in other ways. Many are denied exercise, companionship, natural diets, and other basic needs, and there are no federal laws protecting them. Even animals whose rearing supposedly meets certain "compassion standards" are commodities. Male chicks are killed soon after birth, even in so-called free-range egg operations. Mother cows in dairy herds are separated from their babies—and male calves usually killed for veal—on even "organic" dairy farms.

It could be argued that some animal foods come with a higher pain cost than others, and many people who are not vegetarian but whose compassion has been aroused by information have stopped eating certain foods. Among these are:

Foie gras, the "fatty liver" from ducks and geese that some gourmets foolishly prize is the result of sadistic force-feeding that results in a diseased liver and an expensive appetizer. *Foie gras* is banned in several countries and was even decried by Pope Benedict.

Veal is another item on the cruelty menu. Calves are taken from their dairy-cow mothers shortly after birth, a horrible separation for both, confined in crates in which they cannot turn around, and fed an anemic diet to preserve the babyish white flesh. Although there is some movement toward "less intensive" veal operations, there are none yet that would invite a 5th grade class for a field trip.

Factory-farmed eggs are another ugly story, one that, like the slaughterhouse I can tell firsthand because I've been to the "batteries" where they're produced. Male chicks are of no use in an egg operation so they are killed, often by suffocation or shredding, soon after hatching. The females, de-beaked and de-clawed, are crammed into tiny cages allowing them no social interaction or any life as a chicken. Many die daily and one worker at a "farm" I visited had as his job to remove the dead birds every morning.

And yet, agribusiness is *one industry* and using animals for food opens the way for abuses. If, for example, there was no demand for dairy, there would be no veal industry. While consideration for the animals involved may never be your motivation for a diet that excludes animal foods, expect that as you adopt some of the principles found here your overall reverence for life will expand. You may not interpret or express that reverence in the way that someone else might, but expect to see it in your life because it will be there. As psychologist Virginia Satir wrote, "Spiritual power can be seen in a person's reverence for life—hers and all others, including animals and nature, with a recognition of a universal life force referred to by many as God."

Food for a Sustainable Planet

This way of eating is as gentle to the earth as it is to animals and arteries. Eating a largely plant-based diet can be just as easy to incorporate into an ecologically aware lifestyle as other responsible practices like recycling cans and recharging batteries.

More than half the water used for all purposes in this country goes to raising livestock; the practice also leads to loss of precious topsoil and to deforestation. A 2006 report from the United Nations Food and Agriculture Organization states that animal agriculture is responsible for 18% of greenhouse gas emissions. *That's more than is attributable to all our cars, trucks, and SUVs.*

In addition to the environmental benefits brought about by eating low on the food chain, there are subtler ways in which simpler eating supports an ecological ethic. Since you'll be selecting natural foods, many of which can be bought in bulk and put in reusable containers, you'll be using fewer packaging materials. You'll be less likely to visit fast-food places with their plethora of disposables, and since you won't have meat scraps, all of your garbage can be composted. With the money you save, you can buy some food that is organically grown, and with more fresh fruits and salads in your diet, you may use your stove less often and save energy. Also, this is clean eating; you will have fewer dishes to wash so you'll use less detergent and hot water.

Eating in this way can also awaken an appreciation for nature in even the most avowed city dweller. Don't be surprised if you find yourself growing parsley and chives in clay pots on your windowsills or raising a crop of alfalfa sprouts on your counter. You might even find yourself planting a tree that, in a few years or several, will bear fruit or nuts. When this was suggested to me, I argued, "Why should I plant a fruit tree? I won't even be living in this house when it gets its first peach." But "Someone will be living there," I was reminded. A tree, then, can be a contribution to strangers and the next generation. And eating from trees, gardens, and fields can be a gift to yourself, one of all sorts of ways that you'll discover to make the love in your life practical and viable.

As you make appropriate changes in what you eat and how you eat a day at a time, you make this a way of life that works for you in the real world, *your* real world. I can tell you that it's worked for me for over twenty years as I've traveled for business and pleasure all over the country and around the world. I had no problems in Tibet or Iceland, and only a few on the Interstate in my native Missouri.

Nourished by Love

- **Choose natural foods from the plant kingdom-fruits, vegetables, whole grains, and legumes.** If you are not ready to become a complete vegetarian, use animal foods more for variety and flavor than as major players.

- **Know that plant foods may be eaten generously.** Have ample portions from the four plant-based food groups (fruits, vegetables, whole grains, and legumes) and use concentrated sweets and oil-rich foods sparingly. If you enjoy salad, eat all you want; just keep an eye on the amount of dressing you're using.

- **Avoid second helpings as a general rule.** When you serve yourself, start with enough. If someone serves you a piddling portion, have more.

- **Rethink the main course.** Make sure that rice, potatoes, or a large salad with pasta or beans in it can fit there. Round out meals with more vegetables, whole-grain bread, and so forth.

- **Use *rich relatives* like nuts, avocado, and dried fruit, sparingly.** (If you're healthy and don't need to lose weight or can handle the extra calories, you can eat more of these.)

- **Go for quality.** You deserve better than junk food. For the most part, leave sugar, grease, and excess salt on their side of the tracks—the wrong side. Caffeine and alcohol consumption should be reduced or eliminated.

- **As a rule, have three meals a day unless you have a health condition that requires you to eat more often.** Sit down during meals. Have a place setting. Try not to rush through the meal. Keep it nice: argue some other time. And don't watch TV at mealtime.

- **If you want a snack, have fruit, raw veggies, or freshly extracted juice such as carrot/celery/spinach or kale/romaine/apple/lemon.** Feeling hungry—not faint, not shaky, just hungry—for a while before a meal is okay, too.

- **Eat only when you're emotionally and spiritually centered.** If you feel that you're about to eat for a fix, even at mealtime, get yourself together first by calling a supportive friend, taking a walk, or writing in your journal.

- **Avoid personal binge foods**. These are the foods that seem to incite overeating or that you obsess over when they're around. A love-powered diet eliminates most of the common ones, but recognize and respect yours, common or not.

- **Leave a little food on your plate**. I've heard it called the *angel bite*. You're not a failure when you don't do this, but you get lots of inner nourishment when you do.

- **Give less power to the scale**. Find a sensible midpoint between frequent weighing and refusing to find out what you weigh. Decide to weigh yourself once or twice a month and stay with that. You will lose weight. Give yourself an edge with exercise. If you have a history of crash dieting, or if you have been bulimic, it may take time for your body to respond to normal, healthful eating with the loss of weight you're looking for. Be patient. Concentrate on self-acceptance and on enjoying the day at hand. Remember that you're working with the laws of nature. They can't be rushed and they can't be cheated. Allow yourself to be a part of the natural process. This is for life, so there's no reason to hurry. Don't be discouraged by a, slow-moving scale. If you want to be impressed by a number, look at your love-powered cholesterol level.

- **Get the help you need**. Continue to ask God each morning for help in eating reasonably that day. Say thanks at night, even if your eating wasn't perfect. Attend Overeaters Anonymous...
  (www.overeatersanonmous.com)
  or another spiritually based support group (OA has meetings in person, online, and on the phone). Read the books that inspire you and keep you on target.

- **Give your wellbeing priority status**. Allow yourself time for meals and food preparation, for meditation, exercise, support group meetings, and whatever else you need. This isn't selfishness—it's self-preservation.

Nutritional Guidelines

A love-powered food plan provides optimum nutrition for your health. Following these guidelines will further ensure that. If you are under a doctor's care, consult him or her about your eating plan. If you are pregnant or nursing, follow the advice of your health care provider. Also visit www.pcrm.org/health/veginfo/pregnancy.html for nutritional information for a vegan pregnancy from Physicians Committee for Responsible Medicine; read the excellent article "Pregnancy and the Vegan Diet," by Reed Mangels, Ph.D., RD, available on the Vegetarian Resource Group's website (www.vrg.org).

1. Eat from the four main love-powered food groups daily: vegetables, fruits, whole grains, and legumes. Use of some healthy fats—nuts and seeds, avocado, a little olive and flax oil—is also fine; just don't overdo. If you wish to continue using some animal products for now, keep your intake moderate and have a plan for making the break for good.

2. Enjoy at least one large salad every day and include in it a variety of leafy greens (romaine, leaf lettuce, spinach) plus other vegetables.

3. Include foods rich in vitamin C such as citrus fruits, cantaloupe, bell peppers, tomatoes, and strawberries.

4. Eat foods with a high vitamin C content along with iron-rich foods. This helps increase iron absorption by your body. High-iron foods include beans, peas, and lentils; dried fruit such as prunes and figs; almonds and cashews; whole grains; and leafy greens (the greens come with their own vitamin C).

5. Include at least two daily servings of calcium-rich foods such as collards, kale, broccoli, oatmeal, soybeans, tofu cultured with calcium sulfate, almonds, sesame seeds or tahini (sesame-seed butter),

calcium-fortified orange juice, or calcium-fortified soy milk or rice milk. Virtually all your food will provide some calcium, and much research indicates that people need less of this mineral on a plant-based diet than on one high in animal protein.

6. Be sure to get vitamin D through moderate exposure to sunlight. While this is of particular concern to dark-skinned people living in northern latitudes, recent research suggests that vitamin D deficiency is wide-spread. Most nutritionists now recommend taking supplementary vitamin D, up to 400 IU daily.

7. Supplement your diet regularly with a source of vitamin B12 to meet the Daily Value of 6 micrograms. B12 tablets contain more than this and may be taken weekly. Although this micronutrient is not naturally occurring in plant foods, many vegetarian foods are fortified with it, including some meat analogs, nutritional yeasts, fortified soy milk, and some commonly available cereals (check the label). Supplementing vitamin D is a good idea for anyone on any diet, since few of us come close to getting an amount through sun exposure to our skin.

8. For a plethora of disease-preventing phytochemicals think *color* and eat a rainbow of foods: blueberries, tomatoes, pumpkin and squash, kale and collards, watermelon. Also include a vegetable from the cabbage family (broccoli, brussels sprouts, cauliflower) on your menu at least four times a week.

9. Don't overdo protein by eating too many beans—a cup a day is plenty. The love-powered diet will keep your protein intake at the proper level. Provided you obtain adequate calories from a variety of natural foods, you will secure ample protein without special foods or food combinations.

10. Be moderate in your use of nuts, seeds, olives, and avocado and be ever so sparing in your use of oil for cooking and in salad dressings to keep fat consumption low. Cut down by water-sautéing, substituting applesauce for shortening in baking, and using non-stick cookware. Even so, if you eat a plant-based diet, it will automatically be fairly low in total fat and very low in artery-clogging saturated fat.

This is an adaptation of a portion from Victoria Moran's *The Love-Powered Diet: Eating for Freedom, Health, and Joy (New York: Lantern Books, 2009).*

EDITOR'S NOTE

The strongest Love-powered diet ever written was written by our Creator, JESUS! To show the Power of His Love, He gave us free will. Genesis 1:29 showed His Love. To control all the disease, sickness and obesity, all we have to do is choose Vibrant Health by changing our lifestyle!—JEF

SET TIMES TO EAT

Paul Nison

"There is a Time to Every Purpose Under the Heaven."

—Ecclesiastes 3:1

People are consuming too many meals too often and it's another reason their health suffers. With good study of Scripture we can see how YHWH's chosen people consumed only two meals a day at certain times and now health teachers are agreeing that these times would be the most ideal times to consume our food. The Scriptures show us the connection between consuming food and the customary times of worship as found in the Scriptures. Usually around the third and ninth hours of the natural day (which correspond to about 9:00 a.m., and 3:00 p.m.).

"They are headed for destruction. Their god is their appetite, they brag about shameful things, and they think only about this life here on earth" (Philippians 3:19). Today we can see the connection between lack of worship, lack of knowledge and giving no thanks to YHWH for our food and the mass amount of meals that people are eating every day. As people lost

the connection with YHWH, they looked toward food as their comfort. Emotional eating and idolizing our foods can get us sick very quickly and this is what is happening on a daily basis.

Natural Time to Eat

"And YHWH said, Let there be lights in the firmament of the heaven to divide the day from the night; and let them be for signs, and for seasons, and for days and years…And YHWH made two great lights; the greater light for the rule of the day, and the lesser for the rule of the night" (Genesis 1:14, 16).

Yeshua said, *"Are there not twelve hours in the day"* (John 11:9)?

At the time that He said this, the people of the world had a number of ways of keeping time. The Scriptural method of keeping time uses sunrise as the beginning of the first hour, and sunset as the end of the twelfth. This means that as the seasons change and the days become longer and shorter, the hours would necessarily, likewise, become longer and shorter.

YHWH's people of old were told not to learn the customs of the nations around them, who were, in one form or another, sun worshippers. (Deuteronomy 18:9). As far back as ancient Babylon, men were devising ways to measure hours of equal lengths. Water clocks, sand clocks, and many others were invented. In the 11th century A.D., an Arab astronomer even developed a sundial which would read in equal-length hours. Yet YHWH's faithful people used none of these as the rule to establish their hours of worship, and thus their meal times. When they were faithful, they retained nature's health laws by receiving spiritual and physical nourishment in a timely manner. The third and ninth hours which were used for the service of the earthly sanctuary varied in length seasonally. Why didn't YHWH give His people a method of measuring equal-length hours if it would have been beneficial to them? The one who was to "think to change times and laws" (Daniel 7:25) didn't stop with trying to change the Sabbath, or the feast days, or the months and years, but has extended his reach even to the hours of the day, and has thereby affected the hours of worship, eating, and sleeping by this attack on nature and her Author.

Sunrise and Sunset

Today, many health researchers are rediscovering that the human body is directly affected by the sunrise and sunset. The period in between is referred to as the *photo-period*. They have been finding that the big experiment of living by the clock, rather than by the sun, is not really best for any natural being. They are also reaching the same conclusion about the staying up late at night made possible by electrical lighting. There has always been a temptation to unnecessarily "burn the midnight oil."

There are conflicts with nature which arise when one eats at the same hours by the clock. In North America in the winter there are only around 10 sixty-minute hours of daylight, while in the summer there are around 15 sixty-minute hours. If one is in the habit of eating supper at 6:00 p.m. each day, in winter said meal would be taken after sunset – a practice which is contrary to good health, as will be explained later.

Perhaps the greatest testimony against the use of equal length hours is the need for *Daylight Savings Time* which was incorporated to compensate for the extra energy used to artificially illuminate the hours when the work hours were out of sync with the day's light. Twice a year, those people of the earth who take their meals by the clock and go on and off *Daylight Savings Time* by adding or losing an hour of a day throw off their entire bodily cycles and bring an unnecessary shock to their systems. It takes some people months to recover from the change in meal times, and no one who follows the practice of eating by the clock (rather than by the sun) is immune from a certain amount of trauma due to the drastic changes.

The purpose of this chapter (based on writing by Brother Doug-Mitchell of www.the-branch.org) is to aid us in being restored to our natural cycles, and to the ensuing health and well being.

Wisdom of old has also spoken of the consequences of eating at the wrong times.

"What sorrow for the land ruled by a servant, the land whose leaders feast in the morning. Happy is the land whose king is a noble leader and whose leaders feast at the proper time to gain strength for their work, not to get drunk" (Ecclesiastes 10:16, 17).

Photo-periods

Where photo-periods are concerned, the natural process is still the same no matter what we eat – our digestion slows down significantly after the sun goes down, and doesn't quicken again until the sun rises. Those who eat a large meal near or after sundown will usually have the feeling that they are not yet finished digesting it when they rise in the morning, even though it may have been 8-12 hours since they ate. This feeling may last an hour or two after rising.

This slow-down in digestion is attributed to the increase of melatonin, which is a major factor in restful sleep. The large meals which are eaten near or after sundown never really get the full assimilation which is possible, and end up robbing the body of its fully refreshing sleep because the digestive system is still trying to do its major work during a time when it should be at rest. Yet when the same type of meal is eaten earlier in the day the body is wide awake and able to complete its work without interfering with the cycles of rest because of the activity of the day and the effects of the daylight.

This one factor of eating large meals towards the end of or after, the daylight hours, alone, is the major reason why many people's biological clocks are on a 25-hour cycle, rather than on a 24-hour cycle. Forcing the body to try and digest a heavy meal during the time that its digestive processes are slowed due to the sun having gone down extends the actual time for the complete digestion of the food and the cycling and replenishing of the digestive juices, and ends up overlapping with the time when the breakfast is usually taken. Eating after the sun goes down and often only a few hours before going to sleep for the night, causes a poor night's rest which was due to a working digestive tract, and by the need for more energy to finish the digestion of the unprocessed load in their system from the late meal. The practice of putting new food on top of that which is not finished digesting causes fermentation in the system and creates gases and toxins which injure the system and need to pass out of the body through the elimination organs—the skin, lungs, kidneys, liver, and bowels—thus unnecessarily burdening them, and causing unpleasant odors, skin conditions, constipation, and other ailments.

The destructive practice of taking late meals is made worse by taking an early heavy breakfast. As the digestive system has not completed its work on the previous night's meal when another large meal is put in it, it is forced to work overtime without its necessary rest and rejuvenation time, thus robbing the system of more needed energy. This also tends to make one's mental and physical powers sluggish and dull in the early hours of the day. Then the early heavy breakfast is usually followed by an equally heavy lunch and similar supper.

So not only is the system strained by all of the work involved in the continual processing of food, but the overabundance thereof is converted into fat or is passed along in a semi-digested state, thereby causing other maladies.

Eating After a Meal

Researchers have observed that when more food is taken only a few hours after eating something the food already in the first part of the intestines is ejected from there even though it has not yet gone through its full processing. As the body doesn't want to expel the contents of the intestines in a semi-digested state, the taking of more food before the previous amount is fully processed causes that previous mass to be impacted together with the mass which preceded it, thereby causing a stretching of the intestines, the creation of unwanted gases and toxins, and a delay in the normal elimination time (constipation). It simply makes sense that one should have as many eliminations as they have meals, but such is rarely the case when people eat three or more meals per day. Researchers have noted that when someone eats a piece of fudge only two hours after eating a meal, the elimination is pushed back four hours. If another piece is taken after just another two hours, the elimination is pushed back eight hours. And so the problem compounds exponentially.

I have attempted to cover as much as I can about the dangers of overeating in this chapter about consuming too many meals too often. I have been teaching for years that two of the biggest causes of disease from a physical standpoint are overeating and under-sleeping and the connection they have with each other. Then I started to teach the real cause of our self-inflicted disease: not obeying YHWH's Word or even worse going directly against it. I am so thrilled to find Doug's web-site that has many more great articles about "The Daily" times to have our meals, and also a great chart to figure out when the 3rd hour and 9th hour start each day no matter what season we are in. I am even more excited to see the example set in Scripture about the daily times to give thanks to YHWH before our meals.

The information about diet is beneficial but we cannot receive any benefit from the food unless we properly glorify YHWH. Even if you are strict in the quality of your food, do you glorify YHWH and thank Him for your food? We move so fast today making time for everyone except the One we should be making time for the most. Those who place so much food upon the stomach, and thus load down nature, should begin to appreciate the truth. They should arouse the sensibilities of the brain to realize the value of the atonement and the great sacrifice that has been made for fallen man. The animal part of our nature should never be left to govern the moral and intellectual. I am thankful for this information and I will waste no time to put it to good use. I pray everyone will search this information out and experience the benefit and blessings that come from being obedient and thankful to YHWH each day.

EDITOR'S NOTE

Paul is an international author and member of the Living Food Summit Leaders from 8 nations. Paul and I met at Hippocrates about 10 years ago. We both started our journey of health at the same place. This is an excerpt from his book, Health According to the Scriptures. I agree that everything has an order, time to eat, drink, sleep, rest, and a gestation period for a baby, seed, nut, etc. that our Creator Jesus gave us. —JEF

9

YOUR HEALING
NATURE JOURNEY

Fred Bisci

Eating Guidelines: *It's What You Leave Out* then it's *What You Put In*. The system really works, but you have to draw on deep reserves of determination, awareness, and commitment in order to achieve your goal of a healthier life. Your part is to understand that intelligent living is a process of lifestyle change, which involves personal accountability and responsibility. Every life event shows you your ability to learn and grow from experience. Remember, with every new experience at first you don't know what you don't know. Then you go on the journey offered by that experience, and by the end you do know. So open your mind and heart in order to get ready to learn, and let's go on the *Healthy Journey*.

The most important aspect of setting your parameters is deciding what food and drink items you will drop from the "Leave Out" list. What items are you willing to leave out of your diet forever, without being overwhelmed? What can you commit to that will be workable for you in everyday life? Some heroic people may simply go ahead and leave it all out. I do not doubt this can be done, and the results would be marvelous. But your parameters have been constructed over your whole life, and they are not easily altered. I suggest that you establish new parameters that you know you can stick to, rather than allowing yourself to be carried away by initial enthusiasm that will not stand the test of time. As I mentioned in Part I, the reason for this is that the worst thing you can do for your body is to force it to change its chemistry, which is what you do if you swing in and out of your set of parameters.

When you stop eating or drinking items from the "Leave Out" list, a reciprocal action of healing occurs in the body. Your physical body does not recognize what you eat or drink as foods but as chemicals— something is either useful for the body or it's eliminated. If you live in an industrialized country, your body has probably become inundated by the over-consumption of processed foods. When it can no longer eliminate the huge amount of chemical residues contained in these foods, it will deposit them as chemical waste in the cells. According to your genetic expression, this will affect various functions of your body.

You will get healthier over time, and ultimately reverse the damage you've unwittingly done to yourself, if you make the following changes:

- **80% plant-based** (fruits, vegetables, nuts, seeds, sprouts) and **20% protein-based** (grains, legumes) foods instead of a high protein or fat-based approach

- **Real Fresh Prepared Foods** instead of processed foods

- **Raw fruits, vegetables, seeds, nuts, and sprouts** instead of canned and conventional items

- **Grass fed beef and organic chicken** instead of commercial beef or chicken

- **A moderate amount of whole grains, legumes, and small amount of animal protein if necessary in the right combinations** instead improper food combining

- **Three meals a day** instead of snacking between meals (letting your stomach empty between meals instead of keeping it full all day)

- **Eating before dark** instead of eating late at night

In order to set your parameters you need to determine what the following ratios will be:

- *Raw/uncooked* to cooked choices

- *Organic* to conventional foods

- *Plant-based* to animal-based foods

- *Vegetables* to animal protein

- *Vegetables* to fruits

- *Vegetable greens* to fats

- *Monosaturated* to saturated fats

- *Low glycemic* to high glycemic fruits

- *Less concentrated proteins* (seeds and nuts) to high concentrated proteins (beef, chicken, turkey, and fish)

Whether you want to eat a vegan diet (plant based—fruits, vegetables, nuts, seeds and sprouts) or a diet that's a combination of plant and animal foods, parameters can be created so you can enjoy a healthy lifestyle. This is where the First Foundation of **what you leave out** becomes very important. When you leave out everything that is harmful to your body, it adjusts to the change in chemistry and takes action to re-establish homeostasis. To facilitate this process, you require an adequate supply of all the essential nutrients. This is one of the keys to your longevity.

So your first task is to build your foundation by deciding what you're going to commit to leave out and what you're going to leave in. The whole secret to following and adjusting to a healthy lifestyle is to create workable parameters and then live within them, regardless of what others may think or say. Living this way may not be popular, but it is true and right for the body.

Juices and Salads

Your meals should begin with a water-plump base of delicious juices and delightful salads. The reason for starting your meals with high water-content food combinations in the form of fresh juices and salads is that water is a solvent and a transport medium, besides having many other functions such as kidney support, maintaining a proper body temperature, dehydration, proper elimination, and excretion from the bowels.

Juices and salads should be made with fresh fruits and vegetables on a daily basis—again; organic produce is preferred when available. Juices should be consumed for all three meals each day, if possible. Try to follow the juice proportions described on page 67. There are plenty of businesses that prepare these juices but the most effective way is to buy a juicer yourself. Juicers that range from the least to most expensive include: Breville, Omega and Norwalk. One of my favorite juices is apple, celery and a variety of greens.

In this water-plump approach, the juices should be drunk first and then be followed up by a large salad. A raw vegetable juice requires less amount of time and energy to digest and assimilate than a salad, and so follow the order. This is a very important process to understand.

Your salad should have a high percentage of greens with a six-to eight-vegetable combination included. The ingredients of the salad can be cut into small pieces so it's easier to chew and digest. The salad dressing should also be made fresh. The ingredients should include extra-virgin olive oil, hemp oil, or flax oil, with lemon or raw apple cider vinegar. A small portion of fresh herbs can also be added.

If you have cooked food in your diet, make sure you eat it after the raw food. The uncooked foods are alkaline and, if eaten first in the same meal, they serve to balance chemically the cooked foods, which are acidic.

Balancing The Scale

The scale that is being introduced here is to do with foods that require greater or lesser outputs of energy and time for their digestion and assimilation.

The Protein Scale

If a person exchanges a protein rich (concentrated) food such as pork with beef, the beef will be the lesser of the two due to its easier digestibility and its lower saturated fat content. Beef exchanged for chicken and chicken exchanged for fish, is another progression revealing greater understanding. The next level will be to exchange fish for lima beans, lentils or chickpeas and then lima beans, lentils or chickpeas for nuts and seeds. As you can see, the scale of beef to nuts represents increasingly easier levels of digestibility, which releases increasing amounts of energy and time.

The Carbohydrate Scale

Grains are classified as complex carbohydrates. This chemical complex is a sugar with two or more molecules. Complex carbohydrates are more easily absorbed than animal protein and more slowly absorbed than simple sugars. As the carbohydrates are absorbed, they are gradually broken down into glucose. This even pace facilitates the process of assimilation. Carbohydrates are scaled in three ways: from more to less energy/time outputs, from most acidic to most alkaline, and from more glutinous to non-glutinous (the amount of gluten they contain).

Gluten is a sticky protein present in some grains, and it is classified as starch. Gluten is hard to digest, which can lead to congestion in the body. There is usually also a high degree of inflammation associated with it, which is a good reason to seek out less starchy, non-glutinous grains. Wheat, oats, barley and rye contain gluten, whereas brown rice, millet, buckwheat, cornmeal, amaranth, and quinoa do not.

Processed grains have the highest level of gluten and form an acid ash. When you process a grain, you heat it and then remove the bran fiber and the germ nutrients. What remains is starch plus added chemicals and preservatives. If you exchange the most processed starchy grains—such as white flour products, pastas, rice, cold or prepared cereals, pretzels, and crackers—with a starchy unprocessed grain such as wheat, oats, barley and rye, the latter would be the better of the two. Starchy grains—wheat, oats, barley and rye—exchanged for brown rice, millet, buckwheat, corn-meal, amaranth, quinoa, gluten-free bread and brown rice pasta represents a progression to an easier level of digestibility. Exchanging your cooked unprocessed grains for sprouted grains is even better.

Sugar-rich foods that are starches and simple sugars, which have one molecule and are classified as carbohydrates, can also be exchanged. At the next level, brown rice, millet, buckwheat, cornmeal, amaranth, quinoa, gluten-free bread and brown rice pasta are exchanged for sweet potato, squash or yams. After that, sweet potatoes, squash or yams are exchanged for carrots, peas and beets—this brings you to the simplest exchange for digestion and assimilation.

Fats

Fats are qualified in two categories as saturated or unsaturated. Satu-rated fats and their associated products are from animals. They harden at room temperature, are a factor in elevating your cholesterol, and clog arteries. Unsaturated fats, which are plant fats, include olive, hemp, flax-seed, and sunflower oils, and nut butters. These oils do not harden at room temperature and are best when cold pressed. The simple exchange is to replace saturated with unsaturated oils. This is an ideal way of get-ting your essential fats.

Vegetables

Mineral-rich vegetable foods are the basis for this water-plump, plant-based approach. They should be eaten at every meal. All green leafy vegetables are loaded with more minerals than vitamins, even though they abound in the latter. The list of mineral-rich vegetable foods are: Leafy Greens, Lettuces, Spinach, Romaine, Chicory, Kale, Boston Bibb, Endive, Collards, Escarole, Arugula, Red Tip, Green Curley, Mesclun, Fennel, Watercress, Chard, Barley and Alfalfa Grasses. Salad Ingredients: Cucumber, Celery, Red or Green Pepper, Tomato (all varieties), Zucchini, Broccoli, Cauliflower, String Beans, Asparagus, Yellow Squash, Cabbage, Okra, Avocado. Sea Vegetables: Dulse, Kelp, Nori, Arame.

Fruits

Vitamin-rich fruits are another important part of this water-plump approach. They are considered the best source of energy with a high vitamin nutrient value, more so than vegetables. They are rich in plant sugars and are almost a direct source of energy, like the sun. The list of vitamin-rich fruits includes: Oranges (all varieties), Grapefruits, Lemons, Limes, Coconuts, Grapes, Raisins, Figs, Apricots, Apples (all varieties), Pears, Peaches, Cherries, all Berries, Plums, Bananas, Kiwis, Medjool Dates, Watermelons, Melons, Cantaloupe, Crenshaw, Honeydew, Papayas, Mangoes, and Pineapples. Avocados and Peppers have been classified botanically as fruits.

Concerning fruit, it is important to consider the glycemic index. As a general rule, berries, cherries, grapefruit and mangoes are low on the scale, while bananas, dates and dried fruits are high. It should be understood that the companion nutrients from the fiber and minerals inside the fruit stabilize the sugars so insulin levels are balanced. Fructose extracted from fruit does not have the same balanced effect in the body, nor do any other refined sugars.

Supplemental Living Foods

When someone changes their diet and eats a high proportion of raw foods, and does it in the correct and balanced manner, they get all the nutrients they need and should not require a lot of supplementation. Some experts recommend mega doses of different types of vitamins. My experience has been over the years that if you have a good dietary lifestyle it is not necessary.

If you are a strict vegetarian, it's a good idea to evaluate to see if you need vitamin B12. If you're not a vegetarian and you're below four hundred pico-grams, you could be symptomatic. Also, if you are living above the fortieth parallel level—in New York City or Alaska, for example—and you're not getting much sunshine, you need to be aware of the potential for a vitamin D deficiency.

I evaluate every person as an individual, with their own lifestyle, physiology, and environment, and I determine what they really need. I then find the cleanest, purest form of the supplement, as close to a natural food as possible, required in low dosages so the body doesn't interpret it as a chemical.

There are various products that are considered to be supplements, which are actually not supplements at all. Enzymes, probiotics, super-green foods (such as chlorella, spirulina, barley, alfalfa, wheat grass juice, and blue-green algae) are food products. I don't consider them to be supplements because they are live foods, which can be extremely beneficial. There are four categories of living foods that I recommend:

1. **Blue-Green Algae, E-3 Live and Wheatgrass Juice**
    These foods come in a juice form or powder. The frozen form of E-3 Live, which I have researched extensively, is a highly nutrient-dense food. All these foods contain chlorophyll, amino acids, antioxidants, vitamins, essential fats and minerals. They are complete raw living foods and are based on a water-plum, plant-based approach for your daily lifestyle. They can be taken at the start of your meal or in between meals.

2. **Systemic Enzymes and Digestive Enzymes**
    Enzymes participate in every chemical function and are associated with every system in the body. There are 3000 metabolic enzyme actions that are known. Any condition that you are experiencing requires the work of these enzymes, which are the backbone of your immune system.

When you eat cooked foods, whose enzymes have been destroyed by heat, you draw enzymes from the body in order to digest the food. This causes your store of enzymes to become depleted, which can lead to many health problems. A raw food diet, on the other hand, maintains your supply of enzymes. Most of us have been eating cooked foods all our lives, and as a result our enzyme bank has become bankrupt. Therefore, supplementing your diet with **systemic enzymes** is highly recommended.

Systemic enzymes should be taken 45 minutes before your meals, in between meals, or 2 hours after your meals. It is usually suggested to take them when you wake up and when you go to bed.

Digestive enzymes are taken with cooked meals. They supply the enzymes required for digestion and so limit the degree to which your body has to withdraw enzymes from your natural pool.

3. Probiotics

Probiotics are friendly bacteria that boost our existing intestinal flora and make a vital contribution to our health. Many people today have problems with the gastro-intestinal tract because it is loaded with all kinds of yeast, fungus, and molds. It's like a sewage system, and probiotics clean the system up. We do obtain intestinal flora from fruits and vegetables, but for most people their lifestyle nullifies the effects. So taking probiotics as a supplement gives you an edge.

These good bacteria take care of proper digestion and help maintain energy and efficiency levels in the body. They facilitate bowel elimination, promote regularity, assist in managing cholesterol, alleviate flatulence, bloating, and belching, increase the availability of nutrients, fight harmful bacteria, fungi, and viruses, and support healthy liver function.

Probiotics are a blend of live populations of good bacteria that colonize the whole digestive system. They should be stored in a cool environment or the refrigerator. This is a living food and is based on a water-plump, plant-based approach. They can be taken in the morning and at night or throughout the course of the day.

4. **Super Green Food: Barley, Chlorella, Alfalfa and Spirulina**
This raw, living food comes in powder form and can be added to your vegetable juice. It contains chlorophyll, amino acids, antioxidants, vitamins, essential fats and minerals. It can be taken at the start of your meal or in between meals.

Enjoy Your Healing Nature Journey

Your spiritual beliefs, your thoughts and feelings, the diet you eat, the chemicals you are exposed to in your food and environment, all have an influence on your quality of life and your genetic expression.

Often, people come to see me for help with psychological ailments like depression or anxiety, or physical illnesses like diabetes or arthritis, and they tell me it runs in their family. Since they consider the problem to be genetically based, they are not convinced that changing their diet will help or that the remedial ability of the body will operate in their case.

Unfortunately, when somebody is already firmly convinced that they cannot be helped, most likely they aren't going to be helped. The change they're hoping for, but don't truly believe in, requires more than just improving their diet and weeding out all the things that interfere with a healthy physiology. It requires giving their body a chance to utilize what I believe is their God-given capability to heal themselves; but their negative beliefs and thoughts interfere with this self-healing process by adversely affecting their chemistry and genetic expression.

Your mind is extremely powerful. You probably know individuals who are fearful of getting sick and always imagine they have some type of disease or illness. They read about some syndrome in the newspaper, or see it on television, and before long they have a few of the symptoms and are sure they have the disease. Another example of the power of the mind over the body is when you experience a lot of mental stress and are unable to sleep, and your immune system is suppressed. Energy goes from the front to the back of the brain and your body thinks you're in the fight or flight response. When that happens, all the vital energy that is needed for proper bodily functioning is diverted to this emergency response and, if this continues, your health deteriorates.

We see a similar process at work with people who are constantly worried about their child's face, and so on. All these types of thinking will have an effect on their genetic expression. I'm not suggesting that you should not worry about anything, but I am saying that you can learn how to deal with all the circumstances of your life so that you feel fulfilled even under trying conditions, which means that the stress will not damage your immune system. I know of people who have gone to doctors and have been told that they have one year to live, and they accepted this pronouncement as a death sentence. And guess what happened—they died right on schedule. To me, this is a tragedy. The mind can kill you and it can keep you alive. Why not choose life?

So don't turn your mind into your enemy by letting it believe that your health challenges are genetically caused, and thus there is no hope for you. Old school genetics held that the DNA controlled the outcome of illness except when something of unknown origin happened by chance. But the latest epigenetic studies show that only 5% of degenerative diseases in our society are actually genetic, whereas 95% are epigenetic. The term "epigenetic" means outside the cell, and so what these studies are saying is that an amazing 95% of our diseases are controlled by what happens outside of the body—by our diet, by the chemicals that are in our food and water and in the air we breathe, and, just as importantly, by the state of our mind and spirit.

So you have to be attentive to your belief system. If you read the newspapers or watch television, even if it doesn't have a conscious impression on you, it will still have a detrimental affect on your health. You may unconsciously tell yourself, "What's the sense of me trying to do anything that's positive? No matter what I do, it's going to end up being destroyed by what's happening in the world today." If you're looking at events in the Middle East, you'll assume there has got to be something terribly wrong because people over there are killing each other in the name of God. How could the good God possibly be blessing this waste of human life? All this hatred in the world, what effect is it having on our genetic expression? And if you look at the politics in this country, well . . ." I'm not a very politically oriented person but I hope that we will have more and more enlightened people getting into political positions so we can make better choices in government and as a country, have a more benign influence on the politics of other nations and on the peoples of the world in general.

Returning to the subject of epigenetics, let's now examine this in a little more detail. From information based on decades of research and clinical practice, we know that the human cell is controlled by environmental signals. Inside the cell there are regulatory proteins that are altered by these environmental signals and then enable the cell to admit the signals. In addition to the regulatory proteins, there are DNA and RNA (the mirror image of DNA), which manipulate proteins in order to control the genetic expression of the cell. What happens is that the regulatory protein exposes the nucleus of the cell so that the information coming from the outside can have an effect on your genetic expression—both in malicious ways that cause disease and in beneficial ways that enhance your immune system and prevent disease.

When the latter occurs, the cell has the ability to replicate itself and to alter your genetic expression for the better based on the environmental signals it received. Critical among the environmental signals are your spiritual beliefs and the thoughts that you entertain, which you should strive to keep positive and optimistic. In contradistinction, if you live in a toxic environment—in your mind, body, spirit, and world—then you're like a fish swimming in a lake filled with poisons. Your very survival is in question.

Of course, the human body is a fantastic biological machine that has the ability to do things that are almost unbelievable. It is designed to continue regenerating and healing itself, even when subjected to tremendous abuse. But the body has its limits, and in today's world most of us have reached them. We may think we're doing fine, because our life expectancy has increased dramatically over the last 150 years. It used to be that living to the age of 50 was an achievement, whereas nowadays people routinely live to be 80 or 90 years old. However, I believe that we are really only scratching the surface. If we can clean up the outside environment and the inside environment (with a cleansing diet), and if we can unite mentally and break free of the old thought patterns that make us believe in the statistical data concerning death and disease (which, because of the influence of the mind on the body, act as a self-fulfilling prophecy), then we can access untapped possibilities of health and longevity that few people ever dreamed of.

I would like to inspire you with the message that the discoveries I have made in my own life apply equally to yours. You can take back control; you can change what you believe and think much more quickly than you may imagine, and as a result you can change your life very rapidly and in amazing ways. It's not something that can easily be described. You must have the experience of this wonderful enlightened consciousness that you hear about, and then you will understand.

You don't have to travel to India to evolve spiritually. It is a gift that we are all meant to have, right here, right now—wherever we are and whatever our circumstances. All you have to do is declare that you are a willing participant in your own healing and enlightenment, that you want a clear mind, a true sense of wellbeing, the vibrancy and vital force that the human body is meant to have, and the awareness of the divine that is your birthright. Take this one step, and Life will take the next one thousand steps for you.

My hope and intention is that this book has succeeded in inspiring you to take that first step, and to go forward on your quest. Once you have tasted a small part of the spiritual feast that is on offer, you'll be convinced that this is the right path for you, and your mind, body, and spirit will be fully engaged in the Healthy Journey. You will have an experience of awakening that will be a joy for you and that you will want to share not only with your loved ones but with everyone with whom you come into contact. You'll experience the feeling I have when I see people who are suffering physically or emotionally, and I know in my heart of hearts that they do not have to experience this—a feeling of great compassion and a desire to reach out and help them.

As you set out on this amazing path that I call the Healthy Journey, whose goal is health and wellbeing on all levels, I wish you the very best of luck. Enjoy the lifetime experience of Real, Fresh Foods.

The human condition is spiritually and vibrationally induced, electrically and chemically empowered, and biologically carried out.

Next Steps

Changing your lifestyle is simple, but at the same time there are so many variables that it is worthwhile consulting with an expert. One inexpensive approach is to participate in our website conferences, which help you to understand the principles in more depth and to work out a plan that is tailored to your specific needs. To find out more, please visit *www.fredbisci4health.com*

EDITOR'S NOTE

We've all heard the saying, "Birds of a feather flock together." It is an honor to have Dr. Fred Bisci, to join this project. I resonate with Dr. Fred Bisci's quote, "The human condition is spiritually and vibrationally induced, electrically and chemically empowered, biologically carried out." No truer words were ever spoken because he has the understanding from the wisdom acquired by putting the knowledge into practice of treating the body as a Temple. I encourage all readers to read Dr. Fred's book, *Your Healthy Journey.* We all can acquire the same understanding with wisdom if we follow Dr. Fred, as He follows Our Lord Jesus Christ on his journey of healing. "They that wait upon the Lord shall renew their strength, they shall mount up with wings as eagles, they shall run and not be weary, they shall walk and not faint" (Isaiah 40:31). —JEF

PUTTING IT INTO PRACTICE

Vicki Rae Chelf ©

"Prove thy servants, I beseech the, ten days; and let them give us pulse to eat, and water to drink. Then let our countenances be looked upon before thee, and the countenance of the children that eat of the portion of the king's meat; and as thou seest, deal with thy servants. So he consented to them in the matter, and proved them ten days. And at the end of ten days their countenances appeared fairer and fatter in flesh than all the children which did eat the portion of the king's meat."
—Daniel 1:12 - 1:15

Daniel chose not to defile himself and the children of Israel with the king's meat and wine. Instead he asked for pulse (beans) to eat and water to drink. They did not suffer from a lack of meat. In fact, they grew stronger. Today, if we want to eat healthy food, it is a little more complicated than simply choosing beans over meat, although that is a great place to start.

In this chapter you will find 24 delicious recipes without the "king's" meat. They are also free of sugar, dairy products, eggs and refined, processed ingredients. Talking about preparing healthy whole foods from

167

scratch is one thing, but doing it is another. Learning to prepare delicious meatless meals is a skill that must be learned, but it is a skill that will serve you and your loved ones for life. "Anyone can cook," as Chef Gusteau, the little character in the Disney film *Ratatouille* was fond of saying. "On the other hand, being a great culinary artist," he said, "was a special gift reserved for the talented few." To make delicious and healthful meals you don't need to be a great artist. You simply need to learn to cook. If you already know how to cook, switching to healthful whole ingredients will be even easier.

Preparing your own food does not have to take hours. I can throw a wonderful meal together in 30 minutes. Of course, when you first learn to cook it will take longer, but like anything, if you keep doing it, it will become easier and easier. The rewards of preparing food from scratch are certainly worth the effort it takes. Not only will your meals be fresher and healthier; they will be tailored to your particular taste. You know better than any chef what you like or dislike, and with a little practice you will be turning out dishes you love with every effort.

As an example of how fresh plant-based foods can transform one's life, I want to tell you about my former neighbor. "Bob" weighed over five-hundred pounds. He was so big that to weigh himself he had to use the freight scale at the hospital. Bob loved to garden and he grew some of the most luscious varieties of fruit you can imagine. Occasionally, I hired him to work in my garden. One day he asked me why I never said anything about his weight, and I told him that I didn't think it was my place unless he brought it up first. The next day, I simply offered him some lunch. It was a tofu sandwich on homemade whole wheat bread with veggie garnishes. His body must have been craving whole grains and plant proteins, because he said that it was the best thing he had ever eaten! His wife started taking my cooking classes and they gave up processed food, alcohol and soft drinks. They also became vegetarian, or at least mostly vegetarian. Within a couple of years my grossly obese friend, looked normal. He could even ride a bike, something that would have been impossible before he lost all that weight.

More recently, my 93-year-old mother came to live with me. When she arrived, she spent most of her time curled up in a fetal position and was barely able to walk. Besides her heart medicine, she was on stomach medicine, an anti-depressant, and something that was supposed to keep her from getting the flu. After the first week, she no longer needed the stomach medicine. Her stomach never hurt and with the high fiber she was eating, she started having one or more bowel movements daily. Within three months, she was off the anti-depressant and the other pill. Now the only thing she takes is her heart medicine and some supplements. She eats a vegetarian, whole foods diet, gets up early, walks everywhere she goes in the house and spends a little time outside daily, weather permitting. She is stronger, more alert and no longer depressed.

If you have decided that it is worth the time and effort it takes to learn to prepare nutritious, healthy food, let's get started with a few basics. I think you will enjoy the recipes in this chapter. They are favorites in my household. First, however, you may need to make a shopping list.

Listed below are some of the staple items that I use in these recipes. It is not necessary to run out and buy them all at once, but most are items that you will probably eventually want to have on hand. To these staples add an abundant and varied array of whatever fruits and vegetables are in season where you live.

Shopping List:

- **Grains:** brown rice, quinoa, spelt, rolled oats, bulgur wheat, whole wheat pastry flour (Make sure that the flour and bulgur are very fresh, and keep them both in covered containers in the refrigerator.)

- **Legumes:** chick peas, lentils, mung beans

- **Nuts, seeds and dried fruit:** flaxseeds, walnuts, almonds, tahini (sesame butter), raisins, unsulfured apricots (Make sure nuts, seeds, and nut and seed butters are fresh when you buy them and store them in the refrigerator or freezer)

- **Oils:** olive oil, coconut oil, flax oil (the flax oil must be kept refrigerated)

- **Herbs, spices and condiments:** Celtic sea salt, balsamic vinegar, tamari soy sauce, miso, ground cinnamon, cloves, turmeric, tarragon, basil, white pepper, mustard seeds, fennel seeds, cayenne

- **Miscellaneous:** arrowroot powder, agave syrup, kuzu powder, sucanat (dehydrated cane juice), non-aluminum baking powder, liquid stevia, dulse flakes

Eat well for less

Price is on everyone's mind these days, and eating well does not have to necessarily cost more. Here are some tips to help you get the most for your money:

- In general, bulk items are less expensive than packaged ones. However, this is not always the case, so it is worth the time to compare prices.

- Bulk herbs and spices are available in most natural foods stores and they are usually several times less expensive than those already in jars, and often fresher.

- Organic whole grains and beans bought in bulk are another great deal. A pound of beans or grain will go a long way.

- Buy produce in season. In winter, unless you live in a warm climate, choose mostly produce that can be naturally stored until spring, such as winter squash, cabbages, root vegetables and apples. Supplement this hearty fare with homegrown sprouts.

- Try buying produce directly from the farmer, or make friends with local gardeners and offer to buy their excess or trade for something you have.

- If you enjoy sprouts, grow them often. They are cheap, easy to grow and do not take a lot of time.

- Learn to make your own veggie milks, nut butters, and breads.

- If you have more rice, soy or nut milk than you can use, don't let it go to waste, freeze it right in its package.

- Most stores will give a 10-15 percent discount if you buy a whole case of any one product. For rice, or soy milk, a case is a dozen cartons. A full-fledged co-op may be too much trouble for you, but you can buy expensive, non-perishable items such as olive oil, balsamic vinegar, tamari, veggie milks, silken tofu, etc. with three or four friends and save.

- A flourmill, soymilk maker and bread machine will save lots of money in the long run.

- Go vegan—meat, fish and dairy are expensive.

- Think fresh—don't be tempted by "natural" versions of junk food, or precooked food.

Sprout for life

Sprouts are edible seeds that have been soaked for several hours and allowed to germinate. If you are looking for a low-cost way to add some freshness to your diet, try growing sprouts. It is so easy that anyone, even children, can do it. It's fun too, because sprouts grow so fast it almost seems like you can see them change from a dry seed into a beautiful baby plant right before your eyes.

Sprouting truly is a testament to the power of God's creation. Although man has invented a plethora of marvelous machines and gadgets, he has never achieved anything that even comes close to the miracle of the seed. Any viable bean, seed or grain can be sprouted. If you are unable to sprout beans, grains or seeds it may be because the ones you are using, have been heated or treated not to sprout.

Growing sprouts has lots of advantages. When beans, grains and seeds are sprouted they transform themselves into a powerhouse of vitamins and enzymes. Grains or seeds retain the B vitamins that were present in the seed before it was sprouted, but the vitamin C level increases 500 to 600 percent and the vitamin A level increases about 300 percent. Alfalfa sprouts contain eight enzymes that help us to assimilate protein, fats and carbohydrates. During the sprouting process nutrients are pre-digested, turning starches into simple sugars, proteins into amino acids, and crude fats into fatty acids. This is why sprouts are known to be easy to digest. Often, people who experience allergic reactions from eating certain grains or legumes can eat those same grains or legumes as sprouts without the slightest problem. Sprouts are low in calories too. Six ounces of mung sprouts contain only 60 calories.

Sprouting provides you with fresh, inexpensive, and in the case of green sprouts, chlorophyll-rich vegetables year around. You know the sprouts you grow are not pesticide-laden or treated with chemicals because you supervise every day of their short growth period. Sprouts are a very clean food too, because they have to be rinsed two or three times a day to grow. Just make sure to rinse them with filtered or distilled water.

Sprouting is also a great way to teach children about life and the wonders of nature. It is an activity that even the smallest child can delight in. The power of a tiny seed to sprout into a living and highly-nutritious plant certainly is an amazing thing. To find detailed instructions on how to grow sprouts, read Susan Smith Jones' book *Recipes for Health Bliss*, published by Hay House. Her detailed and informative chapter on sprouting includes an easy-to-follow chart on how to grow all kinds of sprouts, so you'll be able to cultivate a sprout garden in your kitchen. (To order, visit: www.SusanSmithJones.com)

"And Jesus said unto them…, 'If ye have faith as a grain of mustard seed, ye shall say unto this mountain, Remove hence to yonder place: and it shall remove: and nothing shall be impossible to you'" (Matthew 17:20).

VICKI'S RECIPES FOR HEALTHFUL LIVING

Here are some samples of healthy, easy and delicious recipes that will help you to add more plant-based whole foods to your diet. They are from my book *Vicki's Vegan Kitchen*. From breakfast to dessert, I'm sure that you can find something that you and your family will enjoy.

RICE APPLE BREAKFAST PUDDING

Here is a way to use up some leftover rice. I like to put it on first thing in the morning, then get a shower or do a few stretches while it slowly cooks.

1	cup cooked brown rice	2	cinnamon sticks
2	apples, cored and diced	8	whole cloves
¼	cup raisins	1 ¼	cup water

SLOW COOKING METHOD:

1. Place all ingredients in a heavy, medium-size saucepan and bring to a boil.

2. Reduce the heat to very low and simmer for about 30 minutes, or until the water is absorbed.

FAST COOKING METHOD:

1. Reduce the water to 1 cup. Place all ingredients in a heavy, medium-size saucepan. Bring to a boil.

2. Reduce the heat to medium and simmer, stirring often for about 10 minutes, or until the apple is tender.

   Yield: 2 servings

173

BLENDER MUESLI

An old-time favorite among health enthusiasts, slightly revised, this is my preferred breakfast in warm weather. The little bit of lemon peel makes it especially refreshing.

Yield: 2 servings

½ cup rolled oats	1 grated apple
2 tablespoons raisins	Fresh, seasonal fruit as desired
2 tablespoons chopped walnuts	(strawberries, peaches, pitted
½ inch square of organic	cherries, grapes, blueberries,
lemon peel	etc.)
6 ounces plain rice, soy or	
nut milk	

1. Place the rolled oats, raisins, walnuts, and lemon peel in a blender. Grind to a coarse flour.
2. Place the mixture in two bowls, and pour the milk over it. Mix well and let sit for about 5 minutes while you prepare the fruit.
3. Add the fresh fruit, mix, and serve.

VARIATIONS:

❖ Replace 1/2 of the rolled oats with wheat germ, corn germ, or oat bran. Apricots, dates, or prunes can be substituted for the raisins, and hazelnuts, almonds or pecans can be substituted for the walnuts.

❖ If desired, multiply this recipe by as many times as you wish, and keep it in a covered container in the freezer.

❖ *Tropi Muesli:* Substitute 2 or 3 dates for the raisins and grated coconut for the walnuts. Use a sliced banana and a ripe mango for the fruit. This is wonderful!

NUT AND SEED TOPPING

This nut and seed blend is a delicious source of omega 3's, fiber, E and other important nutrients. Have it ground up and ready to spoon over porridge, or fruit. Yield: about 2 1/4 cups

1 cup flaxseeds
½ cup almonds
½ cup sunflower seeds

¼ cup date sugar, optional
1 tablespoon cinnamon, optional

1. Place the flaxseeds in a blender and blend until they are ground. Transfer them to a glass jar.
2. Add the almonds and sunflower seeds to the blender. Blend again. The almonds and sunflower seeds do not have to be finely ground.
3. Add the other ingredients to the jar and shake to combine the ingredients. Refrigerate and use within 2-3 weeks.

TAHINI-CARROT SPREAD

Everyone seems to enjoy this quick and healthy spread. When you make it, don't use a food processor to grate the carrots. It is much better if the carrots are grated on the small holes of a hand grater.
Yield: about 1 cup

½ cup tahini
2 tablespoons water
1 tablespoons balsamic vinegar
1 tablespoon tamari

1 cup finely grated carrots
¼ cup nutritional yeast
1-2 cloves garlic, pressed

1. In a medium-size bowl, combine the tahini, water, vinegar, and tamari. Mix with a fork until thick and creamy.
2. Add the remaining ingredients and mix again. If the spread is too dry, add another tablespoon of water. Serve as a spread in sandwiches, wraps, on crackers. or mounded on top of a green salad.

CILANTRO PESTO

This recipe is sometimes called "chelation pesto" because two of its ingredients cilantro and garlic are reputed to help detoxify the body of heavy metals. Dulse is a sea vegetable. Dulse flakes are ready to use. Just sprinkle them on dishes for extra minerals and a salty taste. This recipe is good without the dulse, but better with it.

Yield: about 1 cup

1   bunch fresh cilantro (2 cups coarsely chopped and lightly packed)
1   cup walnuts
¼   cup flax oil

1-3 cloves garlic
¼   teaspoon sea salt, or slightly more to taste
¼   cup dulse, sea vegetable flakes (optional)

1. Place the cilantro and walnuts in a food processor with the bottom chopping blade.
2. Start blending, and then add the oil, garlic and salt through the top. Scrape the sides of the food processor when necessary.
3. Transfer the mixture to a small bowl. Add the dulse, if desired, and mix well. Serve with bread or crackers.

GAZPACHO SUPREME

This gazpacho is a made in a juice extractor. The addition of carrots mellows the tomatoes and imparts a luscious sweetness to this refreshing, cold soup. Make sure that all the vegetables are chilled before you begin, and serve it as soon as possible after it is made. People have told me that this is the best gazpacho they have ever tasted.

Yield: 6 servings

4	medium tomatoes (or enough for 3 cups juice)	½	green bell pepper, chopped,
3	cloves garlic	1	tablespoon red wine vinegar, or lemon juice
4	medium-large carrots (or enough for 2 cups juice)		Pinch of sea salt to taste
1	medium cucumber, grated	1	teaspoon dry basil, or 2 tablespoons freshly chopped basil

1. Core the tomatoes and run them through a juice extractor. Save the pulp and transfer both the juice and the pulp to a bowl. It is important that you juice the tomatoes before the carrots because you do not want the tomato pulp that you will be using, to be mixed with the carrot pulp, which you will discard.
2. Run the garlic through the juicer. It is not necessary to peel it first.
3. Juice the carrots and add the carrot/garlic juice to the tomatoes.
4. Add the remaining ingredients. Mix and serve immediately.

MY BEST END OF SUMMER VEGETABLE SOUP

The tomatoes in this soup are left raw, so they should be perfectly ripe and luscious. This provides an unexpectedly fresh taste to what at first glance seems to be an ordinary soup. If tomatoes are out of season, you can make this soup with tomato puree from a jar, and it will still be very good.

Yield: 4 to 6 servings

2	medium potatoes, 2 cups diced	2	cups water
3	medium carrots, 1 ½ cups sliced	6	bay leaves
½	pound green beans, 1 ½ cup broken into 1-inch pieces	1½	pounds tomatoes, 3 medium
2	small turnips, 1 cup diced	¼	cup yellow miso
4	cups chopped greens, from the 2 turnips, may substitute collards or mustard greens	2	teaspoons dry basil or 2 tablespoons chopped fresh basil
		1	tablespoon balsamic vinegar
		½	teaspoon white pepper

1. Clean and chop the vegetables. Place them in a large, heavy kettle with the water and bay leaves. Cover, and bring to a boil.
2. Reduce the heat and simmer, covered over low heat for 20-25 minutes until the vegetables are tender.
3. While the vegetables cook, wash the tomatoes and cut them into big chunks. Place them in a blender and blend to a puree. Add the miso and blend again.

Add the tomato mixture to the soup along with the basil, balsamic vinegar and the white pepper. Mix and serve. You may reheat the soup, if desired, but don't cook it.

VARIATION: Cut the kernels off of one or two ears of fresh, tender sweet corn, and add it raw along with the tomato puree.

SPELT SALAD

A similar salad is a traditional dish in Tuscany. Add the chick peas if you want to make a complete meal out of it. This is a perfect dish to bring along to a potluck or dinner party.

Yield: 4 to 6 servings

1 cup whole spelt berries, soaked
   6-8 hours, rinsed and drained
2 cups water
½ pound green beans, in
   ½-inch pieces
1 cup cooked chick peas
1/3 cup thinly sliced red onions

½ cup pine nuts
2 tablespoons olive oil
1 ½ tablespoons balsamic
   vinegar
½ teaspoon sea salt
   Freshly ground black pepper,
   to taste

1. Place the spelt berries in a medium-size pan with 2 cups water. Cover, bring the water to a boil and cook for about 45 minutes, or until tender.
2. While the spelt is cooking, steam the green beans until just tender. Don't over, or under cook them. Set aside to cool.
3. Place the cooked spelt in a large bowl with the steamed green beans and chickpeas. Add the remaining ingredients. Serve warm, at room temperature, or chilled.

FLORIDA SALAD

Citrus and avocados are in season at the same time and are wonderful together. Pummelos are similar to pink grapefruit, but bigger, slightly less juicy, and sweeter. If you can't find a pummelo substitute a large grapefruit. The pink of the pummelo or grapefruit makes a pretty color combination with the ruby red radicchio and green avocado. To make it really spectacular, add the seeds from one pomegranate.

Yield: 4 to 6 servings

1	large Florida avocado, or 2 California avocados, diced	1	small head radicchio, chopped
2	pink grapefruit or 1 pummelo, peeled, seeded and chopped into bite-size pieces	2	cups arugula, coarsely chopped
		¼	medium red onion, thinly sliced
½	bulb fennel, chopped		Favorite Flax Oil Vinaigrette

1. Mix together all the ingredients in a large salad bowl.
2. Add the flax oil vinaigrette to taste. Serve immediately.

FAVORITE FLAX OIL DRESSING

I use this dressing more than any other. My cooking students love it and many of them have adopted it as their own. It is good over any green salad, raw or cooked vegetables, and even simple bean or grain dishes.

Yield: 1 cup

½	cup flax oil	1	teaspoon tarragon
¼	cup balsamic vinegar	1	tablespoon Dijon mustard
¼	cup tamari	1	or more cloves garlic, pressed
		2	tablespoons roasted garlic
	OPTIONS:	1	teaspoon agave syrup

1. Combine flax oil, vinegar and tamari in a small jar.
2. Add the options of your choice, (Substitute olive oil, or walnut oil for the flax oil, and substitute wine vinegar, raspberry vinegar, lemon juice, or lime juice for the balsamic vinegar), and shake before serving. Dressing will keep in the refrigerator for up to 2 weeks.

MUNG DAHL

Mung beans are said to be both strengthening and detoxifying. Therefore, they are an especially healing food. Cooked into a traditional Indian dahl they are delicious. Korma seeds can be purchased in any Indian grocery store. Serve over brown basmati rice and accompany with a vegetable curry.

Serves: 4 to 6

1-inch piece ginger, peeled	½ teaspoon fennel seeds
1 large tomato, coarsely chopped	¼ teaspoon korma seeds, opt.
	½ tablespoon ground turmeric
3-4 cloves garlic, peeled	1 tablespoon ground cumin
1 cup coarsely chopped onion	4 cups cooked mung beans
2 tablespoons olive oil	1 teaspoon sea salt, or to taste
1 teaspoon mustard seeds	cayenne, to taste

1. Place the ginger, tomato, garlic and onion in a food processor. Blend briefly - it's okay to leave a few lumps in the puree.
2. Heat the oil in a large, heavy kettle. Add the mustard seeds, fennel seeds and korma seeds. Stir over medium-high heat until the seeds begin to pop.
3. After the seeds pop, stir in the blended tomato mixture. Add the turmeric and the cumin. Stir and cook over medium heat for about 10 minutes.
3. Add the cooked mung beans and salt. Simmer the dahl, stirring occasionally, for about 10 minutes more. Add cayenne to taste.

CHICK PEAS IN SPICY TAHINI SAUCE

Use this easy recipe to quickly dress up a can of chickpeas or, better yet, cook the beans from scratch.

Yield: 3 to 4 servings

1	tablespoon olive oil	1	tablespoon arrowroot
1	cup chopped onion (1 medium)	1	tablespoon lemon juice
1	teaspoon dry basil	2	tablespoons salsa (hot or mild to taste)
2 to 3	cloves garlic, minced	2	tablespoons tamari, or to taste
¼	cup tahini	2	cups cooked and drained chick peas
1	cup cool or room temperature water		

1. Heat the oil in a large skillet. Add the onion and the basil. Sauté for about 5 minutes or until the onion is translucent. Add the garlic. Continue to sauté until the onion is tender.

2. Stir in the tahini and half of the water. Cook, stirring constantly, until the sauce thickens. Remove the skillet from the heat.

3. In a small bowl, mix together the remaining water with the arrowroot, lemon juice, salsa, and tamari. Add it to the mixture in the skillet. Add the chick peas and stir over high heat for about 3 minutes until the mixture boils and thickens.

4. Serve on a bed of rice, millet, or pasta and top with garnish. Accompany with a green salad.

Garnish: sliced roasted red peppers, chopped fresh tomatoes and minced fresh parsley or cilantro

LENTIL-CARROT LOAF

This is a recipe that my cooking students enjoy.
Yield 4 servings

3 cups carrots, cut into 1/3-inch thick slices

1 ½ cups lentils, cooked and drained

½ cup finely chopped onions

½ teaspoon sage

1 teaspoon curry powder

2 tablespoons tamari

1 cup rolled oats

½ cup chopped walnuts or pecans

2 tablespoons finely chopped parsley

1. Steam the carrots until tender. Drain the carrots, and, reserve the water to make the Red Pepper Sauce.
2. Mix together the cooked carrots and lentils. Mash them coarsely with a potato masher. Add the remaining ingredients and mix well.
3. Pack the mixture into a well-oiled loaf pan. Decorate the top of the loaf with nut halves if desired.
4. Bake at 350°F for 35-40 minutes, or until firm and golden brown.
5. After baking, let the loaf stand for about 5 minutes and then unmold it onto a serving platter. For an attractive presentation, surround the unmolded loaf with sliced ripe tomatoes, or any other colorful vegetable. Serve with the Red Pepper Sauce.

RED PEPPER SAUCE

The pretty color and mild flavor of this sauce make it a delicious accompaniment to veggie croquettes and loaves. Yield: about 1 ½ cups

1   red bell pepper, cut into chunks
½   cup water
2   tablespoons tahini
1   tablespoon plus 1 teaspoon arrowroot

¼   teaspoon sea salt, or to taste
Dash of cayenne, to taste
1   tablespoon fresh minced basil

1. Place the bell pepper, water, tahini and arrowroot in a blender. Blend until very smooth and creamy.
2. Pour the mixture into a saucepan. While stirring constantly with a wire whisk, bring the mixture to a boil. Reduce the heat and add the remaining ingredients. Mix well.
3. Sprinkle with basil before serving.

SNOW PEA STIR-FRY WITH QUINOA, SCALLIONS AND AVOCADO

This recipe is so simple that it is almost not a recipe, but if the vegetables are garden fresh, it is divine. It makes a wonderful light summer meal. Yield: 3 to 4 servings

1   cup quinoa
2   cups water
2   tablespoons unrefined sesame oil
1 ½ pounds snow peas, trimmed

1-2 tablespoons tamari, to taste
3-4 chopped scallions, chopped
2   thick wedges avocado per person

1. Rinse the quinoa and place it in a medium-size pan. Add the water. Cover, bring to a boil, reduce the heat and simmer for about 20 minutes, or until the water is absorbed.
2. When the quinoa is almost done, heat the oil in a large skillet or wok. Add the peas and stir over high heat for 2 minutes, or until they are nice and hot.

3. Add the tamari and stir quickly. Remove from the heat and add the scallions. Cover for about 1 minute while you dish out the quinoa.

4. Top the quinoa with the vegetable mixture. Distribute any juice that is left in the bottom of the pan over each serving. Serve immediately garnished with thick wedges of ripe avocado.

BULGUR SWEET POTATO PILAF WITH APRICOTS

This pretty dish cooks quickly and has a subtly sweet flavor and the crunch of walnuts.

Yield: 3 to 4 servings

1	tablespoon unrefined sesame oil	1	teaspoon sage
1	stalk celery, finely chopped	¼	cup dried, apricots, thinly sliced
3 to 4	cloves garlic, chopped	½	teaspoon turmeric
2 ¼	cups boiling water	½	cup walnuts
1	vegetable bouillon cube		Freshly ground black pepper,
1	cup bulgur wheat, rinsed		to taste

1. Heat the oil in a large skillet. Add the celery and the garlic and sauté for 3 to 4 minutes.

2. Place the bouillon cube in the boiling water to dissolve. Keep hot.

3. Add the bulgur to the skillet with the celery and garlic. Stir and add the sage. Stir for a minute or two and add the apricots and the turmeric. Mix well and add the hot water. Cover immediately because the mixture will sizzle and splatter.

4. Reduce the heat to low and simmer for 5 minutes, or more, depending on the coarseness of the bulgur, until all the liquid is absorbed. Fluff with a fork and top with walnuts. Serve with a simple green salad.

OIL LESS "STIR-FRIED" VEGETABLES

Low in calories and full of flavor, this quick and easy dish uses broccoli and a variety of mixed vegetables. Serve it plain over rice, or turn the cooking water into a sauce, as indicated below.

Yield: 2 generous servings

1 cup water or vegetable stock	1 tablespoon grated ginger
2-3 tablespoons tamari	1 cup sliced onion (1 med. onion)
A few drops roasted sesame oil (for flavor)	2 stalks broccoli
	1 red bell pepper or 1 carrot
2 cloves garlic, minced	4 cups mung bean sprouts

1. Place the water or stock, tamari, roasted sesame oil, garlic, and ginger in a wok or large skillet.
2. Cut the broccoli flowerets into bite-sized pieces. Peel the broccoli stems and cut them into strips. Slice the pepper or carrot into strips.
3. Bring the liquid in the wok to a boil. Add the onions, broccoli, and carrot (if you are using a carrot). Stir the vegetables with a constant shoveling motion as if you were stir-frying with oil. Cook over high heat stirring constantly, for about 2 minutes. Add the pepper (if you are using a pepper) and the bean sprouts. Continue stirring until the bean sprouts reduce in size.
4. Cover the wok, reduce the heat to medium, and let steam until tender (about 3-5 minutes).

TO MAKE A SAUCE: Reserve the leftover broth to use for soup stock, or make it into a sauce to serve with the dish. To make a sauce, dissolve 1 tablespoon of arrowroot or kudzu powder in 2 to 3 tablespoons cool water. Add it to the vegetables at the end of cooking, and stir until the liquid boils.

VARIATION

Use any desired combination of vegetables that lend themselves to stir-frying (such as mushrooms, Chinese cabbage, and summer squash) to replace the ones in the recipe.

BEETS WITH TOPS

Beets and their tops cooked together like this are delicious.

Yield: 4 servings

4 medium beets, with their tops, cleaned and sliced	1 or more cloves garlic, pressed (optional)
1-2 tablespoons olive oil	1 teaspoon tarragon
1-2 tablespoons lemon juice	Pinch of sea salt, to taste

1. Place the sliced beets in a pan with about 1 inch of water in the bottom. Place the greens on top of the sliced beets. Cover and steam for about 20 minutes or until both the beets and the greens are tender. From time to time check the water level, adding more water if necessary. .

2. In a small bowl, mix together the olive oil, lemon juice, garlic, tarragon and salt.

3. When the vegetables are done, remove them from the pan with a slotted spoon and place them in a serving bowl. Pour the dressing mixture over the vegetables. Toss and serve.

EDITOR'S NOTE

It's impossible to obey a law unless you know what the law is. Whether you understand gravity or not, you will pay the same price if you step off a high rise building!

When our taste buds are clouded, with dead "food," we desire or prefer addictive dead "food." Our taste buds become vibrantly alive when we treat them with living food. When you consume raw, living food, prepared by a gourmet chef, you are not aware that it is not cooked! Our body craves the food we feed it. Choose living food instead of addictive, counterfeit, substitutes for food and your prayers will be answered! You will receive the blessings of the Healing Nature of Jesus! —JEF

FLAXSEED MUFFINS

A muffin similar to these was used in a study at the University of Toronto. In the study, women with newly diagnosed breast cancer consumed one muffin containing 50 grams of ground flax per day. A control group ate muffins without flax. By the end of the study, the tumors were significantly reduced in the women who ate the muffins.

Yield: 24 muffins

1 ½ cup flaxseeds (2 cups ground)

1 3/4 cups whole-wheat pastry flour

1 tablespoon baking powder

½ teaspoon baking soda

1 tablespoon cinnamon

¼ cup sucanat

1 cup raisins

2 tablespoons finely minced tangerine peel (organic)

3 cups rice milk

1. Grind the flaxseeds in a blender. Unless you have a high-powered blender, this will have to be done in two or three batches.
2. Place the flaxseeds in a large bowl along with the flour, baking powder, baking soda, cinnamon and sucanat. Mix well. Add the raisins and the tangerine peel. Mix again.
3. Pour the rice milk into the bowl with the dry ingredients, all at once, and quickly mix until well blended. If you mix it too slowly the batter will become thick and hard to stir.
4. With a ¼ cup measuring cup, ladle the batter out into well-oiled and floured muffin tins. Bake at 350 for 25 minutes.

BLUEBERRY CRUMBLE

This desert contains very little sweetener, but is plenty sweet to the taste. It is also good with blackberries, peaches or pears.
Yield: 6 servings

1	cup whole wheat pastry flour	1	teaspoon vanilla
1	cup walnuts	1	teaspoon liquid stevia
¼	cup coconut oil	4	cups fresh or frozen blueberries
2	tablespoons sucanat		

1. Place the flour, walnuts, coconut oil, sucanat, vanilla and stevia in a food processor. Blend until the nuts are ground and the ingredients are combined.

2. Wash the blueberries, picking out any stems or damaged berries and place them in the bottom of an 8"X 8" oven dish.

3. Spread the flour mixture over the berries. Bake at 350 for 30 minutes or until the berries are bubbly and the topping is lightly browned.

STRAWBERRIES IN ROSEWATER SAUCE

I love this easy, but elegant recipe. The rose water makes it special,.
Yield: 4 to 6 servings

4	tablespoons kuzu root starch	1	teaspoon rose water (available at stores that carry products from the Middle East)
5	tablespoons water		
4	cups unsweetened mixed berry juice		
2	pints fresh sliced strawberries		

1. Place the kuzu starch in a small bowl or cup and mix with the water. Stir for a minute until the kuzu is dissolved.
2. Place the juice in a medium-size saucepan and add the dissolved starch. Mix well, and bring to a boil while stirring constantly. Continue to cook for 1-2 more minutes. Transfer to a bowl to cool.
3. When cool, add the strawberries and the rose water. Serve chilled.

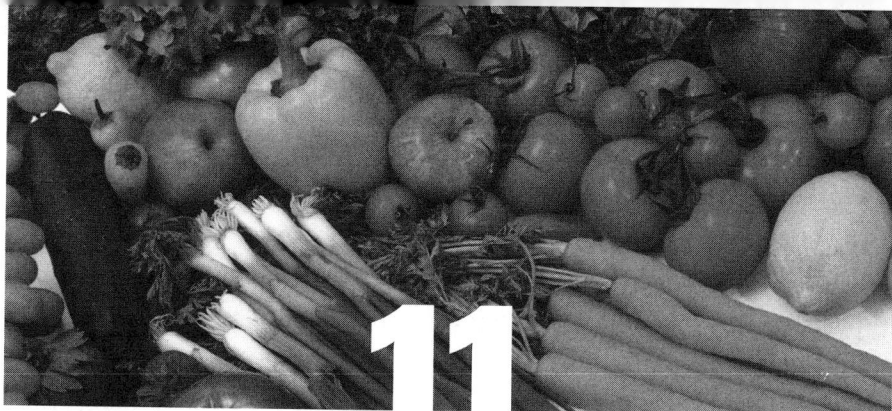

PRINCIPLES FOR ACHIEVING OPTIMAL HEALTH

Based on *God's Original Diet for Man*

Olin Idol, N.C., C.N.C.

It is with great excitement and anticipation that I approach this subject. I will be exploring with you a Biblical concept that is unfamiliar to the masses and ignored by others. It is a concept that will empower you to make choices that will have a positive impact not only on your own personal health, but that of your loved ones and others as you share with them what you learn. I trust that by the time you conclude this chapter you will have committed to make those changes that will allow you to enjoy a level of health you never thought possible. The information that follows could even save your life.

Before we see what the Bible sets forth as the ideal diet, we want to look briefly at the current health situation most people find themselves in today. It is painfully obvious that what we are doing is not working and that some drastic changes need to be made if we want to enjoy a long, healthy life.

Our Current Situation

Almost everyone we know would like to live as long as possible and en-joy optimal health throughout life. Unfortunately, that is not the reality experienced by most people today. Our approach to health care today is to treat symptoms with drugs, surgery, and/or radiation. Approximately 2 million people have toxic reactions to properly prescribed medication annually! Over 106,000 people die from these prescribed medications each year. That is the equivalent of an aircraft carrying 290 people crash-ing each day killing everyone on board.

Over 120,000 people (another jet liner with 328 people on board crashing every day) die each year due to hospital medical errors. Adverse reaction to prescribed aspirin kills 1600 children each year. (*Improve Your Health ProActively*, Maurice Pisciottano, D.C & Richard Barrett, D.C.) What would happen to the aviation industry if they had a track record of this magnitude?

Advancements in medicine over the past hundred years have al-lowed us to live to a ripe old age in the twenty-first century. According to the CDC, the life expectancy in the US for men born in 2005 was 75.2 years, and 80.4 years for women, a significant increase over the respective 46.3 and 48.3 years in 1900. (http://www.cdc.gov/nchs/data/hus/hus07.pdf#027) However, our quality of life is rapidly declining as compared to that of our ancestors.

The majority of deaths in the early 1900s was primarily due to in-fectious diseases such as tuberculosis and diphtheria, which have been practically eradicated in the U.S. and other industrialized nations given the increased practice of good personal hygiene, better sanitation, and improved living conditions. In 2005, however, the CDC lists heart dis-ease cancer, stroke, chronic lower respiratory disease, and diabetes as the five leading chronic disease killers in the U.S. (http://www.cdc.gov/nchs/data/nvsr/nvsr56/nvsr56_10.pdf)—these degenerative diseases often begin to manifest symptoms by the age of forty or earlier, thus taking a huge toll on the quality of life we have now and could have in our later years.

Years of scientific research indicate these chronic, degenerative diseases, their symptoms, and the deaths associated with them are directly or indirectly the result of poor dietary and lifestyle choices. The CDC confirms that over 70% of all deaths today are the result of those diseases and thus a direct result of our dietary and lifestyle choices. If we want to enjoy a quality of life in our latter years, we must learn how to take control of our health and not rely on the medical community. We must learn the biblical principles for optimal health and apply those to our lives.

Biblical Warning

In the book of Proverbs we read these words of warning: *When you sit down to dine with a ruler, Consider carefully what is before you, And put a knife to your throat if you are a man of {great} appetite. Do not desire his delicacies, for it is deceptive food* (Proverbs 23:1-3 NASB). These words were penned about 3,000 years ago. If they held a valid warning back then (and they did) how much greater is that warning for us today?

Often when we think of the Bible, we think strictly in terms of the spiritual. Yet, the Word of God has quite a bit to say about diet. While it is not necessary, today science is validating the truth of the scriptural teachings regarding the benefits of an optimal diet as we shall see as we examine the biblical perspective on health.

Discussing any issue from a biblical perspective is an awesome opportunity as well as a challenging responsibility. It is critical that we hold true to the teachings of the Word of God and that we allow the Holy Spirit to lead us in all truth. I take this opportunity very seriously and trust that as you read this chapter you will prayerfully ask the Holy Spirit to open your mind to the truth of God's Word and that He will lead you in understanding the truths from the Word and direct you in applying them to your life personally and in sharing them with others.

The day and age in which we live is not unlike the Greek world in the days of the early church when much of the New Testament cannon was written. The worldview at that time was that the answers to life's questions resided in wisdom of great teachers. It was thought that by simply following the teachings of men and women of intelligence and charisma they would find the answers and enjoy a better life.

We live in a day and age much like the Greek world in that respect. The overwhelming majority of the population of the Western world today looks to doctors of the medical profession and the drugs of the pharmaceutical industry for answers to their health challenges. We see the dismal results of this mentality today. This is not unlike the Greek world in the days of Christ. In the Gospel of Luke chapter 8, we read these words in verse 43 & 44: *Now a woman, having a flow of blood for twelve years, who had spent all her livelihood on physicians and could not be healed by any, came from behind and touched the border of His garment. And immediately her flow of blood stopped* (NKJV).

There never was a time in history when so called 'Health Care' costs more than it does today in the US and delivered less in quality of life and health. Today's 'Health Care' allows men and women to live longer lives than our ancestors of a century ago lived but the quality of life in those later years is greatly diminished.

There must be an alternative to the way we approach health today. In this chapter, we are going to look at a biblical perspective on health and what I believe the Bible presents as the ideal way to nourish the human body.

Eternal Consideration

Before we go any further, I want to be clear that while our diet and lifestyle are critically important in determining our quality of life, what we eat today is not a spiritual issue. It is not a sin to eat certain foods. Abstaining from certain foods does not make one person more spiritual than another. What we choose to eat will impact our physical health, our length of life, and our ability to serve God to a great extent. Our years of service may be cut short due to poor dietary choices. But, as important as our physical health is, our spiritual health is vastly more important.

The most important decision each of us has to make is in regard to where we spend eternity. Jesus Christ, God's son laid aside His deity.

Through the virgin birth, He became flesh. He lived a sinless life and willingly went to the cross and paid the ultimate penalty for our sins so that by simple faith in His substitutionary death we can have eternal life. We can accept His death on the cross as payment for our sin debt and have the assurance that once this temporal life on earth is over that we will spend eternity with God in heaven. Not only can we be assured of an eternal home in heaven, but as a believer in the Lord Jesus Christ, we have the opportunity of living a supernatural life here on earth as God's representative as we serve Him. (Romans 10: 1-21 and 2 Corinthians 5:17-21.)

God has provided a physical body as the home for our eternal soul and spirit. As a believer in the Lord Jesus Christ, our body is also the temple of the Holy Spirit (1 Corinthians 6:19-20). He has entrusted the care of that body to us and we are to present it a living sacrifice, holy, acceptable unto God. In Romans 12:1-2 we read: *I beseech you therefore, brethren, by the mercies of God, that ye present your bodies a living sacrifice, holy, acceptable unto God, which is your reasonable service. And be not conformed to this world: but be ye transformed by the renewing of your mind, that ye may prove what is that good, and acceptable, and perfect, will of God* (KJV).

Unfortunately, most believers have conformed to the world in the way they live and eat. They suffer the same physical problems and fight the same diseases as the rest of the world around them. I suggest to you that we should be separated from the world not only in spiritual matters but in our diet and lifestyle.

If we go back to the book of Genesis in chapter 1 we find a brief synopsis of the creation of the earth and everything upon it. In Genesis 2:7 we see a detailed description of God's creation of the first human being—Adam. *And the Lord God formed man of the dust of the ground, and breathed into his nostrils the breath of life; and man became a living soul* (KJV). It is very interesting that man's body was formed or fashioned from the dust or the elements of the earth. God breathed the breath of life into this body of dirt and it became a living soul.

In Genesis 1:29 after the overview of creation we read: *Then God said, "I give you every seed-bearing plant on the face of the whole earth and every tree that has fruit with seed in it. They will be yours for food* (NIV). God has just created the first human life and He now instructs His new creation in feeding that marvelous creation. He placed Adam and Eve in a perfect environment and gave them a raw plant-based diet (a diet of living food) as found in nature to be the perfect food for the newly created body.

While it is not implicitly stated here, we learn from reading Genesis 3:22 that mankind had been created and entrusted with a body capable of enjoying eternal life here on earth in a perfect environment. God placed only one stipulation on Adam and Eve, that they not eat the fruit of only one tree in the midst of the Garden of Eden. That I believe was to be just a simple test of their free will and obedience to God. We learn in Genesis 3 that they failed this test and as a result the first sin was committed. In Genesis 3:22b - 23 we read, *and now, lest he put forth his hand, and take also of the tree of life, and eat, and live for ever: Therefore the Lord God sent him forth from the Garden of Eden, to till the ground from whence he was taken.* In verse 4 we learn that God placed a cherubim and flaming sword to keep man away from the tree of life. God did not want man to live for ever in his sinful condition.

I want to use the passages in Genesis 3:22b-23 to demonstrate that God entrusted to man a marvelous body that was not subject to death (only after man sinned was he under the penalty of spiritual death [separation from God] and ultimately physical death. God told man in Genesis 1:29 how to ideally nourish the human body that was fashioned from the elements of the earth. The living plants God placed upon the earth, which take up the elements from the earth were to keep man's body replenished with the elements (from the earth) that were necessary to sustain human life in a state of optimal health.

When God breathed into man's nostrils the breath of life, man became a living soul. There is no reason to believe there was any change in man's body after he sinned. Only now man has been cut off from the tree of life and is under an ultimate penalty of physical death. His living body was no doubt just like man's body today as all of mankind is the result of Adam and Eve's procreation. God had instructed them in Genesis 1:28 to *Be fruitful, and multiply, and replenish the earth, and subdue it* (KJV).

The Miraculous Human Body

We know from science today that man's body is made up of trillions of cells – possibly as many as 100 trillion. These cells form tissues, blood, lymph fluid, etc. and organs. We know each cell is a living organism that carries out hundreds of functions each and every minute of every day. Each cell must take in nutrients that are derived from the foods we eat. Each cell uses those nutrients to create energy and to fuel the metabolic functions that support life. The metabolic processes that take place create a cascade of events as well as toxic by-products that must be eliminated. We will take a closer look at this process.

As procreation continues throughout human history the female egg is fertilized by the male sperm. This begins the process of procreation at the cellular level with the union of these 2 cells. Each cell begins to multiply over the next several months. Tissue, organs and ultimately a human body is formed. In approximately nine months after conception, the baby is delivered, takes in that first 'breath of life' and a new living human being is born—very much like the breath of life in Genesis 2:7 when God breathed life into the body of dust He had fashioned for man.

Within a few short minutes, ideally this new life is placed at mother's breast where by natural instinct it begins to nurse at mother's breast. The first fluid from the mother's breast the first day or so is colostrum. The colostrum is rich in vital protective factors that mother imparts to this new life. (*Understanding Nutrition*, 8th edition, Whitney and Rolfes, 1999, Wadsworth Publishing Company)

God's ideal nourishment for the newborn of any mammal species is the milk of the mother. The first fluid is colostrum which provides the newborn with important immune and protective factors that are critical for optimal health. Unfortunately, today the vast majority of newborn infants never receive these vital protective factors and start life off with a deficit from the day of birth. With God's natural design for nourishing an infant often being ignored from day one, how can we expect that baby to grow up with optimal health? God's ideal nourishment for a newborn baby is exclusively mother's breast milk for at least the first 6 months.

Lessons from Nature

When we observe God's creation in nature apart from man's interference we find mammals giving birth to healthy offspring that nurse mother's milk until the ideal weaning time for that species. After weaning, the offspring in nature will instinctively live on raw foods as found in nature whether the species is herbivorous or carnivorous as long as mankind does not interfere with nature. In nature, we do not find wild animals that are obese and sickly except again where there is interference in the natural processes by man.

We saw earlier that the ideal food for man was the raw plant foods God supplied in nature. It is not until some 1600 years after man sinned and the earth has been destroyed by flood waters that we see God gives man permission in Genesis 9:3 to consume animal flesh. Since man was created with a body capable of enjoying eternal life here on earth if he simply obeyed God, time was irrelevant until man sinned and came under the penalty of physical death. We really don't know how long Adam and Eve lived in the perfect environment before time became a factor. We can establish from the various ages provided for Adam and Eve's offspring that it was a little over 1600 years after their sin that God judged earth's inhabitants by flood and spared only Noah and his family to repopulate the earth.

The Word of God gives no explanation as to why God allowed the eating of animal flesh at this time. We can only conclude that in the beginning at creation God's ideal for mankind was raw plant-based foods. When we read the book of Isaiah, in chapter 11 where the millennial kingdom (the 1000 year reign of Christ on earth after the seven-year tribulation period) is discussed, we see again that mankind will apparently be restricted from eating and killing animals for food. In the context of chapter 11 we find no hostility in the animal kingdom. The cow and bear shall feed together and their young shall lie down together (vs. 6). The lion will eat straw like the ox (vs. 7). *They shall not hurt nor destroy in all my holy mountain: for the earth shall be full of the knowledge of the Lord, as the waters cover the sea* (Isaiah 11:9 KJV).

It seems reasonable that if God created man with a physical body capable of eternal life and that the nourishment for that body was to come from living plant foods, and that ultimately in the millennial kingdom man will again nourish his body with living plant foods, this may just be the ideal way to nourish the human body today if we are to enjoy optimal health.

Things Were Different in Biblical Days

In suggesting that a plant-based diet is the ideal biblical diet for mankind we need to look at some concerns that are often raised. While God allowed the eating of animal flesh after the flood, and even instructed it on certain occasions it was never the main part of the diet. The animals of biblical days were not raised the way they are today. They were not loaded with hormones and antibiotics. The plant based foods were the main stay of the diet and these foods were nutritionally dense, free of toxins, and were able to offset any negative aspects of the limited amount of animal flesh in the diet.

In biblical days, man lived in an environment that was free of toxins and pollution. His water was pure and uncontaminated. The air he breathed was pure and it was much easier to maintain an optimal level of health. Man was physically active and did not have televisions and computers to spend hours in front of each day. He walked most of the places he traveled.

In contrast today, our foods are at best nutritionally deficient even when grown organically compared to just a few decades ago, let alone compared to a few thousand years ago in biblical days. Our environment is polluted with thousands of chemicals. Animals that feed on food stuff that is full of toxic chemicals concentrates the chemicals in their flesh and when mankind eats the flesh or drinks the milk, he receives a heavy concentration of these chemicals and toxic poisons. Fish are contaminated with pesticides, PCBs, mercury and other pollutants from mankind's 'progress.' Our bodies are undernourished at the cellular level and over burdened with a load of toxins that cannot adequately be eliminated on a diet that is based on foods from animal sources.

As we saw earlier, life begins at cellular level with the union of the male sperm and the female egg. Life begins at cellular level, is maintained at cellular level and ends at cellular level. As long as each cell is provided optimal nutrition, and timely and efficient elimination of toxins it functions optimally and we enjoy optimal health. When this process is compromised we begin loosing our health very slowly at the cellular level. If impaired cellular function isn't corrected, after years or decades of abuse, the body begins to manifest symptoms of ill health and chronic degenerative disease usually appears.

The Hallelujah Diet®

How do we meet the needs of the body at the inner most cellular level today? The Hallelujah Diet based on principles found in Genesis 1:29 is the most optimal diet I am aware of today. We will review the fundamental concepts of the Hallelujah Diet here. For a more in-depth look and a look at hundreds of testimonies from folks who adopted the diet and lifestyle you may want to visit www.hacres.com.

In observing the principles of Genesis 1:29, the Hallelujah Diet is an exclusive plant-based diet, free of all animal source foods (including sea food). It consists of about 80 to 85% raw plant based foods and 15 to 20% cooked plant based foods and an abundance of freshly extracted vegetable juice along with some discrete supplementation.

Raw foods are important because the heat sensitive enzymes (those nutrients that are heat sensitive) have not been destroyed. By the time a raw food is heated to a temperature of 122 degrees, the life-force – the enzymes have been all destroyed.

Cooked Food

Why include cooked food if Genesis 1:29 was a raw, plant based diet you might ask? As we mentioned earlier, our foods today are nutritionally deficient when compared to just a few decades ago, let alone to those available in Biblical Days. With the inferior quality of our foods today, it is difficult to take in enough calories on a raw plant based diet without eating an excessive amount of fruits and fats. We can take in more calories in a smaller volume of cooked food to help meet the metabolic needs as well as energy needs of the body than we can with raw foods exclusively. With the high quality and nutrient density of the foods in biblical days, it was not difficult to consume the volume required to support optimal health. We simply have difficulty processing the volume of raw foods and fiber today required to support optimal health at cellular level.

Also, the vast majority of our population is addicted to cooked foods. The inclusion of some cooked food on a daily basis satisfies that addiction and makes the diet and lifestyle easier to follow. There are also some nutritional benefits in cooked foods. Just a couple examples are: 1) Lycopene in cooked tomatoes is much more readily available and more efficiently assimilated than from raw tomatoes. 2) Beta carotene and some other phytonutrients are more bio-available in cooked carrots and other vegetables as the cell structure is broken down in the cooking process releasing these nutrients more efficiently than in the fibers of these foods when eater raw.

Why Fresh Juice

Fresh vegetable juice also plays an important role in nourishing the body optimally at cellular level. Again, one may ask why advocate juicing if you are looking at Genesis 1:29 for our dietary principles. As mentioned earlier our foods today are nutritionally deficient and we can't physically process the volume of fiber that would be present in the amount of raw foods we would need to consume for an optimal nutritional intake. Most people have been eating the Standard American Diet (SAD) for years before they learn of the importance of a plant-based diet. Most of us need to maximize the nutrients at cellular level as rapidly as possible. The juice of fresh vegetables is the quickest way to accomplish this.

In his classic book *Live Food Juices*, H.E. Kirschner, M.D. relates how he used carrot juice therapeutically in treating several patients over half a century ago in his private practice. Regarding the benefit of fresh vegetable juice, Dr. Kirschner had this to say, "Then too, if modern research is correct, the power to break down the cellular structure of raw vegetables, and assimilate the precious elements they contain, even in the healthiest individuals is only fractional – not more than 35%, and in the less healthy, down to 1%. In the form of juice, these same individuals assimilate up to 92% of these elements. The juice of the plant, like the blood of the body contains all the elements that build and nourish. It is a well-known fact that all foods must become liquid before they can be assimilated" (*Live Food Juices*, H. E. Kirschner, M.D., 1975, H. E. Kirschner Publications, Monrovia, CA).

By eating a primarily raw plant based diet with a moderate amount of cooked vegetables, legumes, whole grains, etc and including 1 to 3 servings of fresh vegetable juice daily, we can supply our bodies with the best nutrition possible today.

Recognizing the nutrient deficiency of our foods, it is wise to consider using a nutrient-rich whole grass juice concentrate such as Hallelujah Acres BarleyMax to insure an optimal intake of trace elements (we are built of the elements from the earth) that may be missing from our foods today. You can read more about BarleyMax at www.hacres.com.

This organically grown juice powder is processed in such a way that the enzymes and heat sensitive nutrients are preserved. It is truly a living food in a concentrated juice powder that when reconstituted in water contains the live enzymes inherent in the raw juice from the barley and alfalfa grass.

Essential Fats

In biblical days, the nutrient density of the foods and lack of processing insured an optimal intake of essential fatty acids, especially the Omega-3 fats. Just a century ago, we maintained an optimal intake with a ratio of about 1 to 1 of Omega-6 to Omega-3 fats. Today, for most folks on the SAD the ration is grossly out of proportion with as much as a 50 to

1 ratio of Omega-6 to Omega-3. While both are essential in that they must be obtained from the diet, the Omega-6 in too great a quantity is inflammatory while the Omega-3 is anti-inflammatory. With such a dramatic imbalance in our intake of Essential Fatty Acids (EFAs) it is easy to see why Floyd H. Chilton, Ph.D. states, "We are unquestionably facing an epidemic in inflammatory disease. By my estimate, approximately half of all Americans suffer from an inflammatory disorder, and more of us are at risk" (*Inflammation Nation,* Floyd H. Chilton, Ph.D., 2006, Fireside, New York, NY). We must insure we meet our EFA needs of Omega-3 today with flaxseed, flaxseed oil, walnuts, or a good clean (free of heavy metals, etc) fish oil such as Carlson's.

Antioxidants and Free Radicals

In view of the chronic inflammation of today and the intense free radical damage our body is subjected to, it is vitally important that we insure we have the maximum antioxidant protection possible. In Biblical days, the environment was pure, the food was nutritionally dense, the intake of EFAs was well-balanced and free radical damage was minimal. Considering all of the previous factors mentioned it is easy to understand why our body is impaired in the production of glutathione (GSH) today beyond the age of 20 years. It is well known that after the age of twenty, the body's ability to produce this Master Antioxidant decreases by 10 to 12% or more per decade and is critically impaired in those suffering with chronic degenerative disease according to Robert Keller, M.D.

When our body is not able to deal efficiently with free radical damage, the DNA, the cellular membranes and various other tissues are subject to free radical damage and our health is impaired at cellular level. While antioxidants like vitamin C, vitamin E, and beta carotene from our food are important in our never ending battle with free radical damage and inflammation, the body's own Master Antioxidant—glutathione is by far a superior free radical neutralizer. Glutathione (GSH) is produced intracellularly by each cell as well as by the liver when the body has adequate nutritional resources to do so. Supplementing with a glutathione supplement is of no value. GSH must be produced within the individual cells and the liver. Dr. Robert Keller, after ten years of research has developed a supplement that has been scientifically proven (in a double blind, placebo controlled, cross-over study) to increase intracellular glutathione by 292% within sixty days of continuous use.

Not only does this product, known as MaxGXL, increase intracellular glutathione, but it also was shown in this study to increase the body's DHEA by 46% and IGF-1 by 40.8%. DHEA and IFG-1 are markers related to levels of human growth hormone, which is the indicator of true biological age. They decrease with age—another factor contributing to aging in this age of nutritionally deficient foods.

Subjects in this study also experienced a decrease of 37% in TNF. TNF (Tumor Necrosis Factor) alpha is one of the three most significant markers of cellular inflammation. This is the one supplement I would not be without. For more information on MaxGXL visit www.911yourhealth.com or call toll free 1-888-572-3132.

B-12

The final area of supplementation we want to look at briefly is B-12. There is no B-12 in a plant-based diet so we want to insure we do not develop a deficiency in this area. In a study conducted several years ago by Michael Donaldson, Ph.D. with a group of people who had followed the Hallelujah Diet for at least two years, just under 50% were found to be deficient in B-12.

(http://www.hacres.com/diet/research/b12_summary.pdf).

One might ask if the Hallelujah Diet is based on principles from Genesis 1:29, why would there be a B-12 deficiency. Surely a B-12 supplement wasn't necessary in the Garden. Great observation! Even just a few decades ago when food was grown on local farms it was not so highly sanitized as it is today. Our produce was harvested, the surface dirt was rinsed off and the food was consumed. On this food were beneficial organisms that, when ingested along with our food, helped keep our friendly bacteria built up in our colon. This good balance of friendly flora produced an adequate amount of vitamin B-12 along with other B-vitamins. Due to our sanitation practices today, our foods contain little of this beneficial bacteria and our balance of friendly bacteria is often depleted.

Antibiotic use, eating animal source foods that contain antibiotics, stress and a host of other factors deplete our friendly bacteria. With no dietary source of friendly flora, many people are not able to produce optimal levels of B-12. In order to prevent a deficiency it is wise to use a sublingual B-12 supplement (preferably a Methylcobalamin form of B-12).

Conclusion

We live in a day and age in which the diet of the average person is excessive in caloric content—thus approximately two thirds of the US population is overweight; and, nutritionally deficient—thus we are lacking in nutrition at the cellular level. Over 70% of deaths today are directly related to poor dietary and lifestyle choices. If we want to enjoy an optimal level of health, we must get back to Biblical principles of health by nourishing our bodies with a well-balanced, primarily raw plant-based diet and use wise supplementation.

I want to encourage you to read and study the first few chapters of Genesis. Look at how God created these marvelous self-healing bodies and how He designed them to be nourished. Look at the scientific research today by such noted scientist as T. Colin Campbell, Ph.D. (author of *The China Study*) and how this research that encompasses nearly a half of century validates the benefits of a plant-based diet. Prayerfully ask God to help you implement a diet and lifestyle that will honor Him with your physical body and allow you to serve Him most efficiently.

Beloved, if you and I as believers in the Lord Jesus Christ are to enjoy a level of health that sets us apart from the world, we must renew our minds daily with the Word of God. We must study information that teaches us how our miraculous self-healing body functions and what best meets the nutritional needs at cellular level. And then, as the Holy Spirit leads us, we will be able to adopt a diet and lifestyle that sets us apart from the world. We will no longer need to depend upon a failing sickness care industry to treat symptoms of a disease ridden body. We will begin to enjoy a level of health we never thought possible. We will be able to indeed offer our bodies as *living sacrifices, holy and pleasing to God.*

I believe Moses was the pattern of a life that was set apart unto God. His death was a pattern as to how God designed our lives here on earth to come to an end. In Deuteronomy 34:7 we read, *Moses was a hundred and twenty years old when he died, yet his eyes were not weak nor his strength gone* (NIV).

Moses lived life to the fullest. He lived a long healthy life. When it was time for his temporal life here on earth to end, his soul and spirit left behind a physical body that was still full of strength and apparently not riddled with disease. If the church (believers of this age) is not raptured before it is my time to depart this life, I'd like to follow the example of Moses—Wouldn't you?

I would like to encourage you to follow the instructions the apostle Paul gave to Timothy almost 2,000 years ago, *Study to shew thyself approved unto God, a workman that needeth not to be ashamed, rightly dividing the word of truth* (II Timothy 2:15, KJV). Along with the scriptures, study the research of noted scientists such as T. Colin Campbell in his book, *The China Study* and see how his research spanning nearly five decades validates the principles found in the diet God first gave to mankind. Implement those principles for thirty days and experience the dynamic benefit of living foods. Enjoy your journey to Optimal Health.

"Optimal Health is built on the foundations of health, and Optimal Health is the result of hundreds of choices you may make that gradually turn your health at any given moment toward Optimal Health or toward Disease. If that decision-making process is not present, you'll still have some level of health—you'll still be alive—but you may be moving toward a disease state rather than Moving toward Optimal Health. Health isn't something you were born with that can't change, like your fingerprints. It's something you must take responsibility for forming" (Source unknown).

I call heaven and earth to witness against you today, that I have set before you life and death, the blessing and the curse. So choose life in order that you may live, you and your descendants (Deuteronomy 30:19, NASB). While the context of this verse deals with spiritual issues, the principles apply in many areas of our life as well as to our dietary choices. We can **choose** to put into our bodies the foods that support **life** and health, not only for ourselves but for our entire family and loved ones so that they may live a life of optimal health.

EDITOR'S NOTE

I agree with Olin Idol's principles for achieving optimal health. I might point out just a few statistics: Autism used to be 1-10,000—it's now one in 98! The statistics are projected to be in 2010, that 50% of our children will be autistic! Children are now acquiring adult on-set diabetes in ever alarming proportions! This is criminal! Our health care budget will be approaching 1 trillion dollars in the next 10 years! 90% of this budget is spent the last 30 days of a person's life! Is this health care or is this sick care? Would you agree that something is wrong? God did not create faulty bodies or faulty body parts!

If you read Time Magazine, they keep revealing that everything is at an epidemic proportion: obesity, cancer, AIDS, heart disease, arthritis, diabetes, osteoporosis, alzheimer's, autism, etc. Would you agree that we have a problem in America today? William Penn said, "A country not led by God, will be ruled by a tyrant...let men be good, and the government cannot be bad." Make the man right, and his world will be right! —JEF

THE HEALING NATURE OF WATER

John Eagle Freedom

To include a chapter on water is to actually teach what our life is all about—to be Filled and Loved-on continuously by the Holy Spirit! Let me explain: When God chose an earthly figure to illustrate the eternal essence radiating from His Holy Being, which gives us Life—He chose water!

In the very Beginning, "*God created the heaven and the earth. And the earth was without form, and void; and darkness [no life yet] was upon the face of the deep.*" [Definition: the ocean at that time covering the entire planet which also represents man who is predominantly a "Water Being" both spiritually and physically!] "*And the Spirit of God moved [shook, brooded, relaxed, fluttered] upon the waters. And God said, 'Let there be Light'*" (Genesis 1:2).

Very interesting pictures are seen in the Hebrew word "moved"— e.g. notice the third definition: "relaxed." Just like the dove, sent out by Noah that couldn't find rest, the Holy Spirit is seeking rest in the temples He made for His Own Glory, but He can't rest until we properly nourish our spirit, soul, and body with Him as our fuel and invite in only the

209

things He has created for our growth and sustenance; (it goes without saying: we can't rest, enjoy perfect health, healing and deliverance until He rests in us) and the single most important physical substance He has ordained for our rest is water!

Remember, on the sixth day in the afternoon, when God stood His ultimate creation up on its muddy pods it was just an incredibly very organized, high tech lump of mud; but when He breathed into its two small apertures at the top, that lump—became a living soul! The account of the creation of our planet and man is very clear teaching us that until God moves us when He breathes His Word into our being, man; also symbolized by the formless ocean, is void of life! That's why Jesus could say, "*It is the Spirit that quickens; the flesh profits nothing: the words that I speak unto you, they are spirit, and they are life*" (John 6:63).

If Anyone Thirst Let Him Come to Me

In the next chapter Jesus is confronted by the religious people who thought they were experts in this eternal life business; but were in reality void of life because they rejected the only one who gave it in the first place! Hear these immortal words of the True Eternal Life-giver… "If any man thirst, let him come unto me, and drink. He that believeth on me as the Scripture hath said, out of his belly shall flow rivers of living water. "*But this spoke he of the Spirit, which they that believe on him should receive…*" (John 7:37-39).

Can you see the same Master in the Beginning breathing life as if He were conversing with a friend, speaking life into Adam with His Word, and then 4,000 years later declaring to the Jews during their holiday season that He is ever willing to breathe His Spirit again by speaking His Words of Life to all who will humbly come to Him?

Jesus would later say, "Whosoever drinks of the water that I shall give him shall never thirst; but the water that I shall give him shall be in him a well of water springing up into everlasting life" (John4:14). The message Jesus gave to us today is clear: We are to first enjoy being properly hydrated in our total being, spirit, soul and body so much that we overflow with abundance of life and health!

Two Examples of Water

Here are two examples of how Jesus used the humble substance that we call water to illustrate the only fuel able to propel us around down here in abundance and then rocket us off to Heaven! Is it any coincidence that rocket fuel is the combining of liquid hydrogen and liquid oxygen, the only two elements of water?! Or, that we've known for a long time that clean-burning engines using only hydrogen and oxygen is the most efficient fuel which after combustion exhausts—pure water! Man's vital, real fuel is the Spirit of Jesus! Jesus called this most precious fuel—living water—and as is the spiritual, so is the physical!

Why is water so important to us? In the very beginning of your life, you were 99.9 % water upon conception. When you were born you were 90% water. You couldn't sit, much less stand. You were totally helpless to do anything against the force of this world—gravity. All you could do was flow with it as it moved you along, just like water can only flow downhill. But as you grew, your bones began to mineralize with calcium, and other minerals began to insert themselves in all the right places designed by your creator so you could stand, walk, run, and even do gravity defying stunts such as jumping. In your adult years now you are 70% water; but tragically, at ever younger ages humans are inserting in their bodies inorganic minerals our Creator never intended to ingest, resulting in them settling in places such as the muscular system causing great pain and discomfort. This particular disease we have named "muscular sclerosis" and even though it sounds so formidable, it's 100% treatable and preventable! All it is, among other factors, is dehydration and/or drinking the wrong kind of water!

There are so many other maladies brought on and exacerbated by malhydration and dehydration that I don't think I need to elaborate on every sickness and disease caused by it, but I have singled out this one to prove that if this "incurable disease" is a simple reflection of improper water and/or lack of it, what other "formidable" modern diseases must bow to the power of water? Short answer—all of them! Sadly, this mineralization, if not flushed out with pure living water, will steadily continue throughout our entire adult life. Joints will become creaky, stiff and painful; movement will become restricted, eyesight will become blurred, hearing will be dulled, and hosts of other symptoms will become pronounced the older we get. Without proper hydration through these years If we make it to 70, our bodies will only be an average of 50% water!

The Right Water

If water is so vital, then what is the "right" water to get? Why aren't we hearing about water's vital importance from the doctors and other professional health experts? The sad answer to the latter is because to simply tell people to drink the right kind of water is too simple and sounds—unprofessional! People don't want to hear from their doctor what their mother would say. So, what is the "right" water: This is still very controversial. There's so much money—billions of dollars at stake, that's why there's such a cover-up to keep you in the dark! Please consider the facts:

> All water, whether it's tap, bottled, spring, filtered, purified, and even distilled have at least one thing in common—they are all positively charged. "Why's that such a big deal," you ask? We need negatively charged water. Change from positive to negative water and it will change your life! Why are the others not as good? First of all, we know tap water is dangerous because of the chlorine, and fluoride added in municipal water supplies because they are both poisons. And those known poisons love to combine with other chemicals already present in our groundwater to create new chains of molecules now able to wreak new kinds of havoc on unsuspecting mankind! Add to the fact that drugs, hormones, pseudo hormones, (which mimic our hormones) and antibiotics are turning up more and more in our city water supplies, with pesticides and fertilizers—you really can't with a clear conscience keep drinking it!

Bottled—what amazing recent exposés have been conducted revealing the contamination and other deliberate unhealthy practices go in to that expensive product! Spring water—though it should be the best, still it is loaded with inorganic minerals the body cannot break down but has to make room for them resulting in the diseases we have mentioned earlier! Now filtered and purified, you're not going to find anything more wrong with it—are you? When produced correctly they're not as bad but they still don't have the healing and health properties what many are saying "miracle" water, or "living" negatively charged water has!

Distilled—which is the purest of the pure, having no minerals whatever, considered by many to be the best, has one flaw—it's too pure! What I mean by that statement is: through extensive laboratory testing we know now that distilled water seeks minerals and other impurities to be stable. That's really a good thing when your body is full of inorganic minerals and toxins, but there's only one problem: it can't differentiate between inorganic and the organic minerals that are vital to our health! So, it indiscriminately goes in and binds to the good as well as the bad and flushes them all out. End result of drinking distilled too long—we suffer mineral deficiencies, and that can cause a host of problems such as arthritis and osteoporosis.

We have what is today known as "living water" because everything it touches becomes clean—very interesting; we have always heard that "cleanliness is next to godliness" from our mothers. This amazing form of H2O is actually negatively charged with a pH of 9.5. Anything over 7.4 is especially good for our minds and bodies because in this alkaline state, unhealthy bacteria, viruses, molds, fungus, cancerous cells and everything else negative to our health cannot flourish, but must die! Someone's about to see it—yes, to take charge of your life; to control the disease-causing agents as even bacteria and viruses, start by changing your water! Change your Water, change your Life!

It has been determined that everybody needs at least one half of their body weight in ounces of water. If you weigh 200, you should drink at least 100 ounces of this miraculous water for optimum health! But not only to maintain—here's where it really gets exciting: It also reverses the damages caused by years of improper hydration and malnutrition! Many incurable modern diseases are being overcome by this simplest of all remedies—even cancer!

We are Water Beings

As I began this chapter mentioning that we are "water beings" both spiritual and physical, it is actually becoming more and more evident that connected with every water molecule is the Spirit of God in a form unlike we can perceive in any other substance!

I again have to wonder: What is the substance in our body that looks and acts the most like water? And where does God say is the life of the individual? Actually there are two substances, and they both illustrate God's own life taking up the largest portion of our body—blood and lymph!

The blood gives life circulating throughout the body pumped by the heart—symbolizing the Holy Spirit. I say it represents the Holy Spirit because none of us can control our own heart and it seems as if it has a mind of its own! When properly nourished and cared for, this tireless servant ceaselessly performs, insuring that "life" continuously reaches every cell of our body! It serves regardless of our brain or spinal column; it is independent but will allow itself to be regulated by our endocrine system. It truly behaves as if it is an outside source of energy! See how dedicated the powerful, loving Holy Spirit consistently gives life to even the minutest and mundane parts of our body? We are totally surrounded and ministered to by His Love and Care! Then after the oxygen—"the life" has been ministered, the blood moved by the heart "cleanses" each cell, taking out the wastes—the by-products of life and expels them out of the body—if the cells cooperate. To carry this even closer to where you and I live: the Holy Spirit provides the means and the system to cleanse our lives from sin, sickness, and negative-health-obstructing toxins—but just like the cell must release them to be removed, so we too must avail ourselves of the means provided by the Holy Spirit and release the things we thought we had to hold on to.

This substance we call blood is the very place where God said He placed our life. *"For the life of the flesh is in the blood, and I have given it to you upon the altar to make an atonement for your souls, for it is the blood that makes atonement for the soul"* (Leviticus 17:11). It's amazing to see how the Gospel—Salvation from sin, Healing, Health, and Sanctification are ingenuously revealed in the body! Let us continue to study it well.

The blood is the same color that symbolizes "redemption"—scarlet red. When the precious Holy Spirit begins to minister His life to our needy cells, He first provides "life"—the oxygen contained in tiny insignificant-looking round packets in serum, and personally delivers this most precious gift to every cell.

This clear water fluid completely fills in all the intercellular spaces around all of our cells. Just like He's completely in control of the delivery system, He's also in complete control; helping every cell reach its optimum efficiency and performance. He's embracing every cell and making sure that they can receive every need abundantly provided for, because He knows their needs since he's right there constantly "closer than a brother." He's lovingly monitoring each cell as if it were the only one!

But now, here's where the immune system differs from the circulatory system: though serum and lymph are clear and almost completely all water, lymph serves to actively expunge all foreign agents missed by the circulatory system. It's like a back-up system to insure that we will always get rid of the poisons and debris from waste products, and keep antibodies and soldier helper cells on target, to mention just a few of its protective functions, but, there is no pump-like organ to drive it! For it to work serving you, you have to cooperate and do your part! Exercise! It's easy to say, "I don't think I'll exercise today," but remember when you discount your exercise routine, you cheat your lymph system, and make it sluggish to where it cannot expel the poisons!

The Unique Characteristics of Water

When we look at water's already known amazing characteristics unique in the chemical world, and that scientists still today cannot explain the mysteries why it behaves differently than any other substance in the universe—to accept what I'm about to reveal to you what was discovered in Japan will make sense! But before I do, let me touch on some more of these unique qualities not seen among any other combinations of elements or substances and you'll see—it's almost like I'm describing the attributes of God Himself!

Water is the universal solvent. Given enough time, water will dissolve anything! It can take anything apart to its basic elements!

Water never decays, or loses potency. Pure water can never go stale, spoil, go rancid, rot, or decompose. It is eternal!

Water is existent in all three states—liquid, gas, and solid all within a very narrow range of temperatures compared to the other substances. All other elements and substances must have extreme cold—minus hundreds of degrees to liquefy and even colder to solidify. In our range of temperatures we know them as gases.

Water is the only naturally occurring substance appearing on planet earth in all three of its states of matter. Every Sunday school child has heard their Sunday school teacher attempt to explain the Holy Trinity as the three states of water: ice—The Son, water—The Father, and steam—The Holy Spirit.

When it freezes, water is the only substance that freezes on its surface. Even in the extreme cold at the poles, life is teeming under the icebergs! This is the ingenious method engineered by our super intelligent God to regulate temperatures and protect ecosystems preserving life both in and out of the water! If, like other substances, water freezes at the bottom, we'd have no marine life and therefore no life on the surface.

Water is the only substance that expands and becomes lighter as it freezes, thus—why ice in your glass goes to the top. Nothing else will do this! Now, finally add to these anomalies of water these incredibly astonishing, shocking 21st century truths recently discovered from Japan about water:

A Japanese researcher attempted to photograph snow flakes for his own study, but kept missing his best shots because no one knew at that time how to preserve a snowflake long enough to make a good picture. Through many years of trial and error he finally came upon just the right temperature to conduct his experiments. His photographs were now stunning the world by his proven methods of photography. Then an amazing thing happened: As he was trying to keep snowflakes from melting, he actually discovered that when one did melt, he learned he could refreeze it, and to his astonishment, they always refroze back to their original shape and design!

This proves again that water does indeed have memory! How do you explain it? This humble Japanese scientist, Dr. Emoto, didn't stop there! If water apparently has intelligence enough to "know how" to come back together perfectly again, what other supernatural characteristics could it possibly have? So, began some of the strangest findings ever in modern science! "If water has intelligence then maybe I can in some way communicate with it," thought Dr. Emoto. To begin "talking with water" he labeled a jug with the words, "I Love You" which when crystallized (made into snowflakes) created the most beautiful patterns seen at any time! Then he took another jug, labeled it, "You make me sick" and it couldn't crystallize! He repeated his experiment to be sure, and every time it was as the first! Then he wrote the name of "Jesus Christ" in every language on another bottle and it was as he expected, crystallized into the most beautiful specimens ever! Then he wrote the names of saints, etc. the results were also beautiful, but when he wrote the names of those who have cursed humanity such as Adolph Hitler, they never crystallized, but took on a grotesque, ugly, colorless form! He taped picturesque landscape scenes on one jug, modern-art on another and you guessed it, only the natural serene pictures turned out beautiful.

Not stopping with visual communications he played classical music to one jug, head-banging rock to another, and sure enough, the classical music jug responded with beautiful crystals, while the other—the same disorganized, confused mess that couldn't even crystallize!

Now, here's where it gets to where we live everyday—vegetables have water—right? What would happen if you take food and put it into a jug like the first that says, "I Love You," and put the same kind of healthy food into another jug that says, "I Hate You"? Dr. Emoto found out—the vegetables in the first jug lasted three times longer!

That should convincingly instruct us humans, since we are mostly water, to take every precaution and surround ourselves with loving thoughts, loving words, loving environments, furnishings, atmospheres, etc. We have the evidence before us today now more than ever, because we are mostly water, every cell (which is also mostly water) in our body "knows" when it is loved; and when it knows it is loved, it wants to work hard serving its master! But if it is subjected to a harsh environment of pride, lust, criticism and hatred, it's easy to see how foreign agents of sickness and ultimately death can destroy its incentive to even live! Just like we're learning about water, we know our cells have incredible intelligence of such a type, that we're not smart enough to figure out! But it first begins with the intelligence of the water in the cell! When the water in our cells knows it is loved, then the water communicates its happiness to every part of the cell and the cell responds by tireless activity selflessly functioning flawlessly; even reproducing perfectly every time!

We don't have to know how water and our cells communicate intelligently, we just know that they do! Like the Incan kipu which told the history of its people in knotted cords that no one can decipher today, so each cell will either be encouraged to flourish or wither; and will communicate either their happiness or misery to their neighboring cells!

It used to be that we called these "simple cells" and thought they were composed mostly of a gelatinous substance incorrectly called, "protoplasm." This was an oversimplification! We now know that each individual cell of our 80,000,000,000,000 (yes, that's 80 trillion) in our body possesses an intelligence that can only be explained when we go to the supernatural explanation again to realize the miracle that every cell can function flawlessly when given the proper materials—and that can only improve our intelligence! That's one of the reasons why our modern fast food is so dangerous—there's no living water, or enzymes; no repairing, and building materials our cells can use!

Another shocking thing to ponder: we know our entire society is being "dumbed down"—could all this be the evidence that the diet fostered by our society is the "dumbest diet" of them all?! Our societal ills are mere reflections of our cells being "dumbed down"! We're mentally and emotionally deficient because there's no intelligence—no life in our food! Our cells are coping with defective materials—and it shows literally on our faces! No life—no intelligence because the vital life substances originally placed by our Intelligent Designer are all executed! And if there's little or no water, because it too has been destroyed—that "food" is also dead filler, not fuel to nourish our cells and it shows.

OUR TEMPLE
REQUIRES WATER

Adapted From:
Honoring the Temple of God
A Christian Health Perspective

Bob McCauley

I baptize you with water for repentance.
—Matthew 3:11

Water is referred to 617 times in the Bible, making it the most prevalent substance mentioned in it. It's mentioned 11 times in the first chapter of Genesis, 54 times in the entire book. Water is the first element mentioned in the Bible [Genesis 1:2–6]. God saved humanity through Noah when the world flooded. The Red Sea parted to save the Jewish people, then defeated their enemies during the Exodus. Moses got water from a rock during their 40 years in the desert [Exodus 17:1–7]. Water is mentioned 53 times in the Psalms alone. Bathing and water purification rituals are mentioned numerous times in both the Old and New Testaments. Jesus was baptized with water; Jesus' first miracle was to change water into wine, which was the commencement of his ministry. He performed several miracles on the Sea of Galilee, including walking upon water.

The prevalence of water in the Bible is no coincidence because water is the most important substance the body requires other than the air we breathe. Water is the cornerstone of health. It is a universal solvent and the body's lubricant. Proper hydration of the body is crucial to human health in countless ways. You will never be truly healthy if you are not sufficiently hydrated. When we begin making water a big part of our lifestyle, we take our first steps toward true health.

Every organ in the body heavily depends on water to function properly and to its capacity. We are mostly water. The average human body is 69% water. The brain is 85% water, bones 35% water, blood 83% water and the liver 90% water. When we become dehydrated, we put our health in immediate jeopardy. Thus, we gamble with our lives without realizing the dangerous high-wire we are walking when we don't drink enough water.

We must drink half our body weight in ounces minimum each day. For instance, if you weigh 200 lbs (90 kg), you should consume 100 ounces (3 liters) of water each day. However, I recommend people drink a lot more because we lose that amount of water through the basic functions of the human body, those of urination, perspiration, respiration and defecation.

Living Water

"Never again will they thirst" (Revelation 7:16 NIV).

Ionized Water has many aliases: *Alkali Water, Alkaline Water, Alkalized Water, Cluster Water, Microcluster Water, Micro Water, Reduced Water, Miracle Water, Ion Water, Ionic Water, Electron Water, Hydroxyl Water, Electrolyzed Water, Living Water.*

Ionized Water is known by many names. Jesus is referred to as Living Water in the New Testament. *Ionized Water* is also often referred to as Living Water because ionization wakes up, enlivens conventional water that is considered sleeping or dead because it is of little good to the body other than to hydrate it. *Ionized Water* goes far beyond that and is a world apart from conventional water.

If we wish to truly honor the temple God has given us and be healthy we need only do three things: *Alkalize, hydrate* and *detoxify the body*. If we achieve this, we can prevent and even cure the body of any disease. *Ionized Water* provides all these qualities and much more. It *alkalizes, hydrates* and *detoxifies* the body more effectively than any other substance. No other water can bring about these results. Running normal tap water through a water ionizer creates a miracle that can help put your body into a position of health you never imagined you could achieve.

Ionized Water is not only the best water we can drink, it is the best substance we can possibly put in our body. Consumption of *Ionized Water* is critical if we wish to bring the body into balance, a state known as *homeostasis*. Fresh and strong is the best way to drink *Ionized Water* once you've become acclimated to it. How long that will take depends on your overall health and toxicity.

Ionized Water is negatively charged and alive with electrons, which our bodies are starved for. Along with its alkalizing and hydrating properties, *Ionized Water* is a liquid antioxidant, which is why it can be considered the best substance we can put in the body. I have become biologically younger by drinking it and you will too.

Water cures, but purified water is a detriment to the health of anyone who consumes it. Purified water is produced by *deionization, distillation* or *reverse osmosis* and should not be consumed for three reasons. It acidifies, leaches minerals from the body and its large size and shape of its water molecule clusters do not hydrate the body well. In fact, long-term use of purified water can leave us dehydrated.

Ionized Water and purified water are exactly the opposite from each other in every regard:

Purified water is acidic; *Ionized Water* is alkaline.

Purified water does not effectively hydrate the body; *Ionized Water* is extremely hydrating.

Purified water leaches minerals from the body; *Ionized Water* provides minerals to the body.[1]

Purified water does not provide the body with oxygen; *Ionized Water* provides the body with oxygen.

Purified water does not scavenge for free radicals; *Ionized Water* does scavenge for free radicals.

Purified water encourages oxidation of the body; *Ionized Water* reduces oxidation.

Purified water has a positive ORP, which is an oxidant. *Ionized Water* has a negative ORP, which is an antioxidant.

The Miracle of Ionized Water

Alkaline Ionized Water is by far the most superior drinking water available. The invention of the water ionizer is one of the great health breakthroughs of the 20th Century. *Ionized Water* is electronically enhanced water created through electrolysis. It is produced by running normal tap water over positive (cathode) and negative (anode) electrodes, which ionizes the minerals in the water creating positive (hydrogen) and negative (hydroxyl) ions. The electrodes are composed of titanium, the hardest metal known, and coated with platinum, which is an excellent and durable conductor.

The magic comes when a membrane separates the hydrogen and hydroxyl ions, creating alkaline and acidic water. These two waters are always produced simultaneously during the ionizing process, 70% *Alkaline Ionized Water* and 30% *Acid Ionized Water*. Therefore, producing one gallon of Ionized Water yields approximately 0.7 gallons of Alkaline Water and 0.3 gallons of Acid Water.

To *Ionize* means to gain or lose an electron. Essentially, the ionization process robs an electron from one molecule and donates, or transfers, it to another molecule. The other water produced during the ionization process contains molecules that have been robbed of an electron. These molecules are known as hydrogen ions (H+) and they are what make the water acidic, resulting in a low pH.

These waters produced by ionization are the exact opposite from one another. Both *Alkaline* and *Acid Ionized Water* have extraordinary properties and benefits, although their respective uses could not be more different. We consume the *Alkaline Ionized Water*. The *Acid Ionized Water* should never be consumed. *Ionized Water* has a beneficial effect on everything it comes in contact with as long as it is used properly. *Ionized Water* is one of the most significant preventative health advances of our generation because it is the most beneficial substance available to the human body.

Alkaline Ionized Water is an Antioxidant that provides the body with an abundance of oxygen, which gives us energy. It possesses a negative charge, or ORP, which is also an antioxidant. It balances the body's pH, which helps prevent disease because it is Alkaline. It is a Powerful Detoxifier and Superior Hydrator because of its small water molecule cluster size.

Antioxidant Qualities

The centerpiece of *Ionized Water* are its antioxidant properties. It is truly miraculous that normal tap water can be instantly transformed into a strong antioxidant. *Ionized Water* has two antioxidant qualities, its negative charge and the presence of hydroxyl ions. Water has a low atomic weight and when ionized it becomes the most absorbable antioxidant known. The lighter an object the more easily it can be absorbed by the body. Other antioxidants have a much higher molecular weight, which make them less easily absorbed by the body.

All liquids have an Oxidation Reduction Potential (ORP), which is the millivoltage (mV), or vibration, it possesses. A negative ORP can reduce, or negate, oxidation. Strong *Alkaline Ionized Water* has an ORP of -50 mV to -450 mV, depending on the source water and how many minerals it contains. The more minerals in the source water, the stronger the *Ionized Water* will be. This low negative number means that the water has a very high potential for reducing oxidation. A beverage that has an ORP of -350 mV is healthier to consume than -150 mV because it negates oxidation of the body more effectively. Therefore, the lower the ORP of the water, the greater potential it has to reverse the aging process of the body at a cellular level.

All fresh squeezed vegetables and fruit juices and vegetables have a negative ORP, some lower than others. However, the word can not be stressed enough. Therefore, they are considered antioxidants because they reduce the potential for oxidation in the body. Conversely, if these juices are heated above 118° F, pasteurized or otherwise processed, the negative ORP antioxidant property is destroyed. In fact, all its rejuvenation properties have been removed and now the food has been transformed into mere sustenance that provides the body with calories, almost no nutrition and helps to acidify it. Enzymes must be present in a food for it to truly be considered a rejuvenating substance. This same principle is true for *Ionized Water*. If it is heated, it will quickly lose its negative charge because the fragile, fleeting electrons will dissipate. Electrons are thousands of times lighter than protons, thus they are more easily dispersed and scattered than protons. However, *Ionized Water's* other properties such as alkalinity and reduced water molecule cluster size remain intact to some degree for a longer period of time.

As a substance oxidizes, its ORP rises. Oxidation means to react with oxygen. Rust is metal that has been oxidized, which is an example of slow oxidization. Fire is an example of fast oxidation. In the human body, oxidation is caused, in part, by free radical damage. Unstable oxygen molecules rob us of electrons, which causes oxidation, leading to accelerated aging and disease. *"One can thrive on half the normal intake of food as long as we consume high electron-rich nutrients."*[2] Any time we put a substance in the body that has a positive charge, we increase the oxidation of the body and therefore accelerate the aging process. As we age, our body's ORP continually rises. The pace at which our body oxidizes is directly related to our diet and the other substances we put in it. Our immediate environment also contributes to the oxidation of the body. Genetics does not determine the rate of oxidation of the body.

Alkaline Ionized Water has a negative ORP, therefore it offsets the positive ORP of our oxidizing, aging body. Thus, we counteract the aging process by consuming negatively charged substances that dampen the positive ORP of our oxidizing body. Realistically, we need to drink at least 1 to 2 gallons of strong *Alkaline Ionized Water* each day if we expect significant slowing and reversal of the biological aging process, which is determined by the health of our cells. Human health equals cellular health. If our body's cells are healthy we be will healthy. If they are not healthy, we cannot be healthy.

Consuming fresh *Ionized Water* puts a mild electrical charge into the body the same way that raw fruits and vegetables do, which is why we feel energized after eating them. Living foods have this charge because they are full of enzymes, electrons and electrical activity, which is facilitated by the mineral content of the plants the same way it is for us. Living foods are bio-photonic, meaning they are created by sunlight (photons) and they are alive with enzymatic activity. Living foods are essentially concentrated sunlight. Thus they are bio-electrical, alive with electrical activity. We are also bio-electrical, meaning that electricity conducts through the body when there are sufficient amounts and varieties of minerals present for electricity to flow. If these minerals are absent from the body it will not function properly. In the total absence of these minerals, the body and its organs will cease to function and we will die. Minerals are critical to all life.

Strong, fresh *Ionized Water* charges the body because it contains large amounts of electrons that encourage electrical activity in the body. *"The more alive something is, the more it is moving from the dense matter of nucleons and protons to the world of light and electrons."*[3] The foods and water that we consume should contain substances that promote electrical activity within us. They provide us with energy and charge the body's internal battery. *Ionized Water* also has a negative charge, or Oxidation Reduction Potential (ORP), that promotes electrical activity in the body. When the body is charged and has sufficient amounts of electrical activity we feel energetic. The brain cannot operate without electrical activity. Every thought we have produces a miniature electrical storm in various areas of the brain, depending on what the thought is. As we stimulate electrical activity in the brain by consuming substances that encourage electrical activity, we are able to think more clearly. It is this constant recharging of the body through living foods and *Ionized*

Water that helps keep us young, active and disease-free.

ORP is the single most important term we need to become familiar with if we want to understand human health. A person's ORP level, although quite difficult to determine reliably, would instantly reveal whether they are in a state of health or disease. ORP is another way to measure the body's vibration. Everything in the universe vibrates. When we are healthy we vibrate within a certain frequency range. If we are sick, we will vibrate at a completely different frequency range, one that reflects our state of unhealthiness or disease.

ORP is a measurement of a substance's ability to either diminish or encourage the oxidation of another substance. When we consume living foods, they diminish the oxidation of our bodies. Thus, living foods rejuvenate us. Living foods are also negatively charged. Cooking living foods oxidizes them, thus raising their ORP. When we consume cooked foods, we add to the oxidation of our bodies and accelerate the aging process. It encourages disease by acidifying the body. Cooked foods burn us up internally by stimulating oxidation since they themselves have already been oxidized with a positive ORP of +400 mV or higher. Animal protein, fried foods, soft drinks and other highly processed foods possess the highest ORP and therefore the greatest amount of hydrogen (positive) ions. A high ORP is an *environment* where disease thrives because it is also a high acid (low pH) *environment*. To reduce this oxidation, this slow-burning fire within us, we must consume substances that possess a negative charge such as *Ionized Water* and raw fruits and vegetables. When we do, the consuming fire of high ORP is extinguished and an alkaline environment is created in the body.

The principals of ORP are the same for *Ionized Water*. The positive ORP of *Acid Ionized Water* increases oxidation because it contains hydrogen ions (missing electrons), which is the *environment* of all disease. The negative charge of *Alkaline Ionized Water* reduces oxidation because it contains hydroxyl ions (extra electrons), which is an *environment* that leads to health.

Consuming *Ionized Water* bathes the interior of the body in a negatively charged liquid, which promotes rejuvenation of each bodily system at a cellular level. For instance, a liver cell is better able to repair itself in a negative ion, alkaline environment than a positive ion, acid environment. When we consume negatively charged substances such as *Ionized Water* this oxidation is retarded and our body's cells are in a better position to repair and rejuvenate themselves. Nothing is better for the body.

A fresh glass of strong *Alkaline Ionized Water* right out of the tap will contain a cloud of tiny bubbles in the water. These are hydroxyl ions, *Ionized Water's* other antioxidant component. The best way to drink *Ionized Water* is as fresh as possible. Drinking cloudy *Ionized Water* with its abundance of electrons is one of the healthiest things we can do.

Some antioxidants possess an extra electron. Others, such as carotenoids, which are natural pigments from foods, retard and reverse aging through chemical processes. *Ionized Water* is an extremely effective antioxidant because it is a liquid with small water molecule clusters, and it is more easily absorbed into the body where it can be of immediate use.

Antioxidants have anti-aging and anti-disease properties because they help return the body's cells to a youthful, healthier, more natural state. As we make *Ionized Water* a part of our daily routine and drink sufficient quantities of it, we begin to bathe the body's cells in alkalinity and antioxidants, as well as hydrating them better than they have ever been. Nothing could be more fundamentally healthier for us.

Free radicals are another example of the environment that encourages disease in our body by causing cellular mutations and other types of cellular damage. Free radical cellular damage is a big part of the aging equation, but it can also be reversed with proper diet and the consistent use of *Ionized Water*.

Free radicals are commonly created from: prescription and street drugs; chemicals (pesticides, herbicides, insecticides, etc.); processed and irradiated foods; food additives and preservatives; heavy metal poisoning; artificial food colorings; polyunsaturated oil, mainly vegetable oils, and rancid oils; trans-fats (partially hydrogenated fats); chlorinated unfiltered tap water; tobacco use; excessive, prolonged stress; cooked foods of all kinds, especially fried foods.

Essentially all disease appears and develops in the body from our diet. Science can determine which genes have been damaged or otherwise altered in an individual, but it has only theories as to why and how the defect actually occurred. Environmental diseases may come from sources such as artificial chemical toxins, heavy metals, radiation, naturally occurring toxic substances, or insect-borne diseases, but these can all be battled and often overcome by the right diet, *Ionized Water*, probiotics, exercise and use of a Far Infrared (FIR) sauna.

The scientific and medical communities are desperately trying to find a genetic link to every disease, including cancer. It is an effort to establish that disease is born in genetic anomalies and flaws, thus curing these diseases lies in the engineering and reconstruction of these flawed genes. These efforts manifest themselves in medications and artificial therapies of every kind. All these efforts are enabling devices designed to allow us to keep eating foods that we love and are accustomed to, but unfortunately lead to nearly all disease. The path to health does not lie in these artificial protocols and procedures, nor will it ever. True health is found only in nature where the reflection of God is also found because it is His creation.

Drinking *Ionized Water* gives you energy. On the surface, it seems like an impossible claim that drinking water could possibly give you energy. Once the hydroxyl ions in *Ionized Water* are donated to free radicals what remains are stable oxygen molecules, which provide the body with more dissolved oxygen. If your blood oxygen level is low, check it before you first start drinking *Ionized Water* and then again a few weeks after you have been drinking it regularly and see the difference for yourself.

Alkalizes and Balances Body pH

The world's written history was recorded on alkaline paper until 1850 when it began to be recorded on paper that used bleach, alum and tannin in the book-binding, all of which are acid. Those original written documents from 1850 forward are disintegrating at an alarming rate. The best that can be done is to scan them electronically and save what is left of the books by realkalizing the remaining paper. However, books printed on alkaline paper before 1850 still survive, often in perfect condition. Acid destroys; a balanced, slightly alkaline pH preserves. Acid destroys life, alkalinity restores and sustains it.

We look everywhere for health when it is never any further than what we put in our body. Alkaline substances belong in the body, not acid ones. *All disease thrives in an acid environment and will not thrive in an alkaline environment.*

If we create an acidic environment in our body by years of consuming cooked foods and other acidic substances such as drugs, alcohol, cigarettes, soft drinks, processed sugar, etc., then we become vulnerable to any disease that invades the body, regardless of its source. The more acidic a person is, the more susceptible they are to disease. This acid environment does not cause disease, but rather creates an environment that disease thrives in. As disease flourishes in the body, it creates a more acidic environment in order to spread further until it consumes the body. Disease is essentially another mechanism that nature uses to recycle something that is no longer a part of itself. Yeast, fungus and mold found in the body are also recycling agents used by nature to dispose of that which no longer belongs to itself. Even if we do have genetic propensities toward certain disease, those diseases can be prevented and overcome by proper diet and hydration of the body. The only instances we find of animals in the wild with chronic disease are those that have been over-exposed to synthetic toxins in polluted areas.

One of the keys to great health and honoring our temple is keeping body pH properly balanced and alkaline. Drinking plenty of *Ionized Water* will help achieve that.

Nearly everything the average person consumes, including cooked and processed foods, acidifies the body tremendously. Nearly all recreational beverages are acidic, including coffee, black tea, commercial juices, sports and energy drinks, milk, soft drinks and alcohol. Stress adds tremendous amounts of acidity to the body, as does pollution. Industrialization has toxified and acidified our environment since its inception. Given the amount of acidity that is added to the average person on a daily basis, it would be extremely difficult for anyone to over-alkalize their body.

I have consumed 1.5 – 2.0 gallons of *Ionized Water* every day for 12 years at a pH 9.5 or higher. I live on a 99% living-food diet, which is alkalizing, and my body pH is always balanced at close to 7.0. I have never measured my body pH and found it to be too alkaline. Over-alkalizing your body will not occur if your approach to health is completely natural. Nature always puts the body into balance when its laws are followed and at the core of homeostasis is a neutral pH. If we wish to determine a person's overall health, the first measurement should be taken is their body pH.

Powerful Detoxifier and Superior Hydrator

Ionized Water is sometimes called *Cluster Water, Microwater* or *Microcluster Water* because of its small molecular grouping. Water molecules typically group in clusters of 10 and can even chain hundreds of molecules together. *Ionized Water* molecule clusters are grouped into six water molecules, thus they are *reduced* in size from conventional water molecule clusters. The *Ionized Water* molecule cluster has changed from an irregular, clumpy shape to a hexagonal shape that penetrates and saturates body tissue much more efficiently than conventional water.

Water ionizers have more than one level of ionization strength, which is important to some people when they first start drinking it. The strong detoxification aspects of *Ionized Water* require that people with accumulated toxins in their body and tissues begin drinking it at a mild ionization level (pH 8.0), then slowly increase the strength of the *Ionized Water* over the following days and weeks until they acclimate to it. When first using *Ionized Water*, headaches, rashes, diarrhea and fatigue are common detoxification symptoms for people who have accumulated toxins throughout their body from poor lifestyle choices such as diet and social habits. These different levels of ionization strength allow people to slowly ease into *Ionized Water* when they first start drinking it in order to mollify these powerful detoxification effects that can be drastic for those who are quite toxic. The micro-cluster structure and penetrating aspects of *Ionized Water* leave less room for anything that does not belong in bodily tissue. Thus toxins are effectively pushed out of the tissue and into the bloodstream to then be eliminated by the body.

The sight of a glass of *Ionized Water* with small bubbles in it is appears innocuous in regard to detoxification. In fact, it is a powerhouse when it comes to getting rid of what is not wanted in the body. A toxin is simply something that does not belong in the body. There are mild toxins and quite dangerous toxins such as heavy metals, asbestos or industrial chemical residue. The average person can begin drinking *Ionized Water* without having a serious *healing crisis*, which is a term sometimes applied to a strong and immediate detoxification that is usually an unpleasant, if not painful, experience. Those most at risk are people who have taken a lot of street drugs, prescription medications or those whose diets consist primarily of processed, fried, junk or fast foods. Also at risk of a strong detoxification are those who have been exposed to environmental toxins such as heavy metals, herbicides and/or pesticides, which are more common than many of us realize.

Ionized Water is deceptively powerful because water is not conventionally thought of as a powerful detoxifier. The body removes toxins that have accumulated in it through the lungs, the kidneys, the bowels and the skin. *Ionized Water* mainly removes toxins from the body through the kidneys and bowels, but also through the skin, which is why drinking it gives you a short term rash, albeit a necessary one. All detoxification symptoms, pleasant or unpleasant, are necessary evils that we must go through. Removing poisons from body after a long time of them being housed there can be a very difficult experience, but in the long run a very healthy one.

As long as we don't consume too much in a short period of time or around mealtime, we cannot drink too much *Ionized Water* once our body has acclimated to it. The more toxins a person has accumulated in their flesh, tissue and cells, the weaker the *Ionized Water* should be when they first start drinking it so any unpleasant detoxification effects are kept to a minimum. If the detoxification symptoms become too strong, reduce the strength of the *Ionized Water* and drink less of it. If a person maintains a relatively good diet, drinks a lot of water, doesn't smoke, drink alcohol heavily, take drugs or medication, they can usually start drinking *Ionized Water* at the highest level (pH 9.5 – 9.9).

Regarding children, the vast majority of them have no trouble drinking *Ionized Water* on the strongest level when they first start because they are too young to have accumulated many toxins in their flesh. Their young, resilient bodies are also able to quickly adjust to the healthy environment that *Ionized Water* creates.

The opposite is true regarding the elderly, who have a lifetime of toxins and heavy metals accumulated in their bodies and are often on medications that also need to be detoxified from their tissue. Children on strong medications or a junk food diet may also suffer these powerful detoxification effects as well.

A balanced state of health is that in which the body thrives and is most apt to operate to its capacity. However, if you change the body's environment through poor diet, meaning foods that have been oxidized by processing or cooking, a buildup of hydrogen ions results. The consequence of this is an acidic state and a low pH. To be healthy again, you need only change the environment of your body by adding alkaline substances that have an abundance of electrons such as *Ionized Water* and raw fruits and vegetables.

Ionized Water reflects the characteristics of living
foods in several ways:
- *Ionized Water* has an abundance of electrons, as do living foods.
- *Ionized Water* has a negative charge, or ORP, as do living foods.
- *Ionized Water* possesses negative ions, as do living foods.
- *Ionized Water* is alkaline, as are living foods.
- *Ionized Water* is hydrating, as are living foods.
- *Ionized Water* is detoxifying, as are living foods.
- *Ionized Water* provides the body with ionic (organic) minerals, as do living foods.

Cooked foods have a deficit of electrons, a positive ORP and an abundance of positive ions. They are dry and dehydrating. They also acidify and add toxins to the body. All these qualities lead to disease and therefore are the exact opposite of what we should put in the body.

Ionized Water mimics many of the same attributes in nature that bring us health. Only nature can bring us true health. Vitamin supplements attempt to mimic nature although with dismal results. Medicine attempts to overcome the natural mechanisms of the body, in an attempt to control, alter or outsmart it. Pharmaceuticals only mask symptoms of disease. They endeavor to manage the crisis that is brought about by disease infiltrating and attacking the body. Symptoms are messengers to us that are the result of the disease. If we interpret them correctly, we will begin to understand what we must do to rid the body of that disease. We take drugs that attempt only to send these messengers away. We should embrace them, not cover them up, for they are trying to speak to us. No drug has yet been invented that cures the body of any disease, nor will one ever be. Pharmaceuticals never lead to health, but only allow people to hobble along a little further as they become sicker until the quality of their lives diminish to a point where the option of death is more appealing than continuing to live with such agony. Disease is a symptom that an imbalance in the body exists. True health is only found in nature because it is God's creation. *Ionized Water* mimics and magnifies the qualities of nature better than any substance known.

How Long Ionized Water Lasts

Alkaline Ionized Water

- **Hydroxyl Ions**: 10 – 20 minutes
  (A small number will remain up to 24 hours)
- **Negative ORP** (mV charge): 18 – 24 hours
- **Alkalinity** (high pH): 3 – 20 days
- **Smaller molecule clusters**: 4 – 18 months

Acid Ionized Water
- Up to 150 days if stored in a cool, dark place, unopened. Exposing Acid *Ionized Water* to the air.
- **Hydrogen Ions**: 30 – 90 minutes
  (A small number will remain up to 24 hours)
- **High Positive ORP** (mV charge): 48 – 96 hours
- **Acidity** (low pH): 7 – 14 days
- **Smaller molecule clusters**: 8 – 24 months

Why Christians Should Fast

"After fasting forty days and forty nights, he was hungry" (Matthew 4:2 NIV).

Fasting is mentioned 38 times in the Bible in 19 different books.[4] Fasting is absolutely the *best* thing you can do for your health at any given time. When you stop eating, you return your body to the healing hands of God, if only for a short period of time. If you are sick, fasting is the quickest way back to health, a shortcut that allows the body to focus on one thing: not digesting food or taking in nutrients, but that of healing itself. Digestion requires a lot of energy from the body. *"Fasting is the great remedy. The physician within!"*[5] The best fast you can do is a water fast and the best water for fasting is *Ionized Water.*

Fasting gives the body a chance to rest, cleanse and repair itself. Matthew records in his Gospel that Jesus fasted. In fact, one of Jesus' fasts lasted 40 days. Fasting is mentioned in the Bible numerous times in both the Old and New Testaments.

You can fast for any length of time over six hours, which would be considered a mini-fast. Fasting one day a month is a great habit to develop. I fast for 24 hours quite often by eating a meal in the evening and then not eating again until the same time the following day. The habit of eating one large meal a day, usually in the late afternoon or early evening, was commonly practiced by ancient warriors, including the Romans, especially before a battle. Fighting on an empty stomach was easier, in part because the body is not burdened with the energy demands of digestion.

The word breakfast means to *break a fast*. Instead of eating something for breakfast, I continue my fast for as long as possible by drinking only water in the morning and often into the early hours of the afternoon. Therefore, I fast for at least 14 hours each day.

Fasting cleanses the body as well as the brain. Clear-minded thinking occurs when the stomach is clear; clouded thinking occurs when the stomach is full.

There are many types of fasting and many ways to fast. For instance, one can fast with *Spirulina* and *Chlorella*, which is extremely cleansing and energizing. I fasted on *Spirulina* and *Chlorella* for 10 days and never had so much energy in my life. A raw juice fast will produce similar results, but is not as intense or cleansing. There are green-vegetable fasts and citrus-juice fasts, but these are not true fasts because we are still putting food into the body. The only *true fast* is a *water fast*.

What you fast on will determine how quickly you expel toxins from your body. For instance, a juice fast will remove 2 – 20 days of accumulated toxins in a day, whereas an *Ionized Water* fast will remove up to 100 days of accumulated toxins in a single day.

If you experience severe headaches, rashes, cramps, stomach or joint pain, dizziness, body aches or nausea, then you are detoxifying too quickly and you need to slow down. The rewards of fasting are many, but it can be a rigorous and painful experience for those who are quite toxic. If you don't feel good while fasting or the pain becomes too intense, then eat something mild such as soup or potatoes and the pain will subside. You will know best when it is time to pull back on the reins.

Detoxification stops immediately when we eat cooked foods of any kind. Cooked foods contain toxins that further poison the body. By eating cooked foods the body has no choice but to stop ridding itself of substances that do not belong in it because more are being added to it.

If you don't feel that you can go it alone, there are clinics and fasting retreat centers that will help you get through a fast. Some people recommend that fasts be supervised in order to make it easier for the person fasting to go through it because of the reassurance and support it can offer. Pain is easier when the sufferer has a hand to hold and shoulder to brace themselves on.

If you decide to fast, try to get some support from those around you. Ask them not to encourage you to eat something even though you may be hungry. After fasting for a couple days your hunger will disappear, although you will still miss the habit of simply putting something in your mouth. Without a doubt, fasting is the best way to jumpstart your health. The advice I have for anyone who is sick, regardless of the disease, is to fast. Fasting cleanses our temple faster than anything else we can do for it.

Acid Ionized Water (External Use Only)

When *Acid Ionized Water* is freshly produced, the small bubbles found in the water are free radicals, which is why *Acid Ionized Water* should never be consumed. *Acid Ionized Water* is also an oxidant because it has a high positive charge or ORP (+700 to 800 mV), which is detrimental to our health. We must avoid substances that encourage oxidation such as cooked foods and *Acid Ionized Water*. As with *Alkaline Ionized Water*, the water temperature and flow rate through the water ionizer are components that will also determine its strength.

We have a symbiotic relationship with trees and plants of every kind. We breathe in the oxygen that they exhale while they breathe in the carbon dioxide that we exhale. A plant's growth and health are significantly enhanced with the regular use of *Acid Ionized Water* and these benefits are unmistakable.

I left my prized hang-basket potted herb garden in the July sun too long one day and forgot to water it. When I found it, the soil was bone dry and every plant was wilted beyond recognition. The desiccated greenish leaves hung over the sides like spaghetti. I could see it was gone. It was easily in the upper 90's and the basket had been out all day a drop of water in two days. I took inside, saturated the leaves, roots and soil with *Acid Ionized Water*, and placed it in the shade. I thought it would help, but I thought it was too late to revive it. However, within 3 hours of watering it with Acid *Ionized Water* it was completely rejuvenated as though nothing had ever happened to it. Something that we thought was on its way to the grave had indeed been resurrected.

If strong enough, *Acid Ionized Water* can kill bacteria on contact. This would require a pH of 6.0 or lower. How effective it is as a disinfectant depends on the strength of the *Ionized Water*, meaning how high the ORP (mV) and how low the pH is. Mild *Acid Ionized Water* produced from tap water using a home water ionizer typically has a range of 700 – 950 mV (pH 4.0 – 5.8), which is quite effective at killing surface bacteria and retarding its growth. It is the high charge, or ORP, in the water is the major factor in killing bacteria followed by an extremely low pH environment.

Acid Ionized Water has a wonderful conditioning effect on the skin and hair because they both are somewhat acidic. Acidic skin is the body's first line of defense against bacteria. Human skin typically has a pH of 5.4 in order to ward off bacteria and infection, and hair typically has a pH of 5.6, although these can vary slightly between individuals.

Applying *Acid Ionized Water* regularly to the skin works as an astringent to tighten it and help remove wrinkles, leaving no chemical residue as other astringents do. The only residue on the skin is water, which of course is harmless. *Acid Ionized Water* soothes and helps keep the skin clear of acne and other blemishes. Skin and hair, even animal fur, respond positively to the conditioning effects of *Acid Ionized Water*. The more *Acid Ionized Water* that is applied on the skin and hair, the better they respond to it and there is no limit to the number of applications one can have each day. *Ionized Water* does have a slight drying effect on the skin, which is why you may want to apply a moisturizer such as shea butter.

Combined with drinking *Ionized Water*, which alkalizes the body internally, skin conditions of every kind such as shingles are dramatically improved. However, this can be short-lived if the root of the problem is not addressed by a fundamental change in diet. For instance, a condition such as psoriasis arises from a poor diet of junk foods and excessive animal protein. Chronic skin problems are a result of toxins making their way to the skin on their way out of the body. People with chronic skin conditions go through life using ointments and creams that allay the symptoms of their disease without ever treating its cause. If the diet is not changed to include more alkaline foods, *Acid Ionized Water* will at best only temporarily relieve skin conditions such as *psoriasis*. In fact, in the case of psoriasis, *Ionized Water* can appear to worsen the condition.

Rashes, cuts, scrapes, even serious wounds, as well as Athlete's Foot and other fungus are dramatically improved with the application of *Acid Ionized Water*. It takes the itch out of mosquito bites and alleviates the pain of stings and other insect bites. It provides relief from poison oak and poison ivy exposure. It is especially effective if the affected area is allowed to soak in *Acid Ionized Water* for 20 – 30 minutes. Excessively dry skin is best treated by soaking it in *Acid Ionized Water*. This is also true of the deep cuts near the fingernail that people experience in extremely cold, dry weather, which will heal in a few days after soaking them in *Acid Ionized Water* for 20 – 30 minutes. I would also recommend a natural moisturizer such as shea butter.

Scalp problems such as dandruff are improved with the consistent use of *Acid Ionized Water*. Eating a proper diet comprised of *Spirulina, Chlorella,* raw fruits and vegetables, as well as drinking *Alkaline Ionized Water,* can entirely eliminate many of these health problems. Health problems are an indication that key nutrients in the diet are missing and that your temple is not properly hydrated. Restoration of the body, our temple, occurs when the health protocols of this book are followed.

Acid Ionized Water has been used successfully in treating diabetic skin ulcers, wounds that open up on the skin, particularly the extremities, due to poor circulation. Drinking *Alkaline Ionized Water* is a great benefit to diabetics because it helps bring the body into pH balance and provides it with lots of oxygen, which increases circulation. Once again, changing the environment of the body with negatively charged hydroxyl ions and electrons helps bring it into a position where it can defend and heal itself.

Acid Ionized Water can be applied to an incredible array of practical and effective applications from skin care and treatment to enhanced plant cultivation. It also has great potential for use in the agriculture and industry. *Acid Ionized Water* is an inexpensive, environmentally neutral technology that will one day become as common as chemical applications are today.

Endnotes

1 "Effects of alkaline Ionized Water on formation & maintenance of osseous tissues," by Rei Takahashi Zhenhua Zhang Yoshinori Itokawa. Study at the Kyoto University Graduate School of Medicine, Dept. of Pathology and Tumor Biology, Fukui Prefectural University)

2 Secrets of an Alkaline Body. The New Science of Colloidal Biology, by Annie Padden Jubb and David Jubb.

3 Ibid.

4 Judges 20:26; 1 Samuel 7:6; 1 Samuel 31:13; 2 Samuel 1:12; 1 Kings 21:9 – 16; 1 Kings 21:27; 1 Chronicles 10:12; 2 Chronicles 20:3; Ezra 8:21 – 23; Nehemiah 1:4; Nehemiah 9:1; Esther 4:3; Esther 4:16; Esther 9:31; Psalm 35:13; Psalm 69:10; Psalm 109:24; Isaiah 58:1 – 6; Jeremiah 14:12; Jeremiah 36:6 – 9; Daniel 9:3; Joel 1:14; Joel 2:12 – 15; Zechariah 7:1 – 5; Zechariah 8:19; Matthew 4:2; Matthew 6:16 – 18; Matthew 9:14; Mark 2:18 – 20; Luke 2:37; Luke 5:33 – 35; Luke 18:12; Acts 13:2 – 3; Acts 14:23; Acts 27:9

5 Paracelsus. Swiss born physician. (1493-1541)

www.watershed.net
bob@watershed.net
The Watershed Wellness Center
Lansing, MI

THE HEALING NATURE
OF ENZYMES

John Eagle Freedom

Of all the amazing discoveries of our modern day concerning health and nutrition, the discovery of enzymes—what they are, how they are vital to health, and how they can be administered like medicine to treat every conceivable disease, (even our modern diseases) is most thrilling!

We now know that we were born with over 4,000 different enzymes in every cell, and that for optimum health and longevity, these enzymes must be replaced regularly!

There has been a predominantly false concept about enzymes fostered by those who should know better leading us to believe that they are true catalysts—unchanged by the reactions occurring with substances—like Superman and brick walls! Instead, enzymes are affected by these reactions and are "used up" and must be replaced at all costs! Enzymes are life, because they are alive!

I can best describe human life as a tightly wound timepiece. The "spring" representing your enzymes is slowly winding down, and if nothing is acting to "wind-up" the spring, then when it reaches its final relaxed position, the clock stops—dies!

The ideal state we think we all desire is one of "no stress." A state of no stress is unrealistic! Life is supposed to consist of "good stress"! But, it's excessive stress that wears us down, spends too many enzymes, and when nothing is "put back in the bank"—the result is an early passing somewhere between 70-90! Did I shock you? "Don't you mean to say, 40-70?" you ask. No, I mean we've got to accept the fact that our ideas of "normal lifespan" and our true potential longevity are very different ideals! "But how can stress be good for me?" you wonder. Think of the good produced when the body, or mind, or whatever valuable is given a challenge—like in resistance weight training: If the muscles encounter no resistance, they will not expand, grow, or become strong; but when confronted with progressively heavier loads, your muscles will "adapt" to the new challenges and will "stretch" to accommodate them! God has designed for each of us circumstantial, unpleasant situations that we might experience ever increasing strength training—morally, spiritually, mentally, financially, socially, and physically! Without challenges and situations to "stretch" us, we would never grow, and know the joy that can only come through overcoming them; life would be one big stagnant boring experience!

What are enzymes?

Enzymes are the catalysts all life depends upon! They are biological, not necessarily chemical catalysts. This means that there is a precious "life force" mysteriously at work in all biological enzymes which are responsible for all the operations our physical lives depend upon! Our bodies require biological substances for every cell to provide all its necessary functions. The cells must have an increasingly complex amount of raw materials to maintain life, generate energy, "know when" to reproduce—even to die—to name just a few of the operations performed by "living" enzymes.

All functions from interpreting data from the nerves and sensory organs, to thinking require enzymes. For enzymes to function, they must be kept in an ideal temperature, and alive! Again, the amazing thing to realize is that normal body temperature, is the ideal temperature for these enzymatic reactions to occur!

Enzymes make reactions happen and happen faster. At normal body temperature, enzymes make all processes happen in our cells faster—and consequently are used up faster.

The Body is such an amazing machine that, even when it doesn't have "all the parts," has ingenious ways of using energy to "manufacture" missing materials, and/or "stealing" them from places in your body that have an abundance—like your bones!

Your body knows, through its enzymes, what has to happen to preserve your life, and it will stop at nothing to protect its vital interests such as your heart and lungs! To insure your vital organs will continue having all the materials they need, muscle tissue will be cannibalized after all the fat cells, or a good many of them have already been burned up to provide the energy needed. This is totally unnecessary and detrimental to good health! Because so much enzymatic activity is concentrated on food digestion, how we supply these enzymes for proper digestion should be priority number one for every human being on this planet!

Actually, Our Creator has already provided the food we need with these necessary enzymes, and it is up to us to preserve them for our own digestion, or else we will weaken our store of enzymes by calling out those vital enzymes for other purposes and converting them into digestive enzymes that are already plentiful in natural, uncooked fruits, vegetables and grains! These digestive enzymes are: Proteases, for digesting proteins; Amylases, for digesting carbohydrates; and Lipases, for digesting fats and they are inserted by our Creator into these true foods to be our agents for digestion serving us—the consumer.

When we consume cooked fruits, vegetables, and grains; it is like a child on his birthday discarding his "Jr. Police Officer Set," and playing with the pretty box! It may appear to be fun, but the box will wear quickly! Wouldn't it be a better investment for the child to play with his new policeman's toy gear so he may get a feel for serving his community as a policeman when he grows up?

What intelligence is behind these humble agents, (called enzymes) for all human, and animal physical life processes? How do they "know" the perfect time to "fire up" hormones, shut down inflammation, nourish the cells, remove wastes, produce the functions each cell is specialized to do, reproduce and die?—to only mention a few of the thousands of processes enzymes are responsible! Thanks to the humble enzymes we know about and the ones we haven't discovered yet, the only way to explain them is, "There just has to be an all-wise, all-loving Creator God!"

How else can you explain that with lightning-fast speed, they can take nutrients and put them exactly where they need to be placed in cells like putting nitro in a top fuel dragster—they know exactly how to become a "telephone" for the cells to communicate with each other—they know how to "order the troops into service," supply them with ammunition, and plan battle strategies—they know how to protect their host by the "fight or flight" mechanism of firing up the adrenals and other glands—and also, keep the brain making decisions, reasoning, remembering, dreaming etc.?

Another way of thinking about enzymes is: they are the "unlimited hands" of the cell! Imagine how cool it would be if we had hands that could go to the grocery store and return while we're still at our work station and bring back the day's groceries never missing a beat! Or how about sending "housecleaning hands" to clean your home while you're in your "cubicle working for the company!" Now you know where the expression "hired hands" came from… Here's one more: you know those robot lawn-mowers? Your enzymes are like those little grass-munchers with artificial intelligence knowing just how to mow your back yard while you relax in your hammock sipping your lemonade. Sometimes the cells get to relax—and enzymes control the length of their breaks too!

Where are these amazing substances like miniature genies found? Unlike Aladdin's genie, these thankless, faceless, miracle-working, silent alchemists humbly go about their work never grumbling or complaining making everything about us "tick." It's time they receive the recognition and the honor they deserve, so I'm going to do everything within my power to put them on the pedestal where they rightly belong!

To be fair: It must be addressed that among the raw flesh-eating people groups such as Eskimos, they have clean arteries and no incidences of the degenerative diseases even though they eat a flesh, and fat diet! Why is that? Because in the raw flesh in every living animal is an enzyme—cathepsin. This unique enzyme effectively breaks down dead muscle tissue when the host animal dies and continues working inside the predator's body! Also, the Eskimos have a custom of setting the meat aside for several days allowing the cathepsin to predigest the meat for them before they eat it. When we boil, barbecue, oven roast, fry, microwave, etc., we kill cathepsin one of these "helping hands" forcing our finite store of enzymes allotted to other vital processes, to do the work of digesting! But they do such a poor job, never getting it done right, that the flesh gets stuck in our arteries! Amazingly, Eskimos are among the healthiest people groups still today living on raw whale blubber, raw fish, polar bear, seal…! Apparently, the diseases in raw flesh foods known in the temperate and tropical zones are unknown in the arctic, so God has provided meat for the Eskimo where no veggies or fruit trees can grow!

The only way to get enzymes is firsthand through consuming plants, or get them second-handed through raw meats! I am not advocating a raw flesh diet! Only, if you are an Eskimo where you have no plants, should you be on this diet!

When you boil out enzymes to produce a drink, stuff 14 teaspoons of refined sugar into it so it'll sit forever on a shelf, so that an unsuspecting person, months later will buy it to get a "sugar and caffeine high," you readily see how it should be classified as the drug it really is and should be forsaken with as much fortitude as any street drug!

And what about this excitotoxin we are familiar with—caffeine? Did you know the "rush" and sudden burst of energy is actually your body reacting to a poisoning experience? Your body is so amazing that the next time it encounters the same level of poisoning, it will have a "trained" response to get rid of it faster—that's why you have to ever increase your intake to get the same euphoric "high" you got the first time you drank one cup of coffee, tea, soda—or even that first cigarette, joint, injection, "fix" or pill! We quickly recognize the latter as poisons, but what about the former list? What is a poison? A poison is any substance that when put in the body is non-nutritious, thereby placing a demand on the body for immediate expulsion! God ingeniously designed our bodies to handle harmful substances entering into our bodies, but He never licensed us to consume known non-foods without eventually paying the price of "starvation" through malnourishment!"

The choice of what you put in your body is up to you, but always remember: there are more things important in life than what you put in your mouth; that's what Jesus said! We want you to live long and healthy so you will learn those other things so you can share them with the world in the years to come!

ENZYMES: THE FOUNDATION FOR WELLNESS

Viktoras Kulvinskas, MS

Adequate cellular nutrition is dependent on a combination of factors: dietary choices, method of food preparation, degree of thorough chewing, as well as the body's functional efficiency in digesting and assimilating food. Eating food-based enzymes is a key to helping your body maximize your genetic potential, even if you sometimes choose less-than optimal lifestyle habits. Using plant-based enzymes increases the availability of nutrients to the billions of cells that are your physical body. Your choosing to "dine with enzymes" can mean the difference between a life of mediocre or marginal health, and the experience of high-level wellness and abundant energy.

What are enzymes?

The word "enzyme" comes from the Greek word *enzymas*, which means "to ferment" or "cause a change." Enzymes are the foundation for all cell regeneration. They play a key role in the transformation of undigested food into the nutrients that are absorbed on the cellular level. With proper nutrition, we have the energy to participate in the dance of the living. An enzyme is a specialized protein structure that carries with it an energetic charge. Enzymes speed up chemical reactions that normally take place very slowly or not at all. It is the energy behind the protein structure that makes enzymes different from other protein-based substances. It is the energetic life principle, sometimes called *prana*, or ch'I, that animates all life forms. The father of modern enzyme therapy, Dr Edward Howell, once said that enzymes emit a "kind of radiation" that can be picked up on Kirlian photographs. Howell can be singled out from other researchers because he stressed that enzymes are not merely expendable, protein-based chemical catalysts that move along chemical reactions. He forcefully argued that enzymes are none other than units of life-energy that use various protein molecules as their carriers.

Enzymes are much more sensitive to destruction by heat or cold than vitamins and minerals. Food cooked over 118 degrees F for more than a half an hour will kill all naturally-occurring enzymes. In the event that dry heat is used, the critical temperature for enzyme destruction is about 150 f. Enzymes are the true workers in and out of our cells. As Dr. Richard Gerber MD states, "the enzymes catalyze specific reactions of chemicals either to create structure through molecular assemblies or to provide the electrochemical fire to run the cellular engines and ultimately keep the entire system working."

There are thousands of different enzymes, so many that one cannot separate enzyme activity with the process of life itself. From moving a muscle to blinking an eye, no biological work can be accomplished independent of enzymes. Without enzymes, the body would be nothing but inorganic matter.

Types of enzymes

Enzymes can be grouped into three main categories. The first category consists of the digestive enzymes, which the digestive system collects, manufactures and secretes to break down food. Examples of digestive enzymes are protease, which digests protein; amylase, which digests starch; and lipase, which digests fat. Each enzyme almost always has only one specific function that it carries out. For example, the enzyme protease only digests protein. The enzyme amylase only digests starches.

The second type of enzymes is composed of metabolic enzymes, which are present in every cell, tissue, and organ and act as biochemical catalysts in the second-to-second functioning of living cells. The metabolic antioxidant enzyme superoxide dismutase (SOD), which is present in all cells, reduces free radical damage, and thus retards the aging process. Raw foods, especially sprouts and algae, are rich in SOD.

The third class of enzymes is made up of various food enzymes, which come from raw, uncooked foods. The process of enzymatic digestion begins when you masticate your food in your mouth. When you chew, you not only mix the enzyme ptyalin from your salivary glands into the food, but allow the food-based enzymes present in the food to be released onto itself. This occurs from the moment that you rupture the cell walls of the food with your teeth.

Most fresh, well-grown produce has at least enough enzymes to digest the specific amount of protein, starch or fat found in the food itself. As a general rule, the higher the caloric content of an uncooked food, the more enzymes Nature will have put into the food to handle the exact amount of nutrients present. Nature is so considerate and thoughtful, don't you think? So, foods high in protein will have a high amount of protease or protein-digesting enzyme. Examples are blue-green algae and sunflower seeds. Foods such as whole oats have a high amount of amylase or starch-digesting enzymes. Foods such as avocados and nuts have naturally-occurring lipase or fat-digesting enzymes. Nature is so balanced—I wish I could balance my checkbook as easily.

One of the myths still held by many health food consumers is that eating a raw vegetable salad alongside an otherwise cooked meal is sufficient to digest the cooked food portion of the meal. The reality of the situation is that since here is a direct correlation between the number of calories in a food and the amount of enzymes present, low-calorie salads have relatively few enzymes to help out in digesting any other food you may be eating. Unless the salad is composed of sprouts (which are naturally high in enzymes because they are young plants), you cannot count on raw salads to be of much help in digesting other foods.

Enzyme Logic in dollars and sense

Let's play a little with the concept of enzymes by using our day-to-day experience of banking as a metaphor. Your body's enzymes can be likened to cash reserves in your own life-force bank account. Each time you eat enzyme-less food, you tax your system by making a withdrawal from this enzyme bank. Meal by meal you decrease your enzyme net worth, which can be equated with your life potential. Since at least half of all enzyme capital in the body is assigned to digesting foods, eating life-less cooked foods in effect puts a continual hold on 50% of your budget. Your individual budget limit is determined by your genetic inheritance.

If one's enzyme capital is frozen in this way, your ability to allocate funds to improve the quality of your life is then on hold to the tune of 50% of your net worth! You'll then have limited enzyme resources with which to make much-needed home improvements (cleansing and rebuilding organs and tissues) and protecting your enzyme life savings via a strong immune system. To complicate matters, your bills are coming due, and guess what, your account is low in funds! You're desperate, so you borrow (take stimulants such as coffee to keep going) because your credit rating (overall health) is bad, due to years and years of withdrawals. You now wish that you had made more enzyme deposits in your life-force bank account, so that you wouldn't be finding yourself in arrears, experiencing energy deficiencies. You get the point. Now that you know how health finances work, start investing in your future health by taking plant-based enzymes today, before life hands you a bill that you can't afford to pay! It could be the best investment, with a return of new youthful energy and freedom from some of the crises of middle age.

Enzymes throughout history

In the 1890s, the forerunners of the modern science of nutrition discovered building-block substances in food. They named these building-blocks *proteins*. At the turn of the 20th century, a new word was coined to refer to a class of food-based, bio-active, organically-bound chemical substances found to be essential for human health. These substances were called *vitamins*. And about a decade or so later, the importance of organic *minerals* in food was recognized to be equally essential to health.

More than 100 years after the birth of modern scientific nutrition, we find ourselves at an exciting juncture. A missing link in our understanding of the life-giving properties of food is being illuminated by the increasing acceptance of the critical role of food-based enzymes for health and longevity. I think that in the near future, the recognition of the impact of enzymes on health will have even more profound repercussions than many of the discoveries related to vitamins, minerals, and proteins have had.

We can begin a discussion of nutrition as it relates to enzymes by talking about our first food: milk. Numerous medical studies and current public health statistics confirm what our prehistoric ancestors knew, that infants who were breast-fed on human mother's milk had fewer health problems than those infants who were raised on pasteurized cow's milk. Aside from the self-evident fact that human mother's milk is ideally suited for human infants and cow's milk is ideally suited for calves, it is significant that the former is unheated and therefore enzyme-rich and the latter is heated and therefore enzyme-poor.

More than 20 years ago, I discovered Dr. Howell's long out-of-print first book gathering dust in the basement of a medical library where I was doing health research. Published in 1939, this limited edition book was entitled, *The Status of Food Enzymes in Digestion and Metabolism*. With much effort I traced its author, who was in his 80s, and found him affiliated with an enzyme manufacturing company he himself had founded in the 1930s. Dr. Howell graciously gave me permission to reprint and update the book under the new title, *Food Enzymes for Health and Longevity*. About a decade later, Howell's classic was again republished in a simplified and popularized version by Avery Press and renamed *Enzyme Nutrition*. With this last release, the long-ignored discoveries of Dr. Howell spread to many health practitioners and seekers of health around the world.

Dr Howell's food enzyme concept

Dr. Edward Howell was the first nutritional scientist to develop a larger experimental and theoretical body of work aimed at answering the complex and critically important question, "what are the connections between food or supplement-based enzyme intake, health, disease, and longevity?" Howell devoted his entire adult life to conducting numerous animal and human experiments in his attempt to strengthen the theory that food enzyme deficiencies promote disease and premature aging, whereas enzyme-rich diets promote good health and longevity. To this end, his book, *The Status of Food Enzymes in Digestion and Metabolism* cited more than 400 research papers, which in his day represented the cutting edge of science. Modern researchers have yet to comprehend fully the implications of that book. As Dr Howell once said, "To say that the body can easily digest and assimilate cooked foods may someday prove to be the most grievous oversight yet committed by science."

Dr. Howell theorized that on a largely cooked, low-enzyme diet, the digestive system borrows enzymes from the body's general metabolic enzyme pool to help digest enzyme-less cooked food. Howell emphasized that the consequences of this adaptive measure were great, in that diverting enzymes from one system to another eventually weakened the functioning of these other systems and the body in general. For example, he argued that the immune system was compromised due to gradual enzyme deficiency and that this set the stage for numerous health problems such as allergies, cancer, and diabetes. If he were alive today, Howell would undoubtedly include AIDS on this list.

In treating his patients, Dr. Howell initially prescribed raw food diets but soon found this to be impractical because many patients lacked the willpower required to stay on such a regime. By 1932, however, he had already developed a plant-based enzyme supplement designed to replace the enzymes lost in a typical cooked food diet.

Dr Howell discovered that enzyme supplements from plant sources were uniquely effective. The following are just a few of some of Howell's basic concepts.

Food enzymes are essential nutrients.

Being more fragile to the effects of heat than vitamins and minerals, food enzymes are destroyed by the high temperature of cooking.

When food is chewed and swallowed in its raw natural state, enzymes immediately go to work in the upper cardiac portion of the stomach.

Eating a low-enzyme, cooked food diet increases the size of the pancreas, a sign that this organ is being overworked. He further hypothesized that this condition is a precursor to various forms of dysfunction such as hypoglycemia, diabetes and metabolic imbalances.

A deficiency of food enzymes in the diet gives rise to "digestive leukocytosis," (excess white cells in the digestive system and blood) which is not the case when raw, high-enzyme foods are eaten.

More than 60 years ago, Dr. Edward Howell began to cultivate one special species of the many aspergillus plants that existed in the plant kingdom. He picked the "oryzae" strain because there were no harmful aflatoxins (a type of poison) associated with this plant. More importantly, however, this strain contained a rich store of the very same enzymes that the human body used to digest food.

For the first time in recorded history, Howell gave the powdered form of these little plants directly to human patients. He found that spergillus orzae was a key to treating a whole host of seemingly unrelated ailments. Because of the success of his clinical work, he dedicated his life to working out a theoretical and experimental platform to explain how these seeming miracles had been accomplished. The development of the "Food Enzyme Concept" in human nutrition was this great man's life's work.

This chapter would not have been written, nor perhaps would I be as alive and healthy as I am today, if it were not for the amazing properties of these "angel-hair-in-appearance" microscopic plants. I have been eating aspergillus plant digestive enzymes for more than 20 years. I have also experimented with other animal and vegetarian-based enzymes such as pancreatin, pepsin, papain and bromelain. I have concluded that aspergillus enzymes are far superior to these other enzyme sources.

Recycling and specificity of enzymes

The editor of the *Scottish Medical Journal* (1966) wrote that "probably nearly half of our daily production of protein in the body are enzymes." In a way, our bodies are like big enzyme factories. There is strong evidence that the body seeks to conserve its digestive enzymes. In the prestigious scientific journal *Science,* Liebow and Rohman (1975) describe an experiment in which it was found that pancreatic enzymes given by mouth can be absorbed intact from the gut, transported through the bloodstream and then be re-secreted into the duodenum by the pancreas. If only my home's heating system were as efficient!

There is an antagonistic relationship between the demands of the digestive system for a continual supply of enzymes and the need of the organs, glands and immune system for enzymes with which to do their work. The competition for enzyme resources can be easily relieved by the consumption of food-source enzymes. Dr. Guyon's authoritative *Textbook of Medical Physiology* (1986) states that the pancreas, stomach and possibly other organs secrete specific digestive enzymes according to the type and quantity of food present. The ingestion of plant enzymes may have been conserving effect on the body's enzyme potential, possibly aiding cell and organ regeneration by digesting the food which normally would have required the body's own pancreatic enzymes.

Co-enzymes make super-enzymes

Organic minerals and vitamins are sometimes bound to enzymes that are integrated into the enzyme structure and are referred to as co-enzymes. According to Dr. Maynard Murray, MD, every naturally occurring organic mineral should be considered essential for optimal health. Minerals are essential for the working of enzymes, and enzymes are essential for the working of minerals. A few examples: if a certain enzyme is lacking an essential co-factor mineral such as zinc, then the enzyme cannot successfully activate vitamin A to do its work.

If a co-factor of vitamin C lacks the proline hydroxylase enzyme, this will lead to impaired collagen synthesis which will profoundly affect muscle recovery and wound healing. Co-enzymes give the enzymes the power to do their work. Medical researcher Dr. Haigivara MD concludes: "Modern science has made it clear that all chemical changes within the cells of humankind are performed by the action of enzymes. It has been found that minerals have much to do with the activities of enzymes. In that sense, minerals can be said to be enzymes for the enzymes."

Enzymes are, without a doubt, the most important and most over-looked elements in nutrition today. A deficiency of merely one enzyme may cause the malfunctioning of an entire metabolic chain reaction in the body, thereby preventing some vital function from unfolding. If the food we eat is rich in enzymes, vitamins, and minerals, it will add to our lives. If it is deficient in any of these elements, this will take away from the total life-force available to us. Vitamins, minerals, and hormones cannot work without the presence of enzymes.

Enzyme deficient diseases

The length and quality of life is directly proportional to the amount of available enzymes in the body. The level of amylase in human saliva is approximately 30 times more abundant in the average 25-year-old than the average 81-year-old. In contrast, whales and dolphins, who live in the perfectly balanced aquatic environment and live entirely on raw foods have no difference in cell enzyme composition in young and old (Murray MD, *Sea Energy Agriculture*).

If one were to analyze the bloodstreams of newborns and elderly persons, there would be little difference noted in the comparative blood levels of most vitamins and minerals in the infant and the old person. Amazingly, however, there are more than 100 times more enzymes present in the bloodstream of a newborn than that of an elderly person! This, to me, is an incredible, startling fact! Given this, can we then not look at premature old age, or for that matter, the aging process itself, as a biological condition with a major characteristic being pronounced enzyme deficiency?

Vibrant, healthy cells have high enzyme activity levels. Enzymes are the spark of life and are what makes living cells and tissues truly alive. It is a dubious strategy to expect energy and aliveness from life and then go about eating all that is dead and lifeless. Dr. Francis Pottenger's famous ten-year study showed just that. He fed one group of cats an enzyme-rich diet, and found these cats maintained their health and vigor throughout several generations. A second group of cats, who were fed a diet consisting of 80% cooked food for several generations. The group of cats, who were fed 80% cooked food, exhibited evidence of degenerative disease. Pottenger's data supported Howell's theories that raw food contains vital factors no longer present in cooked food. The SAD (Standard American Diet) has a much higher percentage of cooked and processed foods than most other diets, hence it does not come as a surprise to see that more than 70% of Americans are suffering from some form of degenerative disease. The excess intake of cooked fats leads to the exhaustion of the body's ability to manufacture sufficient amounts of lipase, the enzyme responsible for digesting fat. This in turn can lead to obesity, adult onset diabetes, and cardiovascular disease. Eskimos, on the other hand, can eat up to a pound of lipase-rich raw blubber each and every day and not have any signs or symptoms of cardiovascular disease. However, when Eskimos began to cook their fats like Westerners, they began to suffer from the degenerative diseases that the Western cultures do.

Another medical researcher, Dr. Paul Kauchakoff, MD, experimented with the effects of cooked and raw foods on the bloodstreams of humans. Dr. Kauchakoff found that eating cooked foods caused an immediate increase in the leucocyte (white blood) cell count in the bloodstream, whereas the same food eaten raw did not change blood physiology. Before this important experiment, medical dictum taught that this was a normal physiological event for leucocytes to increase in the blood and migrate to the intestines as soon as food entered the mouth. The strongest hypothesis formulated to explain this phenomenon is that in the body's wisdom, white blood cells collect enzymes from the body's enzyme reserves and migrate to the digestive system to aid in the digestion of the cooked food. Every cooked meal can then be seen as a significant stress on the immune system, speeding the exhaustion of enzymes and ultimately shortening your life.

Enzymeless diet speeds aging

Dr. James B Sumner, Nobel prize recipient and Professor of Biochemistry at Cornell University, wrote in his book *The Secret of Life-Enzymes*, that the "getting old feeling" after 40 is due to reduced enzyme levels throughout the body. Young cells contain 100 times more enzymes than the old cells. Old cells are filled with metabolic waste and toxins. In the textbook *Enzymes in Health and Disease*, co-edited by Dr. David Greenberg PhD, Chair of the Department of Biochemistry at the University of California School of Medicine at San Francisco, this editor suggests that for optimal health, longevity, and the reduction of many of the diseases of old age, the use of proteolytic (protein digesting) enzymes should begin about the age of 40 and should optimally continue for the rest of the life-span.

In a similar vein, Dr. Max Wolf, MD, in his book *Enzyme Therapy*, strongly endorses the use of plant-based enzymes. Dr Wolf states: "Indigestion due to greasy foods is common… Plant-based enzymes are helpful for weak digestions common in old age, or for digestive disturbances. Enzymes are helpful with large rich meals or hard-to-digest foods. Preparations fortified with plant lipase, prevent postprandial (after eating) discomfort or gallbladder attacks."

Enzymes fight free radicals

Free radicals are not holdovers from the 1960s, but are highly-reactive, electrically-imbalanced molecules that damage other cells by trying to unite with them in a sort of sexual harassment on the cellular level. When this happens, the cell wall is ruptured and the contents of the cell spills out and begins a cascade of reactions that causes more free radicals to form. Free radical formation is not always pathological but is a natural event that occurs in the process of living. Eating poor foods and living an unhealthy lifestyle can increase free radical formation. However, our body manufactures special antioxidant enzymes (i.e., superoxide dismutase) to remove free radicals before they create cellular damage. In youth, our cells are able to produce sufficient amounts of the metabolic enzymes superoxide dismutase and catalase, which enable them to defend themselves by neutralizing free radicals. As we age we need to provide the cells with sufficient support, so that they can continue to maintain that balance.

Plant versus animal enzymes

Animal-based enzymes work very powerfully on food when the optimal acid-alkaline (pH) environment that these animal-based enzymes require is present. What animal enzyme manufacturers, and those that prescribe these products, do not tell you is that the optimal conditions necessary for animal-based enzymes to work optimally do not correspond to the actual *in vivo* (in the body) conditions of the human gastrointestinal tract. Outside of this narrow, optimal range, animal enzymes do not work as well as aspergillus plant-based enzymes.

Pepsin, which only digests protein, is taken from pig carcasses and works if (and only if) the acid environment stomach reaches a pH of 3 or less. This is not always the case, especially in humans who need supplemental pepsin in the first place. *Pancreatin*, which is taken from cow carcasses, works best in the neutral or slightly alkaline environment of the duodenum at a pH of between 7.8 and 8.3. These conditions are also not always present.

In contrast, plant-based aspergillus oryzae enzymes function well in the wide pH range actually found in the human gastrointestinal tract. Aspergillus oryzae plant enzymes are active in the stomach during the first 30 to 60 minutes of the meal. When the acidity of the lower (pyloric) stomach climbs, the aspergillus enzymes are temporarily inactivated. As it passes into the alkaline environment of the dueodenum, aspergillus becomes re-activated again.

Enzyme products help the "SAD" one

The National Digestive Diseases Information Clearinghouse in Bethesda, Maryland published these 1993 statistics for the US, as follows: 116,609 digestive system cancer deaths; 20 million cases of gallstones; 66 million reports of "heartburn" each month; 20 million cases of irritable bowel syndrome; 191,311 total deaths due to digestive disease; 22.3 million work-loss days due to chronic indigestion; 9 million work-loss days due to acute indigestion; 4.5 million hospitalizations due to indigestion; 13% of total hospitalizations due to digestive disorders; 5.8 million digestive system surgeries; and 7% of the total number of surgeries performed were digestive system related.

Indigestion brings in its malodorous trail a host of symptoms and discomforts such as heartburn, gas, bloatedness, nausea, burping, bad breath, body odors, headaches, abdominal pain, insomnia, nightmares, allergies, fatigue, constipation, diarrhea, irritable bowel syndrome, diverticulosis, cramps, spasms, skin problems, acne, pimples, food allergies, antacid dependency, post-meal mental fatigue, lack of concentration, memory loss, and nervousness. What are the harmful consequences of chronic indigestion? When food does not digest properly, starches go sour, proteins putrefy and fats turn rancid. Important nutrients become unavailable to the billions of cells that clamor for them. Excess acidity or alkalinity can set in, resulting in aches and pains and a loss of energy that is sometimes mistaken for psychological depression. The electro-voltage potential of your cells declines, leading to premature aging. To compensate for this generalized lack of energy some of us eat sugar or caffeine to "jump start" ourselves so we can "keep on going." If this negative cycle persists, we *will* keep on going—to an early grave.

Furthermore, chemical energy is stored in a molecule known as adenosine triphosphate (ATP). By way of enzymatic action, food is transformed into energy and then stored in the ATP molecules in our cells. The less efficient is our digestion, the less ATP energy will be created. Furthermore, when digestion is inefficient, fermenting and putrefying food has to be neutralized by our immune system, which requires ATP energy to do the cleansing.

The enzyme effect on allergies

Allergies are among the most common and costly of all health problems, afflicting an estimated 73 million people at a cost in excess of over 1.5 billion dollars a year. Nine percent of all patients seeking medical care at a physician's office do so for allergies. (*Asthma and other Allergic Disease, NIAID, NIH Publ. 79-387, 5/79*) Allergies can be caused by an innumerable variety of substances, including food, pollen, dust, molds, drugs, cosmetics, toiletries, fabrics, poison ivy, etc. These allergens can enter your body through your food, the air, your skin, and even via medical injections.

Food allergies evoke a wide variety of symptoms, including fatigue, nervous tension, headaches, dizziness, nasal congestion, runny nose, itching, rashes, abdominal cramping, nausea, vomiting, and diarrhea. Foods high on the allergy list are milk, wheat, corn, eggs, seafood, and chocolate. Many people are also allergic to berries, citrus, and tomatoes. It is possible to be allergic to any food, including whole natural foods. However, I have observed that many people who are allergic to unsoaked or cooked seeds, nuts, and grains are no longer allergic to them when they are sprouted or soaked, or if they take food enzymes. Why does this positive change take place? The enzymes in these foods become enlivened with the sprouting process. The complex allergenic elements of these foods, i.e. the gluten found in wheat, become predigested and/or neutralized by the action of these enzymes.

Many foods contain these hard-to-digest elements. Dr. Howell cited experiments that showed that bacteria, yeast cells, large protein molecules, and fats can slip through the walls of the intestines and into the bloodstream. If this happens the already stressed immune system will not be able to deal with these undigested food elements and foreign proteins floating around. He further demonstrated that protective enzymes in the bloodstream break down these substances and absorb or neutralize them. In this connection, it was also found that if enzyme levels were too low, allergies developed. When supplemental enzymes were administered and the measured enzyme level in the blood had significantly increased, the allergies disappeared. The allergic reaction itself is the body's way to remove the allergen from the system. If this allergic reaction is suppressed by medication, then the body is forced to store the allergen in the body. The long-term effect of suppression is the eventual development of degenerative disease.

Dr. Cory Resnick, in *Plant Enzyme Therapy*, discusses practical approaches in treatment of food allergies: "By digesting dietary protein, plant enzymes administered orally at mealtime work to decrease the supply of antigenic macromolecules available to leak into the bloodstream. In addition, orally administered plant enzymes which have themselves been absorbed intact may help to 'digest' antigenic dietary proteins which they encounter in the bloodstream" (*Pizzome et al, '92*).

Enzyme fasting and healing

When you fast or go on a liquid diet of raw fruit and vegetable juices, your digestive system no longer has to produce enzymes. According to what Dr. Howell refers to as the "law of adaptive secretion," the enzyme potential, no longer directed into digesting food, can now be utilized by the general metabolic pool. These enzymes are now free to repair and rejuvenate the tissues and organs that need attention in other parts of the body. Many a seriously ill person has surprised family, friends, and doctors by healing themselves of seemingly incurable diseases when they adopted a total life-enhancing regime that included a high enzyme diet including supplementary enzymes, sufficient rest, appropriate exercise, positive mental attitude, and a conducive social and physical environment.

For a person who is run-down and toxic, it is not impossible to adopt such a program at home, but for those who are sick, the supervision of a competent health professional is strongly advised. One can also travel to the health centers that specialize in education and/or healing people who are dedicated to regaining their health. A few places in Europe include Josef Issel's Ringberg Clinic in West Germany, and Dr Essen's Vita Nova in Sweden. In the Unites States, Hippocrates Health Institute of West Palm Beach, Florida provides a beautiful residential setting where one can learn by doing.

Can children use plant enzymes?

Most children have strong digestive systems. However, the fact that they can digest less-than-optimal cooked foods does not automatically make these foods ideal for the future unfolding of their maximum health potential. Sure, kids will digest the foods served them and still be full of youthful energy, but the same health principles hold for children as they do for adults: namely, that the process of aging is accelerated when enzyme reserves are squandered by the burden of digesting excessive amounts of cooked food.

Plant enzymes and medication

If you are under medical care or taking oral medication of any kind, there are steps you should take to avoid any inactivation of an enzyme supplement by your medication. Sprinkle plant enzyme powder *on the food itself* instead of taking the capsules or powder directly into your body. Make sure, however, that the food has cooled down a bit or else the enzyme powder will be damaged by the high heat of your food. In this way, the predigestive action of the enzymes will work directly on the food and not have to come in contact with the drugs that may be in your stomach.

Despite the long-overdue surfacing of the truth about enzymes, don't be surprised if your family doctor still downplays the importance or even the existence of enzymes in foods. Traditionally, segments of the medical community take a conservative posture on many issues. In fact, the majority of doctors, dieticians and nutritionists do not fully appreciate the contribution of food enzymes to health maintenance and the prevention of disease. At the conclusion of this chapter you will probably know more about food enzymes than most physicians!

Do plant enzymes survive gut acids?

Less than one fifth of all medical schools in the United States teach even the elementary aspects of nutrition. Of those that do teach it, the true role of food enzymes is rarely if ever taught. According to the prevailing accepted dictum, enzymes found in foods are destroyed by the hydrochloric acid of the stomach and are virtually no use in the digestive economy. However, Dr. Howell has shown that as soon as particular food is masticated in the mouth, the enzymes begin to digest the food. This has been confirmed by Finnish Nobel Prize winner Artturi Virtanen. When the food reaches the first part of the stomach, (upper cardiac stomach) the food enzymes are still actively working. It takes up to 50 minutes for the hydrochloric acid level to rise to the critical level where the acidity of the hydrochloric acid could inactivate the food enzymes in the food. Until this level is reached, the food enzymes are still working. What is more, not all foods stimulate hydrochloric acid production appreciably. Foods like fruit, spouts, grasses and many raw vegetables do not cause hydrochloric acid production to increase rapidly or in any great quantity. In this environment enzymes present in food have a longer time to do their work. According to Howell, even though saliva enzymes shut off in the presence of acid, food enzymes are not markedly disturbed.

After taking enzyme supplements, many people immediately feel a difference in the ease in which their food is digested. They also report an overall boost in their energy level. Others do not report any dramatic subjective improvement. The latter case is probably due to the relatively good health enjoyed already or the fact that the "blood of youth" has not as yet faded. Whether you feel any immediate subjective improvements in your health as a result of taking enzymes is not as important as your understanding how enzymes do their work of enhancing digestion and assimilation, boosting the immune system and contributing to your body's total vitality.

In conclusion

Outside the human body, enzymes can produce dramatic effects very quickly. Enzymes are used in the process of making bread, wine, cheese, etc. Enzymes are used in laundry detergents, septic tanks, and in dissolving massive accidental oil spills. In these cases, there is no denying that enzymes do their work. Why then is there so much resistance to accepting that food enzymes do work in the human body?

In nature, all undomesticated animals eat an enzyme-rich diet. They live out their lives, largely free from degenerative diseases. The human animal is the only species that nourishes itself on a cooked, largely enzymeless diet. Our longevity and our well-being could be increased if we ate more whole foods with an emphasis on uncooked foods.

When food is cooked there is a reduction in the bioavailability of protein, vitamins, and minerals so that your cells get much less nutrition. Unless you cook at 118 degrees Fahrenheit or below (as in sun-drying or dehydrating foods), you will completely destroy all of the enzymes present in the food.

Dr. Howell's powerful words say it all:

"There is no other mechanism in the body except enzyme action to protect the body from any hazard. It is ambiguous to say that "nature cures" when we must know that the only machinery in the body to do anything is enzyme action. Hormones do not work. Vitamins cannot do any work. Minerals were not made to do any work. Proteins cannot work. Nature does not work. Only enzymes are made for work."

EDITOR'S NOTE

The power, wisdom, and Love that Viktoras reveals and shares with the world comes from the dedication, discipline, purpose, passion and obedience he lives his life with. Better known as the "grandfather" of living food, honors us with this chapter on enzymes.

If the only thing the rapidly aging "baby-boomers" take from this book and the generations that follow is the understanding of the importance enzymes contribute to the Lifeforce within us, it would return many of them to the vibrant life of their youth, and eliminate their pain, sickness, obesity, and disease as part of their life! It is my belief, by putting into practice the laws of nutrition, and proper hydration, we can return to a vibrant society that will live in Love, Peace, Joy, and Happiness!

Thank You—Viktoras for the Love you have shown to the world all these years!

—JEF

A NEED FOR CHANGE IN THE DEFINITIONS OF NUTRITION, MEDICINE AND HEALTH

T. Colin Campbell
Jacob Gould Schurman Professor Emeritus of
Nutritional Biochemistry, Cornell University

Working as a co-author with my son Tom (now in medical school), we published in 2005 a book, *The China Study. Startling Implications for Diet, Weight Loss and Long-Term Health*. It was an account of how I became enthralled with a message about diet and health, after spending more than 40 years with my many students and colleagues doing experimental research on the relationship with food and health, mostly at Cornell University. I have now begun a second book that, in many ways, is the theoretical and philosophical bases for the evidence reported in *The China Study*. The following is a version of the intended introduction to this second book that hopefully will be published in early 2009. I wish to describe a very different way to think about the words, health, nutrition and health. It is a way that is more consistent with the natural order of things.

In 1983, in my Cornell University laboratory, we showed that we could turn on and off early cancer development in experimental animals (rats) simply by changing the amount of a nutrient being consumed. Equally amazing, when cancer was turned off for a relatively long time, its growth could be restored using these same simple nutrient intake changes, but in the opposite direction. These effects were dramatic in so many ways. Cancer growth either was vigorous and robust or it was totally shut down. Only modest nutritional changes were required to cause major changes in cancer development, forward and backward. The results of this research were first published 25 years ago.

And what was the experimental nutrient that we used to turn on cancer development? It was animal-based protein, the nutrient that almost everyone has long revered for good health, including myself, because of its completeness and its biological quality. Our love affair with protein, especially the really good kind from animal based foods, started very early. Shortly after its discovery by Gerhard Mulder in 1839, the famous chemist Justice von Liebig then went on to exclaim that animal-based ('high quality') protein "was the stuff of life itself!" Its name was derived from the Greek word, proteios, "of prime importance," a nice baptism, come to think of it.

In my laboratory, we studied this protein effect on cancer in dozens of experiments in many different ways and published our results in multiple papers in the very best peer-reviewed scientific research journals. We learned so much. We learned how it worked at the biochemical level and it was not what I expected. But I also learned that results like these were much too dramatic and provocative for the kind of nutrition that my colleagues and I were taught. Therefore, we had to do our research very carefully if we were to survive in the research community and successfully compete for the necessary but very competitive funding.

During these early days of our research, I was invited to give a lecture at the Fels Institute of the Temple University School of Medicine by the Editor-in-Chief of the leading cancer research journal in our field ("Cancer Research").[1] After my lecture and at dinner, I told him

---

1   I am speaking of Professor Peter Magee who was serving with me on a National Cancer Institute panel reviewing grant applications for research funding.

of a new experiment that we were planning, one that might be even more outrageous. I wanted to compare this remarkable nutrient effect on cancer growth with the well-accepted effect produced by a really potent chemical carcinogen (a cancer causing chemical). I suggested that a relatively modest change in nutrient consumption might be even more significant for cancer development than consuming a potent carcinogen. I asked him, if we actually were to get such results, whether he would consider highlighting our findings on the cover of his prestigious journal. He was skeptical of my hypothesis but nonetheless agreed to consider it. His skepticism, and that of most of our colleagues at that time, were well entrenched. Cancer occurs, so the story went, because of chemical carcinogens and viruses and genes, not because of modest changes in nutrient consumption. What heresy!

With these new experiments, which concerned the early growth of cancers, we succeeded more than I expected.[2] But my hope for publishing these exciting results on the cover of our association's journal was dashed. My Editor-in Chief colleague was now retired. His replacement and his Editorial Review Board were changing policy. They were inclined to dismiss nutritional effects on cancer. They primarily went so far as to assign the review of any papers on the nutritional effects on cancer, good or bad, to a new untested journal,[3] a good way of relegating such nutrition-related research to second-class status. They wanted papers that—in their minds—were more intellectually stimulating, ideas like figuring out how cancer works in molecular terms, especially if these ideas concerned chemicals and genes and viruses. Investigating nutritional effects on cancer was almost akin to non-science.

At about this same time, I presented a plenary paper at the World Congress of Nutrition in Seoul, South Korea, when we had even more convincing evidence of this remarkable protein effect. A good sized audience of researchers was in attendance and during a question and answer period, a well known advocate for consuming more, not less, protein arose and lamented (literally whining), "Colin, you're talking

---

2   Later confirmed for full tumor development(7)
3   Cancer Epidemiology, Biomarkers and Prevention

about good food! Don't take it away from us!" He did not question the validity of our research results but seemed to be concerned that I was questioning his personal love for this nutrient. A storm was brewing! A sensitive nerve was bared. There's also a sad part of this story. My questioner, younger than I, since traveled to greener pastures at an age too young, suffering an ailment spurred on by his reverence for animal-based protein.

During those years, we also were investigating the cancer altering effects of other nutrients on other experimental cancers. One of our studies involved a similar on-off effect of dietary fat on the development of experimental pancreatic cancer. Although less spectacular and less ominous than the protein effect, it made the cover of the official research journal of the U.S. National Cancer Institute. These new findings only added to our observations of the effect of modest nutritional changes on cancer.

We continued to follow our research leads wherever they led us and, as time passed, these leads were proving to be more and more promising, yet also more and more provocative. They began to foreshadow a much larger story about diet and health, a story of great societal moment. We studied different dietary factors, different disease and health endpoints, and different so-called mechanisms. Gradually, my understanding of nutrition learned early in my career was beginning to unravel. But on a more constructive note, my understanding was beginning to expose a fascinating interconnecting world that encouraged our moving beyond experimental laboratory rodent studies to some unique human studies. One was a Buffalo, NY, study of nutrition and breast cancer occurrence and progression in a cohort of 81 women, another an unusually comprehensive and unique study of 6500 adults and their families in rural China. Increasingly, I was reminded of how little we know and how much there is yet to learn. I was becoming more and more convinced that there really is a little known world of science, which has much to offer. It is a world even beyond pure science that was very old even ancient, a world that modern day scientists overly concerned with details have wanted to marginalize.

Now many years later as I write these words, I sense an urgency to re-define words like nutrition, medicine, and health. I now think of these words more as biological and philosophical concepts and less and less as mechanical and architectural entities; like knowing exact chemical structures, functions and physiological concentrations. The sand at the seashore cannot be described by spending a lifetime studying a single granule of sand in the laboratory and never going to the seashore. The biological complexity that best describes these concepts of nutrition, medicine and health is grossly ignored throughout society, both by the lay public and by the professional. In doing so, we have a tendency to value exacting chemical structures, functions and concentrations. Concerning ourselves only to the complexity of biology is even constraining because it is only part of a considerably more expansive and interconnecting world of social complexity that can be described in all manner of ways, economically, philosophically, historically, and environmentally, to name a few. I now sense something substantially more than these complex systems. This 'something' has been marinating in my mind for many years, becoming ever easier to describe during the past 15-20 years. I believe this "something" can be described as a unifying hypothesis, as we like to say in science, whereby we propose all encompassing and reasonably simple solutions to very complex problems.

Many scientists in past years have wrestled with this idea of a unifying hypothesis in an attempt to explain, at least in part, the enormous complexity of the underlying biology of health. I am sure that I have been influenced in some way by those previous writings but cannot know how much. But this I do know. Whatever now remains of those previous discussions, they are not operating very well in the public's understanding of nutrition, medicine and health. I can only say this: my current views are strongly influenced by the research results that we produced in my own laboratory. They do not spring from any preconceived ideologies or special agendas. I have loved learning wherever it has taken me and now I find that my understanding of health has gone far beyond those narrowly-focused hypotheses addressed early in my career.

My career has included both a long-standing laboratory-based experimental research program (about 40 years) and—of equal importance—an active participation in diet and health policy development (about 20 of those 40 years). It began with those narrowly-focused experiments on dietary protein and cancer development that set in motion my future career choices. But in addition to my experiences in the research laboratory, it has been my experience in the diet and health policy boardrooms that encouraged my consideration of a greatly expanded worldview on diet and health, now coming to rest on the following relatively simple lifestyle recommendations:

> Consume whole plant-based foods while minimizing even eliminating animal-based foods and plant-food fragments (e.g., sugar, oil, refined flour, etc.) that have been formulated into processed foods. Be sure to include adequate exercise, water and sunshine exposure and think of this program not as a diet but as a lifestyle that becomes your life.

Undoubtedly, you have heard these recommendations before but I am convinced that only a very few people really know their true significance. "We are what we eat" is an age-old aphorism that preceded, by many centuries, these recommendations, yet it is as appropriate today as it was at the dawn of human history. These modern day recommendations not only give substance to that aphorism but also invoke a wide spectrum of very practical ideas and practices that support my present worldview.

However, as I was becoming familiar with this new worldview, I was becoming more and more frustrated doing experimental research according to the paradigm that had nourished for so long my intellect and fed our research group generous amounts of funding. It seemed that I had no choice but to tell my story and a book for the public seemed to make the most sense. Public taxpayers were paying for our research[4] and

---

4   At least 99% of our funding came from the National Cancer Institute (of NIH) and other public taxpayer supported agencies.

they deserved to know how we spent their money. A book also would have the added advantage of getting feedback from readers, thus engaging the public in a much needed discourse.

So, about 3 years ago, I published, with my son, Tom, *The China Study* that documents some of the evidence and personal experiences of my 45 or so years in science that were reconfiguring my world, both personally and professionally. *The China Study* was written to document my evidence and experiences, a first order of business before telling my larger worldview, the subject of this second book.

Tom had graduated from Cornell in Theater Arts, was exceptionally bright, was doing theater in Chicago and was a very talented writer, assistance that I needed. In writing the book with me, Tom then became deeply involved in the science itself and quickly became a true coauthor, not only re-writing my drafts but also writing original material. He now is finishing up medical school, planning to be a doctor of a different kind.

Amazingly, our book has sparked an unexpectedly large public response. It is now a national best-seller, is generating a very large number of unsolicited reviews from people claiming all manner of health benefits, and has been consistently ranked # 1 in the category "Preventive Medicine" and #1 to #5 in the various "Nutrition" categories on the www.Amazon.com website. Reader reviews, more than 440 as of this writing, have been overwhelmingly positive. Eighty-four percent are 5-star, the highest rating. When 4-star reviews are added, it is 90%. But for a small minority of reviewers, it occasionally generates unusual hostility. Even so, for every hostile 1-star review, there are thirteen 5-star reviews. These latter reviews are exceptionally complimentary but, ironically, one of my favorite comments comes from one of the most hostile critics. When asked by another Internet correspondent why he was consistently attacking each and every complimentary review of our book on www.Amazon.com, he replied, "Because [our] book is the most dangerous." Very nice comment. Indeed![5]

---

5 Amazon.com has since deleted his material from their website and banned further submissions because of his offensive and unacceptable behavior. What a loss!

My education has continued since the book's publication 3 years ago. I especially appreciate the feedback received during the 250 plus lectures that I have presented to a wide variety of professional and lay audiences. Many people have told of unusually promising health benefits when they put into practice the message in our book. Many readers have personally told me how they have even saved their lives by adopting this lifestyle while most others tell that they lose weight and gain energy and a sense of well being not previously experienced. The health benefits are unusually diverse and profound, ranging from the elimination of humdrum colds and headaches to the reversal of serious diseases like cancer, heart disease and multiple sclerosis.

The health benefits coming to my attention, however, are not only those from readers of *The China Study*. Clinicians and other authors, who promote the same or very similar messages, tell of similarly remarkable benefits for their patients. These clinicians are providing or had already been providing for many years the 'proof of concept' that makes my interpretation of the scientific evidence much more credible. Drs. John McDougall (MD) and Caldwell Esselstyn, Jr., (MD) became my first new physician acquaintances when the results of the China project were first publicized in 1990 as a cover story in the science section of the *New York Times*. The remarkable clinical experiences and great personal courage of these distinguished physicians within their professional communities were described in our book, *The China Study*. They and others already had pioneered this kind of medicine before our book and *The New York Times* article were published. Dr. McDougall has practiced this kind of medical practice on more than 8000 patients for more than 35 years and has resolved all types of illnesses. Dr. Esselstyn and Dr. Dean Ornish (18, 19) were 'curing' advanced heart disease, to use the word that Dr. Esselstyn uses. Dr. Alan Goldhamer (DC), because of a personal experience of mine, shared with me the results of his health care practice that solves illnesses much more effectively than seems possible in most of the traditional practices. Dr. Terry Shintani (MD) in Hawaii is having great success with the indigenous population who are experiencing truly excessive rates of obesity and type II diabetes. Dr.

Hans Diehl (DSc) has pioneered an exceptional community-based program that has been offered in more than 250 communities, involving 50,000 attendees, with pre- and post-clinical evaluations. These were my first primary care acquaintances. Then, in more recent times, I came to learn of the practices and exceptional clinical experiences of Drs. Neal Barnard (MD), Joel Fuhrman (MD), Pamela Popper (ND) and Brian Clement (MD). Yet, there are many more primary health care professionals now using with great success this diet-centered approach in their clinical practices. It may surprise some readers that throughout medical history physicians have demonstrated impressive successes with a (plant-based) diet centered approach to medical practice to restore and maintain health but they are not well known because mainstream medical practitioners have consciously and intentionally ignored them. I know this is a strong statement but the differences are huge between mainstream medical practice, which ignores a role for diet, and a medical practice that takes seriously a role for diet. The differences can be described in many ways but one of my favorites is to say that it is the difference between life and death itself. I hope in this book to stimulate dialogue on the way that we think about health and medical practice, taking into consideration these very different approaches.

In my experience, public discussion of diet and health issues is far too often passionate, personal and dominated by self-righteous ideologies. Consider this: There are those who passionately like the plant-based health message in our book primarily because it is consistent with their passion for animal rights as their first priority. But for some, their priority is so single issue-oriented that they passionately despise the findings of our experimental animal studies even though these findings were critical to the development of my own thinking that now finds common ground with the views of these critics. For me, this matter of laboratory animal experimentation is an unresolved dilemma. As told in our previous book, I cannot defend our studies on ethical grounds. I can only say with confidence that the information gained was critical in my thinking. In contrast to my critics who decry my prior use of experimental animals, there are those at the other extreme who ironically question my findings and my views because I am a "rabid animal rights activist," as one outspoken critic has said. These critics tend to represent the status quo, often wanting to protect the marketing of their health products and services—with little or no governmental restrictions. For them, their view is a sacred matter of personal freedom. Although both of these extremist groups are relatively few in number but loud in voice, the vast majority of the public remains relatively uninformed, confused and too often contemptuous of what they consider to be official information of any kind. In the meanwhile some of the animal rights activists consider me lacking compassion for animal rights while some of their opponents claim the opposite, namely that I am an animal rights activist!

In effect, two ideologically motivated groups, each representing minor proportions of the public, create, dominate and even manage the so-called public debate about diet and health. Unfortunately, they create a highly polarized and confused public discourse while the rest of the public mostly remains on the sidelines wondering when and where the truth might be told. Unquestionably, this 'debate' is also undemocratic because those with the most capital, although few in number, still control information development and dissemination. Creating public information on diet and health in this kind of environment tends to drift into self-serving propaganda that favors one or the other point of view.

For those with a vested financial interest, it is not difficult to interpret scientific evidence in a way that serves their special interests. I can cite numerous first-hand experiences to support this view. In the research community, the vast majority of nutrition and health researchers sincerely believe that they are doing their studies in an honest, transparent manner. Overt personal dishonesty is not the problem. I repeat: overt personal dishonesty is not the problem. Rather, the problem arises from the very narrow channel with which we frame our questions, prioritize our research funding and report and interpret our results. We do things according to who's paying the bill and setting the rules for our research system leaving open multiple interpretations of the same results, depending on who does the interpreting.

Deciding what's real and what's not real in the world of health information is exceptionally daunting. Being in the profession for as long as I have been and seeing first-hand how health information is created and used leaves me extremely frustrated. We are slaves to a system of health information that values money far more than personal health.

Confused and unable to determine how reliable a new health claim might be, many people, at best, will fall back on that old expression, "Honest people looking at the same evidence will have honest differences of opinion on its interpretation." Of course, this is often true. But, too often it is an unfortunate cop-out because saying this also reflects an inability to understand the information. For me, it takes time and some familiarity with the research methodology and underlying biology to understand such information. I personally may know the research group making the claim and, when I don't know I can easily access on-line the original manuscript. I can empathize with the difficulties and frustration that others not trained in this field must be having.

The health information that is told to the public on an almost daily basis is highly vulnerable to serious abuse. I have seen far too much of it. I have found that information that is most vulnerable to abuse is crafted by organizations with scientifically sounding names that are influenced, behind the scenes, by special corporate interests. Here is a briefly discussed example that was previously presented in *The China Study*.

In the late 1970s, I was serving as congressional liaison for our combined biomedical societies[6] and, because of this position, was appointed by our societies' Public Affairs Office as an ad hoc member of a new "Public Nutrition Information Committee" of our professional nutrition society. This committee was being established by our 'prestigious' society, so the story goes, to help reduce the massive public confusion about nutrition. Naively, I initially accepted and even was enthusiastic about

---

6 The Federation of American Societies for Experimental Biology and Medicine that was comprised of six of the major biomedical research societies (nutrition, biochemistry, pathology, pharmacology, immunology and physiology). I was a member of the nutrition and pharmacology societies and am still a member of the nutrition society.

the committee's mandate until I attended the first couple of meetings and learned of the multiple and serious personal conflicts of interests of the committee's 17 members. Some of these conflicts bordered on the obscene and I gradually became very uncomfortable with their agenda and voiced my concerns. After a couple years, a newly elected president of our parent society, aware of my concerns, became disenchanted, disbanded the committee and appointed me as committee chair. In turn, my new committee colleagues agreed to abandon our assigned mandate of being the arbiters of public nutrition information. It became clear to me that a committee like this wanted to arrogantly dictate what is fact and what is not, a perfect opportunity for mischief making by their industry associates who had the resources and personal incentives to do so. It was an attempt to control public nutrition information through an agency that sounded objective, highly professional and above the fray.

I regret saying that the execution of medical research is not as open to challenging ideas as I once thought. Spin is a well-honed practice that is as mischievous in the medical community as it is in the political community—and equally dangerous.

My laboratory was the benefactor of generous amounts of funding from the research 'establishment' for many years and for this, I am grateful. But I now realize, both as a recipient of these funds and as a peer-reviewer of research grant applications of other researchers, that for professional development in this field, our hypotheses and our studies need to fit reasonably comfortably within a framework that is intended to serve the wealth of the few at the expense of the health of the many. Harsh words? You bet, but I will defend this view in this book.

This is a small part of the dark side of the 'science' that is so often used to underwrite our health care system, which is now so inept, irresponsible and expensive. I say 'inept' because of an inability and even unwillingness of the system to properly articulate a role for nutrition in maintaining health and preventing even treating illness (e.g., medical students don't get trained in nutrition). I say 'irresponsible' because the system uses large amounts of taxpayer money to serve itself instead of the taxpayer. I say 'expensive' because the U.S. has the highest per capita health care costs and one of the lowest rankings in health care quality of all industrialized societies. Even though this system is hugely complex, it nonetheless relies on a reasonably well-defined scientific philosophy that is channeled in a direction that does not serve the public's interest in health.

I propose an alternative health care model that I believe to be far more productive and far less expensive than the present model. It rests on a reliable understanding of the nutritional power of whole plant-based foods to create and maintain health. The scientific evidence for this nutrition-based model is discussed in our previous book, *The China Study*. The clinical evidence is being provided by physicians working with real people with real problems. The historical evidence, acquired over a very long time, also is remarkably consistent. Unfortunately, however, it has been ignored or, in many instances, distorted by those 'in power' for self-serving reason—at the expense of billions of unnecessary deaths.

On a more positive note, understanding the supporting scientific evidence for the health benefits of wholesome, freshly harvested and minimally processed plant-based foods can be very rewarding, both intellectually and practically. It depends on a deeper understanding of the reality of biological complexity and the nature of multifaceted evidence. Replacing these plant-based foods with animal-based foods won't create these same benefits. Using fragments of the plant-based foods (e.g., sugar, unsaturated cooking oils, re-saturated oils to produce fats[7], isolated nutrients, etc.) won't do it. Fortifying foods with specific nutrients, often used in the formulation of processed foods, won't do it. The health hypothesis having the most potential depends on the virtually unlimited but highly integrated biological mechanisms of wholesome plant-based foods to nourish. While scientists seem to be confounded and confused with these issues, the public is showing some signs that they are beginning to get it. The majority of the public, for example, now seem to agree that eating vegetables and fruits and grains is a healthy thing to do.

---

7   Re-saturated (i.e., hydrogenated) oils give rise to trans fats.

So why do I call this idea merely an hypothesis rather than a proven fact, if I am so confident of the evidence? I prefer leaving open the idea that we do not yet know all there is to know about these foods. We need more information, for example, on whether these foods should comprise 100% of the diet for each and every individual or whether 90-95% might be satisfactory, whether a somewhat different food selection is needed for different ages and different activities, and whether cooking and storage methods affect nutritional activities. I therefore like staying with the word 'hypothesis'. But for many scientists in the experimental research community, it is not appropriate to use this overly suggestive word because it is not sufficiently focused. According to them, hypotheses should be reserved for investigating one event and one component at a time. Accordingly, an hypothesis that simultaneously addresses the effects of virtually countless components at the same time violates the very essence of what science ought to be. Focus is lost. But I strongly disagree with this view and, if necessary, I am quite happy to be labeled a heretic.

On this idea of heresy, I will even venture further and expand my hypothesis into realms beyond traditional science. In fact, it is the very breadth of this hypothesis that especially intrigues me. I see breadth at all levels of biological and social organization. It is a breadth that ranges from the microcosm to the macrocosm, that is, from the 'depth' of subatomic particles 'up' through atoms and molecules and cells and organs and intact bodies to whole societies of people and other ecologies of life to the outer reaches of the universe.

Understanding the implications of this concept of breadth, in many ways, begins with our understanding of the ability of food to nourish. Understanding this ability means understanding nutrition. Understanding nutrition and its broader implications will not happen if we solely depend on hypotheses on its bit parts. Otherwise, our progress in creating a more healthful world will not happen. And finally, understanding why we misunderstand nutrition helps to explain why we humans, do things that neither serve our own personal interests nor the interests of our societies and our environment.

I've read 1,000's of books on nutrition. Over 20 books on water alone. Out of all the books I've read, after the Bible, Dr. T. Colin Campbell's book, *The China Study* brought me closer to God, than any other book.

Dr. Campbell is perhaps most noted for his famous statement: "There is a cure for cancer, and all other diseases—it's called your immune system!"

I never understood how "A Loving God" would deal so harshly as to condemn a child offender, as Jesus said, "Better that a millstone be tied to their neck and cast into the sea," and then in the Old Testament, God says that He will visit the iniquity of the fathers upon the children to the third and fourth generation. After reading T. Colin Campbell's book, *The China Study*, the iniquity (sins) of the fathers I now understand, was not referring to the whoremongering, or winebibbing, it was referring to the food that the father and mother put in their mouths, because it created DNA decline in their unborn offspring! Dr. Campbell proved that it takes three or four generations to reverse the DNA damage. I was visiting with my friend, Dr. Norman Shealy, sharing with him my understanding, and I was so excited, I said, "Norm, all we have to do is raise three or four generations and feed them properly and we'd be back to what God created!" Norman then asked me a question, "John, how long does it take to replace every cell in the body?" I answered, "Seven years, Norm." And he replied, "All you have to do is to remain on your lifestyle for 28 years!" I would encourage every man, woman, and child to read Dr. Colin Campbell's book *The China Study* and to look forward to his new book out this year.

Thank you, Dr. Campbell for your dedication, discipline, determination and desire, to reveal the TRUTH you uncovered. You brought me back to God.

—JEF

TEMPLE TENDING
AND TRIMMING

© Dr. Leslie Van Romer

"Do you not know that you are the temple of God and that the spirit of God dwells in you? If anyone defiles the temple of God, God will destroy him. For the temple of God is holy, which temple you are" (I Corinthians 3:16-18).

Spirit, Mind, and Oops! Body Too?

As a Christian, you walk the spiritual path. You seek a meaningful personal relationship with God and God's Son. You worship, pray, and ask for His guidance to live in His light and His love. Fully aware of your imperfections—you are human after all—you try to emulate Christ, His wisdom, and His example.

For as conscientious as you are about your spiritual awakening and growth, if you are like most Christians (and indeed most people) in the United States, you sorely neglect God's temple—your body—the very place God created to house His spirit on earth. After all, you are conditioned and entrenched in a culture ruled by spoiled taste buds, pervasive excess, depleting food and lifestyle habits without regard to consequences, and quick, no-effort fixes.

283

God expresses Himself and His work through you. As every mindful Christian knows, a well-functioning body is critical to that expression. If you are held hostage in a body that is plagued by excess weight, persistent pain, an imminent life-robbing disease, and/or so little energy that it's difficult to get through your day, how can you effectively serve God with peak performance of spirit, mind, heart, and body? The simple answer. You can't. At best, your service will be compromised. At worst, you won't be able to serve Him at all.

Yet, knowing full well how your body *should* look, feel, and perform, when you look in the mirror, are you happy with what you see? Be honest. Is the reflection a shining example of God's intended holy temple? Or are you like most Americans—overweight and frustrated by the image looking back at you?

You have to admit—you don't get it. You are a bright, hard-working, responsible, conscious, grateful God-loving Christian. How can you be right on track with your spiritual maturity and your ever-strengthening connection with God and His Son, but feel so helpless and hopeless when it comes to what should be the simple task of losing weight and keeping it off—for good?

Stuck and No Way Out

There's no denying. You are trapped in a body that is far removed from the perfect vehicle God created for carrying out His work. How did you get stuck in those layers in the first place?

Just as God offers, give yourself some grace, or in layman's terms, give yourself a break. When it comes to weight and choosing God's best-for-you foods, you didn't have a fighting chance since birth. You were birthed from the loins of this culture and our culture created monsters —food monsters. Just as all food monsters, we want to eat what we want when we want it—and not necessarily those foods that are conducive to permanent weight loss and health gain.

Sure, God gifted you free will and the freedom of choice, and ultimately you are the one responsible for you and your decisions. However, if, from the beginning, you weren't given the correct information in your physical environment, how do you know which foods are your true weight warriors and health heroes?

Think back. Your mother taught you which foods to eat—the same foods she was given by her mother, and so on back through the generations. Little did your mother know that she filled you with too many foods that were high in fat, cholesterol, salt, sugar, and/or calories, such as beef, chicken, pork, fish, cheese, milk, eggs, Wonder bread, mayonnaise, butter, and dried-up boxed cereals. These foods, stamped with Mom's seal of approval, along with doctors, teachers, pastors, and government officials, are still your favorites. Nature's best, fresh fruits and vegetables, were relegated to small side dishes or fell into the one-apple-a-day regiment. In fact, the infamous Four Food Groups, with the highlighted meat, cheese, milk, refined sugar, breads, and cereals seared into your brain, probably still demands dominance in your diet and life.

To add layers to the layers, starting in the 50s and 60s and escalating with each decade, our nation was bombarded by convenience foods, processed foods, refined foods, packaged foods, fast foods, junk foods, not to mention the vast array of sugar-loaded, caffeine-loaded, calorie-loaded, and nutrient-empty drinks. The consequence of conditioning and mindless eating, worsened by the drastic decrease of exercise, was self-evident: a whole nation of people who were overweight, frustrated, tired, tired of being tired, aging prematurely, and staring into the face of early disability and death.

Americans found salvation to their big fat problem, or so they hoped: diets. However, whether touting high protein, low carb, high carb, low fat, concocted liquid meals, or just grapefruits, diets revealed their one common denominator: they don't work. The proof may be as close as your own mirror.

Desperate to be slim yourself, you've hopped aboard and gone round and round that all-American diet-go-round more times than you care to admit. Your diets probably went something like this. You planned. You fussed. You counted. You measured. You weighed. You deprived. You starved. You craved. You snuck. And you guilted. You lost. You gained. You lost. You gained. You lost, and ultimately you gained, maybe even more than you lost in the first place. You beat yourself up—you're good at that.

No matter what you tried, the results were always the same. You looked in the mirror and were terribly unhappy with what you saw. Each unsuccessful attempt to lose weight and keep it off made you feel lazy, weak, or undisciplined. You felt like a miserable failure, one more time, at trimming God's temple. So you gave up. What's the point? No matter what you tried, your weight crept up and your health and energy spiraled down. You vowed to give up diets forever—until the next quick-fix, no-effort, fat-burning-while-you-sleep diet came along appealing to your desperation to be thin.

The good news: you didn't fail, the diets failed you. Most diets-of-the-day are designed to fail. Sure, you may lose weight at first, but because they restrict, deprive, and literally starve you—of calories *and* nutrients – they are temporary at best. Who can follow strict food laws, eat baby-size portions, and live without enough essential nutrients forever? Apparently, almost no one.

The tough news: If you want to reclaim control of your weight, body, and health, it's up to you, with Christ's helping hand, to jump off the diet-go-round. It's up to you, not your doctor, spouse, or mother, to shift your thinking, defy demanding taste buds, and break free from cultural bondage. Is your body, your life, and feeling good about yourself worth that supreme effort and lifelong vigilance? By virtue of the creation of God's holy temple, absolutely!

Fat Stats

Other than the corrosion of your self-esteem and ignoring, even disrespecting, God's clear intent, what is so bad about excess weight? Too much body fat pervades deeper than right beneath the skin. Fat infiltrates and accumulates in and around vital organs, inside blood vessels, and throughout muscles and soft tissue. Fat clogs, maims, and kills. Behold a few fat stats. Decide for yourself whether the supreme effort you make today to feed God's house with His best-for-you foods is worth a healthy, vibrant tomorrow for you, and especially for your children.

1. There are now more overweight people on the planet (1 billion) than starving people (600 million).

2. Over 66% of Americans are overweight; at least 34% obese with thirty or more extra pounds.

3. The biggest tragedy of all—over 25% of our children are overweight or obese.

4. 30 to 40% of our children will get type 2 diabetes in their lifetimes, a totally preventable disease. One soft drink or sweetened drink a day increases a child's risk of becoming obese by 60%. That doesn't count all the other high fat, high sugar, high calorie foods and pseudo-foods that children put into their bodies every day. As adults, we are responsible for feeding our children and creating the tragic fat dilemma they are facing.

5. If a child is thirty pounds overweight when she reaches twenty years old, her life expectancy decreases by twenty years. At that rate, your worst nightmare could become a reality—you could outlive your child.

6. Overweight has now surpassed cigarette smoking as the nation's leading cause of preventable death. Yet, we scoff at cigarette smoking and condone and, indeed, encourage overeating and eating the worst-for-you foods.

7. Overweight adults significantly increase their risk for type 2 diabetes, hypertension, heart disease, cancer, high triglycerides, high cholesterol, sleep apnea, lung disease, gastrointestinal diseases, and degenerative arthritis.

8. Risk of heart disease is two to three times higher in obese people.

9. Twenty pounds of extra fat at twenty years old to middle age doubles the risk of postmenopausal breast cancer.

10. The risk for colon cancer increases by three to four times in obese people.

11. Compared to eating no poultry, eating poultry once a week increases risk of colon cancer by 55%. Eating poultry four times a week increases colon cancer by 200-300%.

12. 80% of people with type 2 diabetes are overweight.

People with a BMI of 30 or above (about thirty pounds overweight) increase their relative risk of getting type 2 diabetes by 3000 percent—a greater correlation than the 2000 percent correlation between smoking and lung cancer.

The scariest part of these statistics is that the fat problem has gone global and continues to mushroom out of control. Now is the time to take control, and it must start with one person—you!

God Created Man and His Perfect Food

"And the Lord God planted a garden eastward in Eden, and there He put the man whom He had formed. And out of the ground the Lord God made every tree grow that is pleasant for sight and good for food" (Genesis 2: 8-9).

To rediscover God's intended best-for-you foods, let's go back to the very beginning—Creation. When God created man in His image, He also created the perfect food to keep man healthy. It makes sense. Those foods grow up from the ground and down from the trees: whole, fresh fruits and vegetables. Combined with sunshine, warmth, water, and carbon dioxide, plants magically mysteriously transform the inert, inedible elements in the soil into nutrients needed for the complete nutrition and proliferation of human beings.

Whole plants, especially fresh fruits and vegetables, provide all the protein (yes, even protein!), carbohydrates, fats, vitamins, calcium, minerals, phytochemicals, antioxidants, beta-carotene, micronutrients, enzymes, fiber, and all those millions of yet-and-never-to-be discovered chemicals necessary for human health and vitality.

The World Health Organization, the American Cancer Society, the American Heart Association, the U.S. government, many physicians, and research scientists agree with God's handiwork: to maximize health and minimize disease, eat more fruits and vegetables, significantly fewer animal products, and less fat, oils, salt, sugar, and refined and processed foods.

The next time you find yourself trapped in a vortex of media, advertising, doctor, author, and glitzed-up celebrity voices screaming for your attention, and your dollars, cut the confusion with one simple question: "Which foods prevent cancer?" The common sense answer: fruits and vegetables. Every doctor, researcher, teacher, pastor, grandmother, mother, father, and child would agree.

Then why do we insist on centering our meals and our lives on meat, fish, pasta, eggs, cheese, milk, brown-color white bread, refined sugar, and cereals—foods which no one has ever claim prevented cancer, heart disease, diabetes, stroke, digestive disorders, or … weight gain?

Because we like these foods and adamantly cling to them. Even if we temporarily take away our food favorites in attempting to lose weight, we are not going to give them up forever! And the simple truth is: you don't have to *if* you fill up on the best-for-you foods first.

One, Two, Three! Temple Trimming Time

"And God said, 'See, I have given you every herb [vegetable] that yields seed which is on the face of all the earth, and every tree whose fruit yields seed; to you it shall be for food'" (Genesis 1: 29).

Time to get practical. Ditch the diets and feeling down in the dumps. *If* you are ready, *really* ready, with doable direction and hope, you can gently transition to God's designer food plan and shed those layers—and this time forever. Incredibly enough—God's original food plan works! Transitioning to the next level from where you are now is as simple (not necessarily easy or quick) as adding 10+10 and following these three rules: Add, Stop, and Wiggle!

Rule 1: Add

Add and fill up first on the best-for-you foods: 10 fresh fruits and 10 different vegetables every day, called *10+10 for Life*®. Think addition, not subtraction.

What is the first thing that pops into your mind when, one more time, you decide to lose weight—starting Monday morning? Something like, "What am I going to "have to" give up?"?

Instead of fretting and moaning about what you "have to" give up, think about what you "get to" add to your day. What a refreshingly freeing weight-loss and health-gain strategy! And which foods do you "get to" add to your day? Why fresh fruits and vegetables of course, your weight warriors and health heroes. These are the very foods that give you the most nutrition for your calorie buck.

Does that mean you can never ever eat your food favorites again? Not at all. You're not going to give up your faves forever and ever anyway, so why pretend otherwise?

It simply means that for all your meals and snacks, you consciously eat fresh, whole fruits and vegetables first, eat enough to fill you up, and then you make other food choices.

Rule 2: Stop

Stop eating when your brain says, "I'm satisfied and full." That's before your stomach begs for mercy. Although this may seem like a no-brainer, this is the hardest 10+10 rule. Somehow that flashing neon light "Enough! Stop Eating!" is easy to ignore when food tastes so good. Unless they are starving and depriving on the diet-of-the-day, most Americans eat until their stomachs are so full and over distended that they are physically unable to stuff more food into themselves—adding up to too many calories that add fat to your fat.

With 10+10 and filling up on fresh fruits and vegetables, that "stop eating" signal from your brain comes through louder and clearer. Carbohydrates from unrefined plant foods, especially fresh fruits and vegetables, satisfy your hunger drive—no, not protein or fat—and trigger your brain's signal to stop eating. If you think about it, as opposed to stuffing yourself with pizza, a baked chicken dinner, or barbecued steak and all the trimmings, how many apples or how much vegetable salad can you eat until you want to stop?

As far as wasting food on your plate, your garbage disposal is replaceable—you are not. Eat the best-for-you foods first, pay attention, and stop eating when your brain tells you to. When you get hungry again, whether it be one hour or three hours later, do the novel thing—eat and watch those choices.

Rule 3: Wiggle!

What do you suppose wiggle means? Moving your body! No, wrong—that was a trick question. Of course daily exercise is important for reaching and maintaining your ideal weight, muscle tone, and health, but you already know that. However, what you may not know is that wiggle room is also key to losing weight.

From the get-go, build flexibility into your 10+10 eating plan. If you are a mere mortal residing on this planet, you are not perfect and will never be perfect. In fact, it's those Patty Perfects who get so exasperated with themselves for not being perfect that one perceived slip-up can lead to negative self-talk and total derailment. *10+10 for Life*® is guilt-proof. You get to wiggle! In fact, the only slip-up is to give up.

So allow yourself that wiggle room. Follow the 80/20 Rule. Eighty percent of the time, when life is routine and circumstances are under your control, whether at home or work, eat impeccably well. Plan, shop, and even prepare ahead if necessary. Wrap your meals around whole, fresh fruits and vegetables, along with sprouts, whole grains (as in brown rice, not breads) and beans, raw nuts and seeds, and, as an extra boost of nutrients and energy, homemade fruit and vegetable juices.

Twenty percent of the time, whether a birthday, anniversary, club luncheon, Sunday brunch with family, or get together with friends, wiggle and enjoy! Just be sure you don't wiggle too much, or you won't lose that jiggle.

Your Designer 10+10 Day

"But be not conformed to this world; but be transformed by the renewing of your mind, that you may prove what is that good and acceptable and perfect will of God" (Romans 12: 2).

Now that you are familiar with *10+10 for Life*® and its three simple rules, let's take a peek at how to apply Add, Stop, and Wiggle to each meal and create a 10+10 day. If you have health concerns, be sure to ask your doctor to monitor your progress.

Breakfast

Think about the three 10+10 rules: Add, Stop, and Wiggle. In our culture, which foods are the most logical choices for your 10+10 breakfast? Fresh fruit. That's simple enough. Add and fill up on God's fastest fast food. Just wash, cut up (sometimes), open mouth, insert, bite down, and chew.

Instead of the all-American sit-down breakfast or that quick cup of coffee and doughnut, graze on fresh fruits throughout the morning. Eat enough whole fruits to fill you up. When satisfied and full, stop eating. Eat more fruit when you get hungry again. You could eat anywhere between four or ten fresh fruits before noon, and the same fruits can be repeated.

For example, your morning grazing may include two bananas, two oranges, two nectarines, two kiwis, a bunch of grapes, a handful of strawberries, and a half of cantaloupe. The whole point is to eat enough to fill *you* up, not to knit-pick about how many grapes you're eating or how many fruits would be equivalent to a half of cantaloupe.

Stop eating your morning fruit about forty-five to sixty minutes before eating lunch. Fruit mixed with other foods can create gas. Eating fruit alone is not a food law; merely a suggestion.

Whether you are used to skipping breakfast or enjoying American breakfasts of dried cereal and milk or bacon, eggs, and toast, eating only fruit in the morning may be a big shift for you. However, it's very do-able. In fact, when transitioning to *10+10 for Life*®, fruit for breakfast is typically the easiest addition to make. And, of course, you've got that wiggle room when you get that urge for your traditional morning favorites. Just don't wiggle too much.

Lunch

Keeping the three 10+10 rules in mind, what are the logical foods for lunch? Fresh, green-leafy vegetable salads made with 10 *different* vegetables. Eating enough salad to actually fill you up may be a new experience for you, especially coming from the handful of iceberg lettuce mentality. Experiment with how much salad is enough for you.

Build your 10+10 salad from green-leafy lettuces and a variety of raw vegetables with different colors, textures, and flavors. You could choose green-leafy, butter, or romaine lettuce, spinach, sprouts, carrots, tomatoes, red or green cabbage, cucumbers, peppers, radishes, onions, broccoli, cauliflower, and avocado. If you cut up all the veggies finely, your salad may be more palatable and easier to eat. Be wise when you select the dressing. If you choose a commercial dressing, be sure it contains no oil, no dairy, and a minimum of sugar, salt, and chemicals.

A tasty alternative to bottled dressings: a finely chopped avocado, half a fresh lemon, and a few sprinkles of organic balsamic vinegar or your favorite vinegar. Stir the salad very well until the avocado coats the lettuce and vegetables, and you've got yourself a tasty, nutritious salad dressing, free from processed oil, dairy, salt, sugar, and chemicals.

Do you "have to" eat salad every day for lunch? No—go ahead and wiggle sometimes. You could choose a meat-free, dairy-free, low-salt soup or a veggie sandwich on sprouted-grain bread, spread with avocado or a low-fat soy-based mayonnaise. Another healthy change-up could be a veggie wrap with raw veggies, hummus, and sprouts, wrapped by a whole wheat tortilla shell. Yum! Or choose, not more than twenty percent of the time, from your old-time lunch favorites.

Voila! Look what you've accomplished! It's only noontime, and you've already added up 4 to 10 fruits and 10 different vegetables, and you still have the rest of the day to go.

Snacks

After feasting on your 10+10 salad, it's normal to get hungry within two to three hours. Again, eat when you're hungry. Snack on fresh fruit, cut up vegetables (keep them on handy), and a small amount of raw, unsalted nuts and seeds (not too many—they're good for you, but pack a bunch of calories).

Later afternoon, around 4:00, is commonly the time of day when foods beckon and tempt. An alternative to fresh fruit and cut-up vegetables is snacking on hot and savory foods, such as homemade vegetable, bean soup, meat-less chili, or a bowl of brown rice and black beans. Fresh, homemade fruit or vegetable juices or fruit-, vegetable-only smoothies can have the same satisfying effect, steering you clear of empty-calorie, sugary, chocolaty, salty, fatty afternoon treats! Big bonus: your appetite will be cut so you fill up quicker and stop eating sooner at dinner.

As far as after dinner snacks, choose healthy foods similar to your afternoon snacks. Whole, fresh fruits particularly satisfy and nourish in those later hours. Stop eating about two hours before bedtime. You'll sleep better and metabolize those calories more efficiently.

Dinner

Due to nostalgic memories and emotional attachment to dinner foods, your evening meal is the most challenging meal to change. After all, dinner is family time and your comforting, relaxing reward for your busy day of work, school, or play. *10+10 for Life®*, with wiggle room for your favorites, helps you gently shift from a high-fat, high-cholesterol, and/or high-calorie traditional meat-, fish-, or pasta-centered meal to a low-fat, no-cholesterol, nutrient-rich vegetable-based meal.

In addition, 10+10 conveniently makes it very possible for you to prepare one meal for your family and you, making your family happy while allowing you to stay on track with your goals. Be sure to include a salad and vegetables—at least for you—to accompany your family's traditional favorite entrées.

Eat your dinner in order with the best-for-you foods first. First eat a 10-veggie salad, probably smaller than your lunch salad, next steamed vegetables, third a more filling vegetable, like potatoes, sweet potatoes, yams, or winter squash. Nix the butter and sour cream, substituting a topping of pureed avocado and tomato, fresh salsa, or stir-fry (in water) veggies. Or, instead of the potato or yam, fill up on a whole grain dish, like brown rice, and/or a legume dish, like black beans, kidney beans, lentils, or split peas.

Once you finish the first three courses of plant foods, ask yourself this simple question: "Am I full?" If yes, then stop eating. Save your body and some dollars too. Put away the meat, fish, or pasta that you may have made for yourself. You or your spouse can eat it the next day.

If your answer is "No, I'm not full," then you can choose more plant foods or the traditional entrée you prepared for your family and yourself. Even if you choose that beef, chicken, fish, or pasta, you'll automatically eat less of the high-calorie, high-fat, and/or high-cholesterol choices without feeling deprived or hungry.

Now look back at your day and be amazed at yourself. Bingo! By suppertime, you've hit the 10+10 jackpot—at least 10 fruits and 10 vegetables in your day, and maybe even more. And it wasn't as hard as you imagined! Just fill up on the good-for-you foods first. Make the not-so-good-for-you foods your last choice.

Beverages

As significant contributors to overall calories consumed, as well as sugar, caffeine, and chemicals, beverages should not be ignored. In fact, in the standard American diet, beverages add up to at least twenty-five percent of total calories consumed. What's the point of conscientiously shifting your food choices if you drown your efforts in liquid calories?

For simple hydration, it will come as no surprise that clean water is the best beverage of choice. As a bonus to hydration, homemade fruit and vegetable juices offer a power-boost of nutrients. All other beverages, some worse than others, deplete your body. Even store-bought juices, unless they are uncooked, are less than ideal. They offer extra calories and very little nutrition.

Honoring God's Temple

". . . I have set before you life and death, blessing and cursing: therefore choose life, that both thou and thy seed may live" (Deuteronomy 30:19)

So there you are—your 10+10 day. You now know a simple plan to mindfully take impeccable care of God's sacred temple – a plan that is doable, gentle, kind, and forgiving. And, just like following any of God's simple principles, it works! Add God's best-for-you foods first. Stop eating when your brain says, "I'm full." And wiggle, but not too much.

Now go for it! It's up to you to incorporate what you've learned into *your* day. And that's the biggest challenge of all—to put God's principles into practice. But if you are willing and ready for the challenge, with prayer, persistence, and patience you will do God's will and what He knows is right for you. You will feed your body as He intended, shed those layers, laser into your core, and be free to be all that God wants you to be – loving in spirit, obedient in faith, bright in mind, and strong in body. With His spirit working its miracles and mystery through His consciously tended and trimmed temple, His unique purpose for you on earth will be fulfilled.

God did not create diseased bodies. He created the perfect body made in His image! And then gave us free will to destroy our temple. All disease, sickness, war, plagues, are opportunities to return to our Creator by being obedient. He told us to treat our body as a Temple, and He would be our Master Healer!

Your 10+10 for Life leads people through baby steps to return to the vibrant health our Creator Designed for us. Jesus said, "Verily, verily, I say unto you, he that believeth on me, the same works that I do, shall he do, and greater works than these shall he do, because I go unto my Father" (John 14:12) Every person on planet earth can accomplish more than Jesus, if they only had the faith of a mustard seed and follow Him.

We are all winners. You won the first race you were involved in—the race for life at conception. You never tried to walk, and you never tried to talk, you accomplished what you set out to do because you saw people walking, and you heard people talking. It was only after you accomplished the three hardest things in your life you heard, "No, Johnny, No, Suzy, you can't do that!" Health is a Decision! Plant the seed of health in your mind and return to the vibrant life that was given to you. Please stop the insanity! Be responsible for your own health and the health of our nation! Every seven years you replace every cell in your body. You will be the same five years from today except for the books you read, the people you associate with, the thoughts you put in your mind, and the food you put in your mouth.

You are definitely a leader, Dr. Leslie. Thanks for contributing your wisdom and understanding to the world through the Healing Nature of Jesus. —JEF

Natural Home Remedies

Ellen Tart-Jensen, Ph.D., D.Sc.

Author of: *Health is Your Birthright,*
How to Create the Health You Deserve

"Jesus said unto her, 'Daughter, your faith has made you well; go in peace, and be healed of your disease'" (Mark 5:34).

S ince I was a little girl and learned about the remarkable compassion and healing nature of Jesus, I have been determined to learn all I could about how to follow his teachings in order to become more like him. I grew up and worked with autistic children, children with learning disabilities, and handicapped children. It was through observation of these children in my classroom that I learned about the healing power of natural foods. When the children would eat foods high in refined white sugar, artificial colorings, and preservatives, they became hyperactive and unable to concentrate. Children who ate whole, natural foods were calm.

My sincere desire to learn about natural healing led me to the work of Dr. Bernard Jensen, who became my mentor for many years and later

299

my father-in-law. He was a man filled with faith and used to quote from the Bible saying, "'we are made from the dust of the earth,' and we must eat the natural foods from the earth or we will become ill." He also said, "God and nature will heal when given the opportunity." I realized that God has provided an amazing plan with laws that when followed will help us to heal. Jesus taught us those laws and demonstrated healing throughout his life. He said in Luke 5:37, "And no man putteth new wine into old bottles; else the new wine will burst the bottles, and be spilled, and the bottles shall perish." I believe this has deep meaning for those of us today. We need to cleanse and purify our bodies and minds of old impurities in order to receive the new – whether it is healthy foods or healing blessings.

Across America, people are realizing the importance of following the laws written within the Bible. We are seeing a rebirth of natural healing. The wisdom of our grandparents regarding natural remedies can play an important role in our health care today. Indeed, a great deal of research is being done world-wide on the medicinal values of plants including fruits, vegetables, and herbs. Each generation grows from experience and over time, we have seen that the extreme over use of antibiotics has created deadly antibiotic resistant bacteria. Throughout the world, there is a growing concern that many illness producing micro-organisms such as bacteria, viruses, fungi and parasites are becoming resistant to the drugs used to fight them. One of the reasons these deadly viruses, germs, and bacteria have become resistant to medications is because of repeated use. Prevention of illness is the key, but when one does get sick, understanding how to use natural remedies that have proven throughout the centuries to heal our bodies without producing harmful side-effects can be very helpful.

In my travels and studies, I learned how the plants of nature can be used as medicine and have used hundreds of natural remedies. I have witnessed tremendous results in myself, my family, and my clients. I have chosen some of the best of those remedies for this chapter. *Please remember before using any natural remedy, it is always best to consult your physician, especially if you are taking any type of allopathic medicine.*

"Behold I have given you every herb bearing seed, which is upon the face of all the earth, and every tree, in which is the fruit of a tree yielding seed; to you it shall be for meat" (Genesis 1:29).

Acne

Our skin is the largest organ of elimination. One of the best ways to heal this organ is to eat a nutritious diet high in fiber including fresh vegetables, fruits, whole grains, beans, nuts, and seeds. Avoid the use of caffeine especially in coffee, black teas, chocolate, and sodas. Avoid sugar, white flour, and greasy fried foods.

The skin mineral is silicon. Silicon nourishes and supports the skin. Foods and herbs high in silicon include red bell peppers, oat straw tea, and the horsetail herb. Horsetail may be taken in capsule form.

Acne Remedies

Wash the face twice daily, morning and night with a nice natural soap that contains tea tree oil. Tea tree oil is a natural antibiotic that will fight infection in the skin. When you wash the face, use a hot wet cotton wash cloth to open the pores. Then rinse the face with cold water to close the pores. Using hot steam and a healing facial mask has proven to be most beneficial. Boil two quarts of water. Pour into a large bowl. Add ten drops of tea tree oil or oregano oil and five drops of lavender oil. Place a towel over your head and hold your face over the steam. This will open and cleanse the pores. After ten to fifteen minutes of steaming the face, apply this facial mask.

Facial Mask for Acne

Break open four to six capsules of goldenseal herb and pour the powder into a glass dish. Add just enough purified water to make a paste. If your face tends to be dry, add olive oil to the powder instead of water. Spread paste onto the acne pimples and leave for 30 to 45 minutes. Rinse face with warm water and when clean, rinse with cold water to close the pores. Use a natural collagen lotion to tighten the pores. Coconut oil is also a great facial lubricant. Avoid cosmetics made with unnatural chemicals. If you feel you must use a powder or cover up make up, check with your health food store for natural ones free of dyes and preservatives.

Age Spots

These brown spots start to appear on the backs of the hands and arms when a person is in their late forties and fifties. When the liver is congested, it may cause these pigments to appear. Too much exposure to the sun can also cause these. A nice liver cleanse can be helpful. A dressing made of lemon juice and olive oil mixed together on a salad goes a long way in keeping the liver cleansed. Don't go out in the sun between 11:00 a.m. and 4:00 p.m. for long periods of time. If you do, be sure to wear a wide brimmed hat or carry a parasol. Also rubbing a slice of lemon or lemon oil on these spots daily has been known to help them lighten and go away.

Allergies

Allergies occur when the immune system and adrenal glands are weak. The adrenal glands are located on top of the kidneys and produce hormones that strengthen immunity. When the body is not strong enough to handle invasive substances such as pollen, dust, and animal dander, it will begin to produce histamines, which cause the allergic responses of sneezing and red, watering eyes. Antihistamines may seem to relieve the symptoms for the moment but do not get rid of the cause. They may also cause drowsiness. It is better to work on strengthening the immune system. Probiotics can help to boost the immune system.

Propolis is a wonderful product made by the bees to protect their hives from bacteria and mold. It comes in liquid and tablet form and has been known to be a tremendous immune booster. Vitamin C and the herb called echinacea also help to boost immunity. Quercitin is a bioflavonoid that helps to block the release of histamine in the body. Nettle is an herb that acts as a natural antihistamine in the body. B vitamins, especially pantothenic acid are excellent for strengthening the adrenal glands. Licorice root is great for boosting adrenal function, but should not be used by those with high blood pressure. Deglycerized licorice root will not raise the blood pressure and helps to balance the adrenal glands.

Anemia

Anemia occurs when the hemoglobin or the protein that carries oxygen is below normal in the blood and there are an insufficient number of red blood cells. Red blood cells are manufactured in the bone marrow. If the body does not have adequate supplies of iron, then not enough hemoglobin will be produced. When a person has anemia, they will become pale and feel tired with no enthusiasm for life.

Taking iron tablets that contain ferrous sulfate can cause constipation and yellowing of the teeth. Better types of natural iron such as ferrous fumarate or ferrous gluconate are preferable. These are well absorbed by the body. Nutrients that help with the absorption of iron are vitamin B12, riboflavin, folic acid, and vitamin C. These should be taken along with a natural iron supplement. This combination of supplements will assist the bone marrow to quickly make new red blood cells.

It is important for a person with anemia to get out into the fresh air and sunshine daily. Do some deep breathing. Iron and oxygen attract one another in the body. Without enough oxygen, the body will not assimilate iron. There are also many natural blood building remedies.

Blood Builder #1

Eat a diet rich in foods that are high in iron such as fresh or dried black cherries, prunes, black mission figs, raisins, currants, blueberries, black berries, apricots, red beets, red cabbage, seaweeds such as dulse, nori, hijiki, and kelp, and dark green leafy vegetables such as kale, collards, chard, spinach and mustard greens.

Blood Builder #2

Drink raw vegetable juices made from foods high in iron such as parsley, cilantro, arugula, beets, beet tops, carrots, and spinach. You may add some apple to give your juice a good flavor. This will help your digestive tract as well.

Blood Builder #3

If you do not suffer from hypoglycemia, candida albicans, or diabetes, drink a glass of black cherry or prune juice daily.

Blood Builder #4

Green super food supplements that build the blood are alfalfa, chlorella, spirulina, wheat grass juice or powder, barley grass juice or powder, and liquid chlorophyll. Chlorophyll is similar in composition to the blood of the plant and builds the blood of the body.

Blood Builder #5

Herbs rich in iron are nettles, yellow dock root, burdock root, dandelion leaf, and parsley, peppermint, spearmint, and thyme. These can be taken in capsule form, as a tincture, or made into a tea.

Blood Building Herbal Tea

2 teaspoons nettle leaves, parsley leaves, and/or dandelion leaves

1 teaspoon red clover blossoms (helps with the absorption of iron)

1 teaspoon peppermint or spearmint leaves

3 cups purified water

Bring water to a boil and add herbs. Then turn off heat and let steep for 20 minutes. Strain out herbs. Drink 2 cups a day.

Arthritis

Symptoms of arthritis include inflammation, swelling, stiffness, and pain in the joints. Most arthritis is caused by acidity in the body. Acidity leaches calcium out of the bones and causes crystals of calcium to form in the joints. Dr. Bernard Jensen called this "calcium out of solution." The pH of our saliva and urine should range between 6.8 and 7.2. It can be tested at any time with a litmus or pH strip.

Fried foods, meat, dairy products, refined grain products such as white flour, and table salt are acidic. Stress also creates a tremendous amount of acidity in the body. Fruits and vegetables help to alkalinize the body. Raw vegetable juices are very alkalinizing and should be consumed often. Celery juice is similar in mineral content to our lymph fluid which lubricates the joints. It nourishes the lymph and helps to hold calcium in the bone.

Herbs that help to relieve inflammation are ginger, turmeric, holy basil, and rosemary. Bromelain is an enzyme from pineapple that also inhibits inflammation. Flaxseed oil, borage oil, hemp oil, and evening primrose oil will help to lubricate the joints. These oils can be used on a salad or taken in capsule form. Japan has now developed a machine that produces hexagonal, highly absorbable alkalinized water called Kangen™ water. This water is proving to be extremely valuable in alkalinizing the body and those with arthritis who drink it are healing.

Epsom Salt/Ginger Bath

If you have arthritis or your muscles are tired and sore from tension after a long day or because you have strained or pulled them, try this Epsom salt/ginger bath.

Add three cups of Epsom salts and one tablespoon of powdered ginger to a tub of hot water. Soak for a minimum of 15 minutes. Rinse off thoroughly. The magnesium in the salt helps to relax the muscles and relieves pain. The ginger helps to relieve pain and promote circulation. You may feel a little weak when you get out of the bath, so step carefully. This bath is not recommended if you are pregnant, have high blood pressure, or open wounds.

Castor Oil Pack

After taking the Epsom salt/ginger bath, rinse well and apply a castor oil pack to any area with pain.

Pour 1/3 cup castor oil in a stainless steel pan and heat but do not boil. Dip a cotton flannel cloth or wool flannel cloth into the warm oil. Lay it on the affected area and put plastic wrap over the cloth. Cover with a towel and place a heating pad on top for one hour on a low to medium heat.

Arthritis Relief Oil

This oil helps relieve the pain of arthritis, aching joints, and muscles. It stimulates blood flow and brings oxygen to the tissues, thereby promoting healing.

6 ounces extra virgin olive oil

2/3 cup dried marigold flowers

1-ounce eucalyptus oil

2/3 cup dried arnica flowers

2 ounces peppermint oil

1/4 cup powdered cayenne

6 ounces wintergreen oil

1/3 cup grated ginger root

Place all ingredients in a quart jar. Let soak for three weeks. Strain and keep in a sterile, glass, airtight container. Use as needed. Be careful not to ingest or get into your eyes!

Asthma

Asthma is a very serious condition that causes obstruction of the air passages. An asthmatic attack can be triggered by allergens such as dust, animal hair, or pollen. Follow the considerations for bronchitis and lung congestion as well as allergies. During an asthma attack it is often helpful to prepare a cup of tea as follows: to one cup of hot water, add ½ teaspoon kudzu root powder or mullein leaf powder, ½ teaspoon powdered ginger root, one dropper of lobelia tincture, and 1/3 teaspoon cinnamon bark powder. Add one teaspoon raw organic honey and sip slowly. These herbs help to bring the circulation of blood through the lungs bringing oxygen and helping to expel mucus. Taking essential oils such as flaxseed oil and hemp oil will help to reduce inflammation. Marshmallow root is also a very soothing anti-inflammatory herb. Magnesium is a great mineral that helps to relax the air passages and open the bronchial tubes. In cases of any type of inflammation in the lungs or body, one must reduce acidity by following an alkaline diet and drinking alkaline water. Be sure to consult your physician before following this program.

Athlete's Foot

Athlete's foot is a persistent fungal infection on the toes and feet. Wear only white cotton socks and change your shoes often. Wear sandals or go barefooted when possible. Expose the feet and toes to the sun. Soak the feet daily in the following solution:

Foot Bath

Fill a basin about two thirds full with warm water. Add food grade peroxide, which is 35% peroxide and very strong. Use 1 tablespoon of food grade peroxide for each gallon of water. If you get the peroxide on your fingers, wash immediately with cold water. If you cannot find food grade peroxide, you may use *raw* apple cider vinegar. Use ¼ cup of vinegar to each gallon of water. Soak the feet for at least one half hour each day. Rinse well and apply garlic oil, tea tree oil, or spray with a colloidal silver spray.

Bad Breath

Chronic, ongoing bad breath comes from putrification going on in the stomach or digestive tract. If you are suffering from bad breath, consider cleansing the intestines. Another cause of bad breath is tooth decay. Visit a natural dentist and make sure to have all decay removed. Avoid using commercial mouth wash. It only masks the symptoms and may kill the friendly bacteria necessary for fighting mouth odors. When you get up in the morning use a stainless steel spoon and gently scrape the coating off the top of the tongue. After each meal, floss well and then brush your teeth with a natural bristle brush and natural tooth paste. Drink lots of purified water to which you have added mint chlorophyll. Chlorophyll absorbs odors and the mint will leave a refreshing taste in your mouth. Rinse your mouth often with a baking soda mouth wash. Baking soda will help to eliminate all odors from your mouth—even if you've eaten garlic or onions!

Baking Soda Mouth Wash

To one glass of purified water, add 1 heaping teaspoon full of baking soda. Gargle throat and rinse mouth thoroughly after brushing and flossing to eliminate bad breath.

Back Ache

There are many things that can cause the back to ache; the number one cause being tension caused by stress. Another cause is gravity. Gravity presses down on the entire body daily and over years of time the discs in the spine can begin to bulge under pressure. This occurs often if a person is overweight or has a job in which they sit all day. When the discs bulge, they can press on nerves causing tremendous pain.

Make sure you have an ergonomic chair that supports the spine. Wear supportive shoes that fit well and are not too tight. Get a posture-pedic mattress that gives with the spine as you move. Lie on a slanting board for at least twenty minutes, twice daily. The slanting board will allow the body to lie at a 45 degree slant with the head down and the feet up. Lying at a slant daily will give tremendous relief to the spine, taking pressure off the vertebrae and discs. Epsom salt baths are high in magnesium and help to relieve back pain. After the bath, rinse well and apply a castor oil pack to which you have added two teaspoons of peppermint oil. Castor oil soothes inflammation and peppermint oil helps to relieve pain by promoting circulation.

Bedsores

Mix two parts slippery elm powder, one part marshmallow root powder, and one part goldenseal root powder with warm purified water, enough to form a paste. Spread on sores and bandage. This remedy helps to relieve soreness and inflammation and also helps get rid of infection.

Bites and Stings

Bee Stings – immediately apply raw honey, mud, or clay. These will help pull out the stinger and reduce pain. Use aloe gel or calendula salve to soothe the area. If you are highly allergic to bee stings, you should wear a medic alert bracelet and be taken to the emergency room. A good homeopathic remedy to reduce the swelling and burning is apis mellifica 12x, 30x, 6c, or 9c. One dose every hour for four hours has been known to be very helpful.

Insect Bites – witch hazel, crushed comfrey or crushed plantain leaves can help relieve the itching and draw out the poison. Jewel weed sap or natural commercial jewel weed spray will also help to relieve the itching.

Natural Insect Repellents – apply lemon oil or peppermint oil to the skin to help prevent mosquito bites. Apply pennyroyal oil to the socks and shoes to repel ticks. Do not put pennyroyal oil on the skin. Eating garlic and brewer's yeast will also help you and your pets avoid being bitten by insects, ticks, and mites.

Serious Spider or Snake Bites - If you are bitten by a black widow spider, brown recluse spider, or poisonous snake, quickly apply crushed plantain leaf and 1 tablespoon Virginia Snakeroot tincture blended can be very beneficial until you can get to the doctor.

Jelly Fish Bites – Immediately apply wet sand or mud on the wound. Raw organic honey is also very helpful in pulling out the barbs and relieving pain. As soon as possible, urinate into a container and soak a cotton ball with the urine. Apply to the bite and bandage with surgical tape. Urine can be most successful in dissolving both the stinger and the poison because of the acidic pH.

Dog Bites – Mix 1 part golden seal tincture, 1 part olive leaf tincture, and one part lobelia tincture and saturate a piece of gauze. Place immediately over the wound. If you don't have those tinctures, pour oregano oil on a gauze and place over the wound. This will help to fight infection until you can get to a doctor.

Bleeding

To stop a wound from bleeding, mix together one part cayenne pepper and one part comfrey powder directly on to the wound. It will sting temporarily, but could save a life. To help prevent vessels from breaking and bleeding in the nose or rectal areas, taking rutin and bioflavonoids can be most beneficial.

Boils or Furuncles

A boil is like a large blister filled with pus from the staphylococcus aureus bacteria. Make a solution of 1 cup hot purified water and ten drops of tea tree oil or eight drops of oregano oil. Wet a cotton wash cloth with the solution and hold the compress on the boil for fifteen minutes, three times daily or until the boil breaks open. Apply a colloidal silver salve to the boil with a q-tip in between compresses. After the boil breaks and the pus comes out, apply the salve with a q-tip and keep it bandaged until it heals.

Body Odor

The skin is supposed to release one to two pounds of toxins per day. The pores of the scalp also release toxicity and the hair collects odors. If we want to smell good, we must keep the internal body clean by eating a healthy diet high in fresh vegetables and fruits. These are high in anti-oxidants that fight body odors. Drinking lots of purified water with 1 tablespoon of chlorophyll added to each glass will gently cleanse the bloodstream and help prevent body odor. Make sure your bowels are working well (at least two to three times per day after each meal) or toxicity from the bowel will come out on the skin.

Dry skin brushing with a natural bristle brush before a shower helps a lot to release bodily odors. Wash your hair, scalp, and body with natural shampoo and soap free of chemicals and dyes. Wear clothing made from natural fibers so the skin can "breathe." Garlic and onions are very good for you, but if you eat a lot of them, the odor will be on the breath and come out on the skin. Rinsing the mouth with 1 teaspoon of baking soda dissolved in 8 ounces of water will keep the breath fresh. Soaking in a baking soda and lemon bath will also purify the pores of odors.

Baking Soda and Lemon Bath

To a tub of warm water, add 3 cups of baking soda.

Cut 4 lemons in quarters and place them in an old stocking. Tie it off and drop into the water.

Soak for an hour. This recipe is so beneficial at removing toxins from the body; you may see a colored ring around the tub when you let out the water.

Use only natural deodorant free of aluminum. Here's a natural deodorant recipe that works really well.

Deodorant

¼ cup clear aloe juice

¼ cup witch hazel

1 tsp. baking soda

4 drops of grapefruit seed extract

10 drops of lavender, lemon, or rose oil

Blend in blender. Store liquid deodorant in a spray bottle. Spray under arms daily as needed.

Bronchitis or Lung Congestion

For helping to release mucus and infection from the lungs and bronchial tubes, put ten drops oil of oregano in four ounces warm water and drink four times daily. Oregano oil helps to fight viruses and bacteria. Rub warm olive oil mixed half and half with oregano or garlic oil on chest. Cover with a warm cotton cloth. Rub feet with the same warm oil mixture and tie cotton cloths around the feet. The onion poultice is another great poultice for any type of lung congestion.

Onion Poultice

Onion poultices help to break up mucus and draw the poisons of colds, bronchitis, flu and pneumonia out of the body.

Peel two to four onions and bake them in the oven until well done. Mash them in a bowl with two tablespoons of warm olive oil. Wrap the mash in cotton cloths and tie them onto the feet. An onion pack can also be placed on the chest. Cover with plastic wrap, a thin towel and a warm heating pad.

Foods that help the body eliminate mucus are onions, garlic, radishes, and lemons.

Bruising

It is normal to bruise occasionally, but when bruising occurs often, the connective tissue in the body is weak. To strengthen connective tissue and prevent bruising, take rutin and bioflavonoids. When a bruise appears, apply a comfrey or cabbage poultice.

Comfrey Poultice

Comfrey poultices are wonderful for sprains and bruises. Comfrey is so powerful in mending and repairing; it has been called knit bone. It is also very helpful in the clotting of blood in cases of heavy bleeding.

Soak one ounce of dried comfrey root in a half cup of distilled water overnight. Simmer for 15 minutes and strain. Blend with one cup chopped fresh comfrey leaf or two tablespoons dried comfrey leaf that has been soaked overnight and simmered for one minute and strained (just use the herb) and one tablespoon of pure virgin olive oil, ten drops of tea tree oil and 12 drops of birch or lavender oil. Spread onto the sprain and cover with plastic wrap.

Bunions

Bunions usually form just under the big toe and can become very inflamed and painful. When people wear pointed toes or tight fitting "stylish" shoes daily for years, too much pressure is placed on the top part of the feet and toes. Shoes that rub on the bone beneath the big toe daily will cause the bone to begin to thicken pushing the big toe inward. This will throw off one's posture and may cause back pain as well.

It is important to wear only wide, comfortable shoes in order to let the toes have room to spread out. Make sure the shoes have plenty of cushion and arch support and this will give optimal support to the foot. Orthotics may even be helpful.

Soak the feet daily for at least one half hour in hot water and Epsom salts with one tablespoon of salt per gallon of water. Rinse feet well and apply a castor oil pack to the area. Castor oil packs are one of the finest things to help relieve the inflammation of a bunion and may even help the extra boney knot to begin to recede. During the day, make a mixture of half lavender oil and half peppermint oil and rub on the bunion. Lavender helps to relieve pain and inflammation and peppermint helps promote good circulation to the area. Blood carries oxygen which helps to relieve pain.

Burns and Sunburns

Drink plenty of alkaline or purified water with liquid trace minerals added to help replace electrolytes in the body. Raw organic honey mixed half and half with wheat germ oil has been known to be one of the finest remedies for healing burns of any kind including sunburn. Aloe Vera has long been known for its healing benefits in the treatment of burns. Plantain and or comfrey leaf powder can be mixed with honey and wheat germ oil or olive oil to heal and soothe burns as well. Moist plantain leaves can be placed over the honey or ointment underneath the bandage to keep the bandage from sticking.

Plantain Poultice

Blend one cup of chopped fresh plantain with four ounces of olive oil and two ounces of honey. Apply to burns. This is also a great poultice for insect bites, bee stings, or animal bites.

Chapped Lips

Apply coconut oil to lips to heal and soothe dryness and cracking. Get more oils into your diet including flaxseed oil and hemp oil and this will lubricate the lips and skin from the inside.

Circulation

If you have cold hands and feet or numbness in the extremities, you need to improve the circulation of your blood. Hot water sends blood rushing through our veins and opens our pores to help release toxins. Cold water slows down the blood and closes the pores. Taking a shower with filtered water alternating with hot and cold greatly improves circulation and can relieve aches and pains. To warm the feet on a cold morning, put a pinch of cayenne pepper in some natural lotion and rub onto the bottoms of the feet. Your feet will stay warm for hours!

Cold Sores

Cold sores or canker sores that appear in or around the mouth can be very painful. They are often caused by a virus and brought on by stress. Spraying the sores with colloidal silver spray or applying colloidal silver directly with a q-tip can help to start the healing process. Silver helps to fight viruses. Another great remedy that helps to heal cold sores is oregano oil. Oregano oil may be mixed half and half with olive oil and applied to the external sores with a cotton swab. Saturate a small piece of gauze with the oil mixture, roll it up and place on the sores inside the mouth. Oregano oil is anti-viral and will help to reduce the pain of cold sores.

Constipation

Constipation is often a magnesium deficiency. Adequate magnesium in one's program can help to promote peristalsis or bowel contractions that move the fecal matter along. Yellow squash and yellow corn are high in magnesium. If foods are not enough, magnesium tablets might be helpful. Start with 250 mg. of magnesium oratate or magnesium citrate, 2x per day. You may take more or less magnesium as constipation improves.

Fiber is also most important for relieving constipation. Eat plenty of fresh fruits and vegetables. Red beet root grated into salads is often all one needs to get the bowels working properly again because beets help the liver and gallbladder to function better. I have also found that when my clients take 4 alfalfa or 10 chlorella tablets together with one teaspoon of flaxseed oil, three times per day before meals, their bowel function will improve. Constipation can be caused by parasites. If you have been tested for parasites, have visited a foreign country, or have abdominal cramping, find and take a black walnut, cloves, wormwood herbal combination.

Digestive enzymes can help to relieve constipation. Well digested food will move through the digestive tract much more easily than undigested food. Probiotics also assist with proper digestion and assimilation. Probiotics help to replace the friendly bacteria that are lost during several weeks or months of constipation. Make sure to find an excellent probiotic with plenty of live friendly bacteria.

A tablespoon full or two of ground flaxseeds should be consumed once or twice a day for better elimination. Ground flaxseeds can be stirred into soups, salads, or cereals for extra fiber. Drink two to three cups of warm flaxseed tea per day. Flaxseed tea is mucilaginous and slippery and helps the bowel to move smoothly. If you have had chronic constipation for a long time, you should learn about colon cleansing and do a cleanse. Cleansing old accumulated fecal matter from the walls of the colon will help the bowel to work much better! I have written how to cleanse in my e-book, *The Simplified Guide to Internal Cleansing* available at www.bernardjensen.com

Flaxseed Tea

Boil one quart of purified water.

Add 4 heaping teaspoons of flaxseeds.

Turn the burner off and let steep for one hour.

Yields 4 cups of tea.

Cleansing Tea

For occasional constipation a tea may be taken before bedtime. A recipe for the tea follows:

1/3 teaspoon cascara sagrada bark powder

2/3 teaspoon of cardamom powder

a pinch of ginger powder

1 teaspoon honey

1 cup boiling water

Pour boiling water over the herbs. Add honey and stir. Cover for five minutes and then drink slowly.

Colds, Coughs, Sore Throat Sore Throat

Colds, coughing, and sore throat are sometimes caused by bacteria, but more often a virus. Gargling with 1 tablespoon of raw apple cider vinegar in a glass of water is most helpful. Raw apple cider vinegar has proven time and again to soothe and often heal a sore throat and stop coughing. You can also make a healing drink.

Raw Apple Cider Vinegar and Honey Drink

To a cup of hot water, add 1 tablespoon of raw apple cider vinegar and 1 tablespoon of raw organic honey. Stir and drink two to three times daily. This drink is very beneficial for relieving sore throats and all types of lung and sinus congestion.

Natural Cough Syrup

Chop one yellow onion and one whole lemon including the peeling into small pieces. Place in a quart sized sauce pan and add two cups of purified water. Bring water to a boil and reduce heat to simmer. Simmer for one half hour. Turn burner off and place all ingredients in a blender. Blend well and strain through a sieve into a sterile glass jar. Add 4 tablespoons raw honey. Stir well and give one teaspoon every hour. Store the syrup in the refrigerator.

Dandruff

Gather ten leaves of fresh spearmint, wash them well and place into a blender. Add a quarter cup of raw apple cider vinegar, one tablespoon of jojoba oil, and five drops of tea tree oil, or oil of oregano. Blend well and massage into scalp. Leave in for about half an hour and then wash with a pine tar shampoo. Supplementing with 25 mg. of zinc daily can also be helpful.

Diarrhea

When a person has diarrhea, there is usually a poison in the system that needs to be released. Taking medicine to stop it prevents the toxicity from getting out of the body. A person with diarrhea should stop eating regular meals. Instead prepare some barley or brown rice gruel, cooking the barley or brown rice well until it forms a mush and then strain. Eat a small bowl of the strained gruel throughout the day. You may also eat a very ripe banana or baked potato.

Teas that are beneficial in stopping diarrhea are red raspberry leaf tea, thyme tea, cinnamon bark tea, and ginger tea. Drink these at various intervals throughout the day separate from food.

With diarrhea, the intestinal tract is usually inflamed. Slippery elm bark or marshmallow root can be taken in tea or capsule form to help coat the walls of the intestinal tract and relieve inflammation. Parasites may be involved when a person has diarrhea. If you have been traveling in a foreign country and get diarrhea, you probably have some type of parasite. The best herbs known to help rid the body of parasites is a combination of wormwood, black walnut, and cloves such as Para Ex. Two capsules, three times per day will usually stop all intestinal cramping and diarrhea if parasites are involved.

Earaches and Ear Infections

Earaches and ear infections can often be relieved and healed using three parts mullein oil and one-part garlic oil. Warm the oil and drop two drops into each ear. Add cotton to keep oil in place. This warm oil is also beneficial in breaking up hardened ear wax.

Ear Drops

Grate 1 clove of garlic into 4 ounces of mullein or olive oil. Let the mixture sit for three weeks in a glass jar at room temperature. Strain and pour into a 4 ounce dropper bottle.

Eczema, Psoriasis

These skin conditions often occur when the bowel and liver are congested and toxic from years of improper eating. Keeping the diet free from sugar, caffeine, alcohol, artificial preservatives, dyes, and colors is crucial. Eating a diet rich in vegetables, fruits, gluten free whole grains, soaked nuts and seeds, and beans is important for healing. Cleansing the bowel and liver is imperative. (See section on Constipation.)

Make sure you are getting plenty of natural oils including flax, borage, and hemp seed oils. Also consume coconut oil and avocados in the diet. Oat straw tea, which is high in silicon (skin mineral) helps to heal the skin. Vitamin E in the form of wheat germ oil has been known to be helpful. Adding 1,000 mg. of vitamin C with bioflavonoids to the program 2x daily can often give the immune system a boost to help improve the skin. Bathing in a bath with one cup baking soda or one cup raw apple cider vinegar can soothe itching. Using the Chickweed/Calendula Oil mixture has proven to be very healing for the skin. Wear only clothing made from natural fibers such as cotton or silk. Synthetic clothing blocks the pores of the skin from proper elimination.

Chickweed/Calendula Oil (rashes, eczema, psoriasis, burns)

2 tablespoons of dry or 3 tablespoons of fresh chickweed
2 tablespoons of dry or 3 tablespoons fresh marigold blossoms
2 cups olive oil

Mix the chickweed and marigold into two cups of olive oil. Pour into a covered glass jar and let sit for two weeks, shaking the container daily. Strain through a cheesecloth and use on rashes, psoriasis, eczema, or burns. Store the mixture in a dark bottle, in a cool place.

Eyes, Tired and Sore

Eyes can become tired and sore from overuse. Staring into a computer all day is often the cause. A lack of sleep or too much reading will also create eye strain. When the eyes are tired, try this soothing eye poultice.

Soothing Eye Poultice

Grate half of a small peeled potato and a quarter of a peeled cucumber. Mix together. Divide mixture in half and spoon onto two 6 inch square pieces of gauze or cheese cloth. Fold edges of cloth over the mixture. Lie down and place a poultice of mixture over each closed eye. Leave on for half an hour and rinse. This is a very cooling, soothing remedy for the eyes.

Eyes, Dry

The eyes may become dry in the winter time when the house is closed up and the heater is on. When the fluids in the eyes dry up, the little vessels in the sclera or white parts of the eyes can break and part of the eye will appear very red.

Each night before you go to bed, rub castor oil on the eyelids – upper and lower and on the eye lashes. Castor oil is lubricating and will help to lubricate the eyes.

The fluids of the eyes are part of the lymph system, so nourishing the lymph daily is important. Celery juice is similar in composition to lymph fluid and helps to feed the lymph with the elements it needs to be healthy. Drink one cup of fresh, raw organic celery juice per day. If you don't like the taste of it, add some carrot and apple.

Fever

Fever or temperature over 98.6 degrees often comes to help the body burn off a bacteria or virus. If the fever goes above 100 degrees, we should work to cool the body down.

Soak in the warming bath I have given below. After the bath, rinse with cool water and get into bed with lots of covers.

Warming Bath

This bath helps to promote sweating, which releases toxins from the skin and can be used with the first signs of fever or flu.

Place one tablespoon each of yarrow herb, peppermint leaf, elder flowers and ground or powdered ginger in a gallon-size pot. Pour two quarts boiling water over the herbs and let simmer for 10 minutes. Strain and pour into bath. Soak in the bath at least 20 minutes.

Cold Compresses

Saturating cloths with very cold water and placing them on the face, arms, and legs will sometimes help to stop a fever.

Foot Bath for Sore Feet

For tired, aching, sore feet, pour two gallons of hot water into a basin. Add one-half cup of sea salt and ten drops of lavender oil to the water. Soak feet for at least a half hour and rinse with cool water. Your feet will feel rejuvenated!

Gingivitis or Gum Disease

Infection of the gums around the teeth occurs when people eat a lot of sugary foods and do not brush and floss their teeth properly. Symptoms of gum disease include red, swollen, and bleeding gums. They can also become quite painful and the teeth may become loose.

Avoiding sugar and eating a healthy diet will help to heal gum disease. Cleansing the intestinal tract often helps to heal gum disease as well. Vitamin C and bioflavonoids are very important for gum repair. The bioflavonoid, rutin will help to strengthen and tighten the connective tissue in the gums. Make sure to floss your teeth carefully after each meal and brush with a natural bristle brush. Use natural toothpaste with antibacterial oils. A water pick is also very helpful as well.

Natural Toothpaste

¾ cup baking soda

¼ cup sea salt

4 Tablespoons of almond oil

1 Teaspoon clove oil, peppermint oil, or cinnamon oil (clove is very antibacterial and best if you have gingivitis)

Apply a small amount to toothbrush and use just as you would any other toothpaste. Store your toothpaste at room temperature in a covered glass container.

Mouthwash for Gum Infections

To six ounces of water, add 5 drops peppermint oil and 5 drops wild oregano oil. Add ¼ teaspoon food grade peroxide OR 1 teaspoon colloidal silver 500 ppm. Swish through gums several times per day and spit out.

Wheatgrass Poultice

After juicing the wheatgrass, take the pulp and add a little of the juice back into it. These poultices are excellent for gum disease. Place them inside the mouth between the gum and the jaw. Wheatgrass juice acts as a natural antiseptic and antibiotic anywhere in the body.

Anti-infection Gum Poultice

4 capsules marshmallow root (break open and use contents only)

3 capsules white oak bark (broken open and use contents only)

2 teaspoons of comfrey or plantain powder

12 drops myrrh oil

12 drops Roman chamomile oil

8 drops thyme oil

6 drops clove oil

3 drops oil of wild oregano oil

Mix all ingredients to form a paste. (Add additional oil or powders to achieve pasty consistency.) Cut a cheese cloth to form a two-inch by one-inch swatch, add paste and roll to form a "Tootsie roll" shaped poultice. Use dental floss to tie off each end. Poultice may be placed between gum and cheek and left there from one to three hours. Use during the day or at night. Store poultices in a plastic bag in the refrigerator.

Hair Loss

Hair loss can be caused by hormonal imbalances, medications, a lack of protein in the diet, and scalp infections.

Hair Remedy

Heat one-third cup of sesame oil in a small glass or stainless steel pot. Remove from burner before it boils and add ½ teaspoon of ginger powder. Massage into scalp and wrap a hot wet towel around the head. Warm the towel again when it cools by dipping it into hot water. Leave towel around head for a half hour. Then wash scalp with a biotin or keratin shampoo from your health store. Do this three times per week. Sesame oil helps to cleanse and nourish the hair follicles and ginger promotes the circulation of blood, which carries nutrients to the hair.

Headache

Headaches are usually caused by sinus congestion, tension, poor circulation to the head, or liver and bowel congestion. They may also be caused by cervical vertebrae that are out of alignment. Eating a good healthy diet and cleansing the bowel and liver will often stop headaches. Check with your chiropractor to see if your neck needs to be adjusted. Lying on a slanting board for 20 minutes, 2 times a day will bring blood flow back to the head. Massaging peppermint oil into the forehead and along the hairline will release tension and stimulate blood flow to the head. Taking white willow bark in capsule form will also help to relieve headaches.

Hemorrhoids

Hemorrhoids are actually swollen veins much like varicose veins located in the rectum. They are often caused by straining with constipation. Follow all suggestions under Constipation. Drinking oat straw tea can help strengthen the walls of the veins and arteries. Take 2000 milligrams of vitamin C with bioflavonoids three times daily to strengthen connective tissue. If hemorrhoids are persistent, take extra rutin, 50 milligrams three times daily. Soak in a warm sitz bath of two quarts of water and one cup of calendula tea and one tablespoon of witch hazel (can be found in liquid form at your health store). Calendula tea is very soothing to hemorrhoids. Witch hazel acts as an astringent and can help to relieve bleeding. Rinse off and apply castor oil to anus and rectum.

Itching

Take a bath with 1 cup apple cider vinegar in bath water. Or dip apple cider vinegar onto a washcloth and apply to itching areas. Apply coconut oil.

Kidney/Bladder Infections

Symptoms will be burning when urinating and/or lower back pain. Uva ursi, parsley, and juniper berry teas have been used successfully in getting rid of kidney/bladder infections. Grapefruit seed extract – a few drops in water three times per day may be helpful.

Avoid sugar. Drink six ounces unsweetened cranberry juice or pomegranate juice from the health food store, four times daily. These juices will keep the bacteria from sticking to the walls of the bladder and thus flush it out of the body. Parsley juice is excellent for strengthening the kidneys. Marshmallow root taken in capsule form – 2, 3x per day will soothe the kidneys and bladder and relieve inflammation and pain. Peppermint oil rubbed on the lower back can help reduce pain and bring circulation to the area. Take a good probiotic such as Preolac on an empty stomach two to three times per day. Probiotics supply friendly bacteria that help to fight bad bacteria. Drink lots of purified water.

Kidney Stones

Kidney stones develop from minerals such as calcium that stick together in the urine. Uric acid crystals may also form stones in the kidneys. When the body becomes too acidic, calcium may come out of the bone and form crystals in the joints or kidneys. Too much uric acid is created when a person eats a lot of meat. Eating fresh vegetables and drinking fresh vegetable juices, especially parsley and celery juice can help to alkalinize the system and dissolve stones. Raw apples, apple juice, and raw apple cider vinegar are excellent for dissolving stones. Drink eight ounces of water with one tablespoon of raw apple cider vinegar added to it, four times per day. Make salad dressings with raw apple cider vinegar and olive oil. Epsom salts baths and castor oil packs help to dissolve kidney stones.

Muscle Cramps

Muscle cramps are often caused by a lack of minerals in the diet, especially potassium. When children start their growth spurt, they will often have leg cramps at night. This is because they are using lots of minerals for growth and not replacing them in their diet. To relieve muscle cramps, mix 2 tablespoons raw apple cider vinegar in 8 ounces water and drink. The potassium in the drink relieves cramps and muscular pain.

Nausea

Nausea can be caused by car sickness or sea sickness. It may also be caused by a stomach virus, vertigo, or overeating. To help relieve nausea, try ginger tea, peppermint tea, or red raspberry leaf tea. Chewing on anise seeds is also helpful.

Ringworm

Ringworm is a fungus that is highly contagious. It looks like a concentrated, red, circular rash that is often raised and itches. An effective remedy for ringworm is:

1 tsp tea tree oil, and 2 teaspoons powdered goldenseal root. Mix together to form a paste. Apply and keep area bandaged for 24 hours. Shower using a tea tree oil soap; rinse well and bandage again. With persistence, ringworm will leave in one to two weeks.

Sprains

When a person sprains their ankle, it will swell and become very painful. This is because tissue and vessels under the skin have been pulled or torn. The body sends extra lymph fluid to that area to help to soothe inflammation. Apply a cool damp cloth or ice pack immediately to help reduce swelling. Later, rub in lavender oil to relieve pain and promote healing. A poultice can also be made.

Sprain Poultice

Blend 1/4th cup chopped cabbage
1 tablespoon dried comfrey leaf powder or 2 tablespoons chopped fresh comfrey leaves
2 tablespoons lavender oil
Add water until the mixture forms a paste.
Apply to sprain and wrap with gauze.

Varicose Veins

Varicose veins look like raised, lumpy, purple areas on the backs of the legs or calves. They most often occur when the veins have lost their elasticity. Taking rutin and vitamin C with bioflavonoids will strengthen the veins. Consuming silicon in the form of oatstraw tea will also tighten the veins. Drink cabbage juice, which is high in vitamin P and C. These vitamins have been found to give strength to blood vessels. Cabbage poultices help to heal varicose veins because they improve circulation and act as an astringent to tighten and heal the stretched tissue in the vascular walls.

Cabbage Poultice

Place one cup of chopped cabbage in blender with one-third cup of raw apple cider vinegar and 1 teaspoon of ginger powder. Blend into a thick paste. Smear paste on varicosities and wrap with plastic wrap. Keep legs propped up through the night on a pillow while wearing this poultice. Rinse well the next day. The ginger in the poultice helps promote circulation.

Warts

Warts are caused by a virus and are contagious. People with strong immune systems do not get warts as easily as those with lowered immunity. There are some great natural remedies for wart removal.

1. Pick a dandelion and rub the sap that oozes out of the stem onto the wart, several times per day.
2. Apply crushed, fresh basil to wart and bandage it. Change dressing daily.
3. Peel a banana and cut the peeling just a bit larger than the wart. Place the inside part of the peeling on the wart and bandage.
4. Slice a clove of garlic and place on the wart and bandage.
5. Pour garlic oil mixed half and half with castor oil onto the wart and bandage.

For any ailment, have faith and pray often. Imagine the beautiful Master Jesus holding your hand and healing your body.

19

STEPS TOWARD A HEALTHIER AND MORE COMPASSIONATE DIET

John Robbins

If, like most Americans, you have eaten meats, dairy products and eggs that come from factory farms, you might want to consider steps toward a healthier and more compassionate diet. If you take these steps, your body will thank you for the rest of your life because you'll be getting more nutrients and eating less junk. And also, your spirit will rejoice because your life will be that much more fully an expression of your respect for yourself and for all of life.

Taking steps toward a better diet can make an extraordinary difference, even if you've eaten poorly for years. One reason is that, although you may think of your body as a permanent structure, most of your body's tissues are actually in a constant state of renewal. The cells lining your stomach, for example, are replaced every five days, while your red blood cells last about four months. The cells in an adult human liver are replaced every three to five hundred days. Even your bones are far from permanent; the entire human skeleton renews itself about every ten years. Almost all the cells in your body are being continually regenerated, so what you eat today literally becomes your body tomorrow.

- Bring consciousness to the foods you eat. Ask whether they are natural, wholesome, and in alignment with the health of your body and your spirit.

- Don't pollute your body. Go to your kitchen cupboard and get rid of any food products that no longer serve your potential to be radiantly fit and healthy.

- Eat slowly, chew thoroughly, digest well. Eat just to the point of fullness without feeling stuffed.

- Whenever possible, shop at local farmers' markets or participate in community-supported agriculture, buying produce direct from the grower. Shop at local natural-foods stores, or at chains like Whole Foods, Wild Oats, and Trader Joe's. Always read labels so that you can select foods with the most nutritious ingredients.

- Save money and packaging by buying in bulk.

- Don't buy or eat anything that contains partially hydrogenated oil. Learn to recognize the smell of rancidity, and don't eat nuts, seeds, or grain products that carry the telltale odor.

- Keep away from high-fructose corn syrup. Replace regular ketchup with organic brands that are sweetened with fruit juice. Look for jams that are 100 percent fruit sweetened (no added sugar).

- Stay away from food dyes (blue 1, blue 2, citrus red 2, green 3, red 3, red 40, yellow 5, yellow 6, etc.).

- Drink soy milk rather than cow's milk. Switch from mayonnaise to a more healthful soy or canola version. Eat whole-soy products like tofu and tempeh rather than meat.

- Eat less meat or none at all. For protein, depend on soy foods, other beans, peas, whole grains, and nuts.

- If you eat any kind of meat, purchase products that you know to be truly free-range and organic.

- If you eat fish, be sure it's low in mercury, and wild, not farmed. To learn about the mercury levels in various kinds of fish, visit gotmercury.org.

- Whenever possible, select fresh fruits and vegetables rather than canned ones. If you are unable to get the fresh produce you want, then choose frozen (without added salt or sugar) over canned.

- Get to know the amazing variety of vegetables beyond French fries and iceberg lettuce. Enjoy eating a wide assortment of fresh vegetables, especially lots and lots of dark green leafy vegetables (kale, collards, mustard greens, spinach, chard, broccoli, etc.).

- Eat an abundance of fresh raw vegetables and fruits.

- Whenever possible, eat food that is in season and locally grown.

- Eat fewer products made with flour (bread, crackers, chips, pastries), and more whole grains, beans, sweet potatoes, and vegetables.

- Buy and eat organic food.

- If possible, grow food. Plant collards or kale in the late summer (or early summer where growing seasons are short) so that you have fresh greens all winter.

- Add your voice to the call for labeling genetically engineered food.

- Pack your own lunch. If you make someone else's lunch, write a love note and put it in with the food.

- Bake with your children. Involve them in making wholesome food. Bake delicious whole-grain muffins with blueberries, bananas, or other fruits they love.

- Serve a green leafy salad to your kids while they are waiting for dinner. In your salads, use romaine and other lettuces rather than iceberg (they have more vitamins and minerals). Also include chopped-up carrots and other vegetables.

- Buy or make healthful desserts and healthful comfort foods.

- Put wholesome snacks such as seeds, nuts, and vegetables with hummus in a conspicuous and accessible part of the fridge.

- Eat many colors. Foods' natural colors are not just treats for the eye but also signs of important nutrients known as antioxidants.

- When you crave something crunchy, try raw vegetables or nuts instead of salty chips.

- Every few days, grind organic flaxseeds in an electric coffee grinder reserved for this purpose. Keep the ground seeds in the refrigerator and sprinkle them daily on your meals. Try them on cereal and salads and in sandwiches and stews.

- Eat plenty of fresh vegetables every day. Make a big pot of vegetable soup, keep it in the fridge in a large container, and heat up small batches throughout the week.

- Eat whole grains, not refined grains. Eat baked potatoes with the skins, not French fries. Eat your own homemade vegetable soups, not the highly salted ones generally available in grocery stores. Look for brands that say "organic" and "low sodium."

- Between meals, drink lots of pure water. Avoid soft drinks and diet sodas. Herbal teas can be comforting as well as healthful, particularly on cold days.

- Use monounsaturated oils such as olive oil and canola oil as your primary cooking oils. Avoid heating oils to the smoking point. For the fat in your diet, eat walnuts, almonds, hazelnuts, sunflower seeds, avocados, and other nuts and seeds.

- Stay away from dairy products and fatty meats.

- Minimize consumption of oils that are high in omega-6 fatty acids, including corn, safflower, sunflower, soybean, and cottonseed oils.

- Shun trans-fatty acids. Stay away from margarine, shortening, commercial pastries, deep-fried food, and most prepared snacks and convenience foods.

- Instead of eating out, invite friends over for dinner. Or invite yourself over to a friend's house for dinner, offering to bring a delicious and wholesome meal.

- Patronize only restaurants that serve healthful food, or at least can accommodate your preferences.

- Instead of soft drinks, make your kids fruit smoothies.

- When you are interacting with people who don't eat the same way as you do, never be ashamed of the steps you are taking toward greater health. Let your enthusiasm and love of life be contagious.

EDITOR'S NOTE

The knowledge that John Robbins is sharing with you, when put into practice will lead you through baby steps into the understanding how powerful your life can be when you awaken the life-force that lies within! To acquire more wisdom, which leads to understanding to healing and to an exciting life of awareness, "Why are we here?" I would encourage everybody to purchase John Robbins books, *Healthy at 100, Diet for a New America: How Your Food Choices Affect Your Health, Happiness, and the Future of Life on Earth, The Food Revolution: How Your Diet Can Help Save Your Life and Our World,* and more. —JEF

20

THE PIG FARMER

John Robbins ©

One day, in Iowa, I met a particular gentleman—and I use that term, gentleman, frankly, only because I am trying to be polite, for that is certainly not how I saw him at the time. He owned and ran what he called a "pork production facility." I, on the other hand, would have called it a pig Auschwitz.

The conditions were brutal. The pigs were confined in cages that were barely larger than their own bodies, with the cages stacked on top of each other, in tiers, three high. The sides and the bottoms of the cages were steel slats, so that excrement from the animals in the upper and middle tiers dropped through the slats on to the animals below.

The aforementioned owner of this nightmare weighed, I am sure, at least 240 pounds, but what was even more impressive about his appearance was that he seemed to be made out of concrete. His movements had all the fluidity and grace of a brick wall.

What made him even less appealing was that his language seemed to consist mainly of grunts, many of which sounded alike to me, and none of which were particularly pleasant to hear. Seeing how rigid he was, and sensing the overall quality of his presence, I—rather brilliantly,

333

I thought—concluded that his difficulties had not arisen merely because he hadn't had time, that particular morning, to finish his entire daily stretching routine.

But I wasn't about to divulge my opinions of him, or his operation, for I was undercover, visiting slaughterhouses and feedlots to learn what I could about modern meat production. There were no bumper stickers on my car, and my clothes and hairstyle were carefully chosen to give no indication that I might have philosophical leanings other than those that were common in the area. I told the farmer, matter of factly, that I was a researcher writing about animal agriculture, and asked if he'd mind speaking with me for a few minutes so that I might have the benefit of his knowledge. In response, he grunted a few words that I could not decipher, but that I gathered meant I could ask him questions and he would show me around.

I was, at this point, not very happy about the situation, and this feeling did not improve when we entered one of the warehouses that housed his pigs. In fact, my distress increased, for I was immediately struck by what I can only call an overpowering olfactory experience. The place reeked, like you would not believe, of ammonia, hydrogen sulfide, and other noxious gases that were the products of the animals' wastes. These, unfortunately, seemed to have been piling up inside the building for far too long a time.

As nauseating as the stench was for me, I wondered what it must be like for the animals. The cells that detect scent are known as ethmoidal cells. Pigs, like dogs, have nearly 200 times the concentration of these cells in their noses as humans do. In a natural setting, they are able, while rooting around in the dirt, to detect the scent of an edible root through the earth itself.

Given any kind of a chance, they will never soil their own nests, for they are actually quite clean animals, despite the reputation we have unfairly given them. But here they had no contact with the earth, and their noses were beset by the unceasing odor of their own urine and feces multiplied a thousand times by the accumulated wastes of the other pigs unfortunate enough to be caged in that warehouse. I was in the building only for a few minutes, and the longer I remained in there, the more desperately I wanted to leave. But the pigs were prisoners there, barely able to take a single step, forced to endure this stench, and almost completely immobile, 24 hours a day, seven days a week, and with no time off, I can assure you, for holidays.

The man who ran the place was—I'll give him this—kind enough to answer my questions, which were mainly about the drugs he used to handle problems that are fairly common in factory pigs today. But my sentiments about him and his farm were not becoming any warmer. It didn't help when, in response to a particularly loud squealing from one of the pigs, he delivered a sudden and threatening kick to the bars of its cage, causing a loud "clang" to reverberate through the warehouse and leading to screaming from many of the pigs.

Because it was becoming increasingly difficult to hide my distress, it crossed my mind that I should tell him what I thought of the conditions in which he kept his pigs, but then I thought better of it. This was a man, it was obvious, with whom there was no point in arguing.

After maybe 15 minutes, I'd had enough and was preparing to leave, and I felt sure he was glad to be about to be rid of me. But then something happened, something that changed my life, forever—and, as it turns out, his too. It began when his wife came out from the farmhouse and cordially invited me to stay for dinner.

The pig farmer grimaced when his wife spoke, but he dutifully turned to me and announced, "The wife would like you to stay for dinner." He always called her "the wife," by the way, which led me to deduce that he was not, apparently, on the leading edge of feminist thought in the country today.

I don't know whether you have ever done something without having a clue why, and to this day I couldn't tell you what prompted me to do it, but I said Yes, I'd be delighted. And stay for dinner I did, though I didn't eat the pork they served. The excuse I gave was that my doctor was worried about my cholesterol. I didn't say that I was a vegetarian, nor that my cholesterol was 125.

I was trying to be a polite and appropriate dinner guest. I didn't want to say anything that might lead to any kind of disagreement. The couple (and their two sons, who were also at the table) were, I could see, being nice to me, giving me dinner and all, and it was gradually becoming clear to me that, along with all the rest of it, they could be, in their way, somewhat decent people. I asked myself, if they were in my town, traveling, and I had chanced to meet them, would I have invited them to dinner? Not likely, I knew, not likely at all. Yet here they were, being as hospitable to me as they could. Yes, I had to admit it. Much as I detested how the pigs were treated, this pig farmer wasn't actually the reincarnation of Adolph Hitler; at least not at the moment.

Of course, I still knew that if we were to scratch the surface we'd no doubt find ourselves in great conflict, and because that was not a direction in which I wanted to go, as the meal went along, I sought to keep things on an even and constant keel. Perhaps they sensed it too, for among us, we managed to see that the conversation remained, consistently and resolutely, shallow.

We talked about the weather, about the Little League games in which their two sons played, and then, of course, about how the weather might affect the Little League games. We were actually doing rather well at keeping the conversation superficial and far from any topic around which conflict might occur. Or so I thought. But then suddenly, out of nowhere, the man pointed at me forcefully with his finger, and snarled in a voice that I must say truly frightened me, "Sometimes I wish you animal rights people would just drop dead."

How on Earth he would suspect that I might have any sympathy toward animal cruelty issues I will never know—I had painstakingly avoided any mention of any such thing—but I do know that my stomach tightened immediately into a knot. To make matters worse, at that moment his two sons leapt from the table, tore into the den, slammed the door behind them, and turned the TV on loud, presumably preparing to drown out what was to follow. At the same instant, his wife nervously picked up some dishes and scurried into the kitchen. As I watched the door close behind her and heard the water begin running, I had a sinking sensation. They had, there was no mistaking it, left me alone with him.

I was, to put it bluntly, terrified. Under the circumstances, a wrong move now could be disastrous. Trying to center myself, I tried to find some semblance of inner calm by watching my breath, but this I could not do, and for a very simple reason, there wasn't any to watch.

"What are they saying that's so upsetting to you?" I said finally, pronouncing the words carefully and distinctly, trying not to show my terror. I was trying very hard, at that moment, to disassociate myself from the animal rights movement, a force in our society of which he, evidently, was not overly fond.

"They accuse me of mistreating my stock," he growled.

"Why would they say a thing like that?" I answered, knowing full well, of course, why they would, but thinking mostly about my own survival. His reply, to my surprise, while angry, was actually quite articulate. He told me precisely what animal rights groups were saying about operations like his, and exactly why they were opposed to his way of doing things. Then, without pausing, he launched into a tirade about how he didn't like being called cruel, and they didn't know anything about the business he was in, and why couldn't they mind their own business.

As he spoke it, the knot in my stomach was relaxing, because it was becoming clear, and I was glad of it, that he meant me no harm, but just needed to vent. Part of his frustration, it seemed, was that even though he didn't like doing some of the things he did to the animals—cooping them up in such small cages, using so many drugs, taking the babies away from their mothers so quickly after their births—he didn't see that he had any choice. He would be at a disadvantage, and unable to compete economically, if he didn't do things that way. This is how it's done today, he told me, and he had to do it too. He didn't like it, but he liked even less being blamed for doing what he had to do in order to feed his family.

As it happened, I had, just the week before, been at a much larger hog operation, where I learned that it was part of their business strategy to try to put people like him out of business by going full-tilt into the mass production of assembly-line pigs, so that small farmers wouldn't be able to keep up. What I had heard corroborated everything he was saying.

Almost despite myself, I began to grasp the poignancy of this man's human predicament. I was in his home because he and his wife had invited me to be there. And looking around, it was obvious that they were having a hard time making ends meet. Things were threadbare. This family was on the edge.

Raising pigs, apparently, was the only way the farmer knew how to make a living, so he did it even though, as was becoming evident the more we talked, he didn't like one bit the direction hog farming was going. At times, as he spoke about how much he hated the modern factory methods of pork production, he reminded me of the very animal rights people who a few minutes before he said he wished would drop dead.

As the conversation progressed, I actually began to develop some sense of respect for this man whom I had earlier judged so harshly. There was decency in him. There was something within him that meant well. But as I began to sense a spirit of goodness in him, I could only wonder all the more how he could treat his pigs the way he did. Little did I know that I was about to find out...

We are talking along, when suddenly he looks troubled. He slumps over, his head in his hands. He looks broken, and there is a sense of something awful having happened.

Has he had a heart attack? A stroke? I'm finding it hard to breathe, and hard to think clearly. "What's happening?" I ask.

It takes him awhile to answer, but finally he does. I am relieved that he is able to speak, although what he says hardly brings any clarity to the situation. "It doesn't matter," he says, "and I don't want to talk about it." As he speaks, he makes a motion with his hand, as if he were pushing something away.

For the next several minutes we continue to converse, but I'm quite uneasy. Things seem incomplete and confusing. Something dark has entered the room, and I don't know what it is or how to deal with it.

Then, as we are speaking, it happens again. Once again a look of despondency comes over him. Sitting there, I know I'm in the presence of something bleak and oppressive. I try to be present with what's happening, but it's not easy. Again I'm finding it hard to breathe.

Finally, he looks at me, and I notice his eyes are teary. "You're right," he says. I, of course, always like to be told that I am right, but in this instance I don't have the slightest idea what he's talking about.

He continues. "No animal," he says, "should be treated like that. Especially hogs. Do you know that they're intelligent animals? They're even friendly, if you treat 'em right. But I don't."

There are tears welling up in his eyes. And he tells me that he has just had a memory come back of something that happened in his childhood, something he hasn't thought of for many years. It's come back in stages, he says.

He grew up, he tells me, on a small farm in rural Missouri, the old-fashioned kind where animals ran around, with barnyards and pastures, and where they all had names. I learn, too, that he was an only child, the son of a powerful father who ran things with an iron fist. With no brothers or sisters, he often felt lonely, but found companionship among the animals on the farm, particularly several dogs, who were as friends to him. And, he tells me, and this I am quite surprised to hear, he had a pet pig.

As he proceeds to tell me about this pig, it is as if he is becoming a different person. Before he had spoken primarily in a monotone, but now his voice grows lively. His body language, which until this point seemed to speak primarily of long suffering, now becomes animated. There is something fresh taking place.

In the summer, he tells me, he would sleep in the barn. It was cooler there than in the house, and the pig would come over and sleep alongside him, asking fondly to have her belly rubbed, which he was glad to do.

There was a pond on their property, he goes on, and he liked to swim in it when the weather was hot, but one of the dogs would get excited when he did, and would ruin things. The dog would jump into the water and swim up on top of him, scratching him with her paws and making things miserable for him. He was about to give up on swimming, but then, as fate would have it, the pig, of all people, stepped in and saved the day.

Evidently the pig could swim, for she would plop herself into the water, swim out where the dog was bothering the boy, and insert herself between them. She'd stay between the dog and the boy, and keep the dog at bay. She was, as best I could make out, functioning in the situation something like a lifeguard, or in this case, perhaps more of a life-pig.

I'm listening to this hog farmer tell me these stories about his pet pig, and I'm thoroughly enjoying both myself and him, and rather astounded at how things are transpiring, when, once again, it happens. Once again a look of defeat sweeps across this man's face, and, once again, I sense the presence of something very sad. Something in him, I know, is struggling to make its way toward life through anguish and pain, but I don't know what it is or how, indeed, to help him.

"What happened to your pig?" I ask.

He sighs, and it's as though the whole world's pain is contained in that sigh. Then, slowly, he speaks. "My father made me butcher it."

"Did you?" I ask.

"I ran away, but I couldn't hide. They found me."

"What happened?"

"My father gave me a choice."

"What was that?"

"He told me, 'You either slaughter that animal or you're no longer my son.'"

Some choice, I think, feeling the weight of how fathers have so often trained their sons not to care, to be what they call brave and strong, but what so often turns out to be callous and closed-hearted.

"So I did it," he says, and now his tears begin to flow, making their way down his cheeks. I am touched and humbled. This man, whom I had judged to be without human feeling, is weeping in front of me, a stranger. This man, whom I had seen as callous and even heartless, is actually someone who cares, and deeply. How wrong, how profoundly and terribly wrong, I had been.

In the minutes that follow, it becomes clear to me what has been happening. The pig farmer has remembered something that was so painful, that was such a profound trauma, that he had not been able to cope with it when it had happened. Something had shut down then. It was just too much to bear.

Somewhere in his young, formative psyche he made a resolution never to be that hurt again, never to be that vulnerable again. And he built a wall around the place where the pain had occurred, which was the place where his love and attachment to that pig was located, which was his heart. And now here he was, slaughtering pigs for a living—still, I imagined, seeking his father's approval. God, what we men will do, I thought, to get our fathers' acceptance.

I had thought he was a cold and closed human being, but now I saw the truth. His rigidity was not a result of a lack of feeling, as I had thought it was, but quite the opposite: it was a sign of how sensitive he was underneath. For if he had not been so sensitive, he would not have been that hurt, and he would not have needed to put up so massive a wall. The tension in his body that was so apparent to me upon first meeting him, the body armor that he carried, bespoke how hurt he had been, and how much capacity for feeling he carried still, beneath it all.

I had judged him, and done so, to be honest, mercilessly. But for the rest of the evening I sat with him, humbled, and grateful for whatever it was in him that had been strong enough to force this long-buried, and deeply painful memory, to the surface. And glad, too, that I had not stayed stuck in my judgments of him; for if I had, I would not have provided an environment in which his remembering could have occurred.

We talked that night, for hours, about many things. I was, after all that had happened, concerned for him. The gap between his feelings and his lifestyle seemed so tragically vast. What could he do? This was all he knew. He did not have a high school diploma. He was only partially literate. Who would hire him if he tried to do something else? Who would invest in him and train him, at his age?

When, finally, I left that evening, these questions were very much on my mind, and I had no answers to them. Somewhat flippantly, I tried to joke about it. "Maybe," I said, "you'll grow broccoli or something."

He stared at me, clearly not comprehending what I might be talking about. It occurred to me, briefly, that he might possibly not know what broccoli was.

We parted that night as friends, and though we rarely see each other now, we have remained friends as the years have passed. I carry him in my heart and think of him, in fact, as a hero. Because, as you will soon see, impressed as I was by the courage it had taken for him to allow such painful memories to come to the surface, I had not yet seen the extent of his bravery.

When I wrote *Diet for a New America*, I quoted him and summarized what he had told me, but I was quite brief and did not mention his name. I thought that, living as he did among other pig farmers in Iowa, it would not be to his benefit to be associated with me.

When the book came out, I sent him a copy, saying I hoped he was comfortable with how I wrote of the evening we had shared, and directing him to the pages on which my discussion of our time together was to be found.

Several weeks later, I received a letter from him. "Dear Mr. Robbins," it began. "Thank you for the book. When I saw it, I got a migraine headache."

Now as an author, you do want to have an impact on your readers. This, however, was not what I had had in mind.

He went on, though, to explain that the headaches had gotten so bad that, as he put it, "the wife" had suggested to him he should perhaps read the book. She thought there might be some kind of connection between the headaches and the book. He told me that this hadn't made much sense to him, but he had done it because "the wife" was often right about these things.

"You write good," he told me, and I can tell you that his three words of his meant more to me than when the *New York Times* praised the book profusely. He then went on to say that reading the book was very hard for him, because the light it shone on what he was doing made it clear to him that it was wrong to continue. The headaches, meanwhile, had been getting worse, until, he told me, that very morning, when he had finished the book, having stayed up all night reading, he went into the bathroom, and looked into the mirror. "I decided, right then," he said, "that I would sell my herd and get out of this business. I don't know what I will do, though. Maybe I will, like you said, grow broccoli."

As it happened, he did sell his operation in Iowa and move back to Missouri, where he bought a small farm. And there he is today, running something of a model farm. He grows vegetables organically—including, I am sure, broccoli—that he sells at a local farmer's market. He's got pigs, all right, but only about 10, and he doesn't cage them, nor does he kill them. Instead, he's got a contract with local schools; they bring kids out in buses on field trips to his farm for his "Pet-a-pig" program. He shows them how intelligent pigs are and how friendly they can be if you treat them right, which he now does. He's arranged it so the kids, each one of them, gets a chance to give a pig a belly rub. He's become nearly a vegetarian himself, has lost most of his excess weight, and his health has improved substantially. And, thank goodness, he's actually doing better financially than he was before.

Do you see why I carry this man with me in my heart? Do you see why he is such a hero to me? He dared to leap, to risk everything, to leave what was killing his spirit even though he didn't know what was next. He left behind a way of life that he knew was wrong, and he found one that he knows is right.

When I look at many of the things happening in our world, I sometimes fear we won't make it. But when I remember this man, and the power of his spirit, and when I remember that there are many others whose hearts beat to the same quickening pulse, I think we will.

I can get tricked into thinking there aren't enough of us to turn the tide, but then I remember how wrong I was about the pig farmer when I first met him, and I realize that there are heroes afoot everywhere. Only I can't recognize them because I think they are supposed to look or act a certain way. How blinded I can be by my own beliefs.

The man is one of my heroes because he reminds me that we can depart from the cages we build for ourselves, and for each other, and become something much better. He is one of my heroes because he reminds me of what I hope someday to become.

When I first met him, I would not have thought it possible that I would ever say the things I am saying here. But this only goes to show how amazing life can be, and how you never really know what to expect. The pig farmer has become, for me, a reminder never to underestimate the power of the human heart.

I consider myself privileged to have spent that day with him, and grateful that I was allowed to be a catalyst for the unfolding of his spirit. I know my presence served him in some way, but I also know, and know full well, that I received far more than I gave.

To me, this is grace—to have the veils lifted from our eyes so that we can recognize and serve the goodness in each other. Others may wish for great riches or for ecstatic journeys to mystical planes, but to me, this is the magic of human life.

DESIGNED FOR HEALTH

Rev. George H. Malkmus, Lit.D.

As I sit down to write this, my heart is very heavy! It is heavy because although the Christian Community has learned how to take care of the spiritual part of man through faith in Jesus Christ, which of course is of greatest importance because it determines where one will spend eternity, sadly, most in the Christian Community are in gross ignorance and darkness when it comes to the physical part of man!

This was brought vividly to my attention when a dear Christian brother and friend, who had been diagnosed with colon cancer a year or so ago, told me last Sunday that the doctors now tell him his cancer is terminal and that he is going to die. When this brother was first diagnosed, he was encouraged to change his diet by both his pastor and myself, but the doctors told him diet couldn't help, so he made no diet change. In fact, the doctor not only told him that a changed diet could do nothing for his cancer, but also told him that, without surgery and chemotherapy, he would die.

So this dear brother listened to his doctors, had the surgery to remove a large section of his colon, which left him with a bag to collect his feces, and accepted all their other medical modalities, including chemotherapy.

Now the doctors tell him he is going to die! Thankfully, he knows the Lord, and is prepared spiritually to die, but physically he is only 60 years old and too young to die. He should still have many years left to live and enjoy life while serving the Lord, but he can't do either if he dies.

On May 29, 1957 at a Billy Graham Crusade rally in Madison Square Garden in New York City, though I had been brought up in church and been baptized, for the first time in my life I realized I was a sinner and in need of a Saviour. That evening I made the most important decision of my life, because, on that night, I opened my heart to Jesus Christ, invited Him into my heart, and, in so doing, took care of the spiritual part of me, and established my future spiritual destiny.

For the next almost 20 years of my life I saturated my life with the spiritual – studying my Bible daily, going to church every time the church doors were open, going to school 4 years in preparation for the ministry, and then pastoring for almost 20 years. During many of those years I had read through the entire Bible annually, while preparing and delivering over 5,000 Bible-based sermons. The spiritual was my passion, not only personally, but I had also dedicated my life to trying to help others spiritually.

The physical part of man

In 1976, at the age of 42, after totally saturating my life with the spiritual for the previous 20 years, I was suddenly brought to the realization that there was another part of me – a physical part. For the previous 20 years, while taking care of the spiritual part of me, I had almost totally neglected the physical part, and as a result, was told I had cancer.

For some unknown reason, for the previous 20 years, I guess I had felt that if I took care of the spiritual part of me, the physical part would take care of itself. Because I had dedicated my life to the Lord and had saturated my life with Him and in the helping of others, there was no need to be concerned about the physical. I guess subconsciously I believed that if I put God first and dedicated my life to serving Him and helping others, God would protect me from physical harm. I was wrong!

God used that cancer in my life to awaken me to the importance of not only taking care of the spiritual part, but also the *necessity* of taking care of the physical part if I wanted to live and continue the spiritual ministry God had given me. Sadly, I am not alone in this neglect of the physical, as I have learned that most in the Christian community are also in gross ignorance, darkness, and neglect, when it comes to the physical.

The average Christian can sit in the average church their entire life and *never* hear a message from the pulpit regarding how to take care of the physical part. Those reading this know what I am saying is true! For while we are devoting almost all of our time in church to the spiritual part of man, at the *same time*, 90% of the prayer requests in our churches are for physical problems.

Why? Because God's people have never been taught that if they neglect the physical part, the physical part will break down and fail them. These physical breakdowns can cause physical problems that can affect their ability to serve the Lord, fulfill their spiritual mission and ministry, and the living of a long and healthy life!

Listen to what God has to say about the physical part.

"I beseech you therefore, brethren, by the mercies of God, that ye present your bodies a living sacrifice, holy, acceptable unto God, which is your reasonable service, and be not conformed to this world..." (Romans 12:1-2a).

In this scripture, the believer is being admonished to take proper care of their physical *"body."* Also, this scripture is telling us that we cannot take proper care of this physical body if we are *"conformed to this world."* And there are other verses dealing with this subject:

"What? know ye not that your body is the temple of the Holy Ghost which is in you, which ye have of God, and ye are not your own? For ye are bought with a price: therefore glorify God in your body, and in your spirit, which are God's" (I Corinthians 6:19-20).

"Know ye not that ye are the temple of God, and that the Spirit of God dwelleth in you? If any man defile the temple of God, him shall God destroy; for the temple [physical body] of God is holy, which temple ye are" (I Corinthians 3:16-17).

In the above verses we learn that because of Christ's sacrifice on the cross and through our acceptance of that sacrifice, our body has literally become *"The temple of God."* Thus: *"you are bought with a price,"* and because we have been purchased by God, we should *"glorify God in* [our] *body."* And if we fail to *"glorify God in* [our] *body,"* and if we *"defile"* [bring harm to this] *"temple"* [physical body], God will *"destroy"* it!

God did not design His human creation to be sick

In Genesis 1:31, after the 6 days of creation had been completed, during which time God made all things – including man – we read: *"And God saw everything that He had made, and behold it was very good . . ."* Friends, God made no mistakes in creation!

In the New Testament, in 3 John 2:1 we read: *"Beloved, I wish above all things that thou mayest prosper and be in health, even as thy soul prospereth."*

From the above verses it is clearly evident that sickness was not a part of God's original design or plan for His human creation. If that be so, and obviously it is, why do we humans get sick? That is an easy question to answer. In Galatians 6:7 we read: *"Be not deceived, God is not mocked: for whatsoever a man soweth, that shall he also reap."*

Sowing and reaping is an irrefutable natural law established by God! Sowing and reaping can have many applications, but in keeping with the subject, we get sick because we are not taking proper care of our physical bodies. We get sick because we are putting things into this physical body that cause it harm. Even though often done in ignorance, we, as a result of putting into our body things that will harm it and that God never intended to enter it, create physical problems within our beautiful God-made physical body temples! Thus: *"My people are destroyed for lack of knowledge . . ."* (Hosea 4:6).

Christians are just as sick as non-Christians

If you were to go into the average church of today, you would find that some 90% of all the prayer requests of the people in that church are for physical healing. Statistically, we find that Christians are just as sick as non-Christians, suffering the same physical breakdowns, to the same percentages, in spite of an abundance of spiritual prayers for healing.

How do Christians deal with physical problems?

Sadly, except for spiritual prayer, the Christian community deals with their physical problems in the identical manner the non-Christian community deals with their physical problems. Both groups go to the same doctors, take the same toxic drugs, allow their bodies to be burned with the same radiation, and mutilated with the same surgeries, in an effort to remove their physical problems. This drugging, burning and mutilating is what I call the world's system of health care. Is there a better way than the world's system of health care? Absolutely!

God built self-healing into each of our bodies

Although God did not design us to get sick, God, in His infinite wisdom, apparently knew that we would get sick because we would not take proper care of our physical bodies, and, thus, He built self-healing into these physical bodies we each possess. We clearly see this self-healing manifested when we cut ourselves – the bleeding to cleanse the wound, the scab to protect the wound while underneath it is knitting the skin back together, and ultimately the self-healing abilities of the body are clearly evident when the scab falls off.

When God created those first two humans, Adam and Eve, He placed within their genetic coding the ability to self-heal, *and this same self-healing* that He placed into Adam and Eve, has been passed down from generation to generation, ultimately to you and me in our genes! Yes, you heard me right! Built right into each one of us is the ability to correct almost every physical problem that comes our way during our entire lifetime without doctors, without drugs, without radiation and without surgery!

As we learn ever more about this incredible physical body temple that God has provided each of us, how can we fail to exclaim words similar to those of the Psalmist in Psalm 139:14: *"I will praise thee; for I am fearfully and wonderfully made . . ."*

My dear friend, there is not a doctor in the entire world capable of healing anyone of anything. Nor is there a drug, radiation or surgery that doctors can use to heal anyone of anything. To go even further – there is not a vitamin or mineral supplement, or herbal or homeopathic concoction that can heal anyone of anything. Here is one that will surprise most – there is not a food, or glass of fresh vegetable juice, or a fast, capable of healing anyone of anything.

No my dear friend, there is nothing that can be done to the outside of the body or that can be placed into the body that can heal anyone of anything. What most folks fail to realize is that the only healing that can ever take place in the body is self-healing and that this self-healing can only take place when we bring conditions conducive to healing about within the body so that the body can do what God designed it to do, which is heal itself.

Man has been looking for centuries, spending untold amounts of money, seeking a cure for the physical ills of man. Yet, in spite of all these efforts and tremendous expenditures, mankind is growing increasingly sicker while the cost of this so-called health care continues to increase. I predict that man will never find the solution to the physical ills of mankind until he realizes that God has already built self-healing into the physical body of man, and all that is necessary to experience true health and healing is to bring conditions about within the body so that the body can do what God designed it to do.

God gave Adam and Eve a healthy diet

In the Bible, in Genesis 1:29, God gave Adam and Eve, and through Adam and Eve to each of us, the very diet He designed this marvelous physical body we each posses, to be nourished with. As we return to that garden diet today, the body receives the nutrients it was designed by God to be nourished with, and thus physical problems usually simply disappear and we no longer experience sickness.

In 1976, after experiencing numerous physical problems for the previous 42 years of my life, culminating in being told I had colon cancer, at the advice of an evangelist friend, I stopped putting into my body substances found outside the Genesis 1:29 garden diet, and started nourishing my body exclusively with the living nutrients found in the garden foods.

The result? Within less than 1 year not only was my cancer gone without the use of any medical modalities, but also gone were all the other physical problems I was suffering at the time, physical problems resulting from the eating of what I call the "world's diet" or frequently referred to as the "Standard American (SAD) Diet." I am now in my mid-70's and have not experienced as much as a cold, the flu, headache or sore throat since making that diet change in 1976.

EDITOR'S NOTE

Dr. George Malkmus, thank you for stepping out in courage and TRUTH. You are truly a leader. I agree with you that the Christian pastors who are the shepherds of the flock and who are feeding the children of the world, need to be reached. Most people know more about the other side of the moon, than their own anatomy! I too, have a problem with the "white coats" impersonating God that have little or no training in nutrition and how the body works! Especially when they give death sentences with no hope for recovery, they are not serving our best interests! I for one, choose not to donate any more of my body parts!

I encourage everyone to be responsible for their own health. Please invite God back into your life, your family, our country, our courthouses, and our schools! Would you want to be where you're not wanted?

Dr. George, I'm proud to be one of your health educators from "Hallelujah Acres," and encourage the readers to join this elite group. I too know the true Healing Nature of Jesus. —JEF

Because of that personal experience, in 1992, my wife Rhonda and I established Hallelujah Acres, a ministry that teaches health from a biblical perspective. Since establishing Hallelujah Acres, millions have adopted what we call The Hallelujah Acres Diet and Lifestyle (very similar to the Genesis 1:29 diet), and tens of thousands have written to tell me that after they stopped eating the SAD diet, and started eating The Hallelujah Diet, they have recovered from over 170 different physical problems and that they rarely get sick anymore.

In conclusion

In the Bible, in Mark 5:25-26, we find clear evidence of the medical communities' inability to bring healing to the physical bodies of that day: *"And a certain woman, who had an issue of blood for twelve years, and had suffered many things of many physicians, and had spent all that she had, and was nothing bettered, but rather grew worse."* Here we are some 2,000 years later, and today we find that the world's system of disease care has not improved.

How many more Christians will have to suffer, be sidelined, and die needlessly and prematurely, at the hands of the Medical Community, before the Christian community realizes that God has not only made provision for the spiritual part of man, but also the physical part? How much longer is it going to take the Christian community to realize that there is a better way than the world's way of dealing with physical problems, and my dear friend, it is called God's way!

HEALING FAMILY PATTERNS

THE WALLS THAT REST
BETWEEN ME AND
ALL I CAN BE

Rebecca Linder Hintze

Author, *Healing Your Family History:*
5 Steps to Break Free of Destructive Patterns

After a dull weekend of housework and "honey-do" chores, I found my husband Shane kicked back in his LazyBoy chair watching an outdoor show on the satellite dish. As I wandered through the room, he made a comment about his frustrating job as an engineer and, once again, shared his secret wish to live his life producing and hosting programs like the one he was viewing. Realizing that there might be more to his comment, I took a seat and initiated further conversation.

For six months, my dutiful husband had been negotiating a promotion at work. Actually, his goal and consequent efforts to get ahead had been underway for years, but during these prior months he had actually been promised a great, new position. Yet, as the days and weeks passed, the job was not fully secured. Interestingly, many of the new job responsibilities were already his, and most people under his jurisdiction knew about the promotion. At that time, Shane was functioning with two jobs: his old one and the new one that was his, but not really. At least he wasn't being fairly compensated for it.

Working hard, not getting paid for it, and struggling to get ahead—this wasn't just my husband's story. A look over his family history on both sides tells the story of person after person who worked hard, didn't get fairly or abundantly compensated, and struggled to get ahead. Shane's experience, though it may have felt like his own, was a direct result of a family pattern that continued to dictate his daily life and the lives of many others.

I took a minute to ask my husband a question. I said, "If you were to close your eyes and pull all the energy out of your body that keeps you from moving forward and prevents you from getting what you want, what would that form of energy look like?"

He responded, "A brick wall."

I continued, "How does the brick wall help you get what you want?"

He said, "It doesn't."

I prompted him further, "But what if a part of you believes that it helps you. Ask that part of you this question: Why do I like this brick wall?"

He opened his eyes with a look of enlightenment and said, "It helps me think out of the box. I have to work hard to get around it, so I learn more and am a more effective problem solver. It helps me do a better job than others."

I thought to myself, "Does it really? How could a brick wall make him feel better about himself?"

A brick wall couldn't be that productive. From where I was sitting, this was clearly an illusion. There must be a better way for him to think out of the box and be good at what he does. Perhaps hard work and smart thinking are the gifts in his family's pattern, but there must be a more effective way that's not so marked with sabotage.

I could see that the wall needed to come down. Yet, as Shane carried on, I realized that the brick wall wasn't going anywhere—at least not that evening. In fact, when I suggested he watch it crumble, he was unwilling. He said the wall was a good thing and he wasn't sure if he was ready to let it go.

Wow! What a realization. The very thing that stood between my husband and what he wanted most was a wall he wasn't fully willing to move.

Every family has hidden belief systems, or false traditions, that are passed down through the generations. We may be aware of the physical history of our ancestors. For example, we may know if we are predisposed to cancer and heart disease, but what of our family's predisposition to emotional and spiritual roadblocks? Since all things are first created spiritually (or, all action originates with thought), our awareness of predisposed family patterns may be as vital to our success, health, and well-being as our knowledge of our family's medical history, if not more so. For Shane, and others like him, financial freedom, less work and more play, and feeling free to reach out and grab a dream will likely never become reality until a false family tradition is identified, challenged, and fully transcended—until that wall finally crumbles.

All families pass down perceptions that become the filters we see through, that color our perceptions of the world. These filters can either help or hinder us. Until we recognize our family's limited thinking patterns, we don't have much of a choice to change them. Since we are raised within our family's reality, becoming aware that there are other possibilities is difficult, if not impossible, without help.

Just like Shane, most of us fight hard to hang on to family traditions. The rebellious "black sheep" family members are not exempt. In fact, they are often the ones who hold on the tightest. In order to effect change, we must not only identify the patterns, but also understand why we work so hard to hold on. When family patterns exist for generation after generation, there is always a reason why. Somewhere within the consciousness of those who hold the pattern, there appears to be a payoff, a seemingly legitimate reason to hold on. In Shane's case, the payoff was the ability to think outside the box, to increase problem-solving skills, and to build strength of will and character. All that was false about his family's perception is that a wall must exist in order to achieve this result. The family pattern became limiting when a wall was produced in order to achieve a desirable outcome.

Most families don't intend to pass down destructive messages to their descendants. In fact, most parents want more for their children than they had for themselves. As in Shane's case, there was good to be found within the family tradition (his family is hardworking, capable, and effective at problem solving). When transcending a family pattern, we don't want to throw the baby out with the bath water, as the adage goes. We want to strengthen our posterity by improving upon the gifts given to us by our families through the process of eliminating the destructive or limiting portions. The goal is to effectively transcend the negative or sabotaging part of our family's beliefs or traditions. We do *not* want to blame, judge, or criticize our families. Such a process creates additional roadblocks, restricting and disabling us.

Interestingly, some scientists today are examining whether thought patterns and feelings that create behavior roam inside our DNA and pass on for generations. With the possibility that our bodies are dictating who we are, how we think, how we feel, what we like to do, and what we eat, it's important to pose the question, "Who are we really?"

Within every human body is a spiritual body. Becoming aware of who we are as spiritual beings helps us to transcend our dysfunctional circumstances and create a more beautiful life. And doing so assists us in accomplishing our mission or purpose in this life, freeing us to experience greater joy and happiness on earth.

Once I was engaged in a conversation with my mother-in-law where she shared a powerful observation. She said, "I know that somewhere inside of me is someone really good—really awesome. But there's all this stuff between me and her, and sometimes she doesn't get to come out as much as she'd like." I believe we all feel that way from time to time. We all have "stuff"—including our false family traditions—that serves as a wall resting between us and all we can be.

Awareness is More than Half the Battle

On a hot, summer evening, years ago, my mother dropped by for a short visit. Her timing left her on my doorstep the night before I was scheduled to host a baby shower for a friend. At the time, I had four small children under the age of six, with three of them one year apart in age. Then, it was a common sight to find me tired and a bit irritable, as I scurried around a house full of dirty laundry, toys strewn in most every corner, and small fingerprints positioned on nearly every wall. My mother walked in the door, took a look around, and asked, "How are you going to have a shower HERE tomorrow?"

That was a good question! Since I was used to sleepless nights after nursing babies year after year, I explained that I would stay up most of the night cleaning and cooking. She got tired just thinking about it! She had other obligations and couldn't stay and help. Within minutes, she was gone, but the comment she made as she walked out the door stayed through the night. She said, "Don't forget those fingerprints on the coffee table."

I couldn't believe it! How did she notice the fingerprints on the coffee table in the midst of dirty carpet, dust, toys, crying children, and the phone ringing? Her comment made me mad. Throughout the evening I thought about what she'd said, why she'd said it, and how her words made me feel. What was the underlying message in her short comment? Why did it spark so much emotion within me?

For those who share my family's tradition of keeping a spotless home, you may relate to some memories from my childhood. I grew up with my grandmother Frances coming to visit, and while she was there—or anywhere—she would walk up the stairs bent over, picking up lint as she walked. If I poured myself a glass of water, then walked away from it for more than a minute, when I returned, my glass would be in the dishwasher. If I used the sink in the bathroom, even if only to wash my hands momentarily, she would wipe the sink with Windex or ask me to go back and clean up. Knowing this, is it any wonder why my mother was keenly able to locate the fingerprints on the coffee table, despite the mess around her?

A clean home and good cooking were paramount for my grandmother Frances and her mother Catherine Stephens (Grammy). I learned from my family that *good* women keep their home clean and cook good food. It was easy to assume that, if good women keep their home clean and cook well, those who don't must be *bad*.

Does that mean that since my home was a mess (a mess that included fingerprints on the coffee table), I was a bad person—that I was less than another, or not good enough? Obviously the answer was no. My home was my number one focus. My family and home environment were well nurtured. Yet despite all my goodness, at that moment I felt like a bad mother, wife, and homemaker.

To this day, I have wonderful memories of visiting my grandmother. Her home was beautiful, decorated to look and feel lovely—and it was "love-ly" to me (a home full of love). I learned at a young age to equate the beauty of a home and a well-cooked meal with peace and love. It is true that a clean home can symbolize order, and order typically feels better than chaos. With all good intentions, my grandmothers and mother taught their children to keep a clean home for many noble reasons. Yet, their message went awry when the worth and quality of a woman, in their opinion, became attached to the cleanliness and beauty of her home.

On that hot, summer night, my family tradition limited me. Despite my mother's good intent, her words left me feeling unworthy. After all, I wasn't in step with the family requirement. My home was far from clean.

Costly Family Beliefs

All families pass along traditions. Some traditions promote success, encourage love, and serve and heal those who choose to participate. Others can be both negative and positive. As with my experience, my family passed along both good and bad. Is there a way to eliminate the bad and keep the good? Absolutely! In fact, teaching readers to do so is the goal of this message. Some family traditions come without any good. Families who pass along dark abuse and hate pass along traditions that must be eliminated in order for a family (even society) to heal and experience long-term joy, peace, and love.

Why should we take the time to identify our family beliefs or traditions? The reason is twofold. Doing so helps us better understand and love others, including ourselves. It also clearly focuses our energy on achieving our goals. Family traditions are limiting or false when they hinder our ability to love, understand, and succeed. Transcending the limited aspects of our family's heritage increases our capacity to achieve our potential. When we are unable to love ourselves, we are unable to love others. Because low self-worth sits at the core of a variety of dysfunctional behavior (e.g., drug abuse, alcoholism, physical and sexual abuse, and other addictions), it is crucial to expose any limited family teachings that may destroy our sense of worthiness.

Most limiting traditions are not spelled out consciously. For instance, I don't ever recall my grandmother saying to me, "Becky, you'd better keep a clean house and learn to cook as well as me, or you'll be a bad person, a flat out failure." She never said that to me. In fact, if she were living and read this, she might even strongly disagree that she ever sent that message to me. After all, my grandmother loved me and would have given just about anything to see that I was happy. She was a wonderful, loving grandmother.

People who love and honor their ancestors often struggle to look objectively at their family history. Loving children and grandchildren often fear uncovering something negative about their relatives. They assume that doing so will make their family appear bad when in fact their family is good. Discovering our limited family patterns doesn't mean that we've established an agenda to criticize our heritage. Rather, it is a process to improve upon it.

Letting go of the false traditions of our forefathers is counsel handed down for thousands of years. In the Old Testament, we read in Ezekiel 20:18: "Walk ye not in the statutes of your fathers, neither observe their judgments..." and in Jeremiah 16:19: "Surely our fathers have inherited lies, vanity, and things wherein there is no profit." Letting go of limited family traditions is a process worthy of undertaking.

Because the indirectly communicated traditions to which I'm referring are passed down in silent form—for the most part based on assumptions—they are more difficult to define than purposefully communicated traditions. For this reason, picking out our family's patterns may seem challenging, particularly if we are fully engaged in them. However, when we become trained to look for them, we can get very good at picking them out. The key is to be willing to see the truth, have an honest intent, and able to listen closely. To open our eyes to our families' underlying messages, we can listen to our own thoughts, silently scrutinize family discussions, and pay close attention to our own conversations with other family members.

We must notice what family members value or judge. We learn a lot when we observe our family's priorities. For instance, if our family values education we might realize that our personal worthiness is attached to our level of higher education. If our family values wealth, we might identify that we've attached our income to our self-esteem.

Many years ago, I was invited to join a family for dinner. We'll call them the "Smith" family. I was aware that the Smith's had a pattern of struggling financially and I knew that some family members wanted to make more money. After dinner, I heard an interesting conversation start up. Several Smith women began commenting on various doctors they knew and expressed how unfair it seemed that physicians earn so much. Mary Smith noted that a particular doctor she knew worked only three days a week and was very wealthy. She continued to describe how unfair it was that this doctor *did not work hard* to earn money, and implied through her expression that this man was "bad" because of the financial success he had attained without working long hours to pay for it. This conversation helped me understand an important, limiting Smith family belief. The subconscious message the Smiths' were sending was something like this: "You have to work hard to have money, and you're a better person if you struggle to make ends meet. People who have lots of money are bad."

Is there any question why this family struggled to get ahead financially? This family valued hard work. They didn't value financial independence. They also didn't value playtime, vacations, or leisure activity. Consequently, this family worked hard, played little, and struggled to make ends meet.

The traditions we are most interested in discovering are the ones that prevent us from loving others and ourselves. All limited family beliefs affect individual self-esteem or self-worth. This is vital information, because, as I said before, a lack of self-love sits at the core of all dysfunction, including: food, sex, and alcohol addictions, abuse, religious frustration and/or anger, and emotional detachment. Any information, teaching, tradition, value, or projection that leads us to dislike or hate ourselves is a form of an illusion.

Other traditions that we are interested in understanding are the ones that prevent us from getting what we want in life. Many members of the Smith family wanted to create financial freedom and more time to play. Under the current family rule, such an opportunity would violate the unspoken family law. Someone who had a lot of money may not need to work hard. Family members would be highly uncomfortable with one of their own showing up in life like one of the doctors they didn't like.

When our family sends us messages that stand in the way of our goals, we may become "double-minded." We are double-minded when part of us wants one thing while part of us wants another. Since our families typically provide a powerful sense of stability, and supply us with much of the love we feel we need to survive, breaking the unspoken family law may seem scary. For this reason, many of us feel stuck. We want and need to be accepted as part of the family, even if its traditions make us miserable.

For some members of the Smith family, their desire for more money and more play left them double-minded. The Smiths are a strong family, devoted to each other and stubborn in their traditions. For those who wanted to make more money, doing so was going to be next to impossible until the unspoken family law was transcended.

When our family beliefs lead us to judge someone or something as bad, we will usually be double-minded about creating what we've judged. For the Smith family, they judged the doctor so it will be difficult for them to become like the doctor. For me, I judged myself by the cleanliness of my home. Unless I heal my self-judgment, it will be hard for me to let my house be dirty without an emotional consequence. This may not surface as a problem if I'm single or married without children. But, for me, it became an issue when I had four kids. As any mother knows, cleaning a home with children in it is like shoveling the snow while it's still snowing. I would have been an emotional mess if I hadn't dealt with this faulty core belief.

Society's Powerful Influence

I once purchased a children's book written by author Max Lucado titled, *If Only I Had A Green Nose*. The story was about a community of dolls who wanted to gain acceptance. In order to feel good and fit in, the characters were willing to change themselves according to the latest styles or trends. Whatever was believed to be the hottest and most acceptable fashion was pushed upon the characters and because of their desire to be loved, they conformed.

Expectations exist all around us. We have parents, leaders, and teachers who expect us to behave and think in certain ways. When we are in our youth, we feel pressure from our friends to measure up (peer pressure). Though we may assume that peer pressure is something we experienced in the past, peer pressure exists for all of us today, despite our age. It is simply the pressure we feel to behave and act like those around us. Though the family seems to have the most powerful influence over our thoughts and behaviors, society plays a significant role in influencing our beliefs about ourselves, our choices, and our behavior.

My brother-in-law lived for several years in the Philippines. He told me that the Filipino people value fair skin. Consequently, even when it's extremely hot outside, it's common to see Filipino men and women covered from head to toe as they try to block the rays of the sun that might darken their skin. The Filipino people aren't the only population sharing this value. Many cultures throughout Asia yearn for whiter skin. I found that interesting, because in the United States the opposite is true. Tanning booths are big business and Americans love to lie out in the sun, hoping to darken their skin. Americans generally believe that a tan makes them look better, while so many others believe a tan makes them look worse.

Many varying beliefs pervade our communities and affect our lives, our world, our sense of self-worth, and our ability to give and receive love. Some communities believe it's good to be friendly, while other communities believe it's better to be reserved or quiet. Some communities believe that the only way to live is to coexist with your extended family throughout life. Other communities believe it's not normal to live with your extended family. Some communities may believe it's better to be black than white, or Muslim than Christian, or European than American. Pervasive beliefs that affect our self image and our ability to love should be evaluated.

A common belief that exists among many communities in our world is the idea that being thin is better than being fat. As a result, many people strive to be skinny so that they fit into their community. In other groups, the opposite is true. Some believe that it's better to be fat than thin.

If we base our self-worth on our communities underlying messages and comply, do we automatically create self-worth? The answer is a resounding *no!* Our sense of worth comes from within, from knowing who we are as children of God, and then accepting ourselves. Whether we're fat or thin, stylish or not fashion conscious, fair skinned or dark skinned, we're happier when we feel good about ourselves. Our worth is inherent, and must be discovered. Complying with the opinions of our communities doesn't always foster a healthy belief in self. In fact, often, it does the opposite. We may feel anxiety trying to fit in, and we may feel less than others in the process.

Believing that we're not "good enough" causes us to beat up on ourselves and this separates us further from Christ. It provokes us to take steps to try to become acceptable. But our steps are often motivated by our fear of not fitting in, feeling valued, or loved. All this doesn't help us find self acceptance. Since low self-worth is the underlying cause of most dysfunctional behavior, the degree to which we adopt unhealthy beliefs and expectations, is worth examining.

I Want to See More Stars

A vital gift we give ourselves is the ability to understand and accept the power we hold to create our own experiences. Becoming aware of the many messages that influence our behavior allows each of us the freedom to step out of present time challenges and move forward. For example, the Smith family members have the ability to create a new financial reality if they are willing to see their family patterns and change them. When they are willing to see the truth and change, they create new opportunities for themselves and their descendants. Until then, they may feel like victims in a world they cannot control—trying to make more money, but barely getting by. All of us are like the Smith's in one way or another. All of us have family or societal beliefs that prevent us from becoming all we can be. For this reason, all of us have a reason to look further into our consciousness for information that may be holding back our families and ourselves.

Becoming conscious is the process of bringing to full-awareness the underlying thoughts, motives, and intentions that govern our behavior. Dr. Harville Hendrix, psychologist and author of *Getting the Love You Want*, shares the following analogy, which helps us understand our consciousness. He writes: "In the daytime, we can't see the stars. We talk as if they 'come out' at night, even though they are there all the time. We also underestimate the sheer number of stars. We look up at the sky, see a smattering of dim stars, and assume that's all there is. When we travel far away from city lights, we see a sky strewn with stars and are overwhelmed by the brilliance of the heavens. But it is only when we study astronomy that we learn the whole truth: the hundreds of thousands of stars that we see on a clear, moonless night in the country are only a fraction of the stars in the universe, and many of the points of light that we assume to be stars are in fact entire galaxies. So it is with the unconscious mind: the orderly, logical thoughts of our conscious mind are but a thin veil over the unconscious, which is active and functioning at all times."

Most of us are trained to look at our subconscious in a way that is similar to the way we observe the universe from our front porch—only recognizing a few stars in a sky full of possibilities. As we work to create something new, we must come to the understanding that there is much more to our consciousness, just like there is much more to our universe than the view of stars seen from our home. Family patterns are accountable for the majority of our consciousness. Thus, understanding these powerful bits of information stored deeply within us is the first step to creating something new.

Years ago, I worked with a woman named Laurine. She was born in the 1930's when few individuals were even consciously aware of a subconscious. Laurine was a spiritually progressed woman who was highly intuitive and very aware of others' thoughts and feelings, as well as her own. Yet, like many others, Laurine blocked much of her subconscious agenda from her conscious mind.

In session, Laurine revealed from deep within her consciousness some powerful family beliefs. Her family's code of unconscious rules included thoughts such as: you are good enough if you do everything right and perfect (perfectionism), you are better if you are educated, you are better if you have lots of money, you are better if others respect you (respect comes when you are educated, wealthy, attractive, and/or perfect), it's very important what others think of you, and you must look good to the world (yet the family had a conflicting belief that you must not look too good or others won't accept you).

Intuitively, Laurine was aware of her family's unconscious code of rules. Further inspection helped Laurine to see that her family laws made it impossible for her to ever feel good about herself—a very harmful circumstance. After the only way she would be "good enough" is if she were perfect. And she wasn't, she is human. Since mistakes are a necessary part of learning and growing, Laurine would forever be stuck. She would never be able to be good enough for her family and for herself. If she couldn't be good enough, how could she love and accept herself? And if she couldn't love and accept herself, how could she love and accept others? Consequently, Laurine was highly judgmental of others and herself and her relationships reflected it.

Laurine unconsciously participated in her family plan throughout most of her life. The family pattern forced her (and others) into a pattern of being dishonest. How could Laurine be honest with herself about her mistakes if she must always be perfect? Being perfect and making mistakes contradict. Rather than see herself (and others) for what she was, she would pretend that she was perfect and that her world was perfect. She hid much of herself from her own self in order to avoid realizing that she was not perfect.

As Laurine got older, she had difficulty remembering anything about her childhood that wasn't perfect. If you asked her about her life prior to our sessions, she would recall a perfect past without flaw. Yet Laurine created for herself abandonment in her marriage, tremendous health problems, a weight problem, financial hardships, lack of companionship, and more. Her present-time dysfunction evidenced some subconscious patterns that produced unhealthy results.

Realizing all of this information consciously, Laurine began to piece together the events of her past with greater understanding. Until she was ready to become aware of the subconscious programming (see a fuller picture of the stars in her universe) she remained a victim with little ability to alter her reality. Once she understood what was going on within her and where it originated, she became empowered and able to create a new reality.

After working with Laurine, it became clear that most of her problem lied in her family's limited patterns. Although Laurine had her own issues about living on this earth, her family's unconscious requirements of what it would take for her to be good enough and accepted, made her life more complicated and contributed to her decision that living on this earth wasn't positive.

Laurine is not alone. We are like Laurine when our issues are created or enhanced by the unconscious family rulebook. Sometimes just knowing is more than half the battle. In fact, many times we only need to make the realization of the illusion in order to change fully.

Cleaning the Hard Drive

Everything we experience in life is recorded by our body/mind. Like computers with complex processing systems and deeply embedded hard-drives, our body/mind contains all the facets of our individual perceptions, including our perception of our family's rulebook. Our personal body computer may change daily as new information is put in and outdated information is replaced by new understanding. Alternatively, our personal body computer may rarely change: running and re-running old data over and over again.

When we lock our family's perceptions into our body/mind computer, our system begins to filter our experiences through the perceptions we have stored. Deciding that we are unworthy or not good enough because begins a cycle of repetition. We begin to see all circumstances through a tainted lens, blocking out other views of reality that may exist simultaneously. Here is a visual example of this concept. When you buy a new car, you become familiar with a new model and color of a vehicle, and from that point on you notice cars like yours when you are driving. You may never before have noticed a car like your new one, but, from the point of purchase on, even after you sell the car, you still notice that color and body type on the road. So it is with each of us in our lives. When we have experiences that lead us to make decisions about our lives or ourselves, we unconsciously go out into the world and notice all other experiences that validate what we believe to be true.

When our brain holds tight to a perception it will attempt to recreate similar circumstances or feelings to validate its decisions. Knowing this, we can understand how families who hold certain perceptions find it difficult to see anything other than their experience (i.e., see other cars on the road). For instance, the Smith family can't imagine themselves experiencing a life without hard work and financial struggle. They don't know how financial freedom feels and they don't even know how to notice or create anything else. The group has functioned with their family's perception for so long that they can't see other realities (i.e., they've always owned the blue Pontiac and consequently they never notice the gold Mercedes—in fact, they don't know they can have a gold Mercedes if they chose to change).

Emotions arise as a result of core beliefs. For example, if I believe that I must be a good housekeeper in order to be a good person, then when someone messes up my house, I become angry. I become angry because the actions of another have directly challenged my worth as a result of my core belief.

Feeling, acknowledging, and understanding our emotions helps us to break down our core beliefs and actually clean our hard drive. It is important to acknowledge our emotions, rather than repress them. Unfortunately, this can be very hard to do. Many in our society maintain a limited belief that it's bad to be emotional—that those who show emotion are bad. Evidence of this unconscious pressure to withhold our true feelings is observed when we hear parents say to their children, "Quit crying. You don't need to cry about that." Or when we hear adults judge or criticize others who show emotion. Our emotions are powerful indicators of what is going on inside of us. Further, our emotions are part of our body's exquisite system for processing through what we've experienced in a day. Crying isn't a bad thing. Sometimes a good cry can relieve stress and leave our bodies feeling peace.

When we understand that our emotions are signs that clue us to our core beliefs, we are more willing to pay attention. Emotions can provide us with the information necessary in order to change our perception, and eventually to begin to see new possibilities (e.g., notice other cars on the road, or create more harmony in a marriage).

As stated earlier, all limited family beliefs affect individual self-esteem or self-worth. When our beliefs challenge the positive way we feel about ourselves, we are bound to experience a flood of negative emotion. These emotions clue us to vital information. If you are suffering from any of the following dysfunctional behaviors—food, sex, drug, and alcohol addictions, relationship failures, abuse of any kind, religious frustration and/or anger, and emotional detachment—it's time to go deep and uncover the patterns and beliefs that are destroying your hard-drive.

Remember, any information, teaching, tradition, value, or projection that leads us to dislike or hate ourselves is a form of an illusion. We are all glorious, spiritual beings with a divine potential. As believers we are all children of God! Sometimes, as we heal, we may find that we hate or dislike our behavior (our choices), but *truth* will lead us to uncover something good within us, not something bad. If you feel emotionally overwhelmed, put your negative emotions to work for you. Let them help you clean your body/mind hard drive of illusions—beliefs that prevent you from loving and accepting yourself.

As you work to heal your family history, you will be most effective if your ambitions incorporate the direction of the Holy Spirit's voice. No matter what the situation, let His voice guide you, because He knows what is best for you. The Holy Spirit is always there for us. We just have to acknowledge Him, Praise Him, thank Him.

EDITOR'S NOTE

I would encourage the readers to turn off their TV's, the largest electronic income reducer in the world! Spend quality time with each other. Poor people entertain themselves, rich people educate themselves and their families. In 1955, America led in every financial index in the world, now we lead in none!

The walls that rest between me and all I can be is the desire to change! I encourage the readers to follow the leaders in this book! —JEF

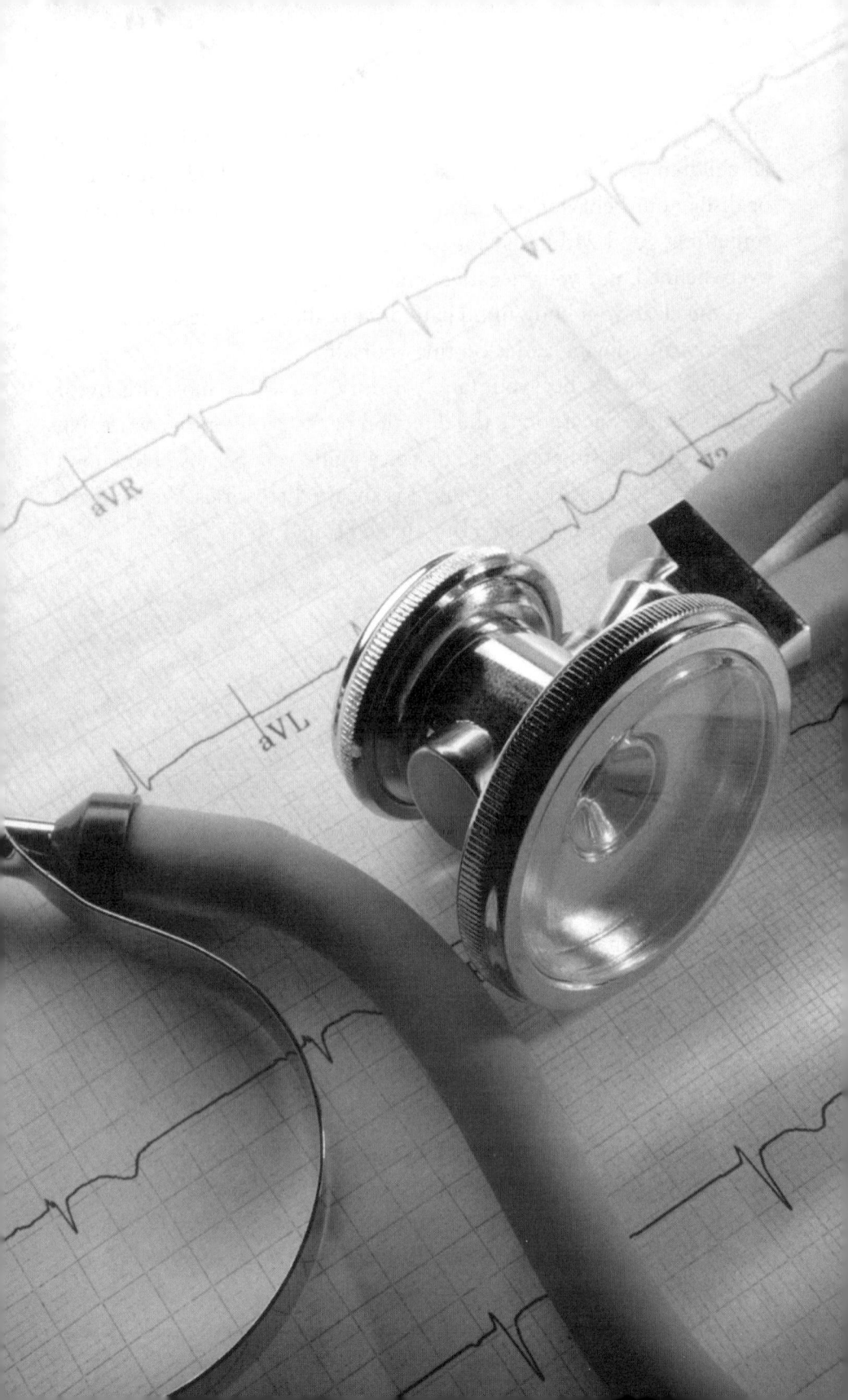

THE ONLY ANSWER TO CANCER™ AND THE ROOT CAUSE OF ALL DISEASE

This is a chapter from: *The Only Answer to Cancer*™

DR. LEONARD COLDWELL

Board Certified: NMD, DNM, PhD, LCHC, CNHP, DIP.PHC
www.InstinctBasedMedicine.com
www.DrLeonardColdwell.com

My childhood memories are filled with feelings of desperation as I listened to my mother's screams, and emergency doctors coming and going from our house. In fact, every day, the first thing I did when I came home from school was run to my mother's room to check and see if she was still alive. She had been diagnosed with liver cancer in the terminal stage and told that there was no hope. She was given two years maximum to live. I was petrified. My fear fueled my ambition to find a cure for my mother's cancer. And so began the driving force that led me to become one of the leading experts on cancer and stress-related illness. It took years of trial and error, studying every kind of therapy imaginable, but in the end I cured my mother, who is alive and well thirty-six years later.

My mother is 74 years old and I have to say that I did make a promise to God. I promised God that if he helped me to cure my mother, that I would spend the rest of my life doing his work to prevent other mothers (fathers) and their children from having to go through what my mother and I had to endure. Unfortunately, in the meantime, I watched my beloved grandmother, father, and seven siblings of my mother die from cancer or some other so-called incurable disease.

I started my quest to find the answer to cancer by studying every successful healing technique worldwide, and I learned about all the alternative or natural forms of healing available. I discovered why people got cancer and how they became healthy after they had it, and why others just died. I became one of the leading experts for cancer in Europe long before I graduated from medical/naturopathic medical school. I then specialized as a general physician in cancer with a particular emphasis on cancer patients who had been deemed incurable by their physicians.

Working with cancer patients, I learned that there is always hope, there is always a way, and there will always be patients that will regain their health, no matter what the diagnosis or obstacles. Most importantly, I learned that I was not the healer, I was only the conduit for my patient to pass on the knowledge and tools and training he or she needed to reactivate the immune system and stimulate self-healing powers so that the patient could achieve optimum health. The bottom line, and the most important lesson I learned from working with over 35,000 patients with so-called incurable diseases, was that no one can cure someone; only the sick can cure themselves. (Many of you know that I am the personal physician to Mega Best Selling Author and Consumer Advocate Kevin Trudeau, as well as the consultant to many of the rich and famous and many of the world's leading companies. I am not working with patients anymore because my goal is to teach and educate and to fight for Health Freedom and Patient Rights amended to the US Constitution.)

There is no magic bullet or fountain of youth, nor are there any shortcuts to life-long health and happiness. We must take charge of our health. We are responsible for our past decisions, actions, or lack of action. Most of us are challenged, looking at the health situation we created, but it is never too late. It is only important to act now, before it gets tougher. We are not failures because we are sick, unfit, or over-weight. We just learned to use the powers of our brains, bodies, and immune systems in the wrong way. All too often, we are brainwashed by the media or misled by people to believe or do the wrong thing. But the good news is that there is always hope. From now on, you just need to act smarter. Make the decision to take charge of your life, happiness, and health right now! Make the commitment to live up to your potential and create the health you deserve.

The Bad Nenndorf Institute for Medical Statistics concluded and published: "Our research shows that Dr. Leonard Coldwell worked with over 35, 000 patients with cancer and other terminal diseases and it is our conclusion that he has the highest cancer cure rate, of all re-searched therapists, in the World—His success rate with cancer pa-tients, that did not have orthodox medical treatment before using Dr. Coldwell's system, is 92.3%" The Berlin Health Institute conducted two clinical studies and came to a similar conclusion in the effectiveness of the Instinct Based Medicine® System. Their conclusion was also that: NPL, Hypnotism, Meditation and other techniques does not have 10% of the effectiveness of Dr. Leonard Coldwell's IBMS™ Stress Reduc-tion System. Our studies concluded that the 20 minute IBMS™ stress reduction sessions equals the relaxation, regeneration and healing of a deep restful sleep of 7 to 8 hours.

The Instinct Based Medicine ® System

Please read my book:
Instinct Based Medicine – How to survive your illness and your doctor www.instinctbasedmedicine.com for more information and techniques.

In my opinion, all illness comes from lack of energy, and the greatest energy drainer is mental and emotional stress, which I believe to be the root-cause of all illness. Stress is one of the major elements that can erode energy to such a large and permanent extent that the immune system loses all possibility of functioning at an optimum level. It is a fact that 86% of all illness and doctor visits are stress related. Stanford University concluded after a major study that 95% of all illness is stress related.

I am referring to the mental and emotional stress that is caused by continuous and/or long-term compromises against you. These vary from person to person, but some examples include living in unbearable relationships and marriages, performing jobs you hate, or hating your boss, or experiencing problems with family, all of which lead to you compromising your sense of self.

Emotional and mental stress comes from living with feelings of constant fear, doubt, hopelessness, lack of self-esteem, worry, and, most of all, always compromising your inner feelings, instincts, and personal needs. The main component of all these energy-drainers is fear. But the Bible tells us over 100 times: Not to fear and to trust in God! Your faith can heal you from fear!

The solution is to start by defining what it is in your life that keeps you from feeling happy. Can you answer the question of why you don't respect yourself enough? Or love yourself? Now identify what needs to change or happen in your life to make you feel good about yourself and your personal environment. What is it that you don't want to do, accept, or take anymore from yourself, your spouse, your children, your boss, or your co-workers? Is there someone in your life that makes you feel badly that needs to go? What are your wildest dreams and goals? Looking at your life, what is it that always takes away your energy, and where do you compromise your personal needs and feelings? Identify everything in your life that keeps you from being your true self, and start working on the development of the true you! This is the first and most important step toward achieving optimum health and happiness. And remember that happiness and hope are the most powerful healers and energy creators in your life. Pay attention to your instincts, listen to your inner voice, and start loving and respecting yourself so that you behave according to your true personality. You need to accept the statistical fact that the medical doctor or medical profession is the number one cause of death in America. That means you cannot rely solely on another person, the MD, with your health and life, but you can rely soley on the Healing Nature of Jesus!

I believe today that the different agencies of the Government, like the FDA and FTC are the leading cause of death in this world because of their manipulations, suppressions, rules and regulations that prevent natural health, natural healing methods, natural cures, healing foods, supplementation and natural healers that do Gods work!

If you do not live your life according to your needs, you will get or stay stressed which will reduce your energy and eventually produce an illness. You are the only one who can change your life and improve your health. So start today by defining, creating, and living your life the way you believe is right and good for you.

Create your own self-healing system: (Here is my personal one for educational purposes only)

Disclaimer: The following information is for educational and research purposes only and does not intend to prevent, treat or cure any condition or disease! If you have any health challenge please consult a qualified health expert before you consider to implement any of the information below! Educate yourself and make qualified and educated decisions about your own health.

What I would personally do if I had any health challenge:

Identify life situations that drain you, make you feel uncomfortable, that make you feel stressed, weak, or unhappy, and find a way to change these negative situations.

Listen to my Radio shows for more information and education: http://www.blogtalkradio.com/TheDrColdwellReport and see the archived shows with the leading health authorities in the world to

learn from the best in Health: http://www.blogtalkradio.com/search/
dr.-leonard-coldwell/archives and listen to my interview with Kevin
Trudeau on www.KtRadioNetwork.com the most educational radio
show for information that the officials don't want you to know about
and to my 4-hour radio interview with my dear friend the world's leading expert on Codex Alimentarius, GMO food and Health Freedom
on www.healthfreedomUSA.org www.naturalsolutionsfoundation.org
and also see my good friend Dr. Betty Martini's website for information
and my interview with her about Aspartame the deadly poison:
www.mpwhi.com , www.dorway.com .
Please donate to these wonderful organizations!

- Breathe effectively into your stomach below your bellybutton. Inhale
  four seconds through your nose, and exhale eleven seconds through
  your mouth ten times in a row and at least three times a day. Also,
  inhale four seconds, hold your breath for sixteen seconds, and exhale
  eight seconds through your mouth ten times in a row at least three
  times a day.

- Create your own destressing program. Escape twice a day for 20
  minutes mentally to a place in nature where you feel free, safe, and
  comfortable. Break the daily stress cycle because stress is not the
  problem; rather, it is ongoing stress that is causing the damage. (For
  my educational stress reduction CDs and training visit www.instinct-
  basedmedicine.com) this is the most endorsed and most sold stress
  reduction system in the world says the Audio Information Journal
  My CD system is endorsed by the world leaders in Medicine and
  Health like Dr. Rima Laibow, Dr. Betty Martini, Dr. Thomas Hohn,
  Dr. Bowersox (leading fibromyalgia expert) and many, many more.

- I would get detoxified twice a year! I use the 21-day all natural full
  body and colon cleanse from www.mybepure.com and for individual
  health challenges I use the highly effective colon, liver, kidney, lym-
  phatic, and chemical cleanses from www.awesomesupplements.com
  and the metal test and cleanse from www.helpingamericanow.com.

- Drink a gallon of water a day, and have half a teaspoon of sea salt with it. Also, take good coral calcium. I use the salt, "Star Dust, from www.greatwholefood.com this wonderful company is a Bible-based operating, product producing company and in my opinion the best all natural or organic whole foods.

- Do aerobic exercise for at least twenty minutes three times a week (just walking is fine). Or seven minutes on a rebounder (Mini Trampoline) each day.

- Eat as many fresh vegetables and fruits as possible, and get a juicer—and use it.

- Health is no accident! Illness is not bad luck or God's way of testing you or genetic based! Every health challenge and imbalance in life is the result of our own decisions and actions. God gave us the power of Free Will. We just need to start using this power in the right way. We are created after God's likeness and we are perfect in God's way until we start to mess up our own health and life. Start taking responsibility for your own life, health, happiness and quality of life and create the life you deserve, desire and that God intended you to have right now! If you have any questions I will answer every email question. Write to instinctbasedmedicine@gmail.com and for free health advice by licensed medical doctors that are trained and use my IBMS™ go to www.goodlifefoundation.com or write to drhohn@goodlifefoundation.com visit my daily blog health freedom information and world health news: http://thedrcoldwellreport.blogspot.com/

Please remember:" There is no incurable disease there are only incurable People that are not willing to do what it takes to get and keep their body in the perfect condition God intended it to be.

In love, faith and respect,
—Dr. Leonard Coldwell

The Dr. Coldwell Cancer protocol:

Educational research information for Cancer patients to enable every-one to make better and educated decisions about his or her own health and life.

Based on my right for freedom of speech I tell you what I would do if I were a cancer patient:

1. I would do a 21-day full body and colon cleansing system from www.mybepure.com .

2. Do the Cancer Protocol
    http://awesomesupplements.com/7335.product.html.

2a. Medical Fact is that cancer cannot grow in an oxygen-rich alkaline environment therefore I would always make sure that my body is slightly alkaline with a pH of 7.36. I would achieve this easily with the Acid-Alkaline Protocol from

    http://awesomesupplements.com/7029.product.html
    that was created after my historical use for my patients.

2b. Very often a correlation between cancer and fungus / Candida over-growth is mentioned in the medical world. To make sure I don't suffer from this Candida overgrowth I would do the Candida Re-mediation Protocol from http://awesomesupplements.com/7066. product.html which was also created after the producer researched my historical use of protocols with my patients in the past.

2c. It is extremely important to cut out the dangerous toxins coming from your water and EMC, Drinking water, showers or bathtubs and Cell phones etc. I would never take a shower without the shower filters from www.ewater.com and would not live in a house without Fred Van Liew's (the owner of ewater.com) whole house water filter system, his under sink osmosis water filter system, as well as his Oxygenation and Revitalization products or his EMF or Electro-magnetic Chaos Protection like his EP 2 Pendant, the cell phone protection. Perfect hydration is one of the most important parts for health I use for myself and everybody. I love his Quanta Water for perfect hydration. I personally use all of his products. For more information www.ewater.com and remember the quality of your water equals the quality of your Health.

3   I would also take Hydrosol silver from www.helpingamericanow.com for every danger of microbial infection and do their metal cleanse and metal test too! There is no substitute for this company and to their products.

4.   I would take vitamin B17.

4.a I would use Baking Soda with real Maple Syrup and warm up one teaspoon of Baking Soda with 5 tablespoons full of Maple syrup. See Dr. Simoncini in Rome, Italy for more information and read his book: *Cancer is a fungus.*

5.   I would take Essiac Capsules
http://awesomesupplements.com/8550.product.html.

6.   I would eat, if I could afford it, only organic whole foods from
www.greatwholefood.com
and eat fresh organic salads, vegetables and fruit.

7.   I would have as much sun as my skin can handle without getting burned. Sun does not cause cancer! In my opinion Sunscreens do!

8.   I would buy an inexpensive juicer such as the Jack Lalanne model and have a lot of fresh juice with a lot of greens added.

9.   I would walk or exercise just a little every day. Or at least 2 minutes 3 times a week.

10. I would eat a vegetarian, all organic, live food diet. Please read the books from my friend Paul Nison www.PaulNison.com the Raw food expert. (*Health according to the scriptures.*)

11. I would take Flora-Zymes, Quint-Essence, vitamin E, and C along with massive amounts of vitamin D (I take 50 000 iU each day until I feel better and 25 000 iU every day but that is just me—you have to do your own research and make your own decisions), and

cal-mag from www.awesomesupplements.com   every day of my life. If I wanted to get more oxygen in my body I would use their Universal Greens.

12. Twice week I would get a full body lymph drainage.

13. Most of all I would use my self-help CD sessions every day. They are the result of 30 years of research, therapy, education and success. For information go to: www.instinctbasedmedicine.com or email to instinctbasedmedicine@gmail.com

**In severe cases I would add oxygen-therapy and or 35% hydrogen Peroxide therapy. I would take (but I don't encourage anyone else to do it!) 8 drops of 35% hydrogen-peroxide in 8 ounces of Aloe juice for at least 35 days. If you decide to use this protocol you need to be under control and advice of a qualified health care practitioner.

After doing all of this I would know I had done everything to address the physical causes of bad health.

In conclusion: There is no substitute for God's living foods, water, air, love and healing power!

Getting rid of the root cause of all disease! Lack of Energy which is usually caused by stress.

I also know that the main cause of Cancer is mental and emotional stress. It's scientifically proven that all illnesses are 84% based on stress and only 16% based on physical elements (As mentioned before the Stanford University states that it is even 95%). Therefore, I would know that I would have to uncover and eliminate the root cause of my personal health challenges to be able to get rid of the symptoms and physical malfunctions. I would have to actively apply the information in my book *Instinct Based Medicine How to survive your Illness and your doctor* (see www.instinctbasedmedicine.com).

After doing all of this I would feel confident that I have done everything in my power to be healthy. I would then let nature, and/or God, do the rest.

Just a reminder: Nearly everyone in my family had cancer! I don't have or will ever get cancer! Today I am considered by many experts as the doctor with the highest cancer cure rate ever and I did not use any chemotherapy, radiation or surgery while I had my clinics.

In my personal experience, and opinion, based on my unmatched results and success, I believe that there is only one Answer to Cancer —Your own! You have to develop and define your own root cause for your own individual health challenge or life imbalance and you have to eliminate these root-causes yourself. When you eliminate your individual root-cause for your personal and unique health challenge, the symptoms, the tumor, the pain and the decay of your own body stops and reverses itself back to God's creation of perfect health. The process of dying stops and life begins again. Therefore the only answer to cancer is: "Your personal, individual answer."

There are amazing healing forces inside the human body and if you use your God-given powers and possibilities you will cure yourself in God's way. You do your part and God will do the rest! For more information please write to me personally at:

instinctbasedmedicine@gmail.com

God bless you and your loved ones.

Dr. Leonard Coldwell—Fighting for you, your health, happiness, freedom to choose, your quality of life, and the constitutional amendment for: "Health Freedom and Patient Rights!"

24

LIVING WITHOUT STRESS
HEALING ADRENAL FATIGUE

Dr. Carolyn Porter

S tress is a killer! This is a strong statement yet is factual. Even the medical profession warns people to lighten up because stress creates unhealthy effects in your body and health, and often contributes to illness and death. Stress causes chemical changes in the body which tear down the adrenal glands, your stress regulator, leading to immune system suppression and eventually disease; it's a chain reaction. Yet people continue to live a life overflowing with stress. It seems puzzling that individuals would continue on a path of stress, but people have been taught to live this way and don't realize they have the power to change it.

Society has been conditioned into striving, producing, pushing, and manipulating to achieve goals that often leave the individuals gasping for air. It's all about the end result with little time to enjoy the journey. Mostly the conditioning is geared towards earning high profits in a competitive setting with a desire to achieve favors, promotions, bonuses, accolades or simply to keep the job. This driving force propels individuals into overwork, overwhelm and over-exhaustion. It seems people do their best to squeeze in as much in a day as possible and they teach their children to do the same as they enroll them in multiple activities and sports. Trying to balance all of this becomes a stressful impossibility, leaving no time to recharge. Then suddenly, the individual is faced with physical symptoms that won't go away so the only thinkable recourse is to visit a doctor and hopefully get some relief with a pill, the quick-fix syndrome of society today.

So what is stress? Stress according to Webster's dictionary is undo pressure, strain, intense force or exertion, or any real or imagined threat and how your mind sees it. We all experience stressful situations from time to time, but if stress becomes a chronic way of life it opens the door for all kinds of detrimental and debilitating physical repercussions. Stress occurs through relationships, diet, lifestyle habits, not enough sleep, too little or too much exercise, finances, chronic pain, which all leaves the individual in a habitual state of unhappiness, judgment, frustration, anxiety, anger and not enough (lack).

Although it may seem impossible to live without stress, it absolutely *is* possible to live stress-free. I was riddled by stress for many years, always pushing to do more even when my body rebelled. Illness struck and I got the message. In later years I learned why I did this and made a conscious choice to transform my entire life. As a result I now live an extraordinary life that is filled with happiness, inner joy, peace, abundance, and so much excitement for life itself that my passion is to help as many *willing* people to change their life into a glorious adventure as is possible.

The adrenal glands, located right above your kidneys, are your stress regulator. They produce two hormones, DHEA and cortisol. They are involved in every system and function of your body. Their main roles are to balance the fluid in your body, keep inflammation under control, and provide you with enough energy throughout the day to live your life. When the adrenals burn out, your body begins breaking down, making adrenal fatigue a core issue whenever you experience any disorder. Through my personal illness and many years of searching for answers, I discovered a huge connection between the adrenals, illness, and the role of stress in health.

Stress has an origin in three main areas: psychological, nutritional, and structural. Let's address each one so you have a better understanding of where it comes from and what is necessary to do so you can let it go. Common stressors are: anger, worry, anxiety, finances, relationship issues, overwhelm, job requirements, illness, shame, guilt, unhealthy diet, lack of sleep, chronic pain, low self-worth, depression, poor digestion.

Psychological Stress has many faces. It is basically from the mental and emotional part of you. This includes your beliefs and your behavior that is a result of those beliefs. First you must understand that your beliefs originate from various people in your life: parents, siblings, friends, teachers, ministers, peers and so forth. The beliefs that you have assumed as yours may in fact be someone else's beliefs that you simply accepted as yours, yet if you took time to think about it long and hard you might realize they don't actually resonate with you. If this is the case, and it often is, there is a relentless internal "battle" going on within you because there are two different beliefs trying to win first place in your mind. This is a stressor.

Many of the beliefs held dear by those in your life have a base in fear. Do you know what fear is? *False Evidence Appearing Real!* Anything based in fear is actually just an illusion because it appears real but really is not. Here is an example. I remember feeling petrified of speaking in front of an audience. In fact, the thought of ever doing this was something I couldn't comprehend because it was too fearful to even imagine. At some time during my life journey I had attached to the belief that public speaking would be too scary to do, that I wouldn't be good enough to do it, and this had developed into a real physical feeling of fear. But people in my life kept telling me I should become a speaker because I had a great deal of information from which others could benefit. I ignored it for many months due to my fear. But then I felt an internal nudge, divine intervention if you will, to get out there and just do it. Finally, I felt so uncomfortable inside knowing I was being guided to do this that I decided to take a speaking training. I was so petrified at the beginning of that training that my clothes were visibly shaking due to my trembling body. I really wanted to run away but I made myself face my fear, shakes and all.

But guess what happened? I did it! I actually completed the training and stopped trembling, and as I began speaking in front of audiences I overcame my fear. What I learned was that my fear wasn't real at all, it was just my belief that created the fear in me. So when I changed my belief about the fear after completing the training, being only a figment of my imagination, my fear went away. I then opened to this amazing realization—my stress was self-inflicted! No matter what you believe about a situation in your life—the stressors that show up—you can change how you view them and create a different outcome. Once I overcame my fear of speaking, I was able to do things I could not have ever imagined in a million years. The original fear is non-existent for me because by doing it I defeated the illusion of it.

So one of the main ways to overcome stressors in your life is to *change your belief about them*, in other words, respond differently to them. It seems most individuals want to control their life, and when they feel out of control they panic and try to get the control back. That is stressful. I learned some time ago that I really cannot control anything, I only think I can. Life happens. Things show up out of left field, which sometimes take us to our knees. The only way to keep on track is to get up, brush off our knees, and keep going. But these obstacles often keep a person down for a period of time, sometimes a long period of time, so that they step into the role of victim. When people live a continuous pity-party, feeling sorry for themselves while repeatedly telling everyone how bad things are, they remain in a low vibration which is based in fear. Whatever vibration you send out, the same will return to you. It's a law of the universe that what you put out you get back, or what you sow you reap. Everything in the universe, including you, is composed of energy, and energetic vibrations can only return the same vibration. Likes attract likes, this is a given, so if your thoughts come from a place of anger from being a victim, you cannot expect anything except more negative experiences to confirm the vibration you sent out.

Letting go of control is not easy for most people, however, it's the only way you can release stress. I like to say, "Let go and let God." Once you realize that things will show up in your life that are unexpected and beyond your control, and that surrender to the challenge is key, you will find an inner peace because you know that God is working out the details to resolve the situation that you couldn't fix anyway, you just thought you could. Instead of fighting the current, if you understand how to flow with what happens, stress disappears.

This is what I mean by responding differently to life's challenges instead of reacting to them.

We all experience the unexpected, but it's in how we deal with them that either gives us peace or stress.

Suppose an unanticipated bill suddenly appears and you immediately get angry. It isn't fair is it because you just got caught up with your bills and began to breathe easier when this new one appeared? You are frustrated because you can't seem to get ahead no matter what and want to blame the world for your misfortune. Now you're in the stress mode but *you have a choice.* You can remain there ranting and raving over this perceived injustice, or you can take a deep breath and simply hand it over to God. Haven't you always made it through similar situations before, and do you not know that God will take care of you now? Here's a little secret – you can get upset or mad as a hornet but it has no effect in solving the problem, so anger or being upset has no value! Perhaps there's a lesson for you to learn about handling money or maybe you need to shift your innermost thoughts to abundance rather than lack. Abundance comes from love and lack is based in fear. Fear creates stress while love creates peace—your choice. And what you choose to think about is what you will create in your life!

The universe is an abundant place with enough resources for every being. Since worry, stress, anger and upset have never solved any problem nor contributed to anything positive, it only makes sense to step away from the expressions of fear and step into expressions of love. In this space you can open to your own *resourcefulness,* which is key to creating the life you want to live. The resources are there—you just have to become resourceful with them. Immeasurable gifts are within you and a power that supersedes any problem or block you may encounter.

When I learned to focus on the good in my life and realized that every challenge had always been resolved with ease once I let go of trying to control the details and outcome, I understood there was no reason to ever feel stress. **Stress is self-inflicted,** *always*. Letting go of the need to be right, or in reality trying to control someone else, you will experience peace. In the whole scheme of things it really has little meaning because we all have the right to our own perception of what is right for us. Letting go of expectations that are from your perception, allows you to accept everyone as they are without judgment, and you experience peace. Forgiveness frees you from stress and allows you to live in love. Hanging on to anger, pain, judgment, blame, guilt, or lack only constrains you in the bonds of fear, and you are the one who suffers. Living through the expressions of love, appreciation, acceptance, forgiveness, abundance, compassion, understanding and kindness, can only bring peace and eliminate stress. Take time to be quiet and meditate to get in touch with your truth so you can restore your faith and connect with God. Become resourceful with the resources presently in your life and you may amaze yourself!

Nutritional Stress can also wreak havoc in your body and health. Hippocrates once said, "Let your food be your medicine and your medicine be your food." Yet many individuals have little concern for their physical shell, the "house" that God has gifted to them along with the responsibility to take care of it during their life. People have forgotten their need for wholesome food and seek the quickie meals and junk food. The processed food, fast food, pesticide-ridden and genetically modified foods do nothing to promote a healthy body, and the continual ingestion of these foods place a significant stress on our bodies.

Our bodies are designed to *consume fresh, wholesome food* brimming over with vitamins, minerals, fiber, healthy fats and all the nutrients we need to be healthy. Choosing the dead, lifeless, mineral deficient food that overflows in our supermarkets and restaurants today places an immense strain on our bodies. Consuming dairy, meat or poultry that's pumped with hormones and steroids in a factory environment or fed grains laden with chemicals rather than allowed to roam on the range or farm, contributes to the overwhelming number of people experiencing estrogen overload, obesity, not to mention multiple diseases and disorders. Would you put oil in the gas tank of your car to make it run efficiently? Of course not. So why do you fill your body's tank with tainted, dead, processed food which prevents your body from running optimally?

Even if you eat wholesome food and are conscious of what is or isn't healthy to consume, when stress rules your life it creates physiological changes in your body that affects the absorption of the nutrients you need for vibrant health. Stress makes your heart rate go up, raises your blood pressure, oxygenation is decreased, and blood is propelled away from your gut so that digestion is completely shut down. This becomes a major problem when you eat under stress even when you are eating healthy food because you won't be able to digest and assimilate the nutrients; nor will you be able to burn calories effectively. As a result, you experience that mid-section weight gain that you really don't want. In addition, within an hour of a stressful event, cholesterol and triglycerides go up while gut flora decreases and you are most likely to experience food sensitivities, reflux, indigestion and heartburn.

Digestion of the food you eat is vital if you want to experience vibrant health. This is a crucial first step for restoring health, and a certainty in the adrenal fatigue scenario. In order to assist in the repair of adrenals and digestion, it is necessary to take plant enzymes with every cooked meal and often needed is Betaine HCL to digest the protein you consume. Betaine begins breaking down the food in the stomach as soon as you ingest the food, particularly the protein, then the food travels to the large intestine and finally the small intestine where plant enzymes are needed to complete the job. Bloating, gas, heartburn, reflux, and heaviness in the gut are all symptoms of improper digestion, a big stressor, a red flag for you to make changes in your life.

A vital element of nutrition is the intake of *water*, one half ounce per pound of body weight every day. Many people are chronically dehy-drated due to their consumption of coffee, carbonated drinks, alcohol, and fruit juices which all tend to deplete the body of nutrients, and the fact that they drink very little water. The beverages mentioned above are loaded with sugar and caffeine and many harmful ingredients that add nothing of value to your health. Drink pure water and refrain from tap water or water in plastic bottles as these add toxic chemicals that do not contribute to your health. Remember that you need water daily to not only replace what you eliminate, flush out toxins while allowing nutrients to be delivered to areas of your body that need them, but also to help regulate your adrenals so they can restore and maintain their important role in your health as a stress balancer.

Include one teaspoon of *Himalayan salt* in your daily diet, often referred to as pink salt. This valuable salt in its pure, natural form, does not cause detrimental effects in your health as table salt can, which is actually a chemical called sodium chloride. Pink salt contains all 84 nutrients needed daily by your body, all the minerals and trace miner-als required for repair and maintenance of your body. For years we've heard about the overused soil that has depleted the necessary minerals from our produce along with the continual use of chemicals and pes-ticides, which rob us of any nutrients we might receive. This salt helps the adrenals repair as it assists in the fluid balance of your body, a role of the adrenals.

Amino acids are needed to repair the adrenals for they are the building blocks of life. Amino acids are found in protein and should be included in every meal or snack throughout the day. Many health professionals recommend a ratio of approximately 30% protein, 50% carbohydrates and 20% good fats at every meal or snack for optimal dietary balance. Good sources of protein are meat, dairy, nuts, seeds, shitake, maitake and portabella mushrooms, beans and vegetables. Equally important is the ability to digest the proteins so the amino acids can be assimilated. All fungus, bacteria and viruses are also proteins so Betaine HCL may be needed to assure proper break down of the protein. It's your first line of defense.

Good fats are needed as part of the balance at all meals and snacks. The good fats help to convert all hormones in your body because hormones require good cholesterol to perform the conversion and the good cholesterol is created from good fats. Good fats to include in your diet are virgin coconut oil, extra virgin olive oil, raw nuts and seeds, avocados, fish—especially cold water fish, black olives, flaxseeds and more. Hormones play a huge role in your health, an example being the adrenal hormones of DHEA and cortisol, and if you do not consume enough good fats, the hormones cannot convert properly and imbalances will occur.

When you are experiencing chronic stress and your adrenals have been affected, it is usually necessary to take some additional nutrients to support the depleted adrenals. Do not ingest an adrenal glandular which is manufactured from animals. Animals do not resonate at the high vibrational level humans do so can never restore your health to the higher vibration. Use organic, pure plant precursors that help restore your adrenals since plants resonate at the higher vibration of humans. Precursors, rather than replacements, help your body produce the hormones needed for vibrant health, always the best way to heal. Most individuals need extra magnesium, B vitamins, extra vitamin C and other nutrients to restore proper adrenal function.

It is not a quick fix, but can positively be healed. My e-Book entitled *Adrenal Fatigue: the Missing Pieces of Your Puzzle*, contains an in-depth detailing for healing this disorder, and can be found at...

www.drcarolynporter.com or www.wheremiracleshappen.com.

Although there is a great deal of information available about dietary suggestions for health, I've only touched upon a few of the basics. There are different perceptions about dietary choices that each individual must decide for himself. Awareness and education is really one of the most important things you can do in your quest for vibrant health, and what works for one person may not work for you, being that we are all unique individuals with different systems. However, do pay close attention to the basic considerations for everyone.

Structural Stress can also be present. Too much exercise can be just as detrimental as too little, just in a different way. Hating the exercise you do and forcing yourself to do it can be quite stressful as well. Keeping your body tight and tense can lead to possible disastrous consequences. Staying in one position for long periods of time can stress your body. Pregnancy and childbirth, although wonderful and natural, can cause misalignment of your spine. Lifting heavy objects improperly may also contribute to spinal misalignment. If pain or discomfort appears, it becomes a stressor and will at some point affect your adrenals and immune system.

What can you do to correct your structural stressors? See a reputable chiropractor to get your spine aligned, then maintain the alignment with regular visits. Most people benefit from walking as humans are meant to walk. Try the physically healthy side of yoga since it stretches and opens the systems and organs so that oxygen, blood and nutrients can reach all areas of your body. If sitting at a computer for periods of time, get up and walk around the room or do a few stretches every hour or so to relax your tense neck and back, and don't forget to flex your fingers to relax them too. Caution: If you are experiencing adrenal burnout, do small amounts of exercise, working up slowly. If you feel exhausted after a walk, you went too far so reduce it next time. Pushing yourself even with a healthy walk can further deplete your adrenals if it exhausts you. Rule of thumb: start slowly and work up, but do get moving!

Sleep is vital for repairing your body and definitely for the restoration of the adrenals. It takes five hours of consecutive sleep (sleep without waking) for your adrenals to heal. Although there are many thoughts about how much sleep is necessary every night, the key element is that you experience all the phases of good sleep, especially the REM period of sleep. This is why most individuals become sleep deprived because they don't sleep deeply enough and cannot remain asleep for at least five hours consecutively. Restoring the adrenals may help you sleep better since one symptom of adrenal burnout is insomnia, due primarily to either elevated or sub-normal cortisol levels. Removing stress from your life should assist you in better sleep.

Eliminating stress and restoring your adrenals is one of the core requirements for vibrant health. To make sure you understand all I've shared in this material, here is a recap of what is important for you to remember to get rid of stress from your life.

Psychological Stress Solutions/Healing Your Adrenals:

- Change your negative thoughts and beliefs to positive ones.
- Discover your own truths.
- Accept your responsibility to make wiser choices. Educate yourself.
- Surrender all challenges and frustrations to God.
- Flow with life to remain in peace.
- Reserve time for quiet and meditation.
- Focus on the good, which is from love.
- Become resourceful.

Nutritional Stress Solutions/Healing Your Adrenals:

- Eat healthy—lots of veggies and fruits, using organic as much as possible.
- Address digestion with enzymes and HCL as they are vital for health.
- Drink pure water, ½ ounce per pound of body weight daily.
- Consume one teaspoon of pink Himalayan salt daily.
- If you eat meat, poultry and dairy, be sure it is free range and free of hormones.
- Include a balance of good protein at every meal and snack to receive enough amino acids.
- Take nutrients that particularly help to restore the adrenals.
- Include healthy fats at every meal or snack.

Structural Stress Solutions/Healing Your Adrenals:

- Visit a reputable chiropractor. Maintain spinal alignment.
- Engage in moderate, enjoyable exercise.
- Try the physically healthy side of yoga—very healing and renewing.
- Learn to lift properly using your legs rather than your back.
- Don't remain in the same position for long periods. Change position; stretch; walk around.
- Take time to relax.
- Get enough sleep, 5 hours of consecutive deep sleep is vital for adrenal repair.

All of the information mentioned in the preceding material is empowering. When you educate yourself with various ways to become healthier in all dimensions and eliminate stress from your life, not only will you feel and look better, but you will *be* better. Life is meant to be enjoyed and considered as an exciting adventure.

Never is it meant to be a struggle or stressful, and how you see it and respond to it is how you experience it. If you find yourself living in fear and don't see life as a wonderful journey, perhaps you could benefit from a spiritual life coach who can help guide you into better responses and thoughts with a new direction so that you can become empowered and experience an extraordinary life. You are a star who is waiting to shine brilliantly, and the choice is yours! *Remember this—the only limits in your life are the ones you place there.*

You are invited to contact the Where Miracles Happen® Institute,
a division of Healing Nature Institute, at
www.wheremiracleshappen.com
or 770-663-3977
for more information or to locate a spiritual life coach. To receive a
free e-Book entitled *Stress Free Living*, visit:
www.drcarolynporter.com.

Star Bright

Endings bring new beginnings...
One door closes, another opens and beckons to you.
Do not waver nor allow fear's illusions to overshadow you
For love surrounds you and angels guide you.
With each step you take, strengthening, growing,
Reaching for the heavens, beautifully empowered,
You are limitless!

Remember, a star shines in its own light.
Always live your dreams.
When darkness comes the beautiful star shines the brightest.
And so it is...
    —Rev. Dr. Carolyn Porter

EDITOR'S NOTE

It is with great appreciation and honor that Carolyn, and her "Where Miracles Happen Institute," now a division of "Healing Nature Institute" is recognized as the first to see the power and vision of joining together with other leaders of the world to offer a virtual campus for learning. Carolyn is a Life-coach who also sees our vision. Our birthright is to enjoy peace, joy, Love, and Happiness with Our Creator and his creation with Vibrant Health!

Carolyn is the first "Coaching Professional" to join, "Healing Nature Institute," where people seeking help can find their way back to vibrant health.

We've all heard: "The Journey of 1,000 miles begins with the first step." I, John Eagle Freedom, want to plant this seed of TRUTH: "The Journey of Health & Wealth begins with the thought of the journey." —JEF

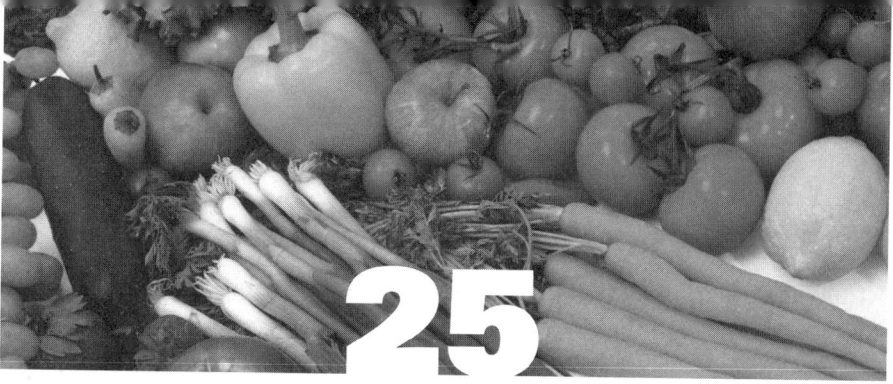

I WAS HEALED,
YOU CAN BE TOO!

Brenda Cobb

When you are willing to make changes in the way you think and in your lifestyle you can change your world! I am living proof of that! It has been many years since I was diagnosed with breast and cervical cancer and every year I feel better and look younger too. My healing journey completely transformed me from a woman with not only cancer, but arthritis, migraine headaches, allergies, depression, fatigue, insomnia, psoriasis, candida, acid reflux, indigestion and heartburn. It seemed that everything in the world was wrong with me and I just took a pill or potion to try to fix my problem. What I didn't realize at the time was that I was adding to my problems by trying to use drugs as a quick fix! Drugs are toxic to the body and toxicity and deficiency are two of the key reasons people develop diseases. Little did I know!

In February 1999 at the age of 50 when I was diagnosed with cancer, my doctors recommended surgery, chemotherapy and radiation. I shuddered at the thought. I remembered my mother telling me she was going to have a mastectomy, and several aunts going through rounds and rounds of surgeries, chemotherapy sessions and radiation that didn't help and only made them worse and in some cases killed them. I thought about other family members and friends who had faced similar situations and their decisions to do drugs and how those drugs made them worse, not better. I just couldn't do that to my body. I told my doctor I wouldn't do surgery, chemo or radiation. I knew there must be a better way to help my body heal itself. He wasn't happy with my decision.

When I received the news from my doctor that I had cancer, I left his office shaking all over. I went to my car and first I cried, then I prayed to God to show me what to do and the way that would heal me! I heard that little voice say, "Go to the health food store." I didn't know what I was going for, but I knew I had to get there. I walked in the store and asked if anyone knew of a book about how to heal cancer without drugs and surgery. I was pointed to a little book *How I Healed Cancer Naturally*, by Eydie Mae. It was the only one on the shelf. When I reached up to take that lone little book off the shelf, I got chills all over my body. It was like a wave of energy that penetrated every cell. Still to this day, it is the strongest "chill" I have ever felt. I knew that was my little book and that it had my answer. I knew that my chills were coming from God as a message for me to pay attention.

I read Eydie Mae's story of how she had cancer and tried surgery, chemo and radiation that her cancer just kept coming back until doctors gave her no hope. Eydie Mae began taking in wheatgrass, energy soup, rejuvelac and veggie kraut and she had a dramatic and total healing. When I read her story I knew in my heart that it would work for me too. So even though I new nothing about healthy eating, I devoted myself to learning everything I possibly could about raw and living food nutrition and a whole new lifestyle. It was amazing. I healed on every level and within 6 months I was free of all my ailments including cancer. My doctors were amazed and I was transformed. Over the next year and a half as I stayed with my new healthier lifestyle even my gray hair turned back to its original color and my eyesight improved to 20/20. I had worn glasses since I was 12 years old, so getting my perfect vision back was quite a gift.

God revealed to me early on that it was important for me to tell other people about the amazing benefits of a healthy raw and living foods program and how to detoxify the body of negative thoughts and emotions, drugs, poisons, chemicals, additives, colors, dyes, heavy metals, parasites, worms, mucoid plaque and all the other toxins that plague the body and keep it from being at its best health. What I understood clearly was that I had to simultaneously get rid of all the toxic stuff accumulated over many years and I had to put in the most perfect nutrition available. I had to give my body every single thing it needed so it could do the job God created it to do. It could heal itself. This became my mission and my passion in life. I started out wanting to heal me, but my desire expanded to wanting to help others heal too. It didn't take me long to realize that God had a real mission for my life and it was all about teaching others what I had learned and helping them heal too.

I have learned so much over the years and have continued to add to my healthy lifestyle protocol. I have realized that optimum health and anti-aging is what most everyone wants. I have learned that there are many facets to complete healing and that it is important to address and heal each part so you can achieve the total and perfect health you desire. The most important aspect of healing is the emotional healing and the mental thinking and to have true faith and belief in what you are doing. What you think manifests in your life. A person must use the power of their thinking and their words to create good health, abundance, prosperity, peace, happiness and joy! You can change what you eat so your body gets the proper nutrition, but if you continue to think in a negative way you will only hurt yourself and you will not heal.

Along with the mental thinking it is equally important to heal the emotional stuff that can sometimes have been hidden for so many years that a person doesn't even realize it is there. Negative emotions and unforgiveness are at the root of all illness and disease and so is stress! Stress can lead to everything from diabetes to heart disease. Stress can create cancer and depression. Stress must be dealt with in a positive and constructive way or it can make a person sicker and keep a person from ever getting well. It's never what happens to a person in life that is stressful; it is the person's reaction to what happens that creates the stress. Change your attitude and you can change your life. This is why emotional healing and mental thinking must be a part of a total healing program.

When people with MS, Parkinson's, lupus or cancer patients, only given a few weeks or months to live, miraculously heal even when doctors thought it would be impossible, this is not happening just by changing the diet. When diabetics are able to normalize blood sugar in just a few days even after they have been a diabetic for twenty or more years, the nutrition is certainly important, but there is much more that is needed. It is the holistic approach of treating the body, mind and spirit that truly brings about complete health.

Another important aspect in healing is to detoxify the body. Toxins make the body sick and toxins build up over many years. Toxic thoughts, foods, drinks, relationships, jobs, drugs, chemicals and a host of other toxins clog up the body and make it impossible for the body to heal itself. You must get out the toxins to heal! Being deficient in vitamins, minerals, enzymes and probiotics is also a cause of poor health! I am not referring to just vitamin pills but the vitamins and minerals from the foods you eat. A pill cannot replace good nutrition. You can supplement with pills, but you can't expect pills to work without a foundation of good nutrition.

Wherever you are right now, remember that your body is capable of achieving the perfect health you desire. If you are sick, you can restore and heal from any disease. If you are well you can increase your energy, gain overall well-being and reverse aging. Aches and pains are not normal and are a sign that the body is toxic and deficient. Sluggishness and fatigue is not natural. The body was created to be energetic and full of life. It is possible to slow up the aging process and to look and feel 10 to 20 years younger with the right lifestyle habits.

Usually the reason people don't do better is because they don't know what to do. Education about you and your body, the right foods, how to cleanse, how to heal emotional stuff and to change your mental thinking, these are some of the most important things you could ever learn. This information is something you have to seek for yourself. Courses on these subjects are not ordinarily offered in mainstream schools. If our school systems put more emphasis on how to achieve real health, it would be just as beneficial if not more so than reading, writing and arithmetic! You can have a great education, but if you are too sick to use it, then what do you really have?

I know the body can heal from most anything because I have personally witnessed miraculous healings of people whom the doctors thought would not get well. It's never too late if a person is willing to do what it takes to get better. Even the most serious of situations and long ongoing health problems can be corrected with detoxification, cleansing, emotional healing, positive mental thinking and good nutrition. If you are sick now, don't wait to make the changes. Do it today! If you're in good health, learn how to stay that way so you don't have to try to fix a problem down the road.

Brenda Cobb is founder of The Living Foods Institute in Atlanta, Georgia and author of *The Living Foods Lifestyle®*, *101 Raw and Living Food Recipes* and seven other books on raw and living foods and natural healing. She teaches a Healthy Lifestyle Raw and Living Food Course at Living Foods Institute in Atlanta, Georgia. 404-524-4488 or 800-844-9876 www.livingfoodsinstitute.com

EDITOR'S NOTE

I met Brenda on my journey of healing and received my first book authored by Dr. Norman Walker, *Colon Health—the Key to a Vibrant Life!* at her "Living Foods Institute" in Atlanta, Georgia.

I resonate with her statement, "Usually the reason why people don't do better, is because they don't know what to do." I would like to add that they do not have a support system in place. This is one of the reasons I have created the on-line virtual campus, "Healing Nature Institute" where global health leaders, such as Brenda, are welcome to feature their quality teaching resources and where students may receive a support system family, so they don't feel like they're going it all alone! Our goal is to offer these courses where they will be accredited towards a degree!—JEF

THE 7 LIFESTYLE HABITS OF INCREDIBLY HEALTHY PEOPLE

Joe Esposito

M ost folks will agree that it is a good idea to take care of their body in order to obtain and maintain good health. The problem is that most people don't know what to do, or, they do know what to do, but don't have the will power to make the changes. If there were a simple, easy to understand, step by step method of improving your life, would you do it? I posed this question to several hundred people and most of them said they would change their lives for the better if they just knew how. I then surveyed extremely healthy people to find out how they can be healthy and still live a "normal" life. The results of that fact finding mission have been compiled into what I call "The 7 Lifestyle Habits of Extremely Healthy People." The following is a simple outline of what they do and how they live their lives.

1. They Don't Poison Their Bodies

Your first step in maximizing your health is to stop polluting yourself. Here are the most harmful foods you need to eliminate.

The Seven Deadly Sinful Foods:
* Alcohol
* Meat
* Dairy
* Sugar
* Coffee
* Soda
* Aspartame

The Evil Runner-ups

All hydrogenated oils, margarine, nuts roasted in oil, creamy peanut butter, fruit in heavy syrup (canned peaches), canned soups, pickles, sauerkraut, snack crackers, potato chips and other chips. Cereals with added sugars, colors and flavorings, white rice, pasta, bread and other refined products.

2. They Nourish Their Bodies With Plenty Of Live Foods

You are what you eat! Make sure your body gets the tools it needs to build a better you.
* Water - drink plenty of pure water.
* Fresh Fruit - Fresh fruit, fruit juices, dried fruit
* Fresh Vegetables - Put on salads or sandwiches. Use sprouts and sea vegetables. Buy organic as often as possible.
* Nuts & Seeds - Raw sunflower, flax, pumpkin: natural nut-butters (almonds, cashews, etc.), Almond milk
* Whole Grains - Whole grain breads, natural cereals, puffed rice, shredded wheat, granolas, Rice Milk.
* Tubers & Squash - Potatoes, yams & Sweet Potatoes; acorn, pumpkin, butternut and spaghetti squash.
* Legumes - Beans, peas, lentils, soybeans and tofu

Supplements can be a great way to ensure that your body is getting all it needs.

3. They Have Structural Integrity

"As the twig is bent, so grows the tree." Accidents, injuries and bad posture all contribute to a break down of the musculo-skeletal system. The danger is that the nervous system will suffer impaired nerve function. This leads to a break down in the signals from the brain that go to the 80 trillion cells in your body. Many diseases are caused by or complicated by a nervous system that is not operating at 100% of its potential.

4. They cleanse & Detoxify Their Bodies

Regular cleansing, fasting and other detoxifying programs help the body free itself of built up toxins. Even a person on a perfectly healthy diet will accumulate waste materials over time, not to mention the build up of chemicals from our air, water and food.

5. They Keep Themselves Fit, Strong and Flexible

Regular weight-bearing exercise and flexibility training are vital to being healthy and preventing disease. You don't have to look like Arnold Schwarzenager, but maintaining good muscle tone and flexibility helps enhance your body's well-being, prevent arthritis and osteoporosis and a host of other ailments.

6. They schedule time for rest and recreation

Giving your body an opportunity to restore itself must be a priority if you want to be healthy. This includes proper sleeping posture, having regular sleep times, meditation and relaxation techniques, and lots of fun! Overdoing anything can and usually does lead to burn-out, which makes you less productive. Remember, this life is not a dress rehearsal; if you are enjoying what you do and could not imagine doing anything else, just keep doing what you are doing. If not, take time out to enjoy life. From what I understand, no one ever said on their death bed, "I should have spent more time in the office and less time playing and having fun."

7. They have passion & Purpose

The number one leading risk factor for not surviving your first heart attack is job dissatisfaction! Spend time doing things you believe in and love to do. The healthiest people live life to the fullest! Maybe your passion is cooking, reading, skiing, being with family or just spending time alone. Right now, think of the one or two things that just make you happy and follow your passion. My mother told me, when I was a child and did not know what I wanted to be when I grew up, "I don't care if you are a garbage man, just be the best garbage man you can be."

Incorporate these simple ideas into your life and see what happens. If I'm wrong, so what, nothing was lost. But if I'm right (and I am), you will see an amazing change for the better in all aspects of your life.

YOUR BODY'S GREATEST ENEMY

Dr. Norman W. Walker

What is Constipation?

The expression constipation is derived from the Latin word "constipa-tus," which translated means "to press or crowd together, to pack, to cram." Consequently, to be constipated means that the packed accumulation of feces in the bowel makes its evacuation difficult. However, a state of constipation can also exist when movements of the bowel may seem to be normal, in spite of an accumulation of feces somewhere along the line in the colon!

The Fact of the matter is that constipation is the number one affliction underlying nearly every ailment; it can be imputed to be the initial, primary cause of nearly every disturbance of the human system. It is vital to stress that constipation affects the health of the colon, upon which the health of the body in its entirety depends.

There are two crimes against nature which civilization indulges in daily. Both beget the most common and popular of our ailments, constipation. One is the consumption of devitalized and refined foods which fail to nourish the organs responsible for the evacuation of waste matter. The other, which is most prevalent particularly among young people, but not much less among the older and more mature, is neglecting to stop everything we are doing when the urge to evacuate the bowels should drive us headlong into the bathroom. Nature is a strict taskmaster.

How Constipation Effects the Colon's Function

If solving the problem of constipation were merely a case of washing out loose material lying free inside any part of the colon, it would not be too great a difficulty to clear the situation. A colonic would most likely be sufficient to take care of its removal. The problem, however, is not quite so simply to dispose of. Constipation involves not only the unnecessary retention of feces in the rectum, but also the retention present throughout the first half of the colon, from the cecum to the middle of the transverse colon. The cecum is found next to the ileo cecal valve at the beginning of the colon.

The wall of this section of the colon is equipped with sensitive nerves and muscles whose function it is to create wavelike motions, known as peristaltic waves, to propel the contents of the colon from the cecum to the rectum for eventual evacuation. This is a distance of approximately five feet.

Besides the formation of these peristaltic waves, this first half of the colon has two other very important functions. First, it must extract from all the residue coming from the small intestine any available nutritional material which the small intestine was unable to collect. For this purpose, it mulches the material which passes into it from the small intestine and absorbs the liquid and other elements through its walls into the blood stream. The nutrition which has thus been extracted from the colon is collected by the blood vessels lining the walls of the colon and is carried to the liver for processing.

Obviously, if the feces in the colon have putrefied and fermented, any nutritional elements present in it would pass into the blood stream as polluted products. What would otherwise be nutritional becomes, in fact, the generation of toxemia. Toxemia is a condition in which the blood contains poisonous products which are produced by the growth of pathogenic or disease-producing bacteria. Pimples, for example, are usually the first indication that toxemia has found its way into the body.

The other important function of the first half of the colon is to gather from the glands in its walls the intestinal flora needed to lubricate the colon. Far too many people, professional and laymen, think that enemas and colon irrigations wash out the intestinal flora and thus deprive the colon of a valuable means of lubrication. Such lack of lubrication only serves to intensify a state of constipation and to generate toxemia.

This fecal incrustation interferes with, if it does not actually prevent, the infusion of the necessary intestinal flora for colon lubrication, the formation of peristaltic waves for evacuation purposes, and the absorption and uses of the additional nutritional elements present in the waste residue coming into the colon from the small intestine.

It does not require much imagination to perceive that the adhesive quality of the feces in the colon is readily susceptible to creating a coating on the inside of the lining or wall of the colon, resembling a layer of plaster in its consistency. It is equally obvious that such a coating, in preventing the normal function of the colon, has the insidious effect of becoming a generator of toxicity, to the detriment of health, happiness and longevity

A Hospital Stay... Canceled

Just a few years ago, a good friend of ours telephoned me from Indiana to tell me that he was scheduled to go into the hospital the next day. "What for?" I asked him. He told me he had a blocked colon and could not defecate. The prolonged retention of feces and stale waste matter in the colon may, and frequently does, result in the blocking of the passage within the colon, making it impossible to have a bowel movement. I asked my friend why, knowing our program, he did not get some colon irrigations. "Oh," he answered, "that's out of the question. The nearest one is 100 miles from here." I told him I would travel 1,000 miles for some colonics before I would allow myself to be taken to the hospital!

As it turned out, my friend took that 100-mile trip and telephoned me a week or so later to say it had saved his life. He was feeling better than he had felt in years, and was going back for some more colonics soon. This is by no means an isolated case; I could fill a book with similar ones.

My study and intensive research on this subject convinces me more than ever that no treatment or healing procedure should ever be started without first giving the patient a series of colon irrigations in order to clean out the colon and remove the incipient source of infection. There is no ailment, sickness or disease that will not respond to treatment quicker and more effectively than it will after the administration of a series of colon irrigations.

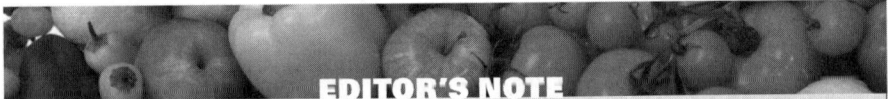

EDITOR'S NOTE

Dr. Norman Walker was my icon. Grandfather of Juicing, author of over 100 books, expert on longevity, he also played a big role in educating many of the leaders today. He saved and extended my life with the priceless information he has placed in his books. Your colon is 80% of your immune system. Dehydration which leads to Constipation is our greatest enemy! I want to thank and acknowledge Book Publishing Company, Summertown, Tennessee for permission to insert this valuable chapter in *The Healing Nature of Jesus*. I would recommend his books which are his legacy to be required reading for anyone seeking to become younger and enjoy vibrant health.

Thank you Dr. Norman Walker. Your long life was not lived in vain.—JEF

28

OUR STORY, OUR PURPOSE

Jackie Graff

During the past 14 years, Gideon, my husband and I have been eating living foods from the trees and the earth. The fruits, nuts, and seeds from the trees, and the greens and other vegetables growing out of the earth, are the foods that God gave us for food (Genesis 1:29). Eating these unaltered foods enabled us to absorb the powerhouse of energy and vitality from the sun; and the air, water, and nutrients within these plant-based foods. This living nutrition has allowed our bodies to self-heal, during which time we have lost, between us, over 150 pounds of fat and toxins; we have boundless energy, normal blood pressure, reduced blood cholesterol, no more depression, no more hot flashes, no allergies, no arthritis, no carpal tunnel, no sinusitis; off medication. During this time we have seen an improvement in our skin, and the disappearance of swollen lymph glands and a breast lump. We have a sense of peace, which we have never had before in our lives. This living enzyme rich nutrition has been a link to a higher relationship with our God and Jesus. "Sprout Raw Food" began because we wanted to share the new life that we have received and take this knowledge to others.

Everything in our life has led to our present purpose and passion: making delicious raw food and teaching others kitchen magic and nutrition science. We went on the road in 2009 with *Raw Food Revival* taking our message to the people about how we regained our health through an uncooked plant-based diet and being conscious of the other requisites of health such as water, exercise, sunshine, sleep, environment, breathing, and prayer. Many paths and directions have brought us to our life's purpose.

God gave me a wonderful talent for making food taste delicious (even when I was cooking unhealthy) and a way of blending textures and flavors, which sets my raw food apart. I have always thought of preparing food as an art form and each dish that I prepared was like painting a picture. The first ingredient in all my food is, Love.

I feel that my talent and creativity has been passed through my ancestors from many generations and lifetimes. My love and passion for preparing food, nursing and caring for others began at the young age of 10 when I was caring for my mother who was bedridden for three months of her pregnancy. My mother was a gourmet cook and from her bed near the kitchen she would guide me in the preparation of food, how to flavor and most important how to correct my mistakes. Because she graduated with a degree in Home Economics, she knew the chemistry of food. Taking care of my mother at this early age molded my life with a love of making delicious food and caring for others, and led me to become a nurse.

In 1969 my mother developed cancer of the breast and had a radical mastectomy, she was 45. The doctors said they had gotten it all and two years later cancer was in her other breast, which she had removed. This time the doctors said they got it all and two years later cancer was in her liver and bones. She had aggressive chemotherapy and radiation therapy and even though they had given her only months to live, she was a fighter and lived for 2 more years… then died from kidney failure due to sepsis (a massive infection), six years after first being diagnosed with cancer. The therapy had made her immune system so weak that she died from a side-affect of this therapy, a kidney infection. Instead of building her immune system to fight cancer and any other disease, her immune system had been weakened to a point that her body fell prey to the bacteria that is around all of us.

My mother and I had tried to figure out why she got cancer. Each time she was diagnosed with cancer, she previously had the "flu." She thought it was an influenza virus that caused the cancer. Why did she get the "flu"? We never related our diet to our immune system. I think she lived as long as she did because she started to supplement with large doses of vitamins and minerals. At the time we never thought about the possibility of getting these nutrients from our food.

As soon as I returned from her funeral and getting her things in order, I came home to face the fact that my dear mother-in-law, was in the hospital to have her breast removed due to cancer. The cancer was in her lymph nodes and after 2 years of chemotherapy and radiation therapy she died…the cancer had spread to her brain. I thought that my daughters had a very bad legacy of breast cancer from both grandmothers, but at the time I was sure there would be a cure by the time they were old enough to get breast cancer. I never stopped to think that our lifestyle or what we were eating could cause this disease. Maybe a healthy immune system could be the answer?

Here we are in 2009 and are we any further ahead? My daughters are 29 and 35 and men and women are still dying with breast cancer or is it the treatment? Do we know why they get breast cancer? We say there are many risk factors. Do we think it could maybe be the toxins we are putting in our bodies from cigarettes, sugar, dairy, alcohol, meat, bread, cooked food, and aspartame? Did we consider that a diet of uncooked fruits, vegetables, nuts, and seeds could boost our immune system to the point that we do not get any disease? I believe now that cancer is just a symptom of a toxic body.

Through my 40-year nursing career, I gained an understanding of anatomy and physiology of the human body and a first-hand knowledge of what is happening to people's health on the Standard American Diet (SAD), and other diets that are supposed to be healthy. As a nurse we were taught therapeutic diets to educate patients only after they already had a disease. How to keep from getting a disease was not part of our curriculum.

Throughout my nursing career I observed that those with chronic and life-threatening diseases were becoming younger and younger. People in their 20's and 30's with strokes and heart attacks. Others were being admitted with multiple system disorders, not just one problem and patients were much sicker now than in the beginning of my nursing career. Patients were being kept alive on long lists of medications, with many side affects. They were alive but were not living; many were unable to enjoy life because of the pain and suffering of their disease or the treatment. I saw many die from the "side-affects" of their surgery, medications, or simply from human error. Our health care system is a disease care system focused on treating after the person is sick. Prevention is touted as a diagnostic tool, which only detects the presence or absence of disease. We could change the health of our country by simply subsidizing fruits and vegetables to make them affordable and quit subsidizing meat and dairy and other foods that make us unhealthy. I now can truly help people heal and learn how their body can heal itself.

Gideon has allowed me to be creative and take different paths, always trusting in my decision. This openness to try new things really led us by accident to the raw food diet thirteen years ago.

At 50 I thought I was a fairly healthy vegetarian. I was 100 pounds overweight, on blood pressure medication and still had high blood pressure, on medication for early arthritis and still had aching joints, antidepressants and was still depressed, taking estrogen and still having hot flashes, chronic sinusitis, and low energy. Gideon, was overweight, had hypertension, elevated cholesterol, and was a smoker. We never drank water, only coffee, diet cokes or beer and wine. Now, how we considered ourselves healthy, I do not know. Despite the fact that I am a nurse and thought I knew about nutrition—I only knew what I had been taught. I only knew part of the story.

As a nurse I learned about a variety of diets for a multitude of conditions such as diabetic, cardiac, and low cholesterol diets. Each of these diets were given after people became ill. I never thought of food as a way to prevent all of the diseases I saw people getting....that was until thirteen years ago.

Our path to healthy eating has taken many years. We had been lacto-ova vegetarians since 1987 when we discovered Gideon's cholesterol was over 350. I had been a gourmet cook for years, using meat, dairy, butter, sugar and anything else I thought would make the food delectable. In my clouded thinking, those low cholesterol diets were for those with high cholesterol and not for me the gourmet cook. I loved to entertain and feed people. My food was known by the many family and friends entertained by us to be delicious and perfectly seasoned but it was killing my husband! Did I think that it could be killing me also?

From my nurse's training I knew what I had to do to get Gideon's cholesterol down… get rid of the animal fat. So out went the butter, cheese, eggs, meat, and later chicken and fish. When we got rid of these high fat, high calorie foods we replaced those calories with high calorie cooked complex carbohydrates and much sugar. My talents for making delicious food evolved into making gourmet low fat vegetarian (this was the low fat, high carb era). We ate much of the high carb foods many vegetarians eat such as potatoes, bread, pasta, beans and rice, and salads. By eating this way, we were able to bring Gideon's cholesterol down into the 250 range, which was still not enough, so he started on cholesterol reducing medication along with his high blood pressure medication both of which had many side-affects. His physician said he would have to take these the rest of his life, but not to worry, many people his age had the same problems. Now as Gideon's cholesterol was going down, our weight was going up because during this era, fat was "bad" and carbs were "good" and we consumed many fat-free products, high in sugar that were on the market.

So what led us to a Living food diet? In 1995, my brother Robert Meadow a brilliant and talented violin maker had been diagnosed with an auto immune disease in which his body viewed his nervous system as bacteria. His body was constantly on the attack, which exhibited itself with various neurological symptoms such as paralysis, seizures, or dysphasia (inability to speak), cardiac arrhythmias and many other neurological symptoms. Doctors had given him a grim outlook for a long life, and informed him that he probably would not live longer than a couple of years. The medical treatment almost killed him. Searching for a way to heal his disease and be free of pain lead him to learn about the raw and living food from a close friend who had been eating this way for many years.

We saw him in New York at Thanksgiving where he shared this new raw food diet, he was chewing wheat grass and eating many things that I thought at the time were very strange. I told Gideon at the time that I "would never eat that way." Well, never say never!

At the time he had been living with different friends in New York and each time that his condition would deteriorate with seizures, frightening these friends, it suddenly was not convenient for him to stay, so he would move to another friend. He went through several friends and was mostly living out of his car in New York City. In a matter of 6 months he had improved his condition so much that he was back to making his violins. I asked him to come live with us so that he could have a place to live, peace of mind, be healthy and make his violins.

We had been vegetarian and decided that we would stay on a raw food diet while he was living with us. Robert had shared with us just how addictive cooked food was and I did not want him to get sick again. I decided that raw food would not hurt us for a while and when he left we could go back to our " healthy" vegetarian diet. After a week or two of eating raw food Gideon and I both felt so much better. We had more energy and a clarity of mind than I had ever experienced before. For the months he lived with us he taught us the basics of the raw food diet and inspired us to continue our quest for learning. The dietary choices that we had been making were catching up with us. We were over fifty and until we had clarity I had thought that many of our food choices were simply making us gain weight. We were eating what I thought was a healthy vegetarian diet.

After several months Robert decided to move back to New York. We were alone eating a raw food diet in Atlanta with no support. We were eating probably between 70-80% raw, depending on the day, trying to find our own path. Reality had set in, we really liked the healthier state we were in, but cooked food is very addictive and we stayed on what I refer to as a roller coaster raw food diet for a couple of years. We had been in what I call "Raw Food Depression," when you love the way you feel but hate what it has done to your social life. This is when my creative juices started flowing. I knew that for us to be able to remain eating healthy like this, we would need a variety of delicious dishes that others would also enjoy. I began detoxing in recipes and at present have created more than 600 delicious original recipes.

We had prayed for a raw food community in Atlanta. And in 2000 started having dinners, which led us to teach others, and for a year and a half we had a restaurant, organic market, and teaching facility. We thought we were following the Lord's plan for us. In 2004 we closed our restaurant and started teaching full time along with a wholesale raw food business. Instead of feeding a few people delicious raw food in Atlanta, we are teaching many from all over the world who will go on to teach others. This is the way we can change peoples lives, helping them to be healthier and eventually change the health of the planet by decreasing the consumption of animals.

We feel that we are following God's plan for us with *Raw Food Revival,* taking our message to the people about how we regained our health through an uncooked plant-based diet and being conscious of the other requisites of health such as water, exercise, sunshine, sleep, environment, breathing, and prayer. Through our international travels, teaching, my recipes and blog, showing people how easy it is to eat a truly healthy living food diet as God instructed us in the beginning with Genesis 1:29, we have our purpose. We can be reached at:

RawFoodRevival.com
or 770-992-9218.

EDITOR'S NOTE

Jackie & Gideon Graff have been very instrumental on my journey to health.

Meeting some of the young leaders in the living food movement at their restaurant, "Sprout Cafe" in Atlanta, Georgia, allowed me to warp-speed my growth to health and awareness. Jackie and Gideon have one of the best teaching styles to keep you on the path to wholeness. I had the privilege of enjoying two Thanksgiving meals prepared in love by them. They are truly gourmet raw-food chefs. You will not be able to distinguish between gourmet, and cooked food! Your taste buds will be tantalized, and you will ask for seconds! It is not the food in your life, it is the life in your food! I encourage every church, societal function, city, etc. that are interested in raising awareness and eliminating sickness and disease from your community, to become a true, Health City U.S.A., and save our children by becoming responsible for your own health!

Please invite our team into your life and the life of your community, unite under the blood of Jesus, and the banner of TRUTH! Host a crusade of TRUTH in your area! Wake Up America!!! Take action now! Come under the Blood of Jesus! Save yourself and this great nation! Learn the TRUTH and He will make You Free!

Please call toll free: 888-572-3132—JEF

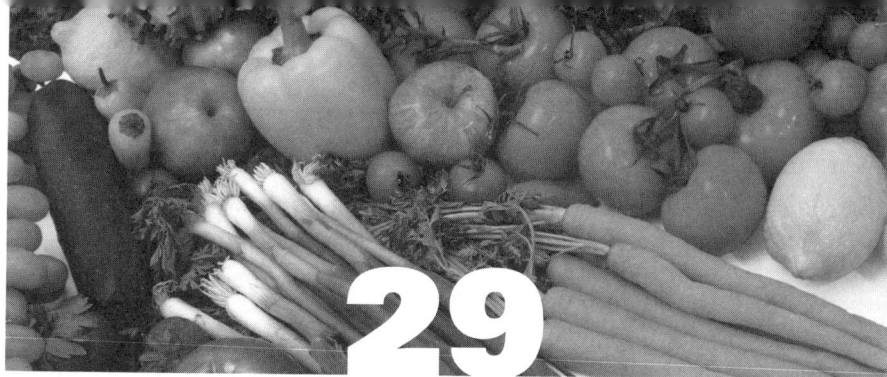

WHAT BUILDS AND WHAT BREAKS DOWN YOUR HEALTH

Michael Saiber, Tamera Campbell, Stanley Arcieri, and Dr. Connie Kennedy

"I give you every seed-bearing plant on the face of the whole earth and every tree that has fruit with seed in it."
—Genesis 1: 29

"E3Live has more bio-available chlorophyll than any other food. In biochemical research circles, the presence of chlorophyll in such high quantities is a clear indication of E3Live's extraordinarily high life force. This inherent vitality helps keep E3Live's wide spectrum of nutrients at their absolute nutritional peak. For me, this partially explains the mystery of how E3Live can have so many positive health benefits."
~ *Karl J. Abrams, Professor of Chemistry*

E3LIVE®: PURE, GOD-DESIGNED, WILD FOOD

We warmly received the invitation to write a chapter on E3Live, a food that stands at the summit of organic, raw and natural foods—wholly due to the genius of the Creator. We are deeply moved to be caretakers of this primordial food, a gift from the wild to humanity.

For your health, we will address both what builds and what breaks down health. For preventing disease, what you eat is no less important than what you do not eat. The renowned Dr. Fred Bisci provides a vital health key in *Your Healthy Journey*. He says that the key is not only in **what you put in** your body but **what you leave out**. We seek to educate people and contribute to waking the nation on both the life-positive benefits of E3Live and the life-negative dangers of eating genetically modified (GM) or transgenic lab foods now available at local supermarkets everywhere. Some of the same MDs that champion E3Live now issue grave health warnings on GM foods. This impacts everyone's health from young children, to pregnant women to the elderly. We will seriously delve into this later in the E3Live chapter.

We invite you to carefully consider what to include and what to exclude in your diet. You may be surprised and shocked, as we once were, to hear conscientious MDs inform us of the hidden health dangers of GM foods. As health missionaries, we encourage you with all our heart to have your friends and family read about the perils of eating GM foods as discussed later in this chapter. You can determine for yourself what is best for your vibrant health and that of your family. Knowledge of what is good and its opposite enables each of us to wisely make life-sustaining choices. Let's begin with the good and then discuss why and what to religiously avoid.

E3Live is literally the rarest natural food found on Earth! It is a raw, wild, all-organic food widely harvested only at Klamath Lake in Oregon's southern high desert. It happens to be the most nutrient-rich food known to humankind. E3Live is a fresh-frozen aqua-botanical known as *Aphanizomenon flos-aquae* or AFA. It is created by the elemental forces of creation and grows in a mountain lake under exceptional conditions. In the winter, Klamath Lake is frozen on top while mineral-rich volcanic hot springs rise up from the lake floor. These and other elemental powers cannot be reproduced in a laboratory. In fact, E3Live has resisted all attempts at laboratory domestication by humans.

HOW E3LIVE IS MADE

The Pacific Ring of Fire holds 2/3 of the world's active volcanoes. It extends through Java, Krakatoa, and Tonga, touching the Northwest USA in the Klamath Lake region of Oregon, the only place on Earth where E3Live is harvested and distributed. Mighty Mt. Mazama erupted here thousands of years ago (with over 40 times the power of Mt. St. Helens' blast in the 1980s), Klamath Lake is thus rich in volcanic minerals. Growing conditions are totally unique. Our mountain lake receives life-giving sunshine 300 days a year and its surface freezes in winter while mineral-rich volcanic hot springs rise up from the lake floor. No one has ever been able to domesticate this wild, all-organic superfood. E3Live, with its volcanic legacy, goes far beyond domestic organic farming. Only the primordial forces of Creation can make E3Live. We are dedicated to gathering this vital, nutrient-dense gift of nature. We harvest E3Live to make its power available to you.

The Hand of Creation alone is responsible for creating the numerous health benefits of E3Live, a single food that is a pharmacopeia unto itself. E3Live has multiple properties that assist our healing, reduce inflammation, improve brain function, promote joy, increase energy, nutritionally suppress food cravings, and generally balance our nutritional needs. It's also beneficial to skin, hair and nails.

E3Live has the very opposite effect of fast food. When a child or adult eats a fast food burger, basically an addictive salt and grease "treat," they will not thereafter want to eat vegetables or salad. When a person takes E3Live, their sense of taste is automatically regulated in a positive direction. There will be a natural movement and a desire to eat healthy foods.

Gabriel Cousens, MD, author of *Conscious Eating* put it this way: "E3Live is specific food for our nervous system, brain function and the quality of our consciousness. More than any other food, it enables us to make a paradigm shift and enjoy a sense of well-being. There's a quality of joy that's really subtle that many people experience." E3Live is a therapeutic food. It makes people feel healthier and motivates them to eat healthier foods. The more you get to feeling better by eating

God-given foods, the more obvious will be the negative health effects of eating fast foods and GM foods. Come to think of it, most fast food is often GM food.

E3LIVE IS THE STANDARD BY WHICH OTHER SUPERFOODS ARE MEASURED

Professional athletes including Olympic Gold Medal winners use E3Live to enhance their performance and increase their recovery times. It is positively recommended by leading MDs in the nutritional field. Its multiple benefits and high nutrient density make E3Live the standard for the entire "superfoods" category.

E3LIVE BENEFITS YOUR BODY, MIND & EMOTIONS

As a multi-function superfood, E3Live has 3 basic system-wide effects:

- It deeply nourishes and provides a smooth energy lift for the body.

- It balances and uplifts your mood

- It tangibly focuses your mind and increases attention span.

E3Live is nutrient-dense. It contains numerous co-factors and an abundance of micro-nutrients. E3Live with its naturally rich array of benefits stands at the opposite pole of lab-created GM food. It provides over 64 easily absorbed vitamins, minerals, micronutrients, EFAs and enzymes. E3Live has more biologically active chlorophyll than any known food. It is nutritionally balancing in a tangible way for people recovering from alcohol or drug addiction. E3Live can help take the edge off of cravings.

SOME REPORTED BENEFITS OF CHLOROPHYLL

- Chlorophyll has been noted to help in the growth and repair of tissues.

- Chlorophyll helps in neutralizing the pollution that we breathe in everyday. It is a good supplement for smokers and those who drink alcohol.

- It efficiently delivers magnesium and helps the blood in carrying much needed oxygen to all cells and tissues.

- Its divalent chemical bond makes it useful as a detoxifier and to help chelate heavy metals lodged deep in our bodies.

- It has been seen to have a good potential in stimulating red blood cells to improve oxygen supply.

- Along with other vitamins such as A, C and E, chlorophyll has been seen to help neutralize free radicals that do damage to healthy cells.

- Chlorophyll is also an effective deodorizer to reduce bad breath, urine, fecal waste, and body odor.

- It may reduce the ability of carcinogens to bind with the DNA in different major organs in the body.

- Chlorophyll may be useful in treating calcium oxalate stone ailments.

- It possesses some anti-atherogenic (arterial plaque) activity as well.

- It can be used to treat infected wounds naturally.

- It has anti-mutagenic and anti-carcinogenic properties.

- It may be helpful in protecting your body against toxins and in reducing drug side effects.

These are only a few of the benefits of chlorophyll on the body. Chlorophyll-rich E3Live is offered as a superfood at the Hippocrates Institute, world-renowned for pioneering wheatgrass juice. Director, Dr. Brian Clement, states: "The most nutritious food on the planet comes from Klamath Lake, it is called E3Live. You will have a longer, higher quality of life when you take E3Live."

GREEN, BLUE, YELLOW AND MAGENTA

E3Live has naturally occurring green, blue, yellow and magenta "light-harvesting" pigments. The most well-known is chlorophyll which is produced by light-harvesting or photosynthesis. Yellow represents a new class of anti-inflammatory agents with healing factors and magenta reflects the presence of beta-carotene. E3Live also harvests or photosynthesizes a beautiful and vivid blue pigment known as Phycocyanin. Phycocyanin from E3Live is unique as a natural anti-inflammatory with positive effects on the limbic system, the emotional center of the brain. In E3Live, we have an aqua-botanical plant that directly converts sunlight into pure cascades of health-giving pigments. Esak Garcia, relates that "Drinking E3Live is like drinking pure light energy. It helps me to maintain high energy levels and fast recovery time." The pure light energy of super-nutrition health pigments are literally in the food. The pristine purity of nature is in E3Live and this helps to renew and feed your cells. We've been harvesting E3Live for years and every day we are thankful and in awe of its power to invigorate, strengthen and provide balance to people seeking to restore their health and come back to a fuller functional life.

E3LIVE PROMOTES JOY AND IS AN ANTI-DEPRESSANT

Dr. Gabriel Cousens is a pioneering MD specializing in nutrition with a clinical background in Psychiatry. He is the author of many books including *Depression-Free for Life*, and is the Director of Tree of Life Rejuvenation Center in Patagonia, AZ. Dr. Cousens writes: "I've had people who've been depressed for years and years, and literally, within a few days after receiving E3Live, their depression lifts. It is a specific food for attention deficit disorders and for depression. E3Live is for peak performance of body, mind and spirit. It helps restore overall biochemical balance by nourishing the body at the cellular level. Include it in any detoxification and rejuvenation program." Dr. Cousens does not recommend drugs for people reporting typical symptoms of depression. A version of E3Live known as E3Live BrainON particularly balances mood and enhances mental clarity.

E3LIVE BRAINON® AND THE LOVE MOLECULE ®

E3Live BrainON is an enhanced version of E3Live. An additional amount of the pure blue Phycocyanin extract from E3Live is added back into E3Live. The Phycocyanin native to E3Live is a complementary blue pigment to its Chlorophyll, the green pigment. Phycocyanin has a special naturally occurring concentration of all-organic phenylethylamine (PEA) along with numerous co-factors. PEA is known as the "Love Molecule." It is also found in chocolate. However, E3Live contains many times over the PEA or "Love Molecule" as is found in chocolate. The main function of E3Live BrainON is to particularly promote clear thinking, optimal cognitive function and to balance mood in a way that is easily felt. E3Live BrainON is often recommended as a superfood to help with attention-deficit disorder. It additionally lifts and brightens mood through the "Love Molecule."

THE "LOVE MOLECULE®" AND
ANTI-DEPRESSION RESEARCH

The "Love Molecule" is scientifically known as PEA. We emphasize that the PEA in E3Live is naturally occurring and is different than synthetic isolates of PEA. Researchers at Rush University and the Center for Creative Development in Chicago conducted a study demonstrating PEA's anti-depressant effects: *"It has been proposed that PEA deficit may be the cause of a common form of depressive illness. PEA produces sustained relief of depression in a significant number of patients, including some unresponsive to standard treatments."*

PEA, the "Love Molecule" was measurably found to be significantly lower in subjects with Attention Deficit Disorder. People using organic PEA from AFA report improved concentration and a better attention span at school and at work.

RUNNER'S HIGH, PEA, EXERCISE AND DEPRESSION

A study by E. Ellen Billett, Ph.D., tells WebMD: "What we are trying to say is now there is more chemical evidence for why runners' high occurs. We hope this information might give doctors more confidence in prescribing exercise for mild depression and as an adjunct to drug therapy." The secret is PEA, the "Love Molecule." A Nottingham Trent University research team in the UK studied twenty healthy young men. The men had their PEA levels measured after one day of no exercise and after one day of moderate exercise. All but two of the men had increased PEA levels twenty-four hours after their exercise. Exercise, even at a moderate level, is a proven anti-depressive because it increases PEA levels in the brain!

The "Love Molecule" or PEA is a key component in E3Live BrainON. E3Live and E3Live BrainON are natural food products to help us in stressful times. Whether we need to give a presentation under pressure, manage a hectic schedule, handle our children's and family's activities, excel at a test or job interview or simply shine in everyday situations, these superfoods are God-designed to naturally balance your mood and increase your focus and attention. This is not any kind of drug with kidney, liver or other side-effects. This is a health-giving feel-good fresh-green food. Above all, it is good for you! This is what super-nutrition can do for each of us, how it can sustain each of us and lead us to live more responsible, functional and enjoyable lives.

E3LIVE IS GREAT FOR CHILDREN!

Tamera Campbell, the CEO of E3live says, "My children, Nicholas and Annie, since infancy, have been getting E3Live by mouth (and through Mother's milk) since they were 2 days old. Nicholas and Annie really love E3Live, and regularly ask for it. Obviously, by their huge smiles, you can see they enjoy it each day. When they were first born, I used a syringe to slowly drip it into their tiny mouths. The syringe not only helped me measure the amount I was giving them, but it helped me control each drop. My children loved the taste of E3Live immediately. After all, they only know what taste I introduce to them! I don't think that it is coincidence—but both babies also seem to enjoy green vegetables over most other foods. I really think it is because of E3Live. There is no doubt in my mind that I see results. They have not been sick since birth, even being exposed to people with colds and flu in public!"

Jennifer, a mother of three writes, "I am writing you this letter in testament of E3Live products for children as we have witnessed first-hand the profound, yet subtle effect it has had on our two year old Jana Aum Kleinberg as well as our three and half month old identical twin girls Naia and Ananda.

E3Live is a staple supplement in our diet for us as well as our three small children. We are frequently stopped in public and asked how old our daughter Jana is. People's first response is 'Wow, she speaks so clearly and she's so deliberate.' We joke that Jana is two going on six! We have found that the use of E3Live dramatically improves her ability to focus and articulate.

We recently took our three children to a pediatric physician for a check up on our (then) ten week old twins who were born six weeks premature. The physician commented on how alert and advanced all three children seemed to be for their age. Despite the twins' pre-maturity, they are advanced in social interaction and hand-eye coordination already!"

"There are very few supplements on the market I would unconditionally endorse—E3Live is the exception."—Amanda Hunter, ND

E3 RENEWME!™ AND E3 AFA® FOR JOINT PAINS

It is gratifying to hear from people who previously used pain-killers like ibuprofen when playing sports or working around the garden happily tell us that they have gotten substantial relief from taking E3RenewMe! When some tell us that they no longer need to take ibuprofen and similar drugs all the time for joint and tendon pains, that is cause for celebration. E3RenewMe! is a proprietary blend of nutritional plant-derived MSM (methyl sulfonyl methane), spirulina, E3AFA, certified organic cayenne pepper, wild-crafted South American camu-camu, E3 AFAMend®, E3 BrainON, tocotrienol & tocopherol (Vitamin E complex), and crystalloid electrolyte sea minerals. In addition to the benefits of E3Live mentioned above, E3RenewMe! particularly focuses in on helping with chronic inflammatory problems.

Many health experts and doctors confirm MSM benefits. They assert that, because MSM is such an effective pain remedy, doctors are often able to lower the dosage of medication they prescribe for patients. Furthermore, MSM is happily free of the side-effects that are frequently caused by prescription pain medications. When we consume this bio-available dietary sulfur, we help to maintain the integrity and elasticity of connective tissues and tendons. Our cell and cell membranes require MSM to assist in the strengthening of proteins, which reinforce the framework of connective tissue. By strengthening this connective tissue, we help prevent pain caused by wear and tear. MSM benefits hair, skin and nails, as well, because it is a vital component of these proteins. MSM works synergistically with the RenewMe! blend for truly maximum benefit. This is in part due to Phycoyanin's anti-inflammatory properties working in tandem with MSM.

If any natural product can cut down or replace a synthetic joint-pain pill, that's great news. Ibuprofen, among many other pills, can cause serious heart problems including stroke. There are also increased gastro-intestinal risks for bleeding, ulceration, and perforation of the stomach or intestines. All these tend to increase with long-term use. The older you are the higher the risk. It can often be helpful to hear what doctors have to say, particularly those who understand the value of eating vibrant foods. Informed MDs know that eating the right foods and using natural remedies are our best first bet before we run to bet our health on any combination of riskier drugs.

For convenience and portability, fresh-frozen E3Live and E3Live BrainON also comes in Refractance Window (gently heated) dried powder and in capsules E3AFA, E3BrainON, E3 RenewMe! and other E3 food products. Powder and capsules let people conveniently enjoy nature's most versatile superfood while on-the-go.

DOCTORS PRAISE E3LIVE

Numerous doctors lavish praise on the E3Live line as a purely natural superfood. Dr. Baxter Montgomery of the Houston Cardiac Association enthusiastically reports, "We have had excellent results with E3Live in our disease reversal program, specifically with cardiac disease, hyperlipidemia, and diabetes. Within a few days of starting to drink E3Live, my staff and I noticed a leap in our stamina during our workouts, an incredible boost in our mental clarity and ability to stay focused, and a decrease in our appetite. Our patients have commented that they are losing cravings for 'the bad foods' as they continue to drink E3Live. We are amazed and overjoyed at the tremendous results we see with regular use of this live super food."

Dr. Fred Bisci, similarly states that "As a clinical nutritionist with over 40 years experience, I'm impressed and delighted at how E3Live helps such a wide range of health problems. I can only conclude that E3Live has the therapeutic versatility of a true adaptogen, nourishing the body and mind on multiple metabolic pathways at the deepest of physiological levels. E3Live's energetic boost is therefore wholesome and lasting, unlike the temporary ups and downs of unhealthy stimulants such as sugar and caffeine."

We have briefly touched upon some of the unique properties of the E3Live superfood line. It's truly the synergy of elements arranged by the Hand of Creation that is most responsible for E3Live's ability to benefit both body and mind. E3Live is a supportive food. It continually tunes the body to a more harmonious state of health. It helps bring the whole system into alignment and influences better food and healthy lifestyle choices.

TAKING RESPONSIBILITY FOR YOUR OWN HEALTH
Choosing between God-made Food and Transgenic Lab Food
As each of us takes personal responsibility for our own health and that

of our families, this will resonate and positively influence other people's health. It is life-critical that we decisively return to fundamental principles and address the health differences between lab-made foods that are genetically modified (GM) by fallible humans and pristine foods like E3Live given to us by the Creator. We have praised the great gift of E3Live. In the same breath, we speak up and rebuke the contrary work of heedless corporations who ignorantly endanger human life by creating and selling GM or transgenic lab-made food.

The Creator gave us sanctified food. He gave us "every seed-bearing plant on the face of the whole earth and every tree that has fruit with seed in it." Food corporations that sell us lab-made GM food would fantasize that they can improve upon the complex balance and inter-relationships among all living things. They even think they can do this without research. Their tunnel vision for profits only shows that when people lose their spiritual bearings and stop caring about the sacred gift of life, they start destroying life!

We now have fish genes in God's fruit, poultry genes in God's fish, animal genes in God's plants and this is to say nothing of growth hormones in milk, insect genes in vegetables, tree genes in grain, and, yes, human genes in pork. There has never been a scientist smart enough to make an apple, a garden or create life itself out of nothing. By knowing spiritual principles, it becomes immediately obvious that man's tampering with the Creation falls short of God's Glory and cannot outsmart the Intelligent Design that created the complex and functional balance of nature. Putting fish genes in tomatoes is not only downright foolish, it risks the very foundations of our health!

The spiritual design behind the Creation far exceeds human intelligence. This is proven too by the multiple health benefits of a naturally occurring superfood like E3Live.

We are honored to be able to bring something beneficial to people. We pray that each of us find some work where we are in service to others. A missionary has a mission to serve others. We are all missionaries. Serving others is the way of heaven, as is taking care of our own living temple, providing our spirit, soul and body the foods it needs to do

God's work on Earth. Love is the food of the spirit just as natural food feeds our bodies. What we physically eat is certainly not everything but it is one essential and accessible way that we can dedicate ourselves to respecting God's Creation, ourselves and our families simply by beginning to put the right food on our plate!

Breathtaking technological developments are a part of our times. Today, scientists can tinker around with DNA, which is like the instruction manual for everything that lives. One company, Monsanto, owns patents on new forms of lab-made life, synthetically derived seed mutations which represent an ever-present danger to replacing the seeds of life created by God. Literally thousands of genetically-modified food products have invaded our farms and our total environment. GM foods are today available in our neighborhood stores. No one knows which ones these are because there are no labeling laws, aside from no research! Who is looking out for us?

Growing or eating genetically altered food can result in unnatural and far-reaching genetic alterations and greatly lower the state of our health. As we begin to see what is going on just below the surface, our choices become much clearer. Ignorance is a killer, literally. Once we understand, it's as simple as choosing life over death.

We may also forgive those who sell GM, over-processed and fast foods. "They know not what they do." They operate out of survival and very often in ignorance. That is why education, if followed by gradual, practical changes (the hard and worthwhile part), will serve one's own health and that of others. An unhealthy nation is not a strong nation. Eating isn't everything but if we eat poorly, the very foundation of our lives is directly weakened. God always asks us to choose.

THREAT OF EATING PROCESSED, FAST AND GM FOODS

As each of us diligently cares after our living temples, the more we will notice and avoid what is detrimental to our God-given bodies. Grace and a sustained effort to live virtuously have helped many a person. When we eat to live with humility and righteousness and cease living to habitually eat GM processed fast food, we free ourselves from food addictions. Producers of fast, over-processed and GM foods do not care about the health of you, your friends or your family. They are more like inadvertent worshippers of the Golden Calf caring mainly about milking you for your money even at the expense of your bodily health and shortening your life-span. There's no care for people here and this is no joke. As we become versed and grasp that our very health is being compromised by lab-made GM food, this will become a wakeup call to every one of us to help wake up those close to us and hopefully the nation at large.

We need to understand that processed foods reduce both the quality and the length of our sacred lives. That's too high a price to pay for eating vegetables mixed with insect and animal genes. If it's bad for lab rats, do not eat the food! Those who sell overly processed food, and let's face an unfortunate fact, unhealthy food is in most supermarket aisles, are not looking out for you, your friends and family. Far from it, money, not health, is their abiding concern. This is as obvious as it is wrong.

Be versed as you read what some MDs are now openly saying. The quality of our lives and that of our nation are literally being compromised and neither the manufacturers of processed GM fast foods nor our government is accountably watching out for us. Truth is, we are being fed food that should not be given to factory-farm animals let alone our children. This is really happening! That is also why so many people are commonly obese and in poor heath today. We can change this for the better with a move toward a healthier life coming directly from the core of our own lives. That responsibility is fully up to us. As we become educated, and that's the whole point, we can respectfully pull away from eating corrupted food and come over to eating naturally pure foods like E3Live to make our bodies shine with vigorous health.

Ann Louise Gittleman, C.N.S., author of *Beyond Pritikin*, *Super Nutrition for Women*, *Your Body Knows Best*, says, "Supplementing our diet with E3Live helps to nourish a body starving for good nutrition. E3Live can balance cravings and regulate appetite. Obesity is frequently associated with both diabetes (high-blood sugar) and hypoglycemia (low blood sugar). E3Live helps to maintain normal blood sugar levels which in turn help normalize the appetite. E3 Live is literally a perfect food containing vitamins, minerals, carbohydrates, and protein that the body needs to be nutritionally supported. E3Live neutralizes acid toxins stored in cellulite, fatty tissues and intracellular basement membranes. E3Live helps eliminate 'hidden hunger,' a main cause of overeating. E3Live's near-instant absorption (when taken on an empty stomach with a little water or juice) can nip in the bud the tendency to overeat. E3Live's adaptogenic (multi-function) properties help us maintain a normal appetite to support both weight-loss and weight-gain."

For the soundest of reasons, athletes in training studiously avoid junk food. Stephen Molitor, a professional boxer, who held an IBF championship, told us of E3Live, "I am amazed by my recuperation time between rounds. E3Live gives me focus like never before." It is always gratifying for us to hear upbeat reports like this from people who enjoy all-natural E3Live. Improving health is our mission. Educating folks on what to eat and what never to eat is part and parcel of this same mission.

Now, let's listen closely to the warnings given to us by MDs about the dangers of genetically engineered foods and why our families should strictly avoid GM Frankenfood and stay with food made by the Creator. Humans may tamper with the creation but are clueless as to how everything interrelates and functions. Those who fabricate GM foods operate in ignorance of the great design behind creation. They know not what they do and for that reason represent a significant danger to the health of every man, woman and child.

GM FOODS CONTRIBUTE TO THE SHARPLY DETERIORATING HEALTH OF AMERICANS

The American Academy of Environmental Medicine (AAEM) has called upon "Physicians to educate their patients, the medical community, and the public to avoid GM foods when possible and provide educational materials concerning GM foods and health risks." They soberly called for a halt on the ingestion of GM foods, for long-term independent lab studies on GM foods, and for our own government to require labeling for GM food.

AAEM's position paper stated, "Several animal studies indicate serious health risks associated with GM food. The risks associated with GM food include infertility, immune problems, accelerated aging, insulin regulation, and changes in major organs and the gastrointestinal system." They conclude, "There is more than a casual association between GM foods and adverse health effects. There is causation," as defined by recognized scientific criteria. "The strength of association and consistency between GM foods and disease is confirmed in several animal studies." In other words, we are being disrespectfully treated exactly like experimental lab animals by being fed unproven and already controversial GM food. Who will stand up for us?

How bad is it? MDs are now increasingly prescribing GM free diets. Consider for yourself what that entails. Dr. Amy Dean, a Michigan internal medicine specialist states, "I strongly recommend patients eat strictly non-genetically modified foods." Dr. John Boyles, an allergist from Ohio, says "I used to test for soy allergies all the time, but now that soy is genetically engineered, it is so dangerous that I tell people never to eat it." Note the word "dangerous." We can choose to eat products like E3Live and cease volunteering to be lab-animals eating unproven and highly experimental GM foods.

Dr. Paul Swanson comments on E3Live, "Those who eat E3Live and gain understanding of higher human health have a new responsibility. That responsibility is first to learn, then to teach." We rejoice with this sound thinking MD who goes on to say, "We are at a turning point in history, a crisis that is both a danger and an opportunity. The native E3Live growing abundantly in Klamath Lake provides an opportunity for humans for something closer to ancient health." This can be a time of restoration or of collapse. We clearly have the power to choose the good path.

Dr. Jennifer Armstrong, President of AAEM, comments on lab-made GM food, "Physicians are probably seeing the effects in their patients, but need to know how to ask the right questions." At this time, an irresponsible hoax is being played on us by the unthinking advocates of GM food. When money is placed above family health by Frankenfood producers, an immoral line is crossed. If we allow US citizens to be fed dangerous GM food unfit for factory farm animals, we betray the future of our own children. World renowned biologist Pushpa Bhargava, upon reviewing over 600 scientific journals, concludes that genetically modified organisms are a major contributor to the sharply deteriorating health of Americans. It is now time to wake the nation!

We can take greater command over our own lives once we have the proper knowledge to inform our choices. If we choose to be responsible, that is, decisively in charge of our own spiritual, mental and physical lives, nothing can stop us! This decision can only come from our core not from political parties or multi-national corporations. Our bodies have been long conditioned to eat foods largely composed of starch, sugar and oily grease and foods composed of salt and over-heated grease. It is not easy to suddenly change and eat nutritious raw foods, vegetables and superfoods like E3Live. The rewards of gradually changing, however, are a life blessed with well-being, balance, strength and liveliness. It takes courage to make a choice. Let's review the very real dangers of eating GM food while keeping in mind the world of difference that health-giving foods like E3Live can make in the quality of our day to day lives.

PREGNANT WOMEN AND BABIES ARE AT GREAT RISK

David Schubert, a Biologist at the Salk Institute strongly cautions that "children are the most likely to be adversely effected by toxins and other dietary problems" related to GM foods. He says without adequate studies, the children become "the experimental animals." This is exactly what we and others from every corner are saying!

Let's take a sober look at the chilling data on GM-fed experimental animals. When GM soy was fed to female rats, as is available at our nearest supermarket, most of their babies died within three weeks compared to a 10% death rate among the control group fed natural soy. The GM-fed babies were also smaller. They later had problems getting pregnant. What does this say for human babies? Who knows? And that's the whole point. The question is who wants to make our families into experimental lab animals? GM food labs and those who market GM food are keeping mum. Our lifeline food supply is now polluted. Who is going to care about feeding your family naturally wholesome food like E3Live made by the Creator if not you?

When male rats were fed GM soy, their testicles actually changed color - from the normal pink to dark blue. Is there a single sound reason why we should eat GM soy? Mice fed GM soy had altered sperm and the embryos of GM fed mice had chaotic changes in their DNA. Mice fed GM corn in an Austrian government study gave birth to fewer babies. They were also smaller than normal. If it is not good enough for mice, do we want human mothers and human children eating this?!

It's not only mice. Reproductive problems have also plagued livestock. Investigations in the state of Haryana, India showed that most buffalo that ate GM cottonseed had complications such as premature deliveries, abortions, infertility, and prolapsed uteruses. Many calves died. Please read your food labels. Cottonseed oil is in many of our human foods. However, due to lobbying, our government does not ask that GM oil be labeled. Much of this oil is likely GM. However, no one considers that we deserve the dignified right to be informed, only to blindly pay for "Frankenfood." Think about this: who is respected more, us or the lab animals? It looks about the same and that is flat wrong.

In the US, about twenty farmers reported that thousands of pigs became sterile after consuming certain GM corn varieties. Which ones were those and are they in our supermarket corn chips? Who knows? No one is saying. Some pigs endured false pregnancies while others birthed bags of water. Cows and bulls also became infertile when fed this same GM corn. In the US, the incidence of low birth weight babies, infertility, and infant mortality are all going up. We can connect the dots enough to say, this must stop. We must stop eating risky GM foods, really stop. That's hard, but certainly not impossible.

AAEM states, "Multiple animal studies show significant immune problems including increase in cytokines, which are associated with asthma, allergy, and inflammation." These are all, as if coincidentally, on the rise among humans in the US.

According to GM food safety expert Dr. Arpad Pusztai, negative changes in the immune state of GM animals are "a consistent feature of all the studies." Monsanto's own research showed significant immune system changes in rats fed GM corn. GM soy and GM corn each contain two new proteins that have allergenic properties. After the introduction of GM soy in the UK, soy allergies spiked up by 50%. It is reasonable to conjecture that the US epidemic of food allergies and asthma is related to allowing GM food into our human food supply without regulation.

The world of apparently disease-causing GM foods stands in sharp contrast to the immune-boosting effects that are yours for the taking when you eat the Creator's foods. As Dr. George Cromack states in *Ageing Well,* "Supplementing your diet with E3Live, is one of the fastest ways I know of kick-starting your return to health." Dr. Brian Clement comments. "If you look at cement, it has cracks and crevices in it. Most of your DNA has little cracks and crevices and pits. What I want you to do is to picture that what E3Live does is fill up those little holes and those little abnormalities. This is important because if people are responsible enough to take charge of their life and start to think positively, eat positively and exercise well, they will live longer and become healthier." We have been conditioned not to want to eat fresh fruits and vegetables. E3Live can help tune the body back to wanting healthy foods.

As we conclude our discussion of GM foods, be versed on another dangerous finding:

GM FOOD MAY STAY INSIDE OF US FOR A VERY LONG TIME.

The only published human study that we know of revealed that GM soy and GM corn could change our regular intestinal bacteria into a pesticide factory possibly adding toxins into our system for years on end. No one knows for sure. This is not out of the reach of possibility. MDs have reported a confounding increase in patients with intestinal problems over the past decade. It is entirely possible that GM foods may be colonizing the gut flora of Americans. Nobody has really researched the human effects.

GM FOODS WARNINGS BY GOVERNMENT SCIENTISTS IGNORED AND DENIED

Scientists at the US FDA had cautioned on these problems in the 1990s. According to documentation released from a lawsuit, the scientific agreement at the FDA was that GM foods were innately dangerous, and might create undetectable allergies, toxins, gene transfer to gut bacteria, new diseases, and possibly unsolvable nutritional problems. They urged that long-term tests be responsibly conducted. Regrettably, the White House, rather than protecting the majority of its citizens, ordered the agency to promote GM food.

Rather than do the badly needed research, the FDA responded by bringing in Michael Taylor, Monsanto's former attorney. He was put in charge of GM food policy. That fox-in-the-hen house policy, in effect today, denies knowledge of scientists' concerns and falsely declares that no safety studies on GM foods are needed. This is untrue, cooked science. It is now the decision of Monsanto and other GM food companies who sell GM foods to people to decide by whim if their GM foods are safe. The conflict of interest is clear cut. Mr. Taylor later became Monsanto's vice president. Corruption in high places had led to the corruption of the very food we daily eat.

We have not had human trials on GM foods. They have not been proven safe, period.

Renowned geneticist David Suzuki states, "The experiments simply haven't been done and we now have become the guinea pigs." He adds, "Anyone that says, 'Oh, we know that this is perfectly safe,' I say is either unbelievably stupid or deliberately lying." There you have it.

If GM foods have aided the well-documented rise of autism, obesity, diabetes, asthma, cancer, heart disease, allergies, reproductive problems, we may, at this point, never be able to track this. Animals fed GM food, in fact, exhibited a wide variety of symptoms. People too may easily react with multiple symptoms which will leave doctor after doctor shrugging their shoulders. Who, after all, is looking out for our friends and families?

There's no need to sit around before taking the caring advice of responsible MDs to stay away from GM foods. For starters, soy or corn derivatives, cottonseed and canola oil, and sugar from GM sugar beets can be avoided unless the label states "organic" or "non-GMO." If you'd like more info on a Non-GMO Shopping Guide, please Email doctor-connie@e3live.com and Dr. Connie Kennedy will get back with you.

If a goodly number of us choose non-GM brands, food companies will probably respond as they did in Europe where they removed GM food ingredients. Self-respecting human beings need not be treated like experimental animals. Our families and friends can enjoy long and happy lives by demanding God-made foods and simply walking away from lab-made GM foods.

Begin to recover your health today by moving away from GM foods and walking toward the Creator's foods. E3Live is a prime health ally. It can help you in your journey to reach the nutritional peak of good health. E3Live will help you to alkalinize your body. Its spectrum of purely natural green, blue, yellow and magenta pigments reflect the presence of fresh chlorophyll and the anti-inflammatory Phycocyanin. Its abundant vitamins, minerals, beta-carotene, antioxidants, trace minerals, co factors and micro nutrients will refresh your cells and promote stamina and recovery time. E3Live's wide spectrum of benefits is the reason why it is renowned as a superfood by MDs and professional athletes. Take the journey toward health along with us. Energize, balance and focus to make this a better, healthier world for ourselves and future generations. We invite you to call us directly at 888-800-7070 or come by and visit our web-site at http://www.e3live.com

This chapter was written by Michael Saiber, Founder, Tamera Campbell, CEO, Stanley Arcieri, CMO and Dr. Connie Kennedy, Board advisor.

APPENDIX 1

SLOW THE AGING PROCESS WITH INCREASED INTRACELLULAR GLUTATHIONE –

THE BODY'S MASTER ANTIOXIDANT

Explore the opportunity

Explore the opportunity to partner with Steven K. Scott (creator of the Total Gym Infomercials) & Guthy-Renker (one of the world's largest direct response television companies) in bringing one of the most scientifically validated nutritional supplements to the world.

The Benefits of Glutathione

Glutathione (GSH) is the body's master antioxidant, produced within each cell of the body. The antioxidants, vitamin C, can give up one electron to neutralize free radicals, and vitamin E can give up five electrons. They each then become a free radical. GSH can neutralize millions of free radicals and never become a free radical. GSH also helps recycle other antioxidants such as Vitamin C and E.

After the age of twenty, individuals lose their ability to produce GSH by about 10 to 12% per decade due to diet and lifestyle, etc. An oral glutathione supplement is of no benefit as it is degraded in the GI tract. MaxGXL provides the building block ingredients with a delivery system that transports them into the individual cells so the cells can produce glutathione.

Each cell is a small energy factory in which the mitochondria produce energy. This energy production and other metabolic processes produce free radicals that must be neutralized. Without adequate levels of GSH, each cell must restrict the production of energy in order to limit the production of free radicals or the cell would self destruct. Thus with low levels of GSH, each cell's ability to function optimally is impaired.

There is no specific result that any one person may expect to experience, as each individual is different. The body knows where increased cellular glutathione is needed most, and that is usually where the greatest benefit is realized.

MaxGXL is now available in veggie capsules as well as gel capsules. It is noted on the packaging that one of the ingredients is derived from shell fish; N- Acetyl D-Glucosamine. This ingredient is so dramatically altered from any resemblance of the shell fish that it does not contradict the vegan lifestyle.

Not only does MaxGXL stimulate the intracellular production of GSH but it also helps to significantly reduce inflammation.

A MaxGXL double-blind, placebo controlled, crossover study recently demonstrated that:

In only 60 days of use, MaxGXL users experienced:

Increase in Intracellular Glutathione – 292%

Increase in DHEA – 46%

Increase in IGF-1 – 40.8% (DHEA and IGF-1 are markers related to levels of human growth hormone, which is the indicator of true biological age. They decrease with age.

Decrease in TNF (Tumor Necrosis Factor-alpha) of 37%. TNF-alpha is one of the three most significant markers of cellular inflammation.

Research on glutathione as well as a brief video as to the impact of IV injections of glutathione with Parkinson's patients is available at http://www.glutathioneexperts.com/gsh-diseases.html (Please note this video is regarding intravenous injections of glutathione.)

Facts About Glutathione (GSH)

Our body naturally creates a powerful antioxidant called "glutathione" or "GSH" to help deal with dangerous daily by-products of breathing oxygen, the toxic intrusions from our air, water, and food, and the by-products of cellular metabolism. While glutathione (GSH) is thousands of times more prevalent and powerful than our body's other antioxidants, (including vitamins C and E) there are four important areas we must understand if we are going to make use of improved glutathione levels.

1. **Glutathione Absorption:** We know that increased glutathione levels cleanse and optimize the cells' function, the function of all of our organs and ultimately our body. How do we increase the GSH levels?

2. Intravenous GSH is costly and a one-shot solution. Oral GSH supplementation is destroyed by digesting it. The GSH components that may get to the blood stream are too large a molecule to get through cell membranes.

3. The answer was developed by Robert Keller, M.D., by creating a high level absorptive blend which contains the ingredients for GSH to be naturally accelerated in the most needed areas of the body.

4. **Glutathione Production:** Glutathione is needed and used in all 100 trillion cells, tens of thousands of times per second. By providing the amino acids and other precursors needed by the cell to produce GSH, Dr. Keller's GXL formula naturally optimizes intracellular health in the areas it is most needed. GSH neutralizes oxidative stress and removes toxins from the cells and body.

5. **Glutathione Recycling:** GSH is not only increased within the cells with the MaxGXL blend by nearly 300% in 60 days, it is also recycled over and over again because of the other ingredients in the GXL formula. This process recycles precious cellular GSH up to seven times!

6. **Glutathione Maximization:** Dr. Keller points out that there are at least seventeen enzymes involved in the production, recycling, and storage of GSH. The supplement blend uses the quercetin,

cordyceps, and sylimarin to maximize and aid these enzymes. An added benefit is the rejuvenation of the many liver functions for creating and storing GSH.

What Experts Say About Glutathione:

"Glutathione is a substance, the levels of which in our cells are predictive of how long we will live. There are very few other factors which are as predictive of our life expectancy as is our level of cellular glutathione. We cannot survive without this antioxidant."—**Earl Mindell, R.Ph., Ph.D.**

"Glutathione is a tri-peptide of the amino acids cysteine, glycine, and glutamic acid. A deficiency of glutathione can cause hemolysis (destruction of red blood cells, leading to anemia) and oxidative stress. Glutathione is essential in intermediary metabolism ... for the detoxification of acetaminophen (Tylenol)."—**[PDR Medical Dictionary. Spraycar. 1999]**

"Without glutathione, other important antioxidants such as vitamins C and E cannot do their job adequately to protect your body against disease."—**Breakthrough in Cell Defense, Allan Somersall, Ph.D., M.D., and Gustavo Bounous, M.D. FRCS(C).**

"No other antioxidant is as important to overall health as glutathione. It is the regulator and regenerator of immune cells and the most valuable detoxifying agent in the human body. Low levels are associated with hepatic dysfunction, immune dysfunction, cardiac disease, premature aging, and death."—**The Immune System Cure, Lorna R. Vanderhaeghe & Patrick J.D. Bouic, Ph.D.**

"As Dr. Lombard points out in his book, "The Brain Wellness Plan," Glutathione is one of the most powerful antioxidants in the body. Depressed glutathione levels are associated with the increased generation of free radicals found in Parkinson's patients, for example, and contribute to further brain cell death."

To order MaxGXL as a Preferred Customer and receive a regular monthly auto shipment please visit http://www.911yourhealth.com.

APPENDIX 2

THE END OF
CARDIOVASCULAR DISEASE

Dr. Leila Lindquist

Karen Hammond was puzzled. "So, Dr. Leila, you have treated me now twice with this thing, and my Raynaud's Syndrome is much improved and I can move my elbow again. What exactly is going on here?" She had suffered with a lack of circulation in her fingers for a few years. Nothing had helped so far. In November she started having excruciating pain in the neck, progression into her left shoulder, elbow, wrist, and also symptoms in the right hand. It finally got so bad, that she could no longer turn her neck and her elbow locked up completely frozen. Some of her fingers were white as a ghost and the skin was starting to peel from the finger tips.

In horrendous pain and unable to type and do her job, she sought care from several physicians, got MRI's, Blood tests, Orthopedic Tests. Besides having Degenerative Joint Disease, she had nothing. No hernias, no Carpal Tunnel, No Rheumatoid Arthritis or Lupus, no Lyme's Disease, no Allergies. Her plight was true mystery. Raynaud's Syndrome is a puzzle in itself. There isn't a known cause, but what is known is that it is triggered by cold and stress.

I explained to her that, " Health is really not black or white. There are many gray areas." Researchers discovered that for many disorders blood tests aren't the standard any more. For many conditions, stool samples, hair tissue mineral samples, dark field microscopy or even Invita Microscopy is required to understand what is going on in the body.

Many Scientists and Medical Doctors consider the BEMER 3000 the Future of Medicine.

We are now entering a new millennium in healing. We are discovering a new dimension of health, way beyond pharmaceuticals and surgery. It all started with the discovery of Quantum Physics and a scientist living in Berne, Switzerland: Albert Einstein. In continuation of studying the relationship between matter and energy, you might have heard of the recent construction in Europe of a particle accelerator (or atom smasher), a device that uses <u>electric fields</u> to propel <u>electrically-charged particles</u> to high speeds and to contain them in well-defined beams and between. We are learning that the smallest particles in our bodies resemble light at lower frequencies, it is all about energy. We can even prove the existence of GOD with quantum physics.

Parallel to all these developments, beginning in the 1960's, German Physicist Prof. Kafka began studying the effects of electromagnetic fields and impulses on the human body. Somebody had found records from a physician with the Name Dr. Bone from 1856. He had treated over 4000 patients in London (England) very successfully with electro magnetism. Sadly, around 1900 pharmaceuticals started to become trendy, and manual therapies were ridiculed. Drugs were quick and easy to take and very successful. Due to the information age, we are more than ever aware of the dangers of drugs. The data collected about side-effects and interactions is scary. Recalls and class-action lawsuits are becoming an expected occurrence. We are now very concerned about how toxic our world has become. There are drugs in the drinking water and in our foods. Synthetics have become an environmental burden for the children of our children and so on. It is very safe to say, drugs have not been the answer to healing. We now battle more epidemic diseases and illnesses than ever: Fibromyalgia, Lupus, Anxiety, Depression, Gastric Reflux, and Cardiovascular Disease, just to name a few. People are toxic, and a toxic body can't heal itself. Of every pill you take, only a small amount is active ingredients, most of it is fillers that end up in your tissues; making you more and more toxic. You think you need more drugs.

Modern Medicine has been trying to find a cure for cardiovascular disease for the last few decades. Currently, cardiovascular disease is the number one leading cause of death in the USA. Dr. Klopp, MD, Director of the Institute of Microcirculation in Berlin (Germany) says: "MD's can temporarily treat the large blood vessels with drugs (beta-blockers) and surgery, but they had until recently no means to successfully treat microcirculation issues." Microcirculation (capillaries, the smallest blood vessels in your body) is the football field, where all the action happens, including the exchange of nutrients and toxins, the exchange of oxygen and carbon dioxide. If you can't get your nutrients and vitamins to the cells all over your body you're not only wasting your money, but you are also starving your cells, which can lead to toxic acidity, cell death, tissue death and organ failure. Once the microcirculation starts having trouble, everything will go downhill. Large blood vessel treatments can temporarily stabilize or symptomatically manage cardiovascular disease, but eventually the microcirculation will bring it all down. Neither MD's nor DC's can successfully heal microcirculation issues with their conventional treatment methods, because there are no chemical receptors in the capillary walls and there are no nerve innervations either. This means, that neither drugs nor adjustments help the capillaries regain normal functioning.

The BEMER 3000 doesn't cure anything, it simply helps the body heal itself.

In 1998 German Researchers discovered, that only a certain bioelectromagnetic impulse was able to restore the microcirculation. "It was a miraculous and unexpected discovery," states Dr. Klopp, "if somebody would have told me, I would have laughed. But I saw it happen with my own eyes, visualized the effects with help of thermography and invitra vital microscopy at our institute!"

NASA has actually used this technology on every space craft. Life outside of the earth's geomagnetic Field is impossible for us. We know

now that part of why it is so important for us and animals to stay active and to move is because moving through earths geomagnetic field charges up our little cell batteries (the mitochondrias). People that sit in front of computers or TV's are exposed to AC current, which causes electronic fog, that slows down those cell batteries, which leads to chronic fatigue, pain and microcirculation and degeneration issues, Fibromyalgia, to name just a few symptoms.

One eight minute treatment with the patented bio-electro-magnetic energy impulse can regulate those issues as much as one hour of exercise. The World Health Organization (WHO) states: "Most illnesses and diseases could be avoided, if people would exercise at least one hour a day." The problem is, in this stressful world, who has time to exercise an hour a day.

The bioelectromagnetic field is the answer! One eight minute treatment has the same effect as one hour of regular exercise! Some of the many health benefits studied are:

- Increase of Microcirculation
- Increase of Immunity
- Increase of Bone Density
- Reduction of Inflammation
- Reduction of Healing time...And many more...

There is barely any condition that hasn't been helped by the BEMER 3000.

Dr. Leila Lindquist, DC, a Swiss native, went to Medical School in Zurich, Switzerland before deciding to come to the USA and learn how to find the cause of disease instead of treating symptoms. She received her Doctorate in Chiropractic in 1999 and has been in private practice since 2000. She is married to Lars and they have three daughters Svenja Millenia, Yolina Seraphina and LivAdiva Minerva.

Lars and Leila Lindquist also own Thor's Gym, a 24-7 Key-less entry Fitness Center, downtown Market Street in Metropolis, IL.

Find out more about the BEMER 3000 by calling toll free 888-572-3132 or our website at:

www.bemeramerica.com/healthcityusa

APPENDIX 3

THE SOLUTION TO INDOOR AIR POLLUTION

Frank Lewis CNHP & Jeff Bennert PhD., C.T.N.

What is Indoor Air Pollution?

Most people are aware that outdoor air pollution can damage their health but they may not know that indoor air pollution can also have significant adverse health effects. It is a fact that in many instances indoor pollution can be more harmful to you than outdoor pollution because there is not as much space for contaminants to dissipate. Studies by the Environmental Protection Agency of human exposure to air pollutants indicate that indoor air levels of many pollutants may even be 2-5 times, and occasionally more than 100 times, higher than outdoor levels. These levels of indoor air pollutants are of particular concern because most people, including many children, spend as much as 90% of their time indoors. In addition, people who may be exposed to indoor air pollutants for the longest periods of time are often those most susceptible to the effects of indoor air pollution. These people include the young, the elderly, and the chronically ill, especially those suffering from respiratory or cardiovascular disease.

We Need Air to Live

We need air to live and if it is filled with airborne air pollutants then our health can be affected. Just think about how important air is for all of us. It is a fact that we can live for weeks without food. We can live for a few days without water but we can live only a few minutes without air. Since we have to have air to live, we will have better health when we have clean fresh air to breathe.

We have to have life-sustaining oxygen in the air to live. Oxygen makes up only 21% of air, but it makes up 65% of the human body. All functions of our body are regulated by oxygen. It must be continuously restored. Oxygen energizes cells so they can regenerate. Our body uses oxygen to metabolize food and to eliminate toxins and wastes through oxidation. Our brain, which consumes 25% of our oxygen supply, needs oxygen each second to process information. In fact, all of our organs need a great deal of oxygen to function efficiently. The ability to think, feel, move, eat, sleep and speak depends on energy generated from oxygen. When oxygen ceases to be available, we die!

Research has shown that in most parts of the world the natural concentration levels of oxygen in our atmosphere are steadily decreasing due to climatic and industrial utilization changes that have taken place over the years. When scientists analyzed the oxygen content of air bubbles trapped in ice-core drillings in Antarctica, they found that the earth's atmosphere at one time contained between 38% and 50% oxygen. Over the years, increased pollution, increased toxins, mass rain forest destruction, and the reduction of other natural oxygen producers have decreased the level of oxygen in our present day atmosphere to below 20%. In over populated countries and urban areas, the oxygen levels fall even lower. Because our bodies are not designed for low-level oxygen consumption, harmful toxins accumulate in our cells, tissues, organs, and blood streams. When the oxygen and pH levels are balanced, the body can re-energize and cleanse itself of toxic substances, which keeps us healthy. Our "Vitality" is directly related to the air we breathe. The cleaner the air, the more energy and vitality we experience and the healthier we remain.

Polluted Outdoor Air is a Problem

In 1997, approximately 52.6 million people lived in areas where air quality levels exceeded the EPA's National Ambient Air Quality Standard for at least one type of airborne pollutant. These areas were primarily the larger metropolitan sections of the country. Today as you might expect the number of people living in these areas has increased dramatically. Unfortunately, however, the pollution created in those highly populated locations is now finding its way into the rural sectors, which were once considered to have relatively clean, pure air. This shouldn't come as a surprise to anyone, especially considering that in 1992 alone US companies reported to the EPA that they had released 1.84 billion (1,840,000,000) pounds of *toxic* chemicals into the air. That's 920 thousand tons *of poison*, in one year! When these amounts of toxic chemicals are released into the air year after year it is no wonder that environmental illnesses have increased so much.

The environmental impact of air pollutants on health, economy and quality of life is significant. Right now, on any given day, there are at least 383 major carcinogens in our environmental air, 5 of which can cause irreversible mutations in the DNA of cells.

Polluted Indoor Air is a Bigger Problem

Recently the U.S. House of Representatives and the Environmental Protection Agency named indoor air pollution the #1 environmental health problem in America. Environmental Protective Agency studies, found levels of some indoor chemicals and toxins 100 times higher than outside levels. Because most Americans spend 90% of their time indoors with building structures closed tightly to conserve energy, there is little or no air exchange, which means we are breathing the same air we took in yesterday, and the day before, and the day before. This can lead to serious health problems.

Indoor air pollution in most homes comes from dry cleaning, synthetic carpets, synthetic furnishings, cleaning products, pets, growing mold, smoking, and personal care products. It may be hard to believe but hair-spray stays in the air for as long as three months. Mold can

grow behind wallpaper, in the ventilation system, under the foundations, in damp clothing, cleaning materials, and the moisture in ceilings,
walls, carpets and drapes. Mold can be so detrimental that it can be the
major cause of frequent headaches and frequent aggravated stomach
problems and even more serious health problems. Mold can present a
serious health challenge and so can various bacteria and viruses that can
be found in your heating and cooling system, garbage, bathrooms, and
even on household pets.

In an effort to have a clean home many people use household cleaners that emit toxic gases and chemicals into the air. It is a fact that
some of the cleanest homes can be the worst homes for allergies and
asthma because of the standard cleaning products we use. The gases and
chemicals from household cleaning and personal cleansing and hygiene
products that hang in the air and invade our bodies (through breathing
and absorption through the skin) are some of the most toxic substances
ever created.

Remember this simple fact, if you can smell it, you are breathing it
into your lungs and absorbing it into your tissues and when your body
accumulates too many toxins you can end up with serious symptoms of
sickness and disease.

Polluted Air Can Seriously Affect Your Health

Scientific studies show that impurities in the air we breathe can cause:
- Premature death
- Increased hospitalization and emergency room visits to treat severe
  symptoms of asthma and other respiratory problems
- More frequent absences from work and school
- Susceptibility to respiratory infections, such as flu and pneumonia
- Elevated risk of heart attack in the elderly and people who have
  heart disease

Indoor Air Pollutants in Homes is Increasing

Over the past several decades, our exposure to indoor air pollutants
is believed to have been on the increase. This may be due to a variety

of factors, including the trend toward creating more energy-efficient, airtight structures, reduced ventilation rates to save energy, the use of synthetic building materials and furnishings, and the use of chemically formulated personal care products, pesticides, and household cleaners.

Many families are inhaling numerous pollutants in their homes without even being aware of the impact on their health. Some common pollutants that affect the air in the home are cigarette smoke, dust, pet dander, droppings from dust mites and other pests. Other additional pollutants are lead, out-gassing fumes from carpets, formaldehyde from particleboard and synthetic materials, chemicals in aerosol sprays, unclean air ducts, fumes from cleaning products, asbestos, the solvent benzene, carbon monoxide, mold, and flame retardants.

"Sick Building Syndrome"

Indoor pollution is not just a problem in the home. Due to exposure to a variety of concentrated pollutants in poorly ventilated offices, "sick building syndrome" and other work-related environmental illnesses are on the rise. People may simultaneously experience extreme fatigue, lowered immune response, and, occasionally, flu-like symptoms. Pollutants are literally overcoming the immune system of people working in "sick buildings."

In the typical office setting, workers may inhale out gassing from carpets as well as pollutants from building materials, office supplies, fax machines, photocopiers, synthetic furniture, and recycled air. Even fellow workers can contribute, with solvents from dry cleaning, chemicals from personal care products, etc. More than 250 pollutants have been identified in a typical indoor office atmosphere. Of course, many of these pollutants are also found in the typical home.

The Solution is Indoor Air Purification

Through the years there had been many different designs and creations of air purifiers, each one better than the last; in an attempt to get clean, fresh, indoor air. In the mid-1980's air purifiers started to make their way into the residential market. This would, theoretically, provide a method to clean the air in homes up to 3000 sq. ft. without purchasing a very expensive in-home filtering system. This was accomplished with the introduction of the ozone producing machines.

Ozone air systems were widely used in the commercial restoration business for fire and flood damage to buildings. These applications utilized corona discharge systems that use a spark on electrically charged plates to simulate lightning. This converted the oxygen (O2) to ozone (O3). The corona discharge method creates very high concentrated ozone. Very high concentrations of Ozone can be lethal so the Federal Regulators banned many high Ozone producing machines.

In the late 1980's it was discovered that a lower concentration of ozone could have an effect on odors, mold and bacteria. The problem was how to create a safe residential air purifier that could produce safe, low concentrations of ozone that would not exceed the .04-.05 parts per million Federal limits. Developing the technology to create safe, low levels of ozone was accomplished in the early 1990's, about the same time as the Federal Government was going after the high ozone residential unit manufacturers. Titanium Dioxide was used as a catalyst to convert ozone to negative ions. This technology enabled the ozone produced from a UVC cell to be converted to safer more effective negative ions and friendly oxidizers.

The most important improvement was the efficiency by which these units cleaned the air. The new cell design created more hydro-peroxides, super-oxide ions and ozone levels were .01-.02 parts per million (ppm) or less. Country or forest air is usually around .01-.02 ppm of ozone. Most people can smell ozone at .01 ppm, and .05 ppm is the federal safe limit for medical devices. The new cell concept also produces hydroxide ions and ozonide ions which broadened the scope of its capacity to purify air. By using technology such as this, with its redundant and friendly oxidizers, the scope of effectiveness has been greatly increased. In 2006, a new technology surfaced that could set the standard for air purification, now, and in the future. This new air purification method utilizes the science of nano-particles or nanotechnology.

Space Age Technology for Air purification

In 2006, a new patent-pending hydro-catalytic nanotechnology, was revealed to the air purification industry by Air Oasis. This catalyst has revolutionized the air purification industry standard. This patent-pending technology has taken air purification to a new level. With the catalyst metals in a nano-sized particle instead of a micron or larger sized particle we are able to insure a more even distribution of metals on the target surface. Utilizing a nano-particle also increases the surface area of any given amount of metals. One gram of nano-sized particles will have up to 100 times the surface area of 1 gram of micron sized particles. This increased surface area increases the rate by which ozone is broken down into different ion structures. The improved dispersion of metals in the coating, applied to the target surface, helps to insure a more efficient way of breaking ozone down to safer levels. This hydrated-catalytic process, utilizing nano-sized (including nano-Nickel) particles, reduces ozone to the safest levels known. This technology is now available.

Clean and Sanitize Your Air

The Air Oasis air purifier uses space age nanotechnology to create negatively charged ions that bind to and destroy positively charged air pollutants. Five precious metals, 4 of which are in nano-sized particles, are painted on metal rings that surround a specially coated UV lamp that produces ozone. As a result, ozone that is produced by the UV bulb is broken down into specific negative ions as it passes by the metal rings. These very safe negative ions (oxidizers) and low level ozone are pushed out of the top of the air purifier out into the air by a fan.

In scientific tests done by West Texas A&M University, negative ions produced by the Air Oasis air purifier were shown to destroy and rid the air you breathe of mold, fungus, smoke, odors, gases from furniture, carpets, paint, hair sprays and cleaning products. The Air Oasis air purifier in additional scientific tests done by West Texas A&M University was also shown to reduce and/or destroy bacteria and viruses, even the very dangerous antibiotic resistant MRSA virus. This air purifier not only sanitizes the air in your home it sanitizes all the surfaces in your house killing germs, viruses and bacteria that can cause colds and flus as well as other more serious sicknesses and medical conditions.

But that is not all this air purifier can do. It can rid your house of dust and dust mites as well as pollens that can cause serious allergic reactions. If you have a dog or cat, this air purifier and sanitizer, will eliminate pet odors making your house smell fresh and clean.

Science has shown that the air surrounding us plays an extremely important role in our health and well-being. We need to breathe clean purified air. The Air Oasis air purifier and sanitizer will clean your air and the negative ions generated by the purifier can help you to think more clearly, sleep more soundly, and stay healthier.

Air Oasis Air Purifiers are Affordable

There are a number of affordable home and commercial Air Oasis air purification units. The most popular home and office units are the Mini that purifies the air in a 500 square foot room. The Mini is extremely efficient and can be used in a bedroom or an office and sells for just $299.99. The 1000, just like its model name implies, covers 1000 square feet of an apartment, small house or office space and it sells for just $399.99. The most effective Air Oasis air purification unit for bigger houses is the 3000. This unit cleans and sanitizes air in a 3000 square-foot house or office building and it sells for just $499.99.

There are commercial units that totally rid a room or house of cigarette smoke, or a gymnasium or locker room of smelly odors and bacteria that start at $549.99 for the portable unit or the same price for the Induct unit that is installed in the duct-work of a 3000 square foot house or office. Air Oasis has an affordable model that meets your needs for clean, fresh sanitized air.

For more information or to order an Air Oasis air purifier please call 1-866-564-3727.

EDITOR'S NOTE

Without the breath of life breathed into us by God, we would be a pile of dirt. I heard a story about some scientists challenging God: "God, we can create life! We've got your secret!" God said, "Bring it on, boys!" God bent down, picked up some dirt and breathed the breath of life and, up popped man! The scientists began their work with a pile of dirt, God said, "Just a minute boys, you've got to create your own dirt first!" Every time you make a copy of a copy, it's less than the original.

Aren't we all glad that God placed our breathing on automatic pilot so we don't have to even think about it. If we had to decide to breathe many people would be dead from lack of air because they just couldn't make a decision to do something healthy for their body. We must have clean air to breathe. Therefore it is vital for you to know that the indoor air in your homes and offices is more polluted than the outdoor air. Since you spend about 80-90% of your time indoors this is a serious problem. The Federal government and various State governments have made a commitment to clean up the outdoor air. You need to decide that it is more important for you to clean up the air in your home or office. For information how to clean your air and sanitize the surfaces in your home or office go to the virtual campus: www.healingnatureinstitute.com.

—JEF

APPENDIX 4

DRINK YOUR COFFEE AND LOSE WEIGHT

Cheers to Fat-Burning Coffee!

B oresha International, Inc. is a company that is perfectly positioned at the forefront of two powerful, global mega-trends.

Headquartered in Concord, California, Boresha provides individuals with an unparalleled business model that combines the second most highly-traded commodity on earth—coffee—with the extraordinary co-operative marketing industry.

At the core of Boresha, which is Swahilian for "to improve," is the mission of improving the lives of others. Whether through its premium organic coffees, its unique business model, or by directly generating charitable income to save the lives of children, Boresha's cornerstone is that of Integrity, Quality, and Making a Difference.

Boresha has integrated two of the largest industries in the world, creating a remarkable vehicle of success for people from all walks of life through which they can actively make a difference in their lives and the lives of others.

The coffee industry serves over 1 billion cups of coffee every day, while cooperative marketing currently exceeds over 50 million participants globally. Boresha's powerful business model allows individuals to capitalize on the unprecedented merger of these two global giants to create their ideal lifestyle.

The purpose of Boresha is clear: to offer the finest premium organic coffees, to create an exceptional business for individuals to live their dreams, to improve the lives of others, and to directly impact the lives of children.

This purpose, combined with the principles of entrepreneurship, ethics, and success, has set the stage for an extraordinary experience for all those involved.

Boresha's organic coffee beans are 100% Arabica. Arabica coffee is the earliest cultivated species of coffee tree, being grown for well over 1,000 years. It produces approximately 70% of the world's coffee, and is dramatically superior in cup quality to the other principal commercial coffee species. All fine, specialty, and premium coffees come from Arabica coffee trees.

Arabica coffee grows only in particular environments with adequate rainfall, temperate climates, good soil (often volcanic), sufficient altitude, and roughly between the Tropic of Cancer and the Tropic of Capricorn. Under the ideal conditions, it can take as many as seven years for the Arabica coffee plant to grow to its full size. After a few years, the plants begin to produce fruit, the seeds of which are the coffee beans.

Our beans are cultivated in the rich soils of small farms located in the fertile, high mountain regions and moist lake areas of Africa. The coffees from this region are complex and have intense berry or floral aromas and have undertones of berries, citrus fruits and chocolate.

Boresha coffee is naturally grown without the use of any artificial fertilizers, pesticides, or other chemical products.

Crafted to satisfy the most diversified and discriminating of palates, our carefully selected exotic beans are roasted in a temperature-controlled environment within a state-of-the-art roasting facility in California.

Boresha coffee is Fair Trade Certified, OCIA and USDA Certified and Infrared Roasted (only a small percentage of beans in the world use this roasting process).

Their flagship product is called "Skinny Science Coffee." Skinny Science Coffee is an Award Winning Breakthrough in Food Science

Technology created by Dr. Ann de Wees Allen and has the first Low Glycemic Coffee Patent ever awarded. Dr. Allen is known as the "Alpha Scientist" and is in the forefront of scientific breakthroughs. She is one of the leading scientists in the world in Food Science Technology. The medical and research community states that Dr. Allen's science and technology is "Twenty Years Ahead of Anyone Else."

Skinny Science Coffee provides *Patented Hunger Control, Balanced Energy, Thermogenic Fat-Burning, Buffered Caffeine and it Combats Stress Related Eating.*

Skinny Science Coffee is the first and only coffee drink designed by Glycemic Index Researchers. Why is this important? Because coffee causes FAT-STORAGE in humans. What is the point of energizing the body and stimulating fat-storage at the same time? The only way to fix coffee so that it does not stimulate fat-storage is to incorporate the Glycemic Index into the equation and to use Buffered Caffeine instead of regular caffeine.

There has been only one patent awarded for Buffered Caffeine and that patent has been incorporated into Skinny Science Coffee. *Buffered Caffeine Delivers Maximum Energy, Maximum Fat Burning and Glycemic Balance.* It is a Fusion of Nature and Science that was named "Breakthrough Product of the Year" by Success Magazine and featured on the front page of the Wall Street Journal.

It negates the fat storing and blood glucose imbalances caused by ingesting caffeine and caffeine-drinks. It programs the body to burn fat and creates maximum energy, instead of storing fat into adipose tissue fat cells. Energy Drinks and caffeinated drinks can cause fat storage and weight gain. The only methodology for blunting that effect is Buffered Caffeine.

Boresha customers describe their *exotic coffee experience* as rich, bold, balanced, bright, intense, wine like, chocolaty, distinctive, fruity, exotic…a very special coffee. Fat Burning Green Tea and other products will be available in the near future.

Find details at www.IGetPaidToDrinkCoffee.com/healthcityusa or phone 1-888-572-3132

APPENDIX 5

CELL PHONE MICROWAVES: WE HAVE TO LIVE WITH THEM, BUT CAN WE?

Fred Van Liew

Have you ever found your head or ear feeling a little hot after talking excessively on your cell phone? Did you think the battery was perhaps heating up your head? Are you aware that your cell phone seeks a signal with microwaves, just like those found in your microwave oven. You cook a hot dog from the inside out when you place it in your microwave oven. Microwaves generate heat very quickly, agitating water, fats and sugars. Your brain is made up of fats, sugars and water. A cell phone is doing the same to your head, your hand or your hip, even more when in use. Once a hot dog is cooked, how do you uncook it? Similarly, can you uncook your brain cells or body cells once they have been cooked?

Cell phones are now a fact of life for the majority of people in the world. It is important to note that it is not just your own cell phone that poses a hazard. Four Billion cell phones are in use today. These are connected to a base station, which makes our exposure to fare-field radio waves unavoidable in the United States, according to Dr. George Carlo's research. Dr. George Carlo, chairman of the Science & Public Policy

Institute in Washington, DC, was originally hired by the cell phone industry to prove that cell phones posed no health hazard. When his research showed the opposite to be true, the industry quickly placed distance between themselves and Dr. Carlo's work. Dr. Carlo's research has consistently used body response and live tissue response as the foundation for testing effective body protection protocols and appliances. The world governments have ignored his findings and sided with industry, with military applications being some of the most hazardous, including spy satellites placing us in a virtual microwave oven day and night, disrupting governing vessel and conception vessel function in our bodies.

The irritating effects of microwaves, particularly from billions of cell phones around the world, are contributing to disrupted DNA repair, a natural God-given cellular design function. Genetic change can occur, and all kinds of symptoms from cell phone use and environmental electronic chaos may manifest from free radical damage, systemic dysfunction and inhibited cellular communication..

These all too common symptoms might include poor sleep, decreased resistance to all forms of stress, autistic behavior syndromes, traumatic stress disorders, multiple chemical sensitivities, organic stress syndrome, and electromagnetic sensitivities. ADD and ADHD in children and adults my be exacerbated by the constant exposure to these microwaves. Excessive fatigue, tingling of extremities, on-going pain from the shoulders up, including severe headaches, are beginning symptoms. Foggy thinking, lightheadedness, unusual memory loss, poor concentration, sensitivity to noise and light and even heart palpitations may manifest. Later symptoms include excessive sweating at night, blood in stool, ringing in ears, persistent nausea, extreme irritability with fits of anger, skin rashes and bumps, vision impairment. (Source, Dr. George Carlo). These symptoms are common, however rarely traced to environmental chaos from cell phones and communication microwaves. Where is our medical community on this? Simple effective protection from this damage, as well as harmonic support for the body, would help prevent or reverse these symptoms.

Cell phone use began in 1984. Before that however, the U.S.

Government knew that when FM radio stations were introduced into a community, melanoma and other forms of cancer increased dramatically. When some FM stations failed, the community where they were located would experience a corresponding decrease in melanoma cancer. This was not made public, and even today most people are unaware of the hazard FM radio signals pose to cellular function. In fact, nearly all communication is now some form of microwave. Little wonder living cells are shutting down and remaining in a protective non-functioning sympathetic state, unable to open back to a functioning parasympathetic state where they can communicate and serve their natural design function. This is often called adrenal disorder, adrenal fatigue or adrenal exhaustion. In fact, the adrenal glands are almost always in perfect function. It is the shut down cells that cannot call for help!

Dr. Carlo points out that electromagnetic fields are the foundation for natural biological function and survival. They are the key to communication within living organisms, and between organisms. Our own DNA has an innate intelligence that allows cells to protect themselves from harmful frequencies and they can positively respond to harmonic or supportive frequencies, if they have the proper support in nourishment and harmonic resources. These exceptionally high vibrational harmonics in the quantum or nano-tesla range are essential, and their presence provides security for cellular function and communication. Lack of these protective, high vibrational harmonics leave cells vulnerable to the irritation from microwaves originating from radiowaves of all types. Perhaps the most harmful are the FM radio waves, spy satellites, cell phone towers, cell phone calls from around the world, and finally the cell phones or the wireless head sets themselves.

Dr. Carlo has shown how much faster and deeper the microwaves originating from cell phone use penetrate into the head of a ten year old compared to the same radiation from a cell phone used by an adult. About eighty percent of brain cells are being affected by cell phone use, according to Dr. Carlo. For this reason, we must consider effective protection for any child using a cell phone an absolute necessity. Adults can make their own choices, however it makes no sense to leave the body defenseless against a personal cell phone, as well as all those calls being made by others that pass through your body every second. These irritate your body cells like the screeching tires of an automobile. You know something bad is going to follow that sound. Well the constant irritation to your cells shuts them down.

The good news is that all cells are adaptive. Given a little help, there is much that has been observed indicating that loss can be restored. God's design is simple. Coherence is found in the Word. Simple, consistent prayer, reading from Scripture and meditation (time spent with God) can provide exceptional coherence. There is no Chaos in the Word. It must be done consistently, and this is unfortunately not a part of most people's daily lives. Like body armor, harmonic support from appliances worn on the body or in a pocket, or placed on a cell phone or computer can produce some serious improvement and is in fact recommended. Choosing one that is effective is not so easy, as we are dealing with very subtle, though powerful energies. Think about the healing power of prayer, or the laying on of hands using one or more of God's Promises to effect healing, and you may understand subtle, though powerful energies. Short term, for a Christian, pulling the blood of Jesus over the body while making a cell phone call can provide from five to fifteen minutes of perfect coherent protection around and within the body. The challenge comes during the rest of the day when you are carrying the phone with you. Testing has shown the Blood protection remains for five to fifteen minutes, allowing you to remove yourself from a bad situation with minimal damage, not remain there. Think body armor for the rest of the day.

So it is in these subtle, though powerful quantum energy technologies that we are finding ways to access and amplify the natural protective harmonic energies provided by God in our environment. These have been artificially though significantly depressed by our man-made electromagnet environment, from the wiring in our homes to all the satellites and communication tools in use worldwide. Even our collective negative and fearful thoughts depress coherent protection. Those appliances that naturally access and amplify whatever left spinning electron coherence that God has provided, known and unknown, appear to show the most promise. In fact, these natural harmonics provide the essential support that allows the body cells to restore themselves to an open parasympathetic state of communication within the body. When the polarized nature of lipid (fat) layers around the body cells get restored, cognitive function and nerve regeneration are immediately improved.

These natural harmonics should be in the water we drink, and the food we eat. However modern water treatment plants do not allow the water to flow over rocks and waterfalls. They add fluoride, chlorine, metal flocculants and other poisons to the water, killing its singing nature, as Dr. Carl Baugh of the Creation Evidence Museum in Glenrose, Texas would say. The dead water coming out of the tap can now be brought back to life using appliances that contain harmonic accessing and amplifying technology, like eMugs, or effective prayer. Yes, a simple prayer *"Father, bless this water (or food) and raise its energy according to your Promises, that it might bring life to my body, in Jesus name"* (Christian prayer example). When one asks this, expecting God to honor it (2 Cor 1:20), the very taste and texture of the water or beverage is improved. This is what structure and harmonics provide. This will also help the cells resist the non-stop assault from man-made environmental chaos.

Unfortunately, this is most likely not enough to protect most people. You should consider effective protection on every cell phone being used by a family member. Blue tooth devices can be even more harmful than the cell phones themselves, needing their own protection (example: www.ewater.com - cell phone bug). Without protection, many people have already had cancer from behind the ear from use of these devices. What is it going to take for us to wake up? Where is the medical community speaking up on this issue? Is the dollar really that much more important than peoples lives?

A final note of caution. Most cell phone protection is only moderately effective at best. Choose carefully, however do choose after you do your homework. Full body protection (example: www.ewater.com EP2 Stress Pendant) plus protection on each cell phone provides the kind of redundancy needed in today's electronically messed up world.

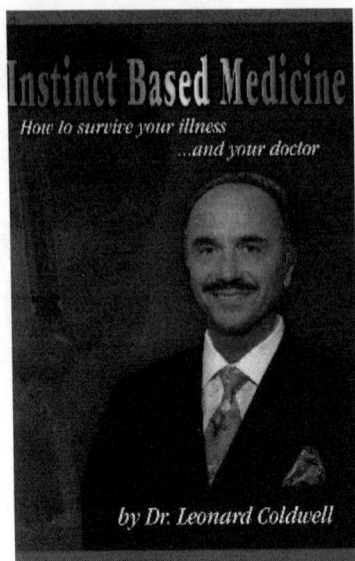

Instinct Based Medicine
How to survive your illness
...and your doctor

by Dr. Leonard Coldwell

Instinct Based Medicine™

Dr. Leonard Coldwell is a health researcher who has spent his career addressing the root cause of disease/illness and how to help patients get rid of the cause of the illness. He discovered that the only way to help his patients was to help them to help themselves, which led him to be known as the "health coach." He does not care about the symptoms of disease/illness because he only addresses the root cause of the illness.

—**Dr. Coldwell** is my personal physician in Europe and his input over the years was extremely valuable for me and the creation of my mega best selling book, *Natural Cures They Don't Want You to Know About.* Dr. Leonard Coldwell is the original natural cures doctor. We are in constant contact, consulting with each other all the time. I am glad that Dr. Leonard Coldwell is now willing to share with the world his secrets for health and healing. In *Instinct Based Medicine*, Dr. Coldwell uncovers the horrifying truth about the medical profession and shows us how to find and eliminate the life circumstances, behaviors, decisions and actions we live with on a daily basis that endanger our health.

This ground breaking book will reach and help millions of people! I ask you to support Dr. Coldwell in his approach to educating and protecting the public from the dangers of modern medicine to give everyone the tools to control their own life and health. Please support this book and help spread the message. I wish my dear friend, Dr. Leonard Coldwell, the biggest success with his book *Instinct Based Medicine*!
—Kevin Trudeau
NY Times Best Selling Author and Consumer advocate May 2008

**Dr. Leonard's book may be purchased at
http://www.instinctbasedmedicine.com/**

BIBLIOGRAPHY

Dangers of Medicine

1. *Confessions of a Medical Heretic,* Robert S. Mendelsohn, M.D. Contemporary Books, Inc. An expose of the medical industry written by a prominent medical doctor (now deceased) who served on the Illinois Medical Licensure Committee, held many faculty and hospital posts and was the former director of Chicago's Michael Reese Hospital. It will open your eyes as to what is going on in the medical industry today. He states that if 95% of the medical industry disappeared, the health of the entire country would improve dramatically. He advocates as little medical care as possible by medical doctors.

2. *Dangers Of Compulsory Immunizations,* Family Fitness Press, Box 1658, New Port Richey, FL 33552. How to legally avoid them.

3. *Immunizations:* The Terrible Risks you Face That Your Doctor Won't Reveal. Robert S. Mendelsohn, M.D., Second Opinion Publishing, 1993.

4. *How To Raise A Healthy Child...In Spite of Your Doctor,* Robert Mendelsohn, M.D. Ballantine Books, New York, Including chapters such as "How doctors can make healthy kids sick," and what to do when your child has an accident, cut, sprain, poisoning, etc.

5. *The Ultimate Rape: What Every Woman Should Know About Hysterectomies and Ovarian Removal,* Elizabeth Plourde, M.T., M.A., New Voice Publications, P.O. Box 14133, Irvine, CA 92623.4133. Why NOT to have any of your female organs removed. Some of the results of having a hysterectomy: high blood pressure, atherosclerosis, bowel and bladder problems, weight gain, depression, death, loss of sexual enjoyment, fibromyalgia, and osteoporosis, and more. Written by a medical technologist and very well researched.

6. *Instinct Based Medicine,* Dr. Leonard Coldwell, Strategic Book Publishing

Enzymes

1. *Enzymes for Autism & Other Neurological Conditions* by Keren Defelice, ThunderSnow Interactive

2. *Everything You Need to Know About Enzymes*, Tom Bohager, Greenleaf Book Group Press

Dangers of Animal Products:

1. *Diet For A New America*, John Robbins, Stillpoint Publishing, John Robbins, heir to the Baskin Robbins ice cream empire, leaves the industry and instead goes into research on the state of the animal raising industry. He describes in detail how the animals are raised, fed, and treated in horrible, shocking and unsanitary ways. He puts forth research supporting the benefits of a vegan diet and also addresses the issue of adequate protein, calcium and iron in a vegan diet in a very scientific manner supported by research. This book will make you never want to go near meat again (or any other animal product).

2. *Mad Cowboy: Plain Truth From The Cattle Rancher Who Won't Eat Meat*, Howard F. Lyman, Scribner, New York. A former cattle rancher and feedlot operator, now considered the country's expert on mad cow disease, tells his story of how he and other feedlot operators raised foods and animals by using unnatural methods such as hormones, antibiotics, pesticides, etc, many of which had been banned. It will make you never want to eat animal products again. Well researched.

3. *Don't Drink Your Milk! New Frightening Facts About The World's Most Overrated Nutrient*, Frank A. Oski, M.D., TEACH Services, Inc., Brushton, New York, 1995.

Vegetarianism/Cookbooks

1. *Recipes for Health Bliss: Using Naturefoods & Lifestyle Choices to Rejuvenate Your Body & Life* / Susan Smith Jones. Hay House, Inc.: www.hayhouse, 2009

2. *May All Be Fed*, John Robbins, William Morrow and Company, Inc., 1992. Very good vegan cookbook.

3. *The New McDougall Cookbook*, John A. McDougall, M.D., the Penguin Group, New York, New York.

4. *Cookbook For People Who Love Animals*, Gentle World, Inc., P.O. Box U, Paia, Maui, Hawaii 96779, Vegan cookbook. Contains no sugar or honey.

5. *Not Milk...Nut Milks!*, Candia Lea Cole. What to feed your child and yourself instead of milk. Over 50 recipes including almond milks, pecan milks, walnut milks, pine nut milks, sesame seed milks, pumpkinseed milks, sunfloweer seed milks, and cashew milks. YUM!

6. *Food For Life*, Neal Bernard, M.D., Three Rivers Press, New York, Vegan cookbook.

7. *Dean Ornish's Program For Reversing Heart Disease*, Ballantine Books, New York 1991

Water

1. *Alkalize or Die*, Dr. Theodore A. Baroody, Holographic Health Press

2. *The Miraculous Properties of Ionized Water*, Bob McCauley, Spartan Enterprises Inc.

3. *Honoring the Temple of God A Christian Health Perspective*. Bob McCauley, Spartan Enterprises, Inc.

4. *Water Crystal Healing*, Masaru Emoto, Atria Books

Raw and Living Foods/Cookbooks

1. *17 Theme Cookbooks*, starting with *Carribean Celebration*, and many other ethnic recipes that substitute healthy ingredients for unhealthy cultural ones by Jackie & Gideon Graff. Go to www.sproutrawfood.org to view and order.

2. **The Hippocrates Diet and Health Program*, Ann Wigmore. Avery Publishing Group, Inc. Raw food recipes as well as explanations of why a raw food diet and wheatgrass are so healing.

3. *The Sprouting Book*, Ann Wigmore, Avery Publishing Group, Inc., Wayne, New Jersey. The benefits of raw food and sprouts and how to easily make sprouts at home.

4. *The Wheatgrass Book*, Ann Wigmore, Avery Publishing Group, Garden City Park, New York. Detailed information on the benefits of wheatgrass and its juice, and how to grow wheatgrass at home.

5. *Sprout Garden*, Mark M. Braunstein, Book Publishing Co.

6. *Living Foods for Optimum Health*, Brian Clement with Theresa Foy Digeroniomo, Prima Publishing, Rocklin, CA, 1998.

7. *Warming Up To Living Foods*, Elysa Markowitz, Book Publishing Company, Summertown, Tennessee, 1998.

Juicing Books

1. *Book of Juicing,* Michael T. Murray, N.D. Prima Publishing. Contains many great-tasting juice combinations. Takes all the guesswork out of "What fruits and vegetables do I juice? The best, most practical juicing book I've seen.

2. *Fresh Vegetables and Fruit Juices,* N.W. Walker, D. Sc., Norwalk Press, Prescott, AZ 1978.

3. *The Juiceman's Power of Juicing,* Jay Kordich (the "Juiceman"), William Morrow and Company, Inc., New York, 1992. Also, any other books he has written.

Emotional Healing

1. *You Can Heal Your Life,* Louise Hay, Hay House, Inc.,

Herbal and Natural Healing Books

1. *Herbal Renaissance,* by Stephen Foster. How to grow your own herbs.

2. *Nontoxic, Natural, & Earthwise,* Debra Lynn Dadd, Jeremy P. Tarcher, Inc. How to avoid toxic chemicals in our households (cleaners, deodorizers, polishes, insecticides, etc.) What easy natural alternatives to use instead, from natural products in the health food store to homemade solutions.

3. *Doctor-Patient Handbook,* Bernard Jensen, D.C. Bernard Jensen Enterprises. The basics of healing and "healing crises." What to expect during a "cleanse." www.bernardjensen.com

4. *Tissue Cleansing Through Bowel Management,* Bernard Jensen D.C. And Sylvia Bell, Bernard Jensen Enterprises. Shows the link between the condition of your bowels and your overall health. Great pictures showing all of the hardened accumulated waste that was drawn out of the bowels during cleansing procedures and pictures of people with diseases before and after the bowel cleansing. The results are dramatic.

5. *Why Christians Get Sick,* Rev. George H. Malkmus. Destiny Image Publishers, Inc.

6. *School of Natural Healing,* Dr. John R. Christopher, Christopher Publications, Springville, UT. Excellent large reference book of herbal formulae, remedies, diseases, natural healing routines.

7. *Medicinal Plants,* (part of the Peterson Field Guide Series), Steven Foster/ James A. Duke, Houghton Mifflin Company. A field guide to identifying therapeutic plants/herbs.

8. *Your Body's Many Cries For Water,* F. Batmanghelidj, M.D., Global Health Solutions, Inc., Falls Church, VA 1997. Tells how many common ailments are due to dehydration.

9. *Bragg Healthy Lifestyle,* Paul C. Bragg, N.D., Ph.D., and Patricia Bragg, N.D., Ph.D., Health Science, Santa Barbara, CA

10. *Cancer Salves:* A Botanical Approach To Treatment, Ingrid Naiman, North Atlantic Books

11. *How I Conquered Cancer Naturally,* Eydie Mae with Chris Loeffler, Avery Publishing Group, Garden City Park, New York, 1992.

12. *Spontaneous Healing,* How to Discover Your Body's Natural Ability to Maintain and Heal Itself, Andrew Weil, M.D., Ballantine Books.

13. *The Cause and Cure of Human Illness,* Arnold Ehret, The Ehret Literature Publishing Company

14. *Raw Food Works,* Diana Store, Raw Superfoods

15. *God's Way to Ultimate Health,* George Malkmus, Hallelujah Acres Publishing

16. *Achieving Great Health,* Bob McCauley, Watershed Wellness Center

17. *The Vitamin Code,* Massoud Arvanaghi, PhD & Mike Yorkey, Garden of Life, Inc.

18. *Patient Heal Thyself,* Jordan S. Rubin, Freedom Press

19. *Healing Inflammatory Bowel Disease,* Paul Nison, 343 Publishing Co.

20. *Health According to the Scriptures,* Paul Nison, 343 Publishing Co.

21. Look for Paul Nison's New Book, *The Daylight Diet* soon to come!

22. *Raw Family,* Victoria, Igor, Sergei, and Valya Boutenko, Raw Family Publishing

Body Building

1. *Raw Power,* Stephen Arlin, Maul Bros. Publishing

Chiropractic

1. *The Chiropractic Way to Health,* Dr. Leila Lindquist, Indialantic Publishing

Nutrition & Beauty

1. *Quantum Eating,* Tonya Zavasta, BR Publishing

Iridology

1. *The Science and Practice of Iridology,* Bernard Jensen, Bernard Jensen Enterprises, CA www.bernardjensen.com

2. *Iridology:* The Science and Practice in the Healing Arts, Bernard Jensen, Bernard Jensen Enterprises, CA. Top of the line iridology text with many full color pictures of irises and explanations of the iris markings. Bernard Jensen is considered one of the fathers of iridology. Excellent for practitioners as well as anyone else willing to learn. www. bernardjensen.com

Anatomy

1. *Atlas of the Human Body,* Takeo Takahashi, Harper Perennial. Excellent, clear, anatomy pictures for those lay persons interested in learning about their own anatomy in order to empower themselves. Good explanations of each system of the body. Best anatomy book for the lay person that I've found.

Women's Books

1. *The Realness of a Woman,* Carolyn Porter, D. Div., Empower Productions, Inc.

2. *Seven Roads to Glory,* Carolyn Porter, D. Div., Empower Productions, Inc.

3. *Angel Love,* Carolyn Porter, D. Div. Empower Productions Inc.

4. *Healing with Color,* Carolyn Porter, D. Div. Empower Productions, Inc.

Retreats/ Spas

1. *"Hippocrates Health Institute"*—1443 Palmdale Court, West Palm Beach, FL 33411. Telephone: 561-471-8876. Reservations only: 800-842-2125. Fax: 561-471-9464.

Feeding the World

1. *Mending the Earth,* Paul Rothkrug & Robert L. Olson, North Atlantic Books

2. *Seeds of Deception,* Jeffrey M. Smith, Yes! Books

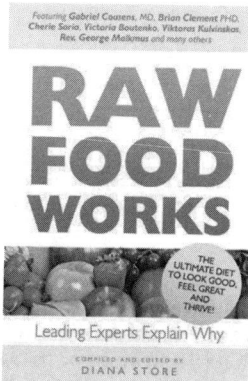

Raw Food Works offers a set of principles that provide a holistic and scientific framework for how the optimum diet works. This framework has one highly empowering idea at its core – that human beings function best on an enzyme-rich diet of unadulterated plant-based foods. Find out from an illuminating cast of contributors how such a diet can give you radiant health and vibrant energy throughout your life!

CONTRIBUTING AUTHORS

*   Victoria Boutenko Author of *Green for Life, Raw Family*, and *12 Steps to Raw Food*
*   Brian Clement, PhD, NMD, LNC Director of Hippocrates Health Institute, Florida, USA. Author of *Living Foods for Optimum Health, Longevity and Lifeforce*
*   Anna Maria Clement, PhD, NMD, LNC, Co-director of Hippocrates Health Institute, Florida, USA. Author of *A Families Guide to Health & Healing*, and *Healthful Cuisine*
*   Brenda Cobb Founder of the Living Foods Institute in Georgia, USA. Author of *The Living Foods Lifestyle, 101 Raw* and *Living Food Recipes*
*   Gabriel Cousens MD, MD(H) Diplomat American Board of Holistic Medicine, Diplomat Ayurveda. Best-selling author of *Spiritual Nutrition, Rainbow Green Live Food Cuisine, Conscious Eating, Depression-Free for Life*, and *There Is A Cure for Diabetes*
*   Rick Dina, DC Teacher of Science of Raw Food Nutrition
*   Dorit Founder of The Green Lifestyle Film Festival and author of *Celebrating Our Raw Nature*
*   Karen Knowler Raw Food Coach and Trainer. Founder and former editor of Get Fresh! Magazine. Former managing director of The Fresh Network, UK
*   Viktoras Kulvinskas MS. Author of the health classic *Survival Into The 21st Century*. Co-founder of Hippocrates Health Institute with Ann Wigmore in the late 1960s
*   Rev. George Malkmus Founder of Hallelujah Acres, North Carolina, USA. Author of *The Hallelujah Diet, God's Way to Ultimate Health, Message of Hope and Healing*, and *Why Christians Get Sick*
*   David Rainoshek MA and Katrina Rainoshek Researchers and Juice Feasting Pioneers/Coaches
*   Michael Saiber and Tamera Campbell Harvesters of Klamath Lake Algae and Founders of Vision, Inc.

PRAISE FOR DR. SUSAN'S NEW BOOK

Recipes for HEALTH BLISS

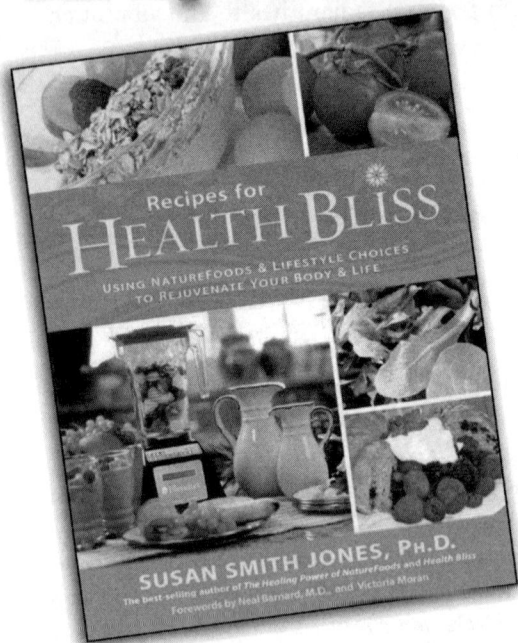

I am a big admirer of holistic health consultant, motivational speaker and author Susan Smith Jones. *Her work with NatureFoods and optimum nutrition is legendary.* I call her the "NatureFoods Lady" because she has been my source of inspiration and information about the wonderful world of NatureFoods for as long as I can remember. After many years of reading her books and articles, I finally asked if she would like to be a Hay House author and write this healthy eating and living series for us. *You'll love this best-selling 3-book set!*

And *Recipes for Health Bliss* is the most beautiful health book on the planet!

— **Louise L. Hay**

This reader-friendly, treasure trove of a book is sure to appeal to anyone who's serious about slimming down; firming up; looking younger; and healing body, mind, and spirit. Learn about the healthiest foods to eat, the best kitchen tips and supplements, the most delicious meals and snacks everyone will love, and other empowering lifestyle secrets from a world-renowned holistic-health and alternative medicine expert, advice columnist, award-winning writer, and motivational speaker. Although Susan Smith Jones has three of America's most ordinary names, her achievements and accolades in the fields of optimal health, personal development, and balanced living are extraordinary. My advice: get a copy of this book for yourself and then get several more copies to give as gifts to all your family and friends. Everyone will love it! And what better gift can you give than the gift of health?

—**Ellen T. Jensen, Ph.D., D.Sc.**, author of *Health is Your Birthright*, president and executive director of Bernard Jensen International: www.bernardjensen.com

Recipes for Health Bliss is a beautiful blend of modern research and ageless wisdom. Dr. Susan Smith Jones's sound nutritional guidance—along with her countless practical food tips and scrumptious recipes—will help you awaken to a new understanding of what vibrant health is all about. Her vast culinary experience will provide you with a better understanding of the specific advantages of the plant kingdom as an excellent source of nourishment. Whether you're 18 or 88 and whether you live in North, Central, or South America; Europe; Asia; New Zealand; Africa; Middle East; India; Australia; or the UK, this book is essential reading and will bring joy and delicious, healthful meals into your life. I wholeheartedly recommend it to everyone!

—**John Robbins**, author of *Diet for a New America*: www.healthyat100.org

Susan's books and work have made a profound difference in my life. As a result, I have lost all my extra weight, healed my body, and am healthier than ever. She has a unique ability to inspire and motivate in a way that makes you feel empowered and know that your health destiny is under your control. I have given the other two books in this series as gifts to countless people.

Now I will have the complete 3-book set with this celebrated book, *Recipes for Health Bliss*—a beautiful collection of her nutritional, culinary, and lifestyle sageness. I've had the privilege of taking several of her culinary classes and am always amazed at how she can take a few simple ingredients and, in minutes, create something dazzling to the eyes and taste buds.

—**Nick Lawrence,** radio and TV talk show host/producer: www.theradiovoice.com

Susan has been an inspiration to me for several years. Her optimistic, faith-filled attitude shines through in everything she says and does. The quality of our health is an integral part of our happiness. With Susan's books and teachings, we have all the tools we need to build solid health and, consequently, strengthen homes and families by passing along traditions that promote happy, healthful, and joyful lives. I'm forever grateful to Susan for her love of nourishing foods and her shining example of healthy living. All of her nutritious and tasty recipes are easy to prepare and enjoyed by my family and friends. *Recipes for Health Bliss*, as well as her complete 3-book set on healthy eating and living, *The Healing Power of NatureFoods* and *Health Bliss*, will enhance your life and keep on giving for years to come. It's the perfect gift set to give for any occasion. Outstanding!

—**Rebecca Linder Hintze,** author of Healing Your Family History: www.rebeccahintze.com

As you read through these beautifully designed pages, you'll feel as though Susan is sitting across from you at your dining-room table, gently and lovingly guiding you on everything you can do to heal and rejuvenate your body, look years younger than your age, and live your highest vision for yourself. As with her other two books in this consummate 3-book healthy eating and living set, *Health Bliss* and *The Healing Power of NatureFoods*, the sage nutritional and lifestyle suggestions here are the very best, and she's a stellar example that her "*Living-Vibrant*" program works. You won't be able to put this book down, unless it's to walk cheerfully to your kitchen to snack on some colorful fruits and vegetables or to make some fresh juice or a smoothie. Ask my 88-year-young mother—she wouldn't be without this book or any of Susan's other delightful and empowering works. Kudos to Susan!

—**Fléchelle Morin,** author of *Kissing or No Kissing: Whom Will You Save Your Kisses For?*: www.nokissing.com

The connection between radiant health and happiness is profound. Susan Smith Jones wisely teaches us in *Recipes for Health Bliss* how we can beautifully nourish and sustain our body by eating nature's sensuous, colorful, delicious, fragrant bounty from the earth — in this way, boosting our "spirit energy."

—**Alexandra Stoddard,** author of *You Are Your Choices: 50 Ways to Live the Good Life*: www.alexandrastoddard.com

You're in for a treat as you read and savor every page of Susan's best-selling, 3-book set. Each book in this series will profoundly change your life for the better, as these dynamic, life-changing volumes (and all of her work) have done for me. I encourage you to read them through once quickly, and then start all over again and read each page slowly, drinking in their magnificence and empowering wisdom. Finally, keep all three books close by, especially in your kitchen or on your bedside table, so you can refer to them often to help you create your healthiest life.

—**Louise L. Hay,** publisher and author of more than 25 books: www.louisehay.com

CRY OF THE NAIL

ALLEN KEMPER

BILL MCCUAN

Hidden beneath the surface, deep down where men dig for great treasures, the Creator of all wealth fashioned the womb where the raw element was birthed that fastened Him to a Tree that grew under His watchful care and provision.

Though a common, ordinary strong metal to man, it became the crucial point upon which mankind's selfish world was turned around upside down; revealing the Greatest Love that the universe had ever seen or will ever see:

The Creator Laying Down His Life for the Created!

Though man was immobilized by the chains of iron made in his rebellion by his own selfish hands, this metal indeed did its dastardly deed immobilizing the Creator of Life that His Life may be imparted; turning the lock of man's utter helplessness thus setting him Free!

Have you the desire for riches? Seek them not! Seek not for gold which turns to powder, or silver which tarnishes! All greatly desired metals can never attain the worth achieved by the humble iron which cried with each blow of the hammer, reverberating throughout all

Time & Eternity...

"I have unlocked the Greatest Treasure of All! Salvation's Vault for Mankind is Permanently Opened! The Greatest Wealth of the Universe is Now Flowing out of Heaven's Vault to You! Come to this Fountain I have Secured for You! Come now to this Saving, Cleansing, Healing, Crimson Flow that I have Caused for You! Do not see me as accursed, ordinary iron—I am the One Key you'll ever need for Everything in Heaven Above, & in the Earth Beneath! Believe in the Flow that I have Caused—Believe in His Blood!"

For more information on the nail go to www.holynail.com

THE ULTIMATE DEMONSTRATION OF THE HEALING NATURE OF JESUS!

Allen Kemper

This nail represents the greatest demonstration of the Healing Nature of Jesus, because there is no greater power in the universe than the power of God's Love! Not only did His Love compel Him to be willing to suffer unspeakable agonies for our Healing, Salvation, and Freedom from all sin, and sickness when He prayed in the garden, "Father...nevertheless, not my will, but Thine, be done" but His Great Heart of Love also compelled Him to perform perfectly, and endure even to the minutest details of suffering described by the holy prophets! Remember, the Prophets saw the future as revealed by YAHWEH thousands of years before! Their prophecies will affect us all the way to the end!

Jesus, Himself many times prophesied of His own sufferings when He taught His followers; one of these is found in John 15:13, "Greater Love has no man than this, that a man lay down his life for his friends."

Before He ever received the horrible nails in His precious hands and feet, He knew it was prophesied of Him, that He would suffer both hands and feet being pierced in a most torturous execution! This was prophesied by King David 1,000 years earlier! And in full knowledge of that—Jesus still said, "Yes, I do Love them that much!"

Jesus knew that the most precious and eternally valuable substance to be given in sacrifice for our sins and sicknesses was His own Holy Blood! Praise His Name! He was willing and actually gave it in Pilate's Judgment Hall for our Healing and emptied Himself entirely of His Most Precious Gift for our Eternal Salvation—at the Cross! Isaiah 53:5 declares, "With His stripes we are Healed!" The word for "bruises" and "stripes" in Hebrew is "marpe" which denotes—a victim so horribly torn and shredded by the cruel sharp metal hooks and bones embedded in the lictor's lash that there could be no distinguishing between one stripe from another!

YAHWEH said, "The Life of the flesh is in the blood, and I have given it to you to make an atonement for your souls, for it is the blood that makes atonement for the soul" (Leviticus 17:11). The atonement prophesied also includes physical well-being and health when we in obedience and Love for Him, steer clear of all that's wrong with our culture fashioned by greedy, wicked men and women intent on defiling our spirit, soul, and body!

Is it too much to ask that we live pure, holy lives to be conduits of His Healing Nature for others? Remember, great eternal rewards will be heaped upon those who will take the challenge to divest themselves of all that's corrupted and unhealthy in our society! Thinking about these rewards far overshadows what you and I think we want so much—health and wealth in this brief life! Remember, Jesus said, "Whoever therefore shall confess me before men, him will I confess before my Father which is in Heaven. But whoever shall deny me before men, him will I also deny before my Father which is in heaven" (Matthew 10:32).

Now, you are privileged to obtain your own replica of this solid, iron, nail of the first century A.D. to help you confess Jesus Christ is your Lord and Savior too, and start (if you haven't already) laying up your treasures in Heaven!

Thanks to the obedience of Bill McCuan, a very diligent TRUTH seeker and personal friend who has pioneered many ways to help share the Love & Healing Nature of Jesus with many, we now have the means to recreate these emblems of His Greatest Love for Us! This means that you can also enjoy using this nail like a key to pry open the doors to many hearts and share The Healing Nature of Jesus with many just like we do! When you do, you'll also experience the same joy welling up in you that we enjoy every day! You'll become so "addicted" that you'll have to tell everyone about His Greatest Love, and His Healing Nature for them too, and get so blessed doing so! You'll have all this "heaven to go to Heaven in" and you'll be so occupied and excited seeing so many turn to follow Jesus, that you'll often have to keep reminding yourself, "The Best is Yet to Come!" "God is not unfaithful to forget your work and labor of love!"

When you have a "key" like this in your pocket, it's not hard to "break the ice" and launch into a mutually interesting conversation with strangers who Jesus Died for too!

It is the Blood that Saves, Heals, Protects, and Cleanses from all defilement! Always be conscious of His Blood over you and your loved ones. When you by faith, appropriate His Blood, then, "No weapon formed against you shall prosper" (Isaiah 54:17).

Read "Cry of the Nail" reverently. Humbly come to Him by faith and ask Him to cover you with His Blood! It is vitally important that you thank Jesus every conscious moment for giving His Blood to protect you and keep you safe from all the wiles of the rogue, enemy spirits, seeking to steal, kill and destroy you mainly through their tactic of suggestions to your mind! Their strategy is to keep you in strife, confusion, doubt and fear! Don't ever doubt God's Word—it's more important that you obey it than if you do everything perfect to enjoy prolonged youthfulness and longevity! You'll never achieve your goal of staying young unless you follow His holy commandments and let His Love fill your heart so much that everyday you enjoy sharing The Healing Nature of Jesus with a lost, confused, and hurting world!

To receive your own witnessing nail: go to
www.healingnatureinstitute.com

EDITOR'S NOTE

My friend, missionary Allen Kemper, has so eloquently spoken the True meaning of The Healing Nature of Jesus, and tied all the authors together.

Our blood empowers us by carrying nutrition and oxygen to every cell of our body. I know in my heart that the Holy Spirit resides in our blood. This is why Our Heavenly Father, after granting us permission to eat all living, moving things instructed us not once, but twice, "Do not eat the flesh with the blood therein." There will be a price to pay if you do! This is where the Jewish, kosher meat comes into play. I believe all the miseries of our civilization begin from disobedience! God invites the world to come under His Blood, not only for our spiritual redemption, but physical, mental, healing, health and wealth! "Wealth without Health is not Wealth!"

Please, for the health of our nation, be responsible for your own health! Wake Up America!!! We, the people have the power when we come under the Blood of Jesus! God, did not create diseased bodies! Man, brought all misery upon himself because of lack of knowledge and understanding that God's laws are in reality loving instructions given to us by the Greatest Dad ever in the universe!

As many of my brothers and sisters that have eyes to see and ears to hear, we need to invite God back into our nation and the nations of the world! Revival is Our Survival! Join us and our Revival of Truth.

Call 888-572-3132 for the latest updates!

—JEF

FROM THE EDITOR

THE LAST CHAPTER OF THIS BOOK IS THE FIRST CHAPTER OF THE REST OF YOUR LIFE!

Congratulations! You've arrived at the last chapter! We've all heard Paul Harvey on the radio, "Now for the rest of the story..."

This book has been compiled and written in Love to you, to reveal the TRUTH that sickness and disease is not created by Our God! It is a penalty that we pay by believing the lies and deception, perpetuated by industries of greed, and governmental lies! We can stop the insanity by educating ourself, and putting the knowledge into practice! We invite you with our prayers and encouragement to join us in our journey to empowerment to live and share God's TRUTH with the world! Receive the wealth that God has in store for you! Health is Wealth!

The power of Jesus Christ abides is in you when you are a believer in Him! That power is called your Lifeforce!

WAKE UP AMERICA!

Our Healthcare, or "sickcare" budget is approaching 1 trillion dollars, 90% of what is spent in the last 30 days of a person's life—this is criminal!

Do you know of anyone suffering from the following symptoms of diseases caused by not treating the body as the temple? do you know of anyone that has lost body parts? Have you lost anyone to premature death and felt the pain of their loss? Have you experienced the pain from divorce and/or other dysfunctional relationship meltdowns?

1. Autism: used to be 1-10,000, now it's 1-98, and the projections are that by 2010, 50% of our children will suffer from our lack of action!

This is criminal! Read Karen Defelice's Book, *Enzymes for Autism & Other Neurological Conditions*. It's a must read to protect our children, written by a mother of two FORMER autistic sons!

2. Obesity: epidemic proportions in all ages!

3. Diabetes: children acquiring adult on-set diabetes at younger and younger ages!

4. Arthritis

5. Cancer: the leading cause of Cancer is fear and stress

6. Fear

7. Stress

8. AIDS

9. STD'S

10. Heart Disease

11. Alzheimer's

12. High Blood Pressure

13. Allergies

14. Fungus Infections such as candida

15. Asthma

16. Multiple Sclerosis

17. Osteoporosis

Remember Dr. T. Colin Campbell's statement: "There is a cure for cancer and all other diseases—it's called your immune system."

Here's my statement, "We know more about the other side of the moon, than we know about our own anatomy."

Are you sick and tired of being sick and tired? Have you made the decision to change your life yet?

Until you make the decision to change your life, you'll be the same five years from now except for the books you read, the people you associate with, the thoughts you put in your mind, and the "food" you put in your mouth (*repetition is the mother of all learning*)?

Dr. Leonard Coldwell, is the best selling author on *How to survive your illnesses and your doctor*, and personal physician to Kevin Trudeau. Trudeau is quoted by saying in his foreword to Dr. Leonard's book,

"Dr. Coldewll is my personal physician in Europe and his input over the years was extremely valuable for me in my creation of my mega best selling book, *Natural Cures they don't want you to know about*. Dr. Leonard Coldwell is the original natural cures doctor."

Baby steps to begin your journey:

- Put into practice the proper water drinking protocol! This is the simplest and the greatest thing to return you to Vibrant Health!

- There's only one disease—the mother of all—Dehydration, Malnourishment, and Acidosis! Drink ½ of your body weight in ounces every day, when your feet hit the floor in the morning, 30 minutes before you eat, drink no water with your meals, it dilutes your digestive juices, drink no sooner than two hours after you eat, when you feel hungry, drink a glass of water, and no water after 6:00 p.m.

- Clean out your cupboard of over-processed "foods."

- Remove your microwave from your kitchen (it genetically alters your food, causes cancer so bad that it's been outlawed by the country that invented it—Russia)!

- Eat more fruits and vegetables.

- Learn the Power of Juicing. Read Dr. Norman Walker's book, Fresh Vegetable & Fruit Juices. Follow Jack Lalanne, a student of Dr. Walker, and Dr. Paul Bragg.

- Learn the Power of Fasting with water, & with Juice.

- Associate with Health Conscious People.

- Watch less TV, read more! Remember, "Poor people Entertain themselves, Rich people Educate themselves!"

- If you don't buy it, you can't eat it, so budget for healthy food!

- Remove sugar and sugary drinks such as soda pop from your eating habits (it takes 30 glasses of water to neutralize the acidity)!

SUGGESTED DVD'S

All DVD'S from the global leaders as listed on the Living Food
Summit II page such as:
Dr. Brian Clement's
"Hippocrates Health Series"
A Way to Complete Health
"Sprouting—The Easy Way"
"Growing Wheatgrass, Sunflower, Pea Greens & Buckwheat
Lettuce"

Viktoras'
Rev. George Malkmus'
"Hallelujah Acres Series"
*How to Eliminate Sickness and Disease
& Others...*

Brenda Cobb's
from her Living Foods Institute
The Secrets of Living Foods

Igor & Victoria Boutenko's
Paul Nison's
Michael Saiber's

"Making a Killing—The Untold Story of Psychotropic Drugging"

"Eating"

"Supersize Me"

"The Mad Cowboy—Howard Lyman"

"King Corn"

"Medicine from the Future—Bemer 3000"

Gary S. Paxton, world renowned composer, entertainer, recording
artist, producer of over 2000 artists! A CD called the Healing Nature
of Jesus. Share it with the world. He has created this song and given it
freely to the world, to the glory of God.

MEET OUR AUTHORS

Drs. Anna Maria and Brian Clement

In his role as a progressive educator, Brian has conducted countless seminars, lectures, and educational programs, traveling extensively to more than 25 countries around the globe. At home in the United States, he has taken the message of this widely successful program to the entire country. In recent years he has been commissioned by government supported organizations to establish, organize, and direct health programs in Denmark, Switzerland, Greece, and India.

Brian has also written numerous books in which he explores the various aspects of health, spirituality, and natural healing. His recent best-selling book, "Living Foods for Optimum Health," has been acclaimed by Marilyn Diamond, co-author of the book *Fit for Life* as "an important and eminently readable book for the new era of self care," and by Coretta Scott King as "a landmark guide to the essentials of healthy living." In response to the growing public demand, he has produced an educational video series on the practical application of Hippocrates Health Institute's Life Change Program, the three-week detoxification and cleansing process that is recognized worldwide as Hippocrates' signature program. In addition, Brian created the Hippocrates Health Educator Program, a nine-week intensive instructional that certifies students to teach the Hippocrates Living Foods Lifestyle, with graduates in over 12 countries.

Anna Maria Clement founded the first living food organization in Scandinavia and was a member of the Natural Health Care Coalition, a government supported effort in unifying the field of complementary health care in her native Sweden.

Anna Maria has been co-director and chief health administrator of

Hippocrates Health Institute situated in West Palm Beach, Florida. She is one of the leading experts in live blood cell analysis, a revolutionary technique in the comprehensive assessment of a person's state of health. She trained in this method under American Biologics in California and assisted their professional staff in furthering their education in this field.

Anna Maria Gahns-Clement is the author of four books on the application of natural health methods in family and children's care. She, also, collaborated in creating a series of books about the Hippocrates Life Change program. She lectures extensively around the country as well as around the globe employing a style that is uniquely down-to earth and sensible approach to teaching practical methods that people can comfortably incorporate in their own lives.

Lee Fredrickson

Lee started his health journey over 36 years ago. He received his doctorate in communications from Louisiana Baptist University. Lee started 21st Century Press over 13 years ago to help authors get their books in print. He has worked with over 100 authors over the years and has formed, along with John Eagle Freedom, Healing Nature Press and Healing Nature Institute. Authors will be encouraged to develop classes based on their books to be offered in a virtual campus environment on the internet.

Susan Smith Jones

For a woman with three of America's most ordinary names, Susan Smith Jones, PhD, has certainly made extraordinary contributions in the fields of holistic health and fitness, optimum nutrition, anti-aging, and balanced living. For starters, she taught students, staff and faculty at UCLA how to be healthy and fit for 30 years. As a renowned motivational speaker, Susan travels internationally as a frequent radio/TV talk show guest, keynote speaker and holistic lifestyle coach; she is also the author of over 1,000 magazine articles (with her picture on many covers) and 20 books. Some of her most popular books include her best-selling 3-book healthy eating and living series published by Hay

House entitled *The Healing Power of NatureFoods, Health Bliss,* and *Recipes for Health Bliss* (referred to as the Blissful Living set) as well as her new book *Be Healthy~Stay Balanced: 21 Simple Choices to Create More Joy & Less Stress.* She also co-authored (along with Dianne Warren) a popular and unique 2-books-in-1, full color nutrition book for children ages 1-10 titled *Vegetable Soup/The Fruit Bowl* that recently won the *Disney iParenting Media Award* for one of the best children's health books. You can order all of these titles and more, easily and quickly, at this toll-free number: 1.800.843.5743 PT. To learn more about Susan, to participate in one of her retreats, to invite her to give a motivational talk to your company, church or business, or to access her many media interviews and free health information, please visit: www. SusanSmithJones.com.

Victoria Moran

Victoria Moran is an American writer and speaker, specializing in books on spirituality and nutrition. She lives in New York City with her husband and stepdaughter. Her articles have appeared in publications including Ladies' Home Journal, Woman's Day, Body & Soul, Weight Watchers Magazine, Natural Health, and Yoga Journal. She has been a guest on tv and radio programs, including two appearances on The Oprah Winfrey Show.

Paul Nison

Raw food chef and Author Paul Nison has been eating a raw food diet since he was diagnosed with Inflammatory bowel disease (Crohn's disease and ulcerative colitis) many years ago. With no other choice but drugs or surgery according to the medical profession, Paul decided to eat a raw food diet. Today he is 100% cured of this so-called "incurable disease." Paul has been featured on The Food Network and in several magazines and newspapers around the world. He travels the world giving lectures on the raw food nutrition and raw food prep classes to show people how easy and fun the raw life can be.

Fred Bisci

Dr. Fred Bisci has a Ph.D. in Nutritional Science. Fred, as he prefers to be called, has had a pioneering, and active practice in New York City for over forty years. He has worked with over 35,000 people all over the world with numerous health issues by helping them change their eating and drinking lifestyles through his Real, Fresh Food approach. His outlook is unique. He looks at biochemical interrelationships, rather than a simple dietary or nutritional standpoint. This biochemical appreciation of how the multiple variables work in the human body are directly related to a lifestyle of what is left out and what is put in. Fred has developed the INTERMEDIATE LEVEL MENU which is the core feature for creating a Healthy Lifestyle Program. His program helps you name your current program and meets you "where you're at." Fred empowers you to set healthier personal parameters through eating and drinking various combinations of food as you commit to a Healthy Lifestyle Program. Fred's main foundation built from his devotion to helping others, combined with his raw food lifestyle for over forty years, has revealed the intimate relationship of real food and the body's God-given ability to always seek health.

Vicki Rae Chelf

Vicki Rae Chelf lives in a yellow 1950's house with solar panels and salvaged furniture in Sarasota, Florida with her husband Jean Renoux. She grows tropical fruits, herbs and vegetables on every inch of her suburban lot. Vicki has written vegetarian cookbooks and taught vegetarian cooking for 30 years. Her first cookbook, *La Grande Cuisine Vegetarienne* stayed in print for over 20 years. Since then, Vicki has written four other cookbooks in French. She is also the author of *Cooking on the Right Side of the Brain, The Arrowhead Mills Cookbook,* published by The Avery Publishing Group, and *For The Love of Garlic,* published by Square One Publishers. She is co-author of *Cooking for Life* with Cherie Calbom. Vicki's latest book is *Vicki's Vegan Kitchen,* published by Square One.

Vicki has owned her own health food store, and restaurant *Le Pommier Fleuri* which she managed for over six years. She has also taught

Western Food Therapy at the East West College of Natural Medicine in Sarasota, Florida. She is the host of Green Connection US, which can be heard at, www.webtalkradionetwork.com. She is the co-host of Truly Sustainable Sarasota on WSLR 96.5 fm.

Vicki is a graduate of the Ringling School of Art and Design with a degree in fine art. She has had one person shows of her paintings in France, the U.S. and in Canada. Vicki also holds a Bachelors of Science in holistic nutrition from Clayton College. She spends part of every summer in traveling and teaching cooking in Europe.

Olin Idol

Olin Idol acquired an interest in health and nutrition over 40 years ago while serving in the military. At that time he began using a multitude of vitamin and mineral supplements, and distilled water while continuing to eat the typical American Diet. This regime was maintained faithfully until the early 90's when he read a book by Rev. George H. Malkmus entitled *Why Christians Get Sick*. The impact of this book on his lifestyle and diet was tremendous—the dietary supplements were tossed aside as was the Standard American Diet (SAD). He embraced a primarily raw plant-based diet and lifestyle. While he had no major physical problem himself, the little aches and pains associated with aging, life-long sinus problems and headaches, and stomach problems simply disappeared.

John Eagle Freedom

John Eagle Freedom is a true-blue American, born and raised in the heartland of America. He has earned his PhD, in the school of hard-knocks and lifetime experiences. John has been self-employed since he was 8 years old. He owned his first grocery store at 17, and his second one when he was 21. He knows the power of the mind, and he enjoys the Healing Nature of Jesus.

He has his own radio show, "Vibrant Life the Hour of TRUTH" on the mightiest radio frequency in Southwest Missouri—KWTO, which can be heard at 560 AM, and streamed live www.radiospringfield.com between 2-3 p.m. Wednesdays interviewing global leaders such as these fellow authors, revealing these life-saving TRUTHS.

John Eagle Freedom has a dream—Building the first Health City U.S.A. in the Ozarks, encouraging fellow citizens to take responsibility for their own health and wealth, and stop all the insanity!!!

He was the visionary and financier of "Vibrant Life Ministries" in Colonial Williamsburg, that has housed over 6,000 homeless men and women in the last 5-6 years. He is also the founder of "Vibrant Life Health Ministries," Springfield, MO, the C.E.O. and founder of Health City U.S.A., and co-founder and executive producer of "Healing Nature Press." John, has been very instrumental in uniting these internationally known best-selling authors and producing *The Healing Nature of Jesus* with God's Gracious help and direction!

Bob McCauley

Bob McCauley, CNC, MH was raised in Lansing, Michigan and attended Michigan State University (BA, 1980 in Journalism). He has traveled extensively, both domestically and abroad, visiting over 32 countries. He published Confessions of a Body Builder: Rejuvenating the Body with Spirulina, Chlorella, Raw Foods and Ionized Water (2000), Achieving Great Health (2005), The Miraculous Properties of Ionized Water, (2006) which is the only book on the market that exclusively addresses Ionized Water, Twelve (Fiction, 2007) and Honoring the Temple of God (2008). He is owner of the Watershed Wellness Center (www. watershed.net). He considers himself a *Naturalist*, meaning he pursues health in the most natural way possible. He approaches health from a Christian point of view.

From 2002-2004 he hosted the radio program *Achieving Great Health,* which was heard by thousands of people each day. His guest included some of the most well-known and respected names in the natural health world.

Bob is a Certified Nutrition Consultant and a Certified Master Herbalist. He is also a 3rd Degree Black Belt and Certified Instructor of *Songahm Taekwondo* (American Taekwondo Association).

Victoras Kulvinskas

Viktoras Kulvinskas, author of *Survival Into The 21st Century*, *The Lover's Diet*, *Sprout For the Love of Everybody*, and other books, is a leading authority on raw foods. He has also contributed articles to many journals. He travels extensively and has given seminars for the World Symposium on Humanity in Canada and Australia and has lectured at many events. Founder of the Hippocrates Health Institute with Ann Wigmore in the late 1960's, he has since done much work and research into the value of living foods and plant enzymes.

T. Colin Campbell

For more than 40 years, T. Colin Campbell, Ph.D. has been at the forefront of nutrition research. His legacy, *The China Study*, is the most comprehensive study of health and nutrition ever conducted. Dr. Campbell is the Jacob Gould Schurman Professor Emeritus of Nutritional Biochemistry at Cornell University and Project Director of the China-Oxford-Cornell Diet and Health Project. The study was the culmination of a 20-year partnership of Cornell University, Oxford University and the Chinese Academy of Preventive Medicine.

Dr. Campbell received his master's degree and Ph.D. from Cornell, and served as a Research Associate at MIT. He spent 10 years on the faculty of Virginia Tech's Department of Biochemistry and Nutrition before returning to the Division of Nutritional Sciences at Cornell in 1975 where he presently holds his Endowed Chair (now Emeritus).

His principal scientific interests, which began with his graduate training in the late 1950s, has been on the effects of nutritional status on long-term health, particularly on the cause of cancer. He has conducted original research both in laboratory experiments and in large-scale human studies; has received more than 70 grant-years of peer-reviewed research funding, mostly from the National Institute of Health, and has served on several grant review panels of multiple funding agencies, lectured extensively, and has authored more than 300 research papers.

He is the recipient of several awards, both in research and citizenship, and has conducted original research investigation both in experimental animal and human studies, and has actively participated in the development of national and international nutrition policy.

Dr. Leslie Van Romer

Dr. Leslie Van Romer is the author of weight-loss, body-best book, *Getting into Your Pants*, and companion WorkBook, called the *Getting into Your Pants PlayBook*. Dr. Leslie, chiropractor, motivational health speaker, and weight-loss cheerleader, writes a weekly e-letter and has produced a series of CDs and DVDs on many different health-related topics, such as diabetes, osteoporosis, aging, menopause, and weight loss. By offering simple direction and hope, she empowers individuals to lose weight and boost their level of health. Dr. Leslie makes you believe in you.

Ellen Tart-Jensen

Ellen Tart-Jensen has been working in the field of nutrition for thirty years. She is a graduate of Appalachian State University, University of New Mexico, and Westbrook University. Having suffered for years with scoliosis, fibromyalgia and severe pain, she searched around the globe for answers. She studied for two years at a natural healing clinic in Switzerland and for five years with Dr. Bernard Jensen at the Hidden Valley Health Ranch in California. Now, she is healthy, vibrant, and free from pain. She serves as President of the Bernard Jensen Natural Health Foundation and is the author of several books including *Health is Your Birthright, How to Create the Health You Deserve* and *The Simplified Guide to Internal Cleansing*. She has a busy practice and travels around the world teaching environmental, whole food nutrition and natural healing principles. Ellen is most passionate about helping young people and adults learn to be healthy with natural therapies and the natural organic foods necessary to be well.

John Robbins

John Robbins is the author of *HEALTHY AT 100: The Scientifically Proven Secrets of the World's Healthiest and Longest-Lived Peoples*.

He is also author of the international bestseller *DIET FOR A NEW AMERICA: How Your Food Choices Affect Your Health, Happiness, and the Future of Life on Earth*, *THE FOOD REVOLUTION: How Your Diet Can Help Save Your Life and Our World*, *THE AWAKENED HEART: Meditations on Finding Harmony in a Changing World*, and *RECLAIMING OUR HEALTH: Exploding the Medical Myth and Embracing the Source of True Healing*.

Widely recognized as one of the world's leading experts on the dietary link with the environment and health, John's work has been the subject of cover stories and feature articles in *The San Francisco Chronicle, The Los Angeles Times, Chicago Life, The Washington Post, The New York Times, The Philadelphia Inquirer,* and many of the nation's other major newspapers and magazines. His life and work have also been featured in an hour-long PBS special titled *Diet For A New America*.

The only son of the founder of the Baskin-Robbins ice cream empire, John Robbins was groomed to follow in his father's footsteps, but chose to walk away from Baskin-Robbins and the immense wealth it represented to "...pursue the deeper American Dream...the dream of a society at peace with its conscience because it respects and lives in harmony with all life forms. A dream of a society that is truly healthy, practicing a wise and compassionate stewardship of a balanced ecosystem."

For further information and to contact John Robbins, visit:
www.healthyat100.org

George H. Malkmus

After becoming a Christian at a Billy Graham Crusade Rally in Madison Square Garden, in New York City in 1957, George H. Malkmus completed four years of schooling in preparation for the ministry. During his nearly 20 years of ministry, he pastored churches in New York, North Carolina and Florida.

However, at the peak of his ministry, at age 42, he was faced with a life-threatening physical problem. He had recently lost his mother to colon cancer, and now he was facing the same condition. His mother, being a registered nurse, accepted the traditional medical treatment of chemotherapy, radiation and surgery with very devastating results. Because of his mother's bad experience with the medical modalities, Rev. Malkmus sought an alternative. In his search he contacted a friend, Evangelist Lester Roloff, who encouraged him to change his diet rather than accept the traditional medical treatments. Over night he changed his diet and almost immediately began to get well. Within one year, not only was his cancer gone but also gone were all of his other physical problems. Now in his mid-seventies, he has more energy than he did as a teenager.

Presently Rev. Malkmus is fulfilling the dream of "Hallelujah Acres" by proclaiming the message "You Don't Have to be Sick" to the world as he travels throughout the country delivering his "God's Way to Ultimate Health" seminar to churches and other interested groups in person and by television and radio. His books and newsletters are virtually going around the world.

You can visit Hallelujah Acres online at http://www.hacres.com

Rebecca Linder Hintze

Rebecca Linder Hintze is an author, speaker, radio show host, and family issues expert, who has worked in private practice for more than a decade, completing thousands of private sessions. Her unique ability to help clients unveil core belief patterns and facilitate the healing of dysfunctional family patterns has made her a leading expert on family issues.

In 2002, Rebecca self-published a workbook called *It's Time to Dance*, and sold out three printings. Her subsequent book *Healing Your Family History* was published in October 2006 by Hay House with a foreword by Stephen R. Covey. *Healing Your Family History* is endorsed by several famed experts, including best-selling authors Christiane Northrup, M.D., James Jones, Ph.D., and Marie Osmond.

Dr. Leonard Coldwell

Dr. Leonard Coldwell is a leading Patient Advocate, expert on cancer and stress related illnesses —Formerly general physician, NMD, PhD, CNHP—Leading health, motivation and success researcher - Consultant and trainer for many companies, organizations, medical institutions, politicians, top athletes and business executives—Founder of the "Modern Therapy Centers" and the "Foundation for Crime and Drug Free Schools and Health for Children." Dr. Coldwell is also President of the World Wellness Organization.

For Information about Dr. Coldwell's newest book go to:
www.instinctbasedmedicine.com

Dr. Carolyn Porter

Rev. Dr. Carolyn Porter has dedicated her life to helping individuals understand their magnificence and the inborn power they have to create the life they truly want and deserve to live. No matter what situations people experience in their life, they have the power of choice, which allows them to step out of their old story of hurt, lack, anger, stress and pain in order to create the life they've always dreamed of living, a life of happiness, fulfillment, abundance, joy and the freedom to enjoy their entire life adventure.

Dr. Porter became an ordained minister in 2000 and continued on to receive her Master and Doctorate of Divinity from Universal Brotherhood University. She has authored multiple books, audios and e-Books, created and facilitates many seminars and workshops, developed and presents Life Skills Speaking Training, Life Skills Coaching Training and Angel Love Practitioner Training. In 2007 she fulfilled a seven year dream by manifesting into reality her healing center called Where Miracles Happen in Woodstock, GA.

You are invited to visit www.drcarolynporter.com and www.wheremiracleshappen.com for more information about Carolyn and her work, and to view and order her products.
You can contact Carolyn at info@drcarolynporter.com, 770-663-3991 or 678-445-3309.

Brenda Cobb

Brenda Cobb founded the Living Foods Institute in Atlanta, Georgia in September 1999 just seven months after she was diagnosed with breast and cervical cancer. She refused the surgery and chemotherapy that her doctor recommended because she had seen her own family members and friends diagnosed with the same type of cancers try the traditional treatments and fail. Brenda set out on a journey to explore a natural way of healing and discovered Raw and Living Foods and Detoxification. Brenda began her healing journey in February 1999 and by September 1999 she was disease free. One of her medical doctors wrote the foreword to her first book praising her for the healing protocol that she developed to help herself and others. Many doctors send their patients to Brenda's Institute in Atlanta when other treatments have failed.

She was awarded an Honorary Cultural Doctorate in Therapeutic Philosophy from the World University in September 2003. She was awarded the Phoenix Award by the City of Atlanta and numerous awards from other organizations for her work. Even though Brenda never makes promises about what her program will do for an individual, many say they have been healed through this amazing and inspiring woman's work.

Brenda's mission to help "Heal the World One Person at a Time" is being fulfilled every day as the internationally acclaimed Living Foods Institute is now known around the world. For more information or to book Brenda to come to your area call 800-844-9876 or in Georgia call 404-524-4488 and visit the website at www.livingfoodsinstitute.com.

Email Brenda at info@livingfoodsinstitute.com

Joe Esposito

Dr. Joseph Esposito, affectionately known as "Dr. Joe" to his colleagues, patients and friends, has become one of the most dynamic, authoritative international speakers on nutrition in the country. He is literally a living reference library of information on nutrition and healthy lifestyles, making him a much-sought after lecturer by corporations, educational institutions, trade shows and conferences, professional and civic organizations and international sports events. Some of the many companies he has worked with include Aetna Insurance, AT&T, Lockheed, Coca-Cola, Deloitte & Touche, and The American College of Chiropractic Orthopedists.

Dr. Norman W. Walker

Walker was born in Genoa, Liguria, Italy to Robert Walker, a Baptist Minister from Scotland, and Lydia Maw. He was the second-born child of the six children of Rev. and Mrs. Walker. As a young man, he discovered the value of vegetable juices while recovering from a breakdown in a peasant house in the French countryside. Watching the woman in the kitchen peel carrots, he noticed the moistness on the underside of the peel. He decided to try grinding them and had his first cup of carrot juice.

Walker advocated a diet based solely on raw plants like vegetables, fruits and nuts. He considered cooked, baked or frozen food dead and therefore unhealthful, saying that "while such food can, and does, sustain life in the human system, it does so at the expense of progressively degenerating health, energy, and vitality." As a strict vegan, he did not recommend eating meat, dairy products, fish or eggs. He did, however, advocate the drinking of raw goats milk. His diet suggestions avoided such staple foods as bread, pasta and rice.

Walker devoted large sections of many of his books to the description of the different organs of the human body, explaining how the digestive system and the various glands work. He considered a healthy colon the key to one's health. He estimated that 80% of all disease begins in the colon. He wrote: "Every organ, gland and cell in the body is affected by the condition of the colon."

Jackie and Gideon Graff

Jackie Graff has been teaching raw food preparation and food science for more than a decade. An RN with 40 years' experience in various areas of patient care and education, Ms. Graff is considered one of the country's top raw food chefs and nutrition consultants.

She continues to teach raw food lifestyle classes throughout the country, is an instructor for Hallelujah Acres® Culinary Academy, and has been frequently quoted in print and broadcast news outlets, including the Atlanta-Journal Constitution, Atlanta Woman magazine, Atlanta Jewish Life magazine, Fox 5 Good Day Atlanta, CNN Headline News, and North Georgia Today. Jackie is the author of 17 theme raw food recipe books, and has produced two instructional raw food DVDs. Jackie also contributed articles to several national and local magazines.

Gideon Graff—along with Jackie has taught raw food preparation for almost a decade. His roles include raw food chef, health coach, and director of Sprout Raw Food, the Graff's consulting and raw food catering and distribution business. He has served as an instructor for Hallelujah Acres® Culinary Academy and Anidawehi Plantation Detoxification and Juice Fasting Program. Gideon has 35 years experience in food and hospitality management. An accomplished public speaker, he is experienced in both conference planning and fund raising. Previously, Gideon and Jackie co-founded and operated the Sprout Café and Shinui Living Food Learning Center, a first-of-its kind center devoted to teaching and promoting the raw food lifestyle in Roswell, Georgia. Together they lost weight, and eliminated many physical problems, resulting in them no longer requiring blood pressure, cholesterol and other medications. They attribute their healthy state to eating raw foods.

Allen Kemper

Allen Kemper began his missionary endeavors in India after graduating from Christ For the Nations Institute in 1976. He has preached and prayed "en masse" for thousands of people for their eternal salvation, healings and miracles—and almost died in South India from an unknown disease! This gripping, story among many others, from his personal experience is told in the book he has authored, *Healings & Miracles for the Third Day*. His blog and website is...

www.godscrafts.com. He can be contacted at:

918-894-1455 / AllenRKemper@yahoo.com

Books written in Love...

should never sit on a shelf. Love has to be given away to enjoy. These contributing authors have given their best. Many of them have offered to give their books free to the congregations of the world with instructions. If you enjoy, resonate with the TRUTH and desire to become part of the solution to Waking Up America, and the world by becoming responsible for your own health, we encourage you to sign your name to this library card, and give this book to your best friend; ask him/her to read it. If he/she agrees, have him/her to pass it on to his/her best friend. Buy another, and start the process again. We need to take massive action to stop the insanity of sickness, disease, and the financial problems America and the world is facing today brought on by our lack of understanding perpetuated by greed, confusion, and disobedience! We the people have the power to save our children! Invite your church, social function, boy scouts, girl scouts, etc., to use our books as fund-raisers with deep discounts to spread the Love of Jesus and His Healing Nature!

Host us and we will come to your city, town, church, any function to spread the word, "You do not have to be sick, diseased or suffering financial woes etc." Wake Up America!

Please Call 888-572-3132 to receive a free gift. If you happen to be the seventh name on this page please call, you will receive an additional gift.

Name:_____

Email:_____

Phone:_____

Address:_____

Name:_____

Email:_____

Phone:_____

Address:_____

Name:_____

Email:_____

Phone:_____

Address:_____

Name:_____

Email:_____

Phone:_____

Address:_____

Name:_____

Email:_____

Phone:_____

Address:_____

Name:_____

Email:_____

Phone:_____

Address:_____

Name:_____

Email:_____

Phone:_____

Address:_____